Something Happened Along the Way

Dedicated to Jeannette (My Inspiration)

You've given me everything and more besides, so much so, that not only am I so proud to have you as my fiancee and hopefully in the not-too-distant future my wife but you're also a very precious friend, "priceless in fact!".
I'll never be in a position to repay you, even though you've never asked for anything in return, but I'll always love you,

Your Paul xxxx

Paul Davies

Something Happened Along the Way

Puerta Publications

Published by Puerta Publications
P.O. Box 45, Worsley, Manchester

British Library Cataloguing-in-Publication Data
A catalogue record for this book is available from the British Library

ISBN 0-9522362-0-6 *paperback*

Photoset in Linotron Ehrhardt by
Northern Phototypesetting Co Ltd., Bolton
Printed in Great Britain by
BPCC Wheatons Ltd., Exeter

Contents

Introduction

> He's a real character that Paul is, what a scream!, how on earth do you put up with him? . . . don't send him for us again, he's down right rude, he's arrogant!

I've heard them all, but it didn't matter to me. I've had them love me, hate me, adore me and despise me, if only they'd known the real me, but they didn't have a clue. They only ever saw the one side of me, the jovial happy go lucky man, who performed for them in the car.

The number of times I've heard these and other similar lines, I could scream, statements like . .

> "You've got it made, big house, fancy cars, you must be loaded!"
> "Eh lad, you don't know your born" . . .

all comments from well meaning good hearted people, as I drove them to and from the airport, but it wasn't their fault, for how were they to know.

Even the rich and the famous who had depended so much on my honesty and loyalty, questioned my ability with scepticism.

> Write an autobiography . . . you're too young to write a book! . . . What have you got to write about? . . . What's so interesting about your life?

Well perhaps it's time to put the record straight, to come clean and to kiss and tell, about a life in which I've lived, loved and lost more than most people twice my age.

So without any further delay, I think it's time for me to put pen to paper and write about the whole experience . . .

ACKNOWLEDGEMENTS

A very personal thank you to my long suffering ex-wife Jean whose patience and love was tried beyond any lengths, "Jean, I'll always love you in a special sort of way, I'm sorry for any hurt I caused you".

Also to Harry her Dad, (a great bloke), Bob and Dave her brothers, thanks for putting up with me and being there whenever I needed you.

As for Joyce and Dad I never knew just how much I really loved you, until now!

To:
Colin (AA)
Marvin Wood
Norman Hill
Cynthia & Ron Humphries
Duncan Thomas
Elton Welsby
Salvador Garcia
Neil Keeling
Sheila Boardman (*Gordon's Bolton*)
Lesley McAllister (*Mitchell's Self Drive, Bolton*)
Carole Stubbins (*British Telecom*)

Thanks, each and everyone of you, for being a good friend.

To the many genuine, decent, appreciative people I've come across in my life, thank you, "You'll know who you are!".

Finally to:
The Alliance and Leicester Building Society, especially Helen Vears.
Doctors Hema & Dilip Gore of Cleggs Lane Surgery.
Hazel Sanderson (Fielding's Solicitors, Bolton).
All at Northern Phototypesetting Co. Ltd., Bolton.

I'll always be eternally grateful, for without your faith, trust, patience and assistance, producing this book would have proved impossible.

To anybody who I hurt as a result of my drinking please accept by sincere apologies, I was sick and I'm sorry, forgive me!

BORN TO STRUGGLE

Chapter One

Insecurity

I was born at ten minutes to ten on the 16th January 1957, delivered at home in Hewitt Street, the second child of Joyce and Eddie Davies, their first being Linda just over twelve months earlier.

Home was typical Lowry scene, a two bedroomed terraced house with outside loo, amongst a backdrop of cobbled streets, it was a working class home, that could boast of neither bath or electric, where the only supply of hot water came via means of a gas geyser in the kitchen, but it was a palace to childhood sweethearts, like my mother and father.

On the 26th January 1958, my mother with the help of my father as midwife gave birth to a second son, Eddie, who was to become more like a twin to me than a younger brother.

Memories of my short time at Hewitt street are few indeed but the recollections of that period of my life, although few, are very vivid, as I distinctly remember spending most of our time playing in the street together, because in those days we experienced a much nicer climate, with summers that were hotter and longer.

One of our favourite pastimes was to spend hours playing with the tar that lay between the cobbles in the road, the intense heat of the day made it a paradise for mischievous kids like us, who took great pleasure in going home as black as the ace of spades. There would be tar everywhere as we would be covered from head to toe in the stuff, but by the time our parents had clapped eyes on us, it would be too late, for within seconds of our arrival home there would be bitumen all over the place, hand prints, footprints, you name it, we'd covered it.

Each Sunday the band and the boy's brigade used to march, whilst people lined the streets gossiping, as they watched the procession pass, more often than not amongst all the commotion, women could be seen on all fours, sometimes in their curlers, as they beavered away either stoning or red leading their steps.

The Salvation army workers habitually rattled their tins, whilst they collected money for their own worthy cause, at the same time Eddie, I and some of the other children would shout at the band leader, goading him to toss up his stick, which was a funny exercise in itself. Whenever he was successful the whole street would cheer and clap, sometimes with an approving "Hooray!", yet failure to make a clean catch would bring boos and jeers from the crowd, how strange, that from the very first time I saw the band leader in front of the procession, I wanted to be that man, "Typical!".

In the latter part of 1959, I found myself standing on a platform at Piccadilly train station accompanying my Mother, Nanna, and Linda. I had no idea why we were there, but I do recall us being dressed in our Sunday best and armed with Union Jacks, as we waited in anticipation for the arrival of the 14.40 express from Dover, which was bringing our Uncle Johnny home.

As the train rolled up to the platform, we all burst into song, waving our flags and banners, chanting "When Johnny comes marching home again", then, as it ground to a halt, our hero appeared with a kit bag slung over his shoulder. Passers by stopped and gazed in amazement, smiling at each other, as we greeted him, but I, like the on lookers had no idea why we'd gone to such effort. "What had he achieved to deserve this acclaim?", I wondered. In my own mind I thought he was a hero coming back from the war, but sadly I couldn't have been further from the truth for, far from being a hero, he was actually a villain returning home, having completed a stretch in Borstal.

At the time both my Dad and Grandad were totally disgusted by the actions of my Mum and Nanna and made their views quite clear, thinking it was both sad and thoughtless of them to portray him as some kind of hero, especially in front of Linda and I, when we were at such a tender age.

I find it strange, but although Linda went with us to Piccadilly and lots of other places, I honestly can't recall her being there, or part of the family whilst we were growing up, in fact, Linda's presence throughout my life is rather vague, something which has always puzzled me.

However one occasion which does stick clearly in my mind, was the time that a photo session was arranged for Linda, Eddie and I, an exercise which was common practice in those days. The idea was that a photographer came around to your home to take a picture of your children, usually sat on the side-board or table. Normally it would be a simple exercise, but with three mischievous, screaming kids present, it took a lot of patience and tolerance, on the photographers part. After much preparation, everything was ready, until Linda started to cry, deciding that she didn't want her picture taken, she then cried when the flash went and by now, matters were being made ten times worse because Eddie and I were becoming rather fractious and getting on Mother's nerves, so in the end, we both got a crack around the ear and we all cried together, it was mayhem! In essence a job that should have only taken a few minutes, took considerably longer, despite the efforts of my mother and the poor photographer, yet the finished article always ended up portraying the perfect child, something any parent would be proud of.

In the September of that year my Mother and Father were offered a flat on the estate where they themselves had been brought up, both of their families still lived there and so we moved to Melland Road in Gorton.

The only memory I do have of this period, was the birth of Carol, my younger sister, delivered by my Dad, during a thunder storm in the early hours on 31st December 1959, whilst we were being looked after and kept occupied in the kitchen, by our Uncle John.

As we played I could hear the constant cries and moaning, as my Mother suffered terrible pain, whilst in labour, she constantly claimed, and still does today, that when giving birth she "dropped us all like rabbits!", but I disagree, for I have never forgotten that night, especially the storm which took place. Listening to my own Mother suffer was bad enough, but the wind and rain constantly lashing the large windows and the claps of the thunder, accompanied by the lightening, made the whole experience a terrifying ordeal.

My first personal experience of fear occurred a year later, in 1960 when my Mum took me for my first day to the nursery, I can't remember whether I cried going, or what I actually felt like, but I do remember us turning that last corner and my Mother saying "You'll be alright, you'll make lots of new friends", with my only response being, "But I love you Mum, I don't want anyone else!".

I just couldn't understand, how the one person, that I adored and depended on, could treat me in such a way, even thinking she'd abandoned me forever, as she disappeared around the corner with all the other Mums as if not to care, leaving me terrified and in the company of total strangers.

I cried myself to sleep that afternoon, while I lay there, with my only comfort being the picture of the rabbit at the end of my little bed, you see we were always made to have a doze in the afternoon and so one of the nursery staff would tell us a story until we were all asleep, but I was so insecure that it took me quite sometime before I settled in and accepted that my Mother was eventually going to return for me.

Once I had settled into my new surroundings, I instinctively picked out a favourite teacher who I immediately became fond of, and although one could say it was ridiculous at such an age, I subconsciously fell in love with her, which tended to make life much more bearable at the time, as I needed someone to take my Mother's place in her absence.

Actually writing this has made me realise, just how hard my Mother and Father worked to look after us and give us the best they could, with us always well dressed and in suitable clothing, whatever the weather.

In the winter we were always well wrapped up, wearing a navy blue gabardine mack, with a hood on, good shoes or wellies and a balaclava, fully armed against any elements we may have to face.

In the summer, we would wear good quality shoes or sandals, nice clean shirts and jumpers, lovingly knitted by my Mother herself, making us the envy of most other children, but there was always one stipulation, which was that Eddie and I always matched, identically!

In 1961 we moved from the flat on Melland Road to Forber Crescent, where my Mother and Father are still living today, but before I tell you about the day we went to view it, I think I should explain a little about the estate that their house is on.

Both the flat and this new house, "Forber" as we have always called it, are on a private trust housing estate, called "Suttons", an estate which had a few advantages in its favour, when compared to living elsewhere. As a result, it was somewhat difficult, even near impossible, to get a flat on there, never mind a house, because any house which did become available was immediately offered to an existing over crowded family, already living on the estate.

An abundance of large families and the fact that many of them had ties in some way through at least a couple of generations, meant that the estate had a sort of "closed community", with a very clannish type of atmosphere, which generally produced rough, but "a down to earth" type of person. They were folk who were always only too happy to help, so it was quite a safe place, where people could let their kids play out, and the neighbours would automatically keep an eye on them without giving it a second thought.

There was a stipulation in the trust, that "Suttons" should always maintain the streets and homes of residents, whilst at the same time keep it's rents as low as possible, which resulted in the estate generally being a clean one, with most of the houses enjoying the luxury of quite a large garden, in fact, there were only a couple of dirty, scruffy streets on the whole estate, but these did tend to have the larger families living in them.

Anyway, the very first time we went to view "Forber" was really exciting, because until then, I'd been far too young to appreciate the previous years I had spent in my Grandad's garden, so this was a new adventure.

"Forber" was a three bedroomed home, with separate inside toilet and bathroom, which seemed enormous to us, especially having spent the last few years living in a flat. The house was situated on a corner and as a result had the added luxury of three very spacious lawns, at the front, back and side, so there was a lot for us three to explore whilst Joyce and Dad were being shown around by the landlord.

You may be wondering why, I have suddenly started to call my Mother by her Christian name, well the only explanation I can give you, is that, for the first time in my writing it feels correct, because all our lives we have called her Joyce and not Mum, why this is? I don't know, it's yet another question, that to this day, remains unanswered.

Viewing "Forber", was also the first occasion I can remember Carol, Eddie and myself in the threesome, we all grew up to be, "Without Linda!", which brings me to what has always been another mystery, as far as we, "The Kids", were concerned, which is, "Why did Linda never live with us?".

We were always told, that Joyce used to go to her Mum and Dads each day to clean up while they were at work, which she did right up until my birth, but apparently, because it was foggy and I was nearly due, my Grandad told her to leave Linda there. After that, she was brought up at "Nanna and Grandads", where it seems story has it, she slept in a drawer for the first twelve months, something which was a common practice in those days, yet having said all this, I and the other kids, are still to this day, unhappy with the explanation.

In the September of 62, I started at Gorton Mount Infants School, with the first day being an absolute nightmare, Joyce took me and left me like all the other Mums did, at the gate, but I wasn't like their kids, I was terrified, just like my first day at nursery. Instead of looking forward to my new school, I dreaded it, as there were a lot more new faces and the school was much bigger. I already knew many of the other kids because we'd come from nursery together and there were a few kids off ' Suttons ', but never the less, there were many children who I'd never seen before, from lots of other local schools, who I didn't know and so I still felt somewhat strange.

As far as I'm concerned, it was at about this time, that all my fears and inadequacies started to manifest themselves in my behaviour, I was insecure, felt inferior and was frightened of anybody who wasn't close to me, such as family. In hindsight, I just couldn't deal with strangers at all, as I'd already adopted a deep seated fear of anyone who was in a position to raise either their voice or temper, consequently any person in authority.

I was so frightened of one teacher, called Miss Dutton, that on one occasion, I was too scared to ask if I could go to the toilet, it was terrifying, I was dying to go and getting more desperate by the minute, but I couldn't say anything. Desperately I hung on, wishing and willing the clock on the wall would miraculously bring the lesson to an end, but that was too much to expect, so I had to sit there suffering in silence, thinking "Could I make it?, can I hang on?". In a moment of sheer madness I even thought, "Perhaps no one will notice!", but in the end it was too late "I'd done it!".

I sat there feeling guilty and remorseful, as others in the vicinity started to sniff, whilst looking around the class, as if to say "Is it him?, her?" or "Who's done it?", I knew it was only a matter of time before the teacher would eventually realise and I'd wish I was dead.

Suddenly, Miss Dutton wanted to know who had done it in their pants, so I reluctantly stood up, sheepishly admitting it was me, then came the humiliation of being made to stand in the corridor until the end of class. The shame of having to stand there with shit running down my leg and that putrid smell was awful, even worse was knowing that eventually the school bell was going to ring and I would be on view for everyone to see. As if that wasn't enough, I then had to suffer the degradation of going next door to the nursery to be "cleaned down and dried out!", once again, fit to mix with society.

Funnily enough, despite being able to remember and describe all of this very clearly, I can't recall the horrendous experience of having to face the class, my family and anyone else who was involved afterwards. Sadly the only person, who showed any sort of kindness and wanted to know what was wrong, or why I was in such a state, was the nursery teacher, who cleaned me up. It seems so sad to me today, that nobody, apart from her, showed any interest or wanted to know what the real problem was which had caused me so much pain, resulting in this mishap.

There were two other occasions, when the same thing happened to another couple of lads, yet when it did, even at that tender age, I felt nothing but complete sympathy for them. I had no ill feelings or bad thoughts, just sorrow and guilt plus the inner relief of knowing it wasn't me as I relived my own nightmare again.

Looking back, I feel that I was odd in other types of my behaviour, for during the playtime periods, I would often make for the iron railings which surrounded the school playground and stare helplessly into the direction of "Forber". From where I stood, I could actually see my Nanna and Grandads, which was at least a mile away and constantly found myself looking, in the hope that by some miracle or other, Joyce would feel me subconsciously crying out for her and that if she did, she would come and get me, but of course that never happened.

The only other thing relating to school from that year, which sticks in my mind, was walking through the gate on the last day of term to start summer holidays.

That six week break was always fun, during which time we were capable of literally anything, especially when we were bored. One such occasion which springs to mind was the time we decided to have a jumble sale, without telling either Joyce or Dad. Whilst Linda and Carol were rooting out some clothes, pots and toys, Eddie and I were setting up a stall with Dad's decorating table and within no time at all a large crowd had gathered, buying stuff as fast as we were displaying it.

During the course of the afternoon, we'd sold nearly everything, which made us about four shillings and sixpence, whilst at the same time giving us all a good laugh in the process. Having completed our first entrepreneurial venture, we only had one thing left to do, which was to clear up, so that by the time Joyce and Dad had arrived home, they were none the wiser.

Later that afternoon, Joyce was making the tea, when she suddenly asked Dad if he had seen the sugar bowl, to which he replied "No". As if by instinct, all attention then swiftly focused on both Eddie and myself, with Joyce asking the same question of us. Once again we also denied any knowledge of it's whereabouts, however with the worst possible timing in the world, Carol appeared having been upstairs to finalise the on going inquisition, but unfortunately, due to her innocence, she replied in a totally honest fashion, "Oh yes !, we sold it on the jumble sale". Joyce looked confused, "What bloody jumble sale!", so we told her about our exciting day, how we'd made money selling our toys, some clothes and some of her pots, at which point she went berserk, "That was my best crystal sugar bowl!!", she screamed, "Who bought it? ". We didn't know the lady by name, so we had to describe her to Joyce, but once she realised who the woman was and where she lived, she made us go and get the bowl back. The basic idea was good, however there was only one drawback to the plan and that was, the old lady's reluctance to sell it back to us, so in the end Joyce had to go round and retrieve it herself, whilst at the same time pay the old girl for her trouble, needless to say, jumble sales in the future were banned!

One of the much nicer things to happen in '62 was due to one of my Dad's brothers "Colin", who unexpectedly arrived at 'Forber ' one day, with this really wild farm dog called "Billy", of course, as soon as we all clapped eyes on the dog, we automatically wanted him.

The dog jumped out of the cab from Colin's wagon and ran around the garden like it was possessed, he was black, with a white chest, had a very shaggy coat and was as wild as they come. Billy was to become more than just a family pet, he was like a third brother (part of the gang) and wherever or whatever we did, Billy was with us, which meant that by the end of that first summer holiday, Eddie, Billy and I had become so close we were like The Three Musketeers, inseparable!

Billy wasn't just a pet, he was our guard dog, so we decided to teach him how to wait for the postman, the paper boy and any other poor sole, who may have the unfortunate task, of having to post any article through our door. Eddie and I spent literally hours with one of us pretending to post papers through the door, while the other one waited patiently with Billy on the other side, ready to pounce. Eventually we succeeded in training him to dive at the letter box, whilst we sat behind the door giggling and tittering, as someone came up the path. Sometimes if it was a newspaper, he could be seen, swinging in mid-air, whilst ferociously growling, with one end clasped between his massive fangs and within a few seconds the paper boy could then be seen running for his life, to get away from "No 2".

Reading any mail or newspapers always proved immensely difficult, sometimes impossible and in some cases it resembled matching up a jigsaw puzzle, with more than just one or two pieces missing. It was always laughable watching my Dad trying his damnedest to pick out horses from the already depleted racing section, forever cursing the dog as he did.

After a while Eddie and I got bored with the original game, so we decided to develop Billy's education further, by training him to hide behind the bushes until his intended victim had cautiously made their approach into his den. Tentatively they would make their way to the front door, in anticipation of Billy's normal reception, but unfortunately for them we'd already changed the rules. Guard lowered and their job completed they confidently turned round to make a hasty exit, only to be confronted at the gate by GUESS WHO?!!

We would literally wet ourselves with laughter, watching and listening to our Billy's prey pleading for help as they stood there pinned helplessly against the wall, but unfortunately for them, they were relying on the Christianity of us two and we didn't possess an ounce of the stuff in our bodies.

Eddie and I spent most of our time playing football and so it was a must that, "Yes, you guessed it!", Billy learnt as well. Sometimes when we were at our most restless and mischievous, we would take him onto the playing fields to watch the league games being played, but Billy couldn't just observe from the touch-line, he had to join in and no matter how many players were involved, it never bothered him, he was capable of spoiling any game!, which is exactly what he did. It was hilarious, as soon as he clapped eyes on the ball he was off, charging ferociously at the player in possession, with the sole intention of getting the ball and keeping it. He would take off at a gallop, whilst at the same time pushing the ball along with his nose, which often resulted in a "Keystone Kops" type of scene, one dog being pursued by twenty odd blokes and a referee chasing all over the field, shouting,

"Who's is this bloody dog?", whilst we sat giggling in our denial, "What dog?".

That first summer holiday we had Billy was great, but it passed too quickly, however fortunately, I had no new school to go to, so I was much more at ease with myself, quietly confident and looking forward to being 'Big Brother ' to Eddie, who was starting his first year at Infant School.

When I think of that second year, I immediately picture my mates and I playing marbles in the soil, flicking cards against the wall, having conker fights and other games that we used to play such as Kick-can, Rally-Ro and Tig-Tag.

It was a very important year, because it was "testing time" for the boys, a very necessary period in any boy's life, where we all had to find out what the "pecking order" was and where we stood in it.

Although I was very nervous inwardly, I always managed to put on a show, pretending to be something that I wasn't, for example, if there were any signs of trouble, I seemed to ward off any threat or challenge with ease, but deep down I realised, that one day I would have to stand my ground and sure enough, it wasn't long before that day came.

All morning in class the lad concerned had continued to goad, calling me "Davies" which I despised, he'd teased and tormented me so much, that in the end I had no option but to accept his challenge of a fight. After dinner, I returned to school, with everybody wondering if there was going to be a scrap, my opposition David Altoft, was playing in the middle of the school field, so I immediately made my way towards him and within a few seconds most of the school were either in the centre of the field or were running towards it, in anticipation. As I walked towards him, my heart thumped at a tremendous rate and I suddenly realised, "God, this is my first proper fight!", deep down I'd never been so nervous, yet I knew that I had to make sure I looked confident, despite my "real" inner feelings. "Altoft", who by now had stopped playing football, stood there waiting, staring right through me and I felt small and vulnerable, amongst a background of violent and aggressive voices, chanting "Fight, Fight, Fight!!", but there was no way on this earth that I, was going to start it. I stood opposite him, nervous and trembling inside, knowing there was no way out, as this was it !, then he threw the first punch and that was all I needed. I retaliated immediately, wrestling him to the ground with an arm lock, followed with a few swift punches to his head, I was desperate to win, knowing it would make life a damned sight easier for the future, so I kept going at him, like a terrier with a rat. My fellow school mates continued to shout and chant, however, it was no longer "Fight, fight!!" but "Davies, Davies, Davies!!", I then realised that they were all on my side now and I'd sort of tasted blood, so I had no other option, but to go for it. Suddenly I felt a smack to the head and my hair being pulled, "Right come on you two!", as both David and I were then lifted by the scruff of our necks to the disagreement and disgust of the crowd, "It was the headmaster!".

For once I felt quite proud of myself, as we were frog marched across the field and playground in to the school building, then made to stand outside his office. Everyone stared at us as they filed passed after the break, but this time I was on show in the corridor for a much better reason than on the last occasion.

That fight lifted me into the "Top Five", which put me in a much safer position, where the only threat to me would come from somebody wanting to challenge my authority, but there was very little chance of that happening, so I confidently enjoyed the rest of that term without threat.

The victory brought about a new confidence in my school life, but home was different, as by now, Eddie, Carol and I were getting older, more inquisitive, whilst at the same time totally confused, "And why not?", for there was our elder sister living in the same road as us, only at the other end with our Grandparents.

The whole family situation affected the three of us at "Forber" in certain ways and at varying times in our lives, but for Linda this was not so, for it appeared that she was constantly spoilt like an only child and treated in a totally different way to us, something which we always resented. It also seemed to me that she was looked upon as an adult, forever listening to the gossip and general "shit stirring" that went on within the family and due to this permanent separation, I never really felt the closeness with Linda that one should feel with a natural sister.

Although living apart from us did have it's advantages for her, because, not only did Nanna and Grandad give her more material things, but they also protected her from the trauma of being brought up in a home, that sometimes had a very aggressive, unpredictable and volatile atmosphere, which could erupt at any given moment.

There were occasions when Grandad, who was considered quite affluent in those days, would drive us all of to the seaside, where any onlooker could be forgiven for thinking we'd gone for a year not a day, as the car would be piled up to the roof with junk. It was a scene which one could only enlighten to the "Clampetts" in "The Beverley Hillbillies", yet in rather similar fashion, despite the chaos, it produced a happy family type atmosphere, where a good day was had by all, in what should of been a total family unit, yet I can still see Linda, always preferring to be with them and not us.

If Nanna and Grandad wanted to go for a walk or do some shopping, whilst we stayed on the beach, you can bet who Linda would want to be in the company of and it certainly wasn't us. The end product of all this, meant that many years later, we became divided as a family, with the small disagreements we'd had, eventually growing into very large resentments.

In 1963 we went on our first trip to Butlins holiday camp, at Pwllheli, which was the first of many, yet still to this day, I don't know how Joyce and Dad coped with it all. We were already excited by the time we'd got there, so you can imagine what they were feeling like after such a long journey. We got off the coach and waited for the luggage, then followed Joyce and Dad into the chaotic main reception hall, where there were people all over the place, checking in and out.

It was one of those many occasions in my life that I stood there and admired my Dad, watching him as he took control of the whole situation, totally in command, always trusting him to sort things out.

During that holiday, the only occasions Joyce and Dad ever saw us, were at the set meal times, where everybody used to eat in the large dinning halls. In a hall there would be hundreds of tables, all set out in rows, in each row there would be perhaps fifteen tables, and eight people would share a table, which is where we were on show the most. Although mischievous, we were always very well behaved and disciplined when in the company of adults, we were always taught to respect our elders and that "children should be seen and not heard", especially when at the dining table, as a result, it was amazing how many people would comment on our good behaviour and table manners, something which Joyce and Dad were always proud of.

Returning home was always sad, but at least this time we could look forward to seeing our Billy, who'd stayed at home, with one of the neighbours looking after him. However, when we arrived home, he was in the house and we didn't have a key, so Dad got out his ladders to climb in through the upstairs window. By the time Dad had got to the top of the ladders, Billy was going spare, the daft sod was so excited by our return he tried to jump out of the window as Dad was attempting to get in. It was so funny, because Dad had such a short fuse and by now, it was ready to blow, needless to say he started cursing and swearing at us all, while we were rolling around laughing, which only succeeded in setting Joyce off, making matters ten times worse. Billy's head kept popping up along side Dad's, as he heard our voices on the garden below and by now Dad was hanging on for dear life, but the more he tried to get in, the more Billy got in his way, which only frustrated Dad even more. At this point the dog was barking and squealing so much that it was really beginning to annoy him, we were now all utterly useless and in uncontrollable hysterics, while Dad was at the window, shouting, "Shut up, the lot of you!, you're all fucking loopy". Each time he cursed, it made us laugh all the more, but he eventually got in, opened the door and Billy flew out to greet us all, then proceeded to gallop around the garden like a mad March hare, with us lot in pursuit, which even made Dad smile, especially as we all cried with joy and happiness.

The next day brought work as usual, Joyce, like her Mum, worked at Marks &

Spencer's, while Dad worked nights at an Engineering Factory, during the day he also had a window cleaning round, which meant we had to be looked after while they were both at work, an honour which usually fell to my Dad's mother, our "Other Nanna".

Although we didn't spend as much time with her as we did with Joyce's parents, she always seemed closer and more sincere whenever we were in her care. We spent hours with her, as we played in the house and in the garden, but she never bothered what we got up to, as long as we were safe.

There were times when we would have the clothes maiden on its side, with blankets covering it like a tent, running all over the place playing Cowboys and Indians, straddling a brush or mop, which was nearest thing we could get to a horse, usually named Silver or Trigger. If we weren't dismantling the house or turning it into a pig sty, then we would all be sat watching very educational television programmes, such as Bill and Ben or Andy Pandy. I remember one lunchtime, she shouted us in out of the garden, to tell us about a programme that was just about to start, called "Tales of the Riverbank". We told her that we had never even heard of it, so she sat us all down on the sofa in front of the telly, with a drink and we watched it together. As kids we always wanted to know the in's and out's of a ducks arse and watching a new programme was no different, so she had to explain every character to us all in detail, which she did, with great patience and lots of love.

Whenever she looked after us, she always made sure that we all got on and played together, that Eddie and I never once left Carol out, yet if we did ever got out of hand, she always came out with her most famous statement, "I'll tell your Dad when he gets in", which never failed, because she knew that those words automatically put the fear of God in us.

"Other Nanna", was much poorer than our other Grandparents, but her genuine love and interest always came through, as she was never ever short of a cuddle for us and was always there if we needed her, although sadly we all grew quite quickly and very much ahead of our years.

As a result of Joyce and Dad's concerted efforts to give us a good home and many luxuries that other kids didn't have, we became quite independent and capable of looking after ourselves at an early age, it was a freedom which led to some hilarious situations and the way we tackled them can only be put down to our own personalities and outlook's on life.

Until children had reached the third year, staying for school dinners was compulsory, but as soon as we could, we chose to be at home for our dinner. For a few years Joyce and Dad had made sure that at least one of them was there to cook for us, but as we were getting older they had more opportunity and freedom to work, so one day, they asked us if we wanted to stop for school dinners, to save us rushing to and from school, but because the food at school was crap, we all voted with an emphatic “No!”.

It was agreed that we would make our own dinner, if we had to, but on most occasions there would be something ready for us and for a few months everything was great, we would come home and enjoy a nice meal, but if there was nothing already made, we would make beans on toast or something similar, we never argued with each other and we all mucked in.

However, one Sunday night, we had just finished our tea, when Dad dropped his proverbial bombshell, “Kids, I’ve cooked your dinner for tomorrow”, a statement which was met with a deadly silence, as we all suspiciously looked at each other, you see, Dad’s problem was that he sometimes thought of himself as Egon Ronnay and boy could he think up some wonderful dishes.

Sitting, waiting for us on the table was the pressure cooker, which immediately told us it was something exciting, leaving us with one major problem, “What are we having now?”. It was time for a “conflab” and as Carol was the youngest, she’d already been given the task of discovering what was on tomorrow’s menu, but when she arrived with the bad news, we were sorry we’d asked, “It’s Pea soup!”.

That Monday morning before we left for school we were all read the usual riot act, which consisted of, no arguing or fighting, everyone had to take their turn doing the dishes, we all had to share with the cleaning up and the last one out had to make sure that the back door was locked.

I’ll never forget getting home that Monday lunchtime, seeing Carol sat there at the table waiting for us, the first thing she said was “Have you seen this shit that we’ve got for dinner?”, of course there wasn’t much to say, for as soon as we saw the thick green gunge with ham floating in it, we just burst out laughing. We decided there and then, that there wasn’t much we could do with the soup, other than get rid of it, but how?, after all Dad always seemed to know everything, as he always “found us out”. After a long deliberation Carol had a great idea, she thought that it was best if we buried it in the garden, and we agreed!, so off we went as if in a funeral procession. Our hysterical laughter could be heard throughout the neighbourhood, as we marched, humming the death tune, into the back garden to give our pea soup it’s burial, suffice to say we got rid of it and made sauce butties instead.

Dads other great achievement, “a la cuisine” was “Bubble and Squeak”, which was usually, left overs from the Sunday dinner. It was so bad that we had to “beef it up” with brown sauce, to make it a little more appetizing, but what annoyed us more than anything else, was at the same time, the kitchen cupboards were full to bursting with a variety of food, yet Dad continued to serve up his own culinary delights.

Consequently it wasn't long before problems started to arise, for the more meals Dad cooked for us, the more we buried, which meant that the soil was being turned over so much, you would have thought we had a giant pet mole in the garden. Within a few weeks, the burial ground was nearly full, and getting more noticeable by the day, so it was time for a change of strategy, which ended up with a decision to start tipping any food we didn't want behind the shed, a secluded place where nobody ever went, except us . . . or so we thought !, for in the not to distant future, we were to discover otherwise.

Like most children, we went through various "fads" and "crazes" in our lives, which ultimately led to money being spent on Joyce and Dad's part and one such notion was our desire to own a pet mouse, it was the start of a new phase, which ended up with us having a multitude of different animals, as well as Billy. Eventually, we'd built up quite a menagerie which consisted of rabbits, guinea pigs, a hamster and some mice, which were all kept in the shed, whilst we also had quite a collection of fish outside in a garden pond.

Looking after our pets was never a problem, we cleaned and fed them daily, but our enthusiasm was severely dented with the first of many deaths. Suddenly animals started dying for no apparent reason, which left us suspecting that there may be some sort of disease in the shed, so we totally dismantled and disinfected all the hutches and cages in it, in an attempt to stop the rot.

Despite all our efforts, the deaths continued and after a few weeks we were both confused and angry, but still undeterred we replaced pets as they died, although eventually we came to the conclusion, that we were being "ripped off" and sold duff animals.

Armed to the teeth with boxes of dead carcasses we descended on the shop, where we were met with an arrogant attitude from the owner, who wasn't interested in our complaint. It was quite obvious that they were used to dealing with youngsters and thought that this would be the end of the matter, but they were wrong, for we were no ordinary children, "We were Davies's!!".

Our immediate response was pre planned at home just in case this happened, so we all trooped around the corner to the Daily Express building, stormed into the reception hall and demanded to speak to the writer of "Action Line", a column which dealt with consumer related problems.

We couldn't have asked for a worse start, as the receptionist was a real old spinster type, who obviously didn't like children and made the fact quite clear as she peered down at us over the top of her glasses, sarcastically questioning why we were there. Without saying a word, we all looked at each other, knowing full well what each one of us was thinking, "Who does this snotty cow really think she is?". With that we lined up the boxes of dead carcasses on her desk, lifted the lids and she was suddenly faced with four stiffs, two white rabbits, one hamster and a guinea pig.

She let out an almighty scream and within seconds we had transformed this cool, efficient, level headed women in to a sick, psychotic wreck, running around screeching, "Oh take them away, get rid of them!!", needless to say the ensuing commotion alerted the attention of the security guards and we were rapidly escorted out of the building, without furthering our enquiry.

In typical "Davies" fashion, we marched back to the shop, giving the owner the ultimatum, "Give us our money back or else!", to which he replied "You must be bloody joking. Piss off!!."

We knew there and then that there was no other option, but to demonstrate outside the shop, so we set up our own protest in typical "Greenham Common" style, intent on reimbursement. We must have looked so comical, for the four of us were dressed as if nobody owned us and by this time we were as black as the hobs of hell, proudly displaying our dead pets in shoe boxes, singing a few choruses of "We shall not be moved" and "We want our money back", bringing our own brand of street entertainment to Manchester city centre. After an hour without any customers, the manager eventually conceded by refunding our money, saying "Don't bother coming back here again!", so we made our way home, content that we'd made our point and had the final say in doing so.

Unfortunately animals continued to die and the mystery carried on, but not for long, as a few weeks later, Eddie, Carol and I were suddenly stopped in our tracks, when we came across, what we thought at the time was a large mouse, which had darted under the shed leaving us all transfixed and absolutely fascinated by it's speed.

Typical of us, we decided to investigate further, so we placed food near the shed, in the hope of a second appearance, which did eventually come, only instead of one small, insignificant mouse, we discovered "It was an army of rats!".

After that, the three of us spent hour upon hour, watching them from the living room, constantly feeding them a wide range of Marks and Spencer's food, without realising, that these animals were in fact, vermin. They were better fed than most of the kids in the area, but it was worth it, for the immense pleasure that they gave us in return, however it wasn't long before Joyce realised that we were all up to something and we accepted that eventually we would have to tell her about our visitors, the only problem was, how?

The answer came a few days later when Joyce was putting her washing out on the line, she suddenly started screaming and in a hysterical fashion came running into the house, proclaiming that she had seen a large rat in the garden. When she had calmed down, we had to come clean and admit that we already knew about them, but we pleaded with her not to let Dad know, but of course, Joyce had no option, she had to tell him.

We already had a good idea, as to how he would react, and sure enough he didn't let us down, for true to form, he went berserk, ranting and raving like a madman, as he called us all the names under the sun.

"Rats!, bleedin rats!, don't talk daft, you're all fuckin crackers, ya barmy, and you Joyce, I'm fuckin surprised at you !", totally convinced that we were all imagining it. To prove our point and Dad wrong, we just needed them to show their faces once, but trying to get our "fury friends" to come out when we wanted, was both frustrating and near impossible, so in an effort to convince him, we all decided to stay in the house, while he put a full apple under the shed, to witness it all for himself. Seconds later, the apple slowly disappeared out of sight, whilst Dad was still making his way back, totally oblivious to the fact. It was so funny, there we were all banging on the window trying to attract his attention, but to no avail and by the time he'd returned we were in hysterics, laughing our heads off, leaving him stood there not knowing why, "Well, how long do we have to stand and wait here for then?". His question was met with a barrage of laughter, which only seemed to anger him more, that was until he realised that it had vanished, but even then he just dismissed it as "a fucking joke", so still not believing us, Eddie took another apple out to finally prove our point, while Dad looked on, "Watch", we said. Straight away another large grey rat appeared and dragged the second apple away under the shed, leaving Dad slightly embarrassed, but definitely shocked, "Jesus !, What the bleedin hell!!".

Although it was difficult for him to believe, he finally had to accept that we were right and once he had, he and Joyce called "The Ratcatcher" in, who came and told Dad that it was a nest behind next doors garden shed. He laid some traps, saying that he would call back within the week and left it at that, although during the next couple of weeks he returned on many occasions to check the traps, while we waited in anticipation, dying to see if he'd caught anything. Despite all his efforts, he never did, although the poison continuously disappeared, which left him quite perturbed, when he tried to perceive the size of the rodents, but after several weeks our visitors moved on, leaving the "Ratman" empty handed, confused and perplexed, saying these parting words to my Dad, "I'd loved to have caught one of those buggers, they must have been enormous!".

Thank goodness they didn't know we'd been operating our own "meals on wheels", serving gourmet dishes such as Bubble and Squeak, Pea Soup, home made curry and other delights that Dad had prepared. Needless to say, we had to stop dumping food and find other alternatives, to save us eating the stuff.

The following couple of years brought more love, laughter and general happiness, but these times were constantly overshadowed with the fits and outbursts of anger, which were part and parcel of the arguments between Joyce and Dad. Constant slanging matches resulted in them throwing damaging accusations at each other and slurring one another's character, which usually ended up with a display of physical violence on my Dad's part. Consequently neither Carol, Eddie nor I, ever knew where we stood, as life was totally unpredictable, with us never knowing how Joyce and Dad would react to any given situation.

A good example of this, was the time that I was learning to write, I and another boy were in competition, writing as fast and as much as we could. By the time I had finished, my story was about five pages long and we had both earned a gold star for our efforts, so I ran home pleased and excited, dying to show the work I had done to Joyce and Dad, "I was chuffed to bits!". However the reception I got at home, was slightly different, "What the bleedin' ell, do ya call this?", Dad ranted. I was totally confused, for on the one hand the teacher was giving me a gold star in reward of my work and on the other, Dad was just pulling it to bits, which left me in a right state, obviously upset and by now crying my eyes out. Eventually he calmed me down and explained that the story was good, but pointed out that the presentation was poor, as I only had three words on each line, so after tea, he showed me how he thought it should have been done in the first place, fitting the whole story on one piece of paper, whilst at the same time condemning the teacher for the way in which she had taught us.

There was also the episode when Joyce brought us home from school, at the time road works were being carried out in "Forber", we were walking down the road, when Eddie and I noticed a pile of sand about fifty yards away, so as soon as we saw it, we were off, both running as fast as we could towards it, "Chaaaarge!". Stood at the side of the road was a "Paddy" workman, who by this time had called out "No !, No missus!", but it was too late, for we were already rolling all over in this pile of sand, throwing it everywhere, putting it down each others shorts, shirts, even socks, we were absolutely covered in it. Meanwhile, Joyce had gone over to the bloke, in response to his shouts, where he told her that it wasn't sand, but in fact, ready mixed brick cement, which immediately prompted her to shout "Eddie, Paul, come out of there!", but we couldn't hear, for we were in a world of our own.

When she finally did pull us out, we were covered from head to toe in the stuff, so she dragged us the rest of the way home, giving us a crack every now and then, "Wait till your father hears about this, he'll go spare, he'll kill the pair of ya!", a statement that always chilled us with fear. By the time Dad had arrived home, Joyce had cooled down and seen the funny side of it all, so she was able to break the news gently to him, saving us from yet another good hiding.

In the first story I went home confident and proud, expecting lots of encouragement, only to be met with verbal abuse and aggression. Yet in the second story, I was put through the hell of waiting hours for a good hiding from my Dad, which never came, sadly both stories depict the total uncertainty and unpredictability that surrounded my whole childhood and general upbringing.

The mid-to-late sixties brought many material changes to our home at "Forber", but it also brought a new awareness to me, of what was happening in and around my own life. My parents had always worked hard to give us a nice home and neither of them were smokers or drank, which meant that through their hard work, we were able to replace many things, such as a new cooker, fridge and many other household goods, but it wasn't those commodities that made the difference. It was the trappings that Joyce wanted to get and Dad didn't, that always caused the rows, for they were the items that he said were luxuries, the things that we didn't really need, however we always put that view down to his background, as he was very Victorian in his attitude, and tight by his general nature, so we just accepted the fact.

Another problem area arose with Joyce working at Marks's, where she was in the company of other women, who, in many cases, came from slightly better backgrounds or nicer areas. She would often come home from work and tell us about her friends, how they lived and how they were improving their own lifestyles, but Dad resented it and on many an occasion, accused Joyce of "trying to keep up with the Jones's", which did tend to cause a lot of animosity. You see, Joyce was always the success behind my Dad, she always wanted to go forward, to progress and do well, but he never liked her working there, he didn't like any of her friends and made his views quite clear on more than one occasion, in fact she was never allowed to go on any works outings, or socialise at all.

If at any time Joyce really wanted anything which would benefit the home generally and he didn't agree with her, she always had to "pay a price" to get her way, with all of us suffering the consequences too, but unfortunately looking back, I have to question, "Was the eventual price worth it?".

One such experience, was the time Joyce fancied having carpet fitted throughout the house, she had saved the money herself, which meant that it wouldn't cost him anything, but you should have heard him "ranting and raving" when she suggested it. The house was in turmoil for several weeks, with Dad regularly accusing Joyce's mates at work, of filling her head with bright ideas, but eventually after a great deal of upset and many tears had been shed, consent from high was given and the carpets were ordered. Joyce was at work the day they were fitted, so you can imagine how excited she must have been after all the pain that she'd been through to get them, however, I'll never forget the look of disappointment on her face when she returned home to discover that the stair carpet had been fitted in the old fashioned way and not wall to wall as she'd ordered. What upset me more than her disappointment, was Dad's lack of interest and support, added to his cocky, "I don't know why you bothered" attitude, which left me feeling both very disgusted and disillusioned to think that my own father could be so uncaring and callous.

A similar row which lasted for a few weeks, occurred when colour television was first introduced, Joyce had wanted one from the very start, but once again her ideas were met with objections from the big "I am", but rather untypically, Dad conceded on this occasion, with less of a fight, which I could only put down to selfishness and the fact that he was able to watch his Gee Gees in colour. Many a time I would walk in to see him crouched in a riding pose, screaming and bellowing encouragement towards his horse on the telly, you see, Dad was addicted to horse racing and seeing him either entering or leaving the bookies was a regular sight. It was at about this time in my life that I realised his gambling problems were beginning to have an effect on our day, as life became totally unbearable if he lost, so we learnt to keep our distance, knowing that his short fuse could ignite without warning, yet in contrast, he could be the perfect Father, if he had backed a winner or two.

Many changes were now taking place at "Forber", as constant refurbishments put it beyond all recognition, with the old kitchen sink being one of the things we were glad to see the back of more than anything else. Just thinking about it brings back many memories of Sunday nights, "bath night!", it was bloody awful, for we had to take it in turns to sit in the sink and be scrubbed down with carbolic soap, by either Joyce or Dad. Then it was time to have our hair examined with the help of the dreaded nit comb, which usually took place in front of the fire, while we all watched the London Palladium. God, it was an horrendous experience, more like a nightmare, we had to sit there, regardless of the excruciating pain, as they continuously dragged our hair with a fine metal tooth comb, whilst searching for the dreaded mites.

If you were unlucky, the exact words that you didn't want to hear, would ring out "Hang on, I think I've got one?", then either Joyce or Dad would press their thumb nail down on the comb, to see if it made a clicking noise, but if it did, YOU HAD THEM!!!

The reason for this escapade was to ensure that you were "clean" for school, before the regular visit from "The Nit Nurse!", a day when many of the kids were sent home with the fearful brown envelope, which informed parents that their child had hair lice. The remainder of that day would obviously be spent tormenting any poor sole who was unfortunate enough to have a letter, needless to say we never got one . . . "We daren't!!".

Another great change, was the transformation from a coal to gas, for the difference it made to our lives was incredible because getting up to a real fire in the morning was a joke. The usual pattern was, first one up had prime position directly in front of the fire, which meant that the other two poor buggers had to snuggle up either side, as we crowded around, trying to get a glimpse of the ever elusive flame.

The only thing I really missed with the change of fires, was not being able to make fresh toast, especially in the winter, as each morning before we got ready for school, we would all sit around the fire, armed with the toasting fork and within minutes be eating toast as fast as we could make it. Then to round things off, Joyce would bring us all a mug of tea each and we would sit there like three little Indians dipping our toast accompanied by best butter into the hot brew, which made one all the more reluctant to move, especially as it had a taste all of it's own.

In 1964 our "other Nanna" died, Dad had found her late one Saturday night, lying at the bottom of the stairs wearing a big smile on her face and it appeared that she'd fallen from top to bottom whilst in a drunken state, yet despite her sudden and sad demise, my own Dad seemed to have coped extremely well with his loss. Although young, we were puzzled as to how he was able to deal with it so well, but his response to our question basically summed it all up, when he said that, "She went the way she had always wanted to go – Pissed!!". Although we weren't that close her death affected me in a funny way, as I was one of the last people to see her alive, for each Saturday evening, Joyce used to send us round to her house with groceries from work and in return she would give us threepence each and sixpence for Linda. However that night she was a little short of change and asked us to tell Linda that she would get her's the next day, but that night she died and so, just for once, Linda missed out!!

> How ironic, that I always felt a special bond with this woman, only to eventually become, like her, "An Alcoholic".

Chapter Two

Confusion

In the summer of that year I was transferred from the Infant to Junior school and yet again I was faced with change, which never agreed with my metabolism. I was really frightened and the fact that I was in totally new surroundings, coupled with the size of the place, terrified me, but there was an added problem. This was the first time in my life that I had ever seen an abundance of new faces in such numbers, an experience which left me feeling totally raw and naked to the world. It was obviously another manifestation of my general inadequacy, which was to follow me throughout my life and once again I was cracking up inside, but somehow I always managed to put a brave face on for all to see.

In no time at all Dad was looking forward to watching me play football for the school team, as this was the first opportunity kids were given to play soccer.

As a father, you can imagine, he was quite excited at the prospect of teaching Eddie and myself to play, but sadly, he had no idea of just how frightened I was of any new challenge that may come along. An announcement that there was going to be a football team brought great excitement to most of the lads, but not for me. This was now the start of a new chapter in my life, it was the beginning of a long, lonely journey, on a path of deceit and lies, the first of which was to my own Dad, when I told him that we weren't having a football team in the first or second years.

The night of the football trials, I hung back and watched from outside the school railings, making sure that nobody saw me. I felt so guilty and unhappy that I cried, knowing in my own mind that I had let my Dad down badly. I was so ashamed of myself to think that I had lied to him, especially when he had so much belief in my football ability, but the guilty feelings were soon shelved to the back of my mind. That year passed quickly and the only other occasions that I felt either guilty or ashamed, were when the team played, or when Dad quizzed me over school football.

The next year, saw Joyce start learning to drive, another example of her being both positive and adventurous, whilst also looking to the future. For nearly four years she'd travelled to and from work in Stockport on the bus, a journey of some four or five miles, more often than not, laden with bags on her return home, so it was common sense for her to learn, "Well!, that's not what Dad thought", for he was against her driving right from the very start. Those driving lessons brought Joyce and us lots of unhappiness, in fact it got so bad at one point, we all had a vote and suggested they weren't worth the aggro, that she should pack them in and forget all about the idea, but undeterred she carried on.

During the course of the next few months there were many fights, as Dad became more aware of the possible freedom Joyce could achieve by passing her test, so it came as no surprise to any of us, when he eventually accused her of having an affair with the driving instructor.

It was now that I started to see him in a different light, less of his good points and much, much more of the evil side to him. Joyce was now beginning to show battle scars, as she would frequently be bruised from fights held the night before and on many occasions she could be heard crying as he hit her, whilst at the same time shouting abuse.

It seemed at times that the only escape from the hell we were living in, came when he was at work on nights, when Joyce allowed us to stay up and watch telly. She never realised why we wanted to be with her, that little bit longer each day, in our own minds it was our way of showing her our love, whilst trying to make up for the pain she was suffering. When she passed her test first time we all breathed a sigh of relief, innocently and naively believing that Dad's domineering attitude and violent behaviour would be a thing of the past, but sadly . .

"We were wrong!".

In 1966 Joyce bought her first car, it was a bright yellow Ford Popular, and to see her drive home for the first time was a most beautiful sight, I loved her so much and was so proud of her and just for that moment it seemed that all the fights, beatings and arguing were worth it,

"But of course nothing was worth all that!!".

The car brought about the expected independence that Dad was always afraid of and needless to say once Joyce was mobile, we went everywhere with her. On the occasions Dad was with us there was always a row, which usually centred on or around driving. Consequently it wasn't long before he started learning himself and being such "a clever shit" within no time at all, he was telling Joyce how to drive, even though, he still hadn't passed his test.

One night we all went out in the car, whilst Joyce gave Dad a driving lesson, which can't have been easy, especially with three kids in the back, but it was a situation made worse by the fact that Dad couldn't stand being told anything, or even worse, laughed at.

Everything went well, until we arrived back home, it was dark and the entrance to the driveway was both narrow and difficult to judge, so Joyce offered to take over, "Eddie love, swop over and I'll take it up the path, you might find it hard to manoeuvre", which was when all hell broke loose. Dad took it as an insult and criticism of his driving capabilities, "What the bleedin ell d'ya think I am, stupid or somethin?". There we were, sat in the car, in the middle of the road with the engine running, tempers at fever pitch and by now the neighbours had either come to their gates or were at their windows, having a nosey. Dad in his cocky, "I'll bloody show her" attitude, suddenly put the car in gear and off we went!

I don't know what speed we went through those gate posts at, but it seemed as if we were travelling at about 30 mph. Joyce shouted

"Eddie!, stop, you're going too fast!, stop!", – but it was too late. I don't know how, but we cleared the gate posts first time, the only problem was that we just kept going on and on and on in kangaroo style.

We finally came to a sudden halt, at the bottom of the garden and that was only because we had crashed through the bushes and into the garden fence. If you thought the other row was a good one, then you should have heard this one. There we all were in the pitch black of the night, covered in mud and crawling amongst the ten foot bushes, all trying to push Joyce's pride and joy, back from the garden fence.

By now, they were cursing and swearing at each other as she told him what a "Clever bastard" he was, while us lot were making matters ten times worse by giggling our heads off.

Amongst all the chaos and laughter, we tried to push the car back, but all our efforts were in vain. Dad said "Oh fuckin leave it till tomorrow, Joyce, it's no good with these lot in this frame of mind", so we did!, the neighbours, God bless them, must have thought, "Oh it's only the Davies's again!".

Dad, being the type of bloke he was, decided to wake us all up early the next morning, in order to save himself any more embarrassment, but his plan didn't work.

Six o'clock in the morning, half asleep, we crept out in to the back garden and so far we had all been quiet, managing to control our emotions, that was until we saw Dad's masterpiece.

There it was, Joyces's bright yellow car, two wheels stuck up in the air, parked up on the edge the rockery, we couldn't help it, we couldn't contain ourselves any longer. We howled with laughter, as Dad stood there, scratching his head, deep in thought, wondering how on earth he was going to get it off. Unfortunately for him, the car refused to budge, so it had to be left there for most of that day, on display, for the rest of the world to see and if to make matters worse Dad failed his first test, but passed his second, a year later which was something Joyce reminded him of for many a year to come.

During that same year, Dad walked out of his job at Fancis Shaws, where he was an engineer on regular nights. The foreman had suddenly decided to change his shift and put him on days, which was considerably less money, so in his own mind it was his way of forcing Dad to seek employment elsewhere, thus enabling him to find a position for one of his own family. However, by their very nature the "Davies's" have always been volatile and impulsive, to say the least and so without any hesitation, he quit on the spot by telling the foreman to, shove the job up his arse.

Instead of coming straight home that morning he went off to look for work and found a job as a milkman at the Express Dairies, a job which only lasted a couple of months, although it wasn't because of the early mornings. The dairy stipulated that staff had to pay for any missing milk and all breakages, what, with children stealing the stuff while he was delivering, then having to collect money from dodging customers, it really proved a hopeless task.

Not long after, Dad noticed there was a window cleaning round advertised in the Post Office, when he enquired about it, he discovered that not only was it local, but it was on our Estate, so he was able to finish on the milk round and begin window cleaning full time.

Having a Dad who was the local window cleaner was more of a hindrance than a help, because you could bet that if we ever we got up to any mischief, he would always find out about it.

One such incident, was the time that we were seen playing on the railway lines, like all lads we did tend to have a fascination for trains and spent many hours playing on the embankment. Quite often we would dare each other to stay on the track for as long as possible, or goad each other into throwing "duckers" at the carriages as they passed. Unfortunately, a teacher spotted us from one of the compartments and the next morning at school, the headmistress made an announcement in assembly, "Would the boys, seen playing on the railway last night, go to my office", but of course nobody went.

During the course of that day, we were individually called to her office, where we were informed of what had happened and consequently severely reprimanded, which was the end of the matter as far as the school were concerned and meant our parents were non the wiser, or so we thought.

A few days later, whilst we were having our dinner, Dad suddenly burst in, "Upstairs you two!!" he shouted and as soon as he said this we knew what was coming, we were going to get a good hiding, care of his big army belt!

As we climbed the stairs Eddie looked at me as if to say, "What have we done now?", but we didn't have a clue. We got in to the bedroom, looking bewildered at each other, waiting for the inevitable to happen. "What have I told you about playing on that bleedin railway?" he shouted, "If I've told you once, I've told you both a thousand times!, I'm not going to bloody tell you again!, don't go near there!". With that he went downstairs, whilst we sat there dumb struck, waiting for him to return, but he didn't, we couldn't believe it!

By now we were totally confused and didn't understand what was happening, he hadn't hit us, but there again, he no longer needed to, because we had already realised the railway was a no go area, it just wasn't worth it.

Later on, towards tea-time, we got home without a care in the world, but as we got in the back door, Dad grabbed us by the scruff of the neck and dragged us upstairs. Ranting and raving like a mad man, he said "What did I tell you this afternoon?, are you bleedin tapped or what?. Get your pants off!". We knew there and then that there was no way out of this one, that it was a matter of "grin and bare it", so we just cried our eyes out, cowering and trembling in fear, whilst he stormed around the room, lashing out in a violent rage, like a demon possessed.

Usually after a good hiding, there was always a period of silence, where the subject was never discussed, so that Eddie and I had time to reflect and ponder over both the crime and punishment, but in this instance, as far as we were concerned, we were guilty of nothing, so we were left feeling both perplexed and confused, wondering "Why?, what have we done?". It wasn't until later that evening, when Dad had calmed down, that the matter was discussed, where it was revealed he had been mislead with wrong information whilst on his rounds.

In actual fact he had been told twice about the same incident, innocently believing we'd disobeyed him, therefore our good hiding was for nothing!

Despite the aggression and violence, we still had many good times together as a family, but deep at the back of my mind I was very weary of my Dad, as I always felt that he was more capable than anybody else of going over the top and snapping. I was convinced that one day, sooner or later, he would commit murder and that either Joyce or one of us would be on the receiving end.

In the September, I started my third year at Gorton Mount and for the first time in my life, thanks to Eddie, my past was about to catch up with me. One evening, he came home with news that he had been selected for the second-year football team, an announcement which left Dad both proud and puzzled, as I had spent the last two years telling him, that the school didn't even have a side. This put me in a very awkward position, Dad started asking questions, wanting to know why I wasn't playing and why all of a sudden there was a team for Eddie's year. I needed to find a new plausible excuse, whilst at the same time cover my backtracks, so I told Dad that I'd missed the trials for that year and that the team for Eddie's term was a new idea. It worked and no further questions were asked, but it didn't ease the guilt or shame that I felt whenever Eddie was playing, for Dad would always be there watching and shouting as encouragement, "Go on Eddie, show em what you can do!". I would spy enviously from a distance, trying to work it all out for myself, I was so good at the game, yet I couldn't stand being watched, especially by my own father. I was distraught, for not only was I letting Dad down, but Joyce as well, which hurt even more, yet I was unable to tell anyone.

Part of that first term had passed, when I was asked to go to the next training session, the third year team had lost most of their games and needed new players, so I was nominated by my mates.

I knew in my own heart, that I couldn't carry on the way I was going, so I went home and told Dad the good news, which cheered him up no end, he was over the moon and so proud of me, but "If only he'd known, how I really felt".

I went to that first training session and without any great effort, was selected for the team, so I only had one other thing left to do and that was to turn up, but I didn't have long to wait, for the next school match followed a couple of days later, which of course was "my big day!".

There was quite a crowd as we came out from the school building and ran towards the field, with everybody shouting, "Come on the Mount, show em how to play!", and all the usual terminology which is associated with football. We lined up, ready to kick off, with me thinking "So far, so good, he's not here, thank God!", then, suddenly, I could here him.

"Come on Paul, we've waited a long time for this, give it to em!". Panic just set in, because deep in the back of my mind, right up until that moment, I'd kept on hoping that I would get a last minute reprieve, that he would still be at the bookies, or perhaps may still be working, but no, he was there.

Despite his presence I played well, in fact everybody thought I was brilliant, even the teacher came over to me when we were getting changed wanting to know why I hadn't played before, so I told him "I just couldn't be bothered". Dad was so proud that evening as we walked home together and for once I felt really good about myself, even more so, whilst he was telling Joyce about my performance.

The next morning I felt ten feet tall, as I walked to school with Eddie and my mates, the difference was amazing, stood in the school grounds feeling as though I was part of a new clique of lads and I was the centre of attraction as they all talked about the game and what a good player I was, it was a wonderful feeling.

That was a good time for me with those feelings lasting a couple of days, although it had quite a long term effect on my character. My outward confidence both in the classroom and in my social activities grew, but within myself I was still the same old insecure Paul, (if only they knew just how much pain I'd suffered deep inside, to get that acclaim.)

Now, for the first time, I was really enjoying school, however, sadly the same couldn't be said for our home life, as every now and then there would be surges of violent behaviour, which invariably ended up with us all on show for the rest of "Suttons" to see and it was around this period of time, that I remember we gave one of our best performances. Joyce had been invited out by a few of the women on the estate, because a family called "The Lambs" were emigrating to Australia, so all the neighbours wanted to give Mrs Lamb a good send off. It was the first time Joyce had ever been asked if she wanted to join in on anything, so she was both pleased and looking forward to going on the night out.

Dad though, had different ideas, because in his mind they were all a bunch of slags and there was no way on this earth that Joyce was going. For once in her life she stood her ground, she was determined to go, no matter what price she had to pay, but she didn't know then, just what that price was going to end up being.

For three weeks we suffered day and night, constant bickering and arguing, which usually ended with Dad smashing up perfectly good furniture, for he would just erupt into frenzied attacks on Joyce and us. There were times when I would have sworn he had the devil in him, as his face would turn red through rage and his blue eyes would look all glassy in appearance.

On this and many other occasions the Police would turn up, having been called by a caring neighbour who was worried about our safety, yet when the Police arrived he immediately transformed himself into a calm and responsible person, rather like "Jekyll and Hyde".

Those mood swings, kept us in a constant state of confusion, which left us never knowing where we stood, with matters always made worse whenever Joyce involved her Mum and Dad. One particular day, Joyce and her Mum stood down the road watching him throwing all her clothes and dirty washing out of the front bedroom window. Even the estate Landlord, Mr Knapman, who lived opposite came out to watch it all going off, as Dad even had the cheek to shout down to him, "Nice, windy day for drying clothes, isn't it". Mr Knapman was the person in charge of the whole estate, he was quite a powerful and influential bloke, not the ideal person to have living opposite you, but that made no difference to Dad when he was in this frame of mind.

I can see it all now, Dad's head popping in and out like a demented Jack in the box, swearing and cursing as he threw each garment into the air. With the help of the wind, Dad certainly made his mark, "What a sight!", four kids and Billy on the front garden, trying to catch anything we could, as if floated down and the more we laughed the more Billy barked, as the poor dog thought it was a game. Our Queen Elizabeth Rose bushes had never looked better, as they displayed a variety of Marks & Spencer underwear and by this time quite a crowd had gathered because Dad was performing well, leaving everyone in hysterics laughing as he offered, "parcels to the poor" and "bargains of the day".

Looking back at this and other incidents, it seems as though we were basically piggy in the middle, for Joyce was as guilty as Dad when it came down to "fuelling the fire".

Despite all the pain and suffering, she always returned home, having left to stay with her Mum, forever conceding to his demands, whilst at the same time seeming to enjoy the extra attention, but unfortunately, they had forgotten all about us, our feelings and the adverse affect their behaviour was having.

Towards the end of that dispute, there was one incident where they held up the traffic by arguing in the middle of the road. Cars were at stand still on both sides, the drivers beeping their horns whilst shouting abuse at Joyce and Dad, telling them to get out of the way, but they just carried on arguing, totally regardless and oblivious to anyone else. That three week period also brought a new man into our lives, he was "The Cruelty Man". Joyce's sister Edith, a so called expert in matrimonial affairs had told her to contact him, but even he couldn't do any good, as Dad frightened him off as well!, so, yet again, he had won, with Joyce eventually conceding and never making the night out.

By now that ever increasing mental and physical cruelty within the home was obviously having a long term effect on my own personal life, not least at school, where I always worked hard and struggled to get through. With my third year at Gorton Mount coming to an end, I only had one awesome task left to complete, which was to take home my yearly school report. That report was the first one that I can remember, simply because the summary said: "Paul works very hard although he does lack confidence!", but all that was soon to change.

The following year I was going to be in Miss Mackey's class, a teacher of high quality, who was well known to everyone as a strict disciplinarian. Linda had just finished the fourth year in her class and had left Gorton Mount in a blaze of glory, so I had a lot to live up to.

That same year Dad started work at the Kelloggs in Trafford Park, where in those days it was an achievement to be given an interview, let alone obtain a well paid job. While he worked there we had cereals coming out of our ears, for whenever a new brand was advertised on the telly we would ask Dad to try and get us some samples and within a few days, he would usually bring home a full case.

Sometimes we would get up in a morning and Dad would come in from doing his night shift, carrying a large box, which was full of plastic toys figures and models, "There you are kids, see if they're any good", where by we would then proceed to empty them all over the floor and have a good rummage through, before going to school.

Joyce's stability at Marks's, plus the fact that Dad also had a good, well paid job, meant that they were now in a better position to change the "Ford Pop" to a bigger family vehicle, so they bought their first "Morris Oxford", which was built like a tank and boy did we need it! With the bigger car we had more comfort on days out, and for our holidays, which brings me to the summer of the "Big Family" trip to Butlins, a trip that consisted of three families from within the Williams side, making an assault on Pwllheli holiday camp.

"What a trip!", it was a week where Eddie and I stayed well out of the way, doing our own thing, with Carol and Linda doing much the same. I think it's best that I try to summarize that holiday by telling you about our entry in the Butlin's 1967 "Happy Families" competition, or should I say our attempt.

Every week at each holiday camp, Butlins had various competitions with one such contest being "The Happy Families". Basically it was a search for the some of the largest, well-represented, but most of all, happiest families on the camp, where the winners got the opportunity to return for the big national final in London.

There were eighteen of us altogether and all week the adults kept going on and on about entering this stupid challenge, even though none of us kids were interested and had no intention of turning up, never the less we were told to be at the hall for no later than one o'clock. At the exact time we were supposed to be meeting, Eddie and I were in the middle of the boating lake, whilst Linda, Carol and our cousin Helen hadn't been seen since breakfast, needless to say, all the others were in the hall panicking and arguing as to our whereabouts. The competition started at a quarter past one with the idea, that a photographer would arrange the groups individually on stage, so that he could take a picture, whilst in line, the judges would ask a variety of questions about the family concerned and the relationships within, in order to obtain background information, making sure that all the entries were genuine.

At half past one, the Davies's were supposed to be on, in our original position, third out of about twelve families, however with five minutes to go, none of us kids were anywhere to be seen. Apparently, behind the scenes it was chaos, the adults were all in dispute, arguing and accusing each other of letting the side down, while Auntie Edith was frantically rushing around looking for Helen screaming "When I get my bleedin hands on her, her life won't be worth living!", with Joyce and Dad sounding as if they were in much the same frame of mind, "I don't know where they are, but I'll kill em when I get my hands on em!". By now tempers and patience were just beginning to boil over, so in desperation a search party was sent out for the five kids who had gone A.W.O.L, which meant our turn had to be delayed.

Meanwhile Eddie and I were still happily rowing away on the boating lake, when suddenly we heard Aunt Edith's dulcet tones, "KIDS!, Eddie, Paul, get out of that bleedin boat, bring it back, NOW!!", she grabbed us by the scruff of the neck and escorted us back to the hall, "Eddie and Joyce are going spare!", she said "Where's the girls?", "Don't know, we haven't seen em since this morning". When we got back Carol, Linda and Helen were still missing and so were Joyce and Dad, who had gone looking for them. Having completed a third body count the organisers had no other alternative, but to once again put us back, so we were now last on and it was a good job!

At three o'clock Linda, Carol and Helen were frog marched in by Joyce and Dad, "Where the bloody hell have they been?" everybody asked, "They'd totally forgotten about it", replied Joyce, "Oh yeah, I've heard that one before!", said Eddie. At this point the only family left before us, were actually on the stage doing their "bit", whilst we were doing our best impersonation of a "Crufts dog show" gone wrong, for we didn't even have a single comb or handkerchief between us. The adults were doing there best to clean the kids up, spitting on their hands and rubbing the dirt off with their fingers, whilst trying to groom our hair to some degree of respectability. Joyce tied Carol's hair in pig tails to try and make it look neater, while Carol had a tantrum, "Joyce, I'm sick of this, it's bloomin stupid", "Carol Stay still!", she replied. By now a couple of the other younger kids were beginning to get restless, so they got a crack, which only made matters worse. It was absolute mayhem, adults arguing, kids moaning and there amongst it all were Nanna and Grandad totally oblivious to all the chaos around them.

Well it was our turn by this time and apart from the judges, the photographer and the organisers, everyone else had gone, with not one of the other families staying, so it was obvious that none of them saw us as a threat to their challenge. It was a good job, because our families attempt so far was bad enough, but once we had got on that stage it was nothing short of a comedy farse, it was a fiasco, something the best comedy writer in the world would have been proud of.

We looked an absolute mess, Eddie and I were ringing wet through from playing on the boats in the lake and God knows what the girls had been doing, they were caked in mud. Although it wasn't their fault, some of our Aunts and Uncles looked so scruffy and poor, you could of been forgiven for thinking that they'd come straight from the "Sally Army".

Another major problem was that each time the photographer asked one of us to stand near someone that we disliked or had fallen out with, he was met with some form of argument or abuse. On top of all that some of the babies were crying just to complete a great "Happy Family" picture, however in the end and after a long struggle, the picture was eventually taken, leaving the tired judges totally confused and bewildered, and the poor photographer shattered, begging us not to go back the following year.

The result and all the pictures were on show in the main reception hall at the end of the week, so we went to look at the photo's with Joyce and Dad on the Friday morning, straight after breakfast, still naively thinking we had a chance of winning. Joyce and Dad suddenly burst out laughing very loudly, "Oh Eddie!", she said "Look at us", Dad couldn't stop laughing, "Bleedin Hell, Joyce!" he replied, "There's no point in buying one, I'd be too embarrassed to show that to anyone!". We couldn't see what was so amusing, so we asked Joyce and Dad, "What's so funny?". They then explained that if we looked at the pictures of all the other families, we would notice that they all looked very smart and immaculately dressed in matching clothes. In contrast we looked very much like, "The Vonn Trap Family" from "The Sound of Music", only, before Julie Andrews had cut up the curtains and made them all new clothes. For days we walked around, naively thinking people were noticing us, because our picture was in the reception hall, what we didn't realise, was that they were probably all saying "Oh look, there's some of that scruffy lot, who were in the happy families competition!".

I hope that I have given you just a little idea of what that family holiday was like and why we kept well away from the rest of the gang for the duration, needless to say, it was the last time we all went away together.

Those summer holidays passed and it was time to go back to school, it was much easier for me this time around, as I was going back to familiar surroundings, for I was now in my fourth year, the oldest form in the school and already established on the football team.

The only draw back, was that I knew it was going to be my most important year so far, and because of my Dad's old ties with my new teacher, I was going to be under very close scrutiny. I decided that I was going to put as much effort as I could into my work, to show everyone that I wasn't slow, whilst also proving that I was just as capable as the others.

For those first few months I worked very hard, doing well in all subjects and generally showed great promise, that was until the day I suddenly became ill. It was late November and I'd felt poorly all day at school, but the teacher constantly refused to send me home, I felt awful, the longer the day went on, the worse I became and by the time it had got to four o'clock I was in a dreadful state. I remember crying as I struggled home, and the relief when I saw Nanna and Grandad's house in the distance, "I'm nearly safe!", but unfortunately, that was the last thing I remember, because shortly after, I collapsed in the road. The next thing I knew, I was lying on the couch in their house, with Nanna, Grandad, Linda and Joyce of course, who had received a phone call at work. When the Doctor arrived he gave me an injection in my thigh, stipulating that under no circumstances should I be moved, as it was pneumonia, but that's it, that's all I can recall, for it was a few days before I came round and realised what had happened, but when I did, it was great!, as I, for once, was the centre of attraction, receiving lots of attention as people kept visiting me with presents.

I really enjoyed the first couple of weeks, but soon realised that all my previous hard work and effort would be to no avail, should I fail to keep up with my studies. Dad was also aware of this, so he went to school to see Miss Mackey and together they worked out the schedule which the fourth year would be following, which enabled me to keep up with the rest of the class.

In the New year, I returned to school, which was a strange feeling in itself, I went back so apprehensive, thinking that I might of have fallen behind the rest of the class, but what a shock I got, for far from being behind, "I was well in front!". You see during my illness Dad had devoted so much of his time to me and my studies, that I inadvertently found myself ahead of the school curriculum, even "top of the class". The results proved that all the extra help, patience and love he had shown me, had paid off, because going back after such a long time, to be credited and acclaimed in the class in such a way, meant that I was now enjoying my work, more than ever before, and for once confident! . . . It was at times like these that he was such a good Dad.

In the final half of that school year a lot of the lads had started going to watch football on Saturday afternoons, which was something that sounded really exciting, so we started pestering Dad about letting us go to Maine Road to watch City. Dad was an out and out Blue, a real true City fan, so the minute we said that we wanted to go to Maine Road, he was over the moon. For weeks we were excited, dying to go and couldn't wait for him to take us, but we accepted that it was all down to when Dad could afford to spare us the time, knowing full well that, he would when he could.

Going to that first game with him was fabulous, something we'd been looking forward to for ages, so proudly wearing our brand new bob hats and scarfs, we set off following Dad's every step, intent on listening to his every word. The whole day from start to finish was a dream come true, a totally new experience which left both Eddie and I drained with excitement, but in no time at all we were back at home boring Joyce with every little detail. Consequently Dad took us to quite a few matches after that, but it wasn't long before we were going on our own, mainly as a result of our independence.

That last term at school was really my most enjoyable and productive, I had worked hard in all my lessons and had done just as well in the football team. In fact, so far that year, I had achieved much more than was ever expected of me, my confidence was at an all time high, and to round things off, Eddie was just beginning to get into odd bits of trouble at school, so I was enjoying being in favour. It seemed that for once, I was having a good time, in which I had a bit of balance, self respect and high esteem, but there was no chance of me getting carried away, because deep down I knew better.

Sure enough, I was right to keep my feet firmly on the ground, for after a routine dental check up, I was told that I would need a brace fitted, to help straighten my teeth out. I was informed that the treatment would begin in the new school term, but that was it, I had no idea of what was involved, all I knew was, that I definitely wasn't looking forward to it, which was just typical of me, because for the first time in ages I had a bit of self confidence and was feeling good, only to brought back down to earth with a bang.

I left Gorton Mount Junior School with a good school report, my head held high and a six weeks holiday to look forward to, but in order to enjoy as much of that break as I could, I needed to put any ensuing problems that would come with the next school year to the back of my mind. However, during the holidays we would sometimes bump into one or two of the older lads from around the area, who would threaten to get us, when we were at the high school the following term. As a result of those threats and stories about bullying, I finished up in one hell of a state and certainly not looking forward to the new school year.

Soon, Joyce was putting the final touches to our school clothes, but this year, I, like Linda, had to have regulation school uniform, so Joyce took us to be fitted out.

Even when we were in the shop I found myself putting on a brave face, trying to hide my fear, but the fact that I hadn't worn long trousers, or ever fastened a tie before didn't help matters. As if all this wasn't enough to cope with, I had the added problem of a new school, with new teachers and literally hundreds of new faces.

It was the Sunday night before school and Dad was showing me how to do my tie, Joyce, Eddie and Carol were waiting to see me in my uniform, so I went upstairs and got changed. I looked in the mirror and cried my eyes out, for I had never felt so scared or vulnerable in my life, all I basically wanted to do, was to curl up and die there and then, but I eventually calmed down, pulled myself together and returned downstairs. "Ooh, don't you look smart!", they all said in a chorus. Carol, God bless her, said "I'll bet your dead excited, aren't you", "Oh yeah" I replied, If she only knew. With my fashion show finished we all watched telly as normal, you know, "The London Palladium", etc, but my mind was elsewhere, as I was as lonely as ever in my head, dreading what tomorrow was going to bring, but that was no surprise to me.

After all my projections of doom and gloom, our first day at school wasn't so bad, as it was only for the new intake of pupils, it was a day that consisted soley of tests, which were used to grade new students, so it passed quite quickly. When I got home Dad was obviously eager to know how the day and the tests had gone, so I told him that I hadn't a clue, mainly because I didn't want to disappoint him, his response to my answer was that, "As long as you've done your best, then nobody can ask any more of you", so with that task behind me I went out to play.

That night Eddie and I played football with all our mates in the street as normal, with the discussion amongst my friends obviously revolving around the next morning and what plan of action we were all going to adopt, in relation to our first real day at "Spurley Hey".

Tuesday morning and it was time for school, most of my mates had to pass our house on their way, so the plan was that they would all call for me.

As I answered the front door, I was confronted by a mass of brand new uniforms, briefcases and absolutely petrified faces, which although clean and bright, were white with fear. I soon discovered that they were all more frightened than I, and were looking to me for leadership, which by it's very nature was the joke of the century. Joyce gave me a quick peck on the cheek, "Good luck luv, don't worry everything will be alright" and by now the tears were starting to appear and I'm wishing she could look and sound a bit more positive. I turned away with the rest of the lads wondering, "Does she know something that I don't?". It was then that I recalled some of my Dads most profound words, "Paul lad, there are two types of people in this world, there are the 'plodders' and the 'leaders', which do you want to be?", so with that in mind, I decided to put a brave face on and take control of the situation, and like the Pied Pier led the rest of the lads to school.

"Talk about being an apprentice con man".

Originally the lads and I, all agreed that we would be safer in numbers, however, things don't always necessarily go according to plan and this was certainly one of those instances, for as we approached the main gate we were ambushed by a gang of second years, leaving us no other option but to scatter in every direction. It was one of those occasions in my life, that I was grateful for being quite fit and athletic, so I just pissed off as fast as my little legs could carry me, looking for a place to hide. I think I would of hidden up my own arse if I could, but eventually settled for hiding around the corner, where I waited until I heard the bell go, then made my way into the yard, where we had to line up . . . I was here, my first day! . . . "What a great start!".

The Second years went straight into the assembly hall, while we had to wait outside, before following them in shortly afterwards. I'd never seen or heard anything like it, the clattering sound of chairs being knocked and smashed together as people kept filing into the hall, mixed with the ever present mumbling noise from everyone talking to each other, as they discussed what they'd been doing during the holiday. A few teachers appeared but everybody carried on talking, then the Headmaster and his deputy arrived on the stage, suddenly there was deadly silence. The Headmaster welcomed us all to the school, as we experienced our very first assembly and shortly after the classes were read out, informing everyone, of what grade they'd achieved in their exams. This was now my own personal moment of truth and in all honesty, because of my low self esteem, I really didn't expect to have done well. Imagine how I felt and my surprise when he suddenly called my name out for the top class, I just couldn't believe it, I was convinced that a mistake had been made and that there was probably another Paul Davies.

I even asked our Form teacher, who then confirmed it, which then meant that throughout the whole of the day I felt that I could have walked on water and I no longer cared about the bullying, the size of the school or anything else for that matter, for all I wanted to do, was get home and tell Joyce and Dad.

When the bell rang at four o'clock I made a "beeline" for home, running all the way, without stopping, dying to spread the news of my achievement, "Well, how did you go on?, what class did you end up in?", "Guess!", I said. So he started guessing from the bottom grades upwards, but within a few seconds, smiled and said, "You didn't make the top one did you?". At that moment, I just wanted to cry, Dad was so proud of me as he stood there with his arm around me and just for once, I felt I was his favourite son, instead of Eddie.

Those first few days obviously felt very strange, they were mainly spent working out our timetables, where I came across one of my first high school hurdles, as I immediately noticed a double period titled "BATHS", which sent a shiver through my spine. I absolutely hated swimming, I couldn't swim and didn't really want to learn, so I knew there was going to be a problem there. Looking through there were an assortment of subjects whose titles alone, scared me to bits, things like Biology, Physics and Chemistry. Every new lesson was like another mini-adventure, a new classroom, new books and a new teacher, basically the unknown and the unexpected, it was fascinating. There were teachers that I took an instant liking to and others that I was very weary and suspicious of, but it wasn't long before I settled in to my new surroundings and everything was going well, I even seemed to have conquered my worst fear of going to the baths, until I had a really frightening experience.

I was still in the learners group, with about five other people and getting both fed up and disillusioned, when I decided to make one last big attempt. It was getting towards the end of the lesson, so I decided to give it one more go, so with as much effort and belief as I could muster up, I made one last push towards the water. I couldn't believe it, I'd finally succeeded, swimming without a float, I was so thrilled with my achievement, even more so when the lesson finished and the swimming instructor told me I could automatically join the swimmers group the following week.

The next time we went to the baths I felt full of confidence, I no longer had butterflies rolling around in my stomach and I had every intention of enjoying each minute of the lesson. I felt so good that if I was asked to swim the English channel, I think I could have done so, however, with fifteen minutes of the lesson to go, everyone was told to walk down to the deep end, either dive or jump in and then swim the full length of the baths. There was only one slight problem here for me, I had neither jumped or dived in more than three feet of water in my whole life, so it was now "panicsville!".

I hung back as all the kids around me entered the water in all types of cocky fashion, diving and jumping from the left and the right, it was like one of those scenes from the films when they're abandoning ship, but for all I cared at that exact moment in time, I could have been on the bloody Titanic. "Oh stuff this!" I said as I jumped, well I think I jumped, it was somewhere in between a jump and a belly flop, whatever it was I suddenly found myself drowning in seven foot of water, with bodies landing all over the place, above, below and behind me. But they didn't seem to have any problem, they just drifted off with great ease, while I struggled, stuck there, doing my impression of Zeberdee with an over active spring, bouncing up and down in a frantic fashion. I eventually got going, I don't know how, but I did, paddling and flapping about for all my worth with only one intention, which was to keep afloat. With all arms and legs splashing, I reached the shallow end where I could finally stand up, totally exhausted and breathing a sigh of relief as I crawled out, "I've made it!", I was shattered, but never before had I been so thankful for being on solid ground. Then I heard the bleeding instructor with his big gob "Once more lads, then you can get changed!". My immediate reaction to his instructions was, "Fuck this, I've had enough, I'm off!", because by now I was just grateful for being alive and certainly didn't fancy my chances of a second attempt, so as I walked back to the deep end, I took a swift detour via my changing cubicle. I had no intention whatsoever of becoming a Mark Spitz or a Johnny Weizmuller, or of furthering my swimming career, so I decided there and then to hang my trunks up, whilst I was still alive.

The day finally arrived when I had to have my brace fitted and Joyce took me to the dentist, I had been on several occasions before for fittings etc, but this was the dreaded day. I think fifteen rounds with Muhamid Ali would of been less painful and certainly more enjoyable than being strapped down in that masochist's chair. For two hours the dentist yanked and tugged at the inside of my mouth, which was pure hell and by the time he'd finished I felt punch drunk, dazed and not knowing where I hurt the most, but when I did finally surface, I looked something like "Hanibal Lector" out of "The Silence Of The Lambs" and felt utterly shit. The amount of metal attached to my teeth was unbelievable, in fact I would have had no problem in playing the part of "Jaws" in the James Bond film, but before leaving, as if to rub salt in my wounds the dentist informed Joyce and myself that I would experience severe pain and that there would be lots of suffering to endure for a few months, "Well, that's something to look forward to, eh!" I thought.

Joyce was also given a letter that excused me from any physical activities, which was the only bright point, to an otherwise traumatic day. That letter gave me the licence to get rid of probably my biggest hurdle for the next coming year, the baths! and I had no hesitation in doing so, although I never used it to skive off P.E or Games, as these were two subjects and their teachers that I took to immediately.

Another favourite was my form teacher, who was the same man that had supervised our tests on the first day, fortunately he also taught me English for the first couple of years which produced a good bond between us. In contrast my woodwork teacher, Mr Quinn was a different kettle of fish altogether, he had the reputation of being a right bastard and boy did he look and sound the part as well. For some reason I always felt more at ease in his presence, probably because of my genuine interest in the subject, which I eventually took up as a career, however, on reflection I always felt much comfier in the company of the few other teachers like him, who had a more direct approach in their methods. There was only one other teacher who really had any great impact on me and that was Miss Page, who taught us French. When we were in her lesson, it was mayhem, she was a real corker and she knew it. We used to spend that much time looking up her skirt and dresses, it was bloody miracle that we even learnt to say "Bonjour", never mind anything else. If she walked around the classroom while we were working, it was hilarious. Each time she passed one of the lads, he would immediately bend down and look up her skirt, with the rest of us waiting in anticipation, then he would signal. It was something similar to a gladiator fight scene, where a thumbs up would mean he'd got a good view, and a thumbs down meant he'd failed, miserably. By the time she had walked down a full aisle of lads, it resembled a Mexican wave, being done with heads, as we all bobbed up and down. The girls in the class used to tut in disgust at our antics, but we didn't care, for there was our heroine, our living fantasy, if only she'd known what she was doing to us. Miss Page was a teacher who I automatically fell in love with the first time I saw her, I had a crush on her from the very start, right through to the final days of my schooling, but it's was only at the very end of my education when I wasn't being taught by her, that she left her greatest impression on me, with something she said to our Eddie that I will never forget.

One day he was manking about and he gave her some abuse, at which she turned around having taught Linda, Eddie and myself and said, "There's only one of you Davies's who will ever do anything with your life and that's your Paul, he's the only one of you, who I hold any high hopes for!", but in hindsight, it's a good job she didn't know just how high I wanted to go.

By Christmas, I was beginning to show my full potential in all subjects and as a result I was nominated to be House captain for sports. Eventually I was chosen to lead our house, in the inter-house games competition and in doing so I attracted the attention of the teacher who was in charge of the football team, which ended up with me being selected for the side. It was as if history was repeating itself, just like in the Junior school the year before, this team had hardly won a game, in fact, they were getting a good hammering every week, so really, I didn't have much to lose. To cut a long story short, I played and played well and was awarded man of the match by both teams, even though we lost 2–1, a performance which brought about a variety of complimentary remarks and comments from both teachers and pupils alike. It surprised me just how fast the news had travelled within the staffroom, one teacher, a Mr Booth who taught us Maths, sat with me for about ten minutes that day talking about football, but it was only then, that I found out we both had something in common, for like myself he was a City fan and from then on every Monday we would have a chat about the matches that had been played over the weekend.

My personal success on the team seemed to be the icing on the cake for me in that first year, as I seemed to go from strength to strength. Yet, despite how well I was doing and feeling, I was still reluctant to go to that first Christmas party at

Spurley Hey, for mixing in crowds was something that had always caused me problems and still does today, but as a child and for part of my teenage years, I put it down to being shy, especially when I was in the company of girls.

The rest of that first year went well and towards that first summer break I felt on top of the world, with only two more hurdles to clear, which were parents evening and my school report, although neither were going to blot my copy book.

Apart from the upheaval at home, which reared its ugly head every so often, those Summer holidays were probably the best that I'd ever enjoyed and to round them off, I had one extra thing to look forward to. In the final week, I had my very last appointment at the dentist to have my brace removed, which was a moment that I'd long been waiting for, knowing that I was finally going to be relieved of all the pain and discomfort that I had suffered. I sat there in the chair as the very last piece was about to be removed, wondering if I, or anybody else would even notice any difference, then suddenly, I experienced the strangest sense of freedom. I arrived home and words can't describe how I felt, as soon as I got in, I ran upstairs to my bedroom to look in the mirror, I was so pleased. For over twelve months, I'd been waiting for this moment to arrive, because for the first time in my life, I felt really and truly confident. I now had the most beautiful problem on my hands, "I had to learn to smile", and within minutes I was outside playing and showing off the new me.

Facing that new term at school was a simple task, especially with this new found confidence I now had. I was also looking forward to taking care of Eddie once again, by being "big brother".

I started that second year off in a really positive manner and completed the first term with ease, a mood which carried on throughout that whole school year, with bonds between certain teachers and myself growing, as a result of the effort I was putting in.

By now people were really expecting a lot from me, in fact, there was very little need for me to do any ducking or diving whatsoever that year, which did make a nice change. I was now going through, what was to become a very rare experience in my life, that was "a bloody good long run", where everything was going well, even Manchester City were winning, something which was very important at the time.

Being a child and growing up is never easy, but being a City fan and living in Gorton at the same time, in those days, made it twice as hard. All our lives we were brain washed into believing that there was only one football team in the whole world, that of course was Manchester United. All anyone ever talked about was, "The Reds" and "Munich", people who we looked up to, who influenced us and who we trusted. Grandad, teachers at school and of course friends who we played with, they were all the same, it was a pain in the arse, each time there was news or sport on the telly, there they were. Any night you cared to pick up the Evening News, they covered the back page. It was that bad, I think they'd have filmed them going to the toilet to have a crap, if they could. The media seemed to grab at any opportunity they could, to dig up the past and once again remind everybody about the air crash. You couldn't move without hearing something about them, as it was like a disease, but there seemed to be no cure. On a Monday morning you could always tell what Saturdays result was, for if United won, all the kids would be wearing red and white scarfs going to school, but if they'd lost there wouldn't be one in sight.

Funnily enough, it was our Grandad, a staunch Red, who inadvertently made us support City, with his bias towards United proving instrumental in our choice of team. I feel he tried to pressure us into following "The Reds", which only succeeded in stirring up our inquisitive nature, which later on, led us to question," Why was it so important?".

We finally discovered the true answer behind this so called United phenomena and having done so, we were both disgusted and disillusioned in Grandad. In our opinion both his actions and his views, were totally wrong and as we were now old enough to start making our own decisions, we felt that perhaps it was time to withdraw slightly from that relationship.

Many questions were answered and mysteries unfolded, as we discovered that the Catholic religion was a key factor behind this terminal disease called United, but if there was still any room for doubt, it was soon expelled from the mind when ' The Reds ' won the European Cup, a victory which led to the local Catholic church and school, painting the information on the roof, for all to see. Although of Christian faith and the Church of England, I was never interested in religion, but one thing I soon realised having grown up between two Catholic schools, in Gorton, was that I neither wanted or needed to understand religion, especially "Micks", as I liked neither.

However during the next few years, things changed on the trophy front, with Joe Mercer and his assistant Malcolm Allison, bringing lots of success to Man City and at long last we dominated the local scene, even gaining European status. To both of them I say "Thanks", for they enabled me to enjoy the rest of my childhood and youth, free of any further suffering at the hands of "The Reds", but even then with United the underdogs of the City, they still always managed to cover the back pages of the bias press, something that all City supporters have had to learn to live with.

That success gave Eddie and myself the opportunity to see some wonderful games of football and what was without doubt, one of the most exciting and enthralling experiences of any boy's childhood, which was our first trip to a Cup Final at Wembley. Dad took us to the semi final, which was played at Villa Park, it was all square and looking like a replay, but with only a minute to go, City scored.

We'd never seen or felt anything like it, the atmosphere was electric,

"We're On The March With Mercer's Army, We're All Going To Wembley!", screamed the City faithful, during a last minute which seemed like a lifetime as the crowd whistled and jeered in an effort to make the ref blow his whistle. When he did, the ground erupted, with sensible human – beings turning totally barmy, throwing themselves around the terraces. When we got back to the car we were drained, we couldn't believe it, our first words to Dad were, "Can we go to Wembley Dad?, please!", and for weeks we were like a couple of bears with sore heads. The bloke who lived over the road from us had already promised Dad that he would get us our tickets, which he did and so our dream had come true, we were on our way to Wembley.

We left home at about ten p.m on the Friday night and walked down to the main road to meet the coach which was taking us down to London. We didn't have a clue what to expect and as we boarded we got the shock of our lives. We were met by a barrage of noise from the back, a mass of harmless, drunken football supporters chanting songs at the top of their voices, it was like a party atmosphere and everyone was enjoying it. The coach stopped at several pubs within the area, each time picking up more fans and by the time we had made our last pick up there was a real assortment of people on the coach, Dads, Grandads, Uncles and kids, etc, all of course were regular seasoned fans. Right from the very start, everybody got on with each other and we all knew that it was going to be one hell of a trip.

At midnight we were only just leaving Stockport, as constant cries to the driver of, "Stan!, can we stop?, I want a pee!" meant that because the drunken fraternity, had to keep emptying their bladders, we hadn't even left Greater Manchester, when we should have been half way there!

We arrived in London at about four o'clock in the morning, obviously tired, but never the less still excited, Stan the driver had dropped us all off at Traffalgar Square, in the centre of the City, amongst all the pigeons and the many other football supporters already there. Dad was at his brilliant best, as he took us all over touring Buckingham Palace, London Bridge, Piccadilly, everywhere, nothing was too much trouble.

We walked our little socks off, never once complaining as we took in all the sights, but although we enjoyed every single minute of it, there was really only one thing we wanted to see.

At one o'clock, we arrived at Wembley Way and for the first time we saw the twin towers of the stadium, “It was just like we’d seen on the telly”. There we were, a mere three foot something tall, covered in scarfs and flags, clasping hold of Dad’s hands as we were being swept along in a sea of bodies. The blue and white colours of the Leicester supporters clashing with the red and black of our fans, accompanied by all the chanting, made it a real carnival atmosphere.

By the time we’d arrived at the gates we were hungry, no starving!!, starving for the experience of a lifetime, for we were finally here, Wembley, at long last.

The sheer size of the place was the biggest shock of all, and that was just the outside, as we walked through the turnstiles and started to climb the countless steps up to the top of the stand, it got bigger and bigger. Eventually we reached the top and those last steps, to be suddenly met with our first view of the pitch and the inside of the stadium. It was absolutely beautiful, the grass was such a lovely green colour, it seemed unreal, as though I was having a dream. I stood there in awe, with Dad on one side and Eddie on the other, as the band marched up and down.

Minutes later we were part of an electrifying experience, as the two teams walked out to the famous Wembley roar.

Even though I was so young, I still got goose pimples, and emotional as we sang “Abide with me” (With the help of a song sheet.) I looked up to my Dad and as I did, I was so, so proud of him, it was one of those times in my life, that I really, really loved him with all my heart.

I remember very little about the game, although I do remember the goal that won the cup for us, and the celebrations that followed when the final whistle blew. For the first time in my life, I experienced feelings and emotions that I’d never done before. The sheer joy, ecstasy and passion of the whole affair are something that go hand in glove with the occasion, and this occasion only, and so I’m sure that anyone else who has experienced the same will know exactly what I mean as they read this.

We left the stadium at about five fifteen in the afternoon, totally drained by the whole experience, so Dad took us back to the centre of London, where we had quite a long wait before being picked up, memories of the next few hours are very vague, although I do remember we didn’t meet the coach at Euston Train Station until midnight, where we started our long journey home, victorious!.

We arrived back home at about half past three on the Sunday morning, with both Eddie and I looking shattered and very dishevelled in our appearance. Dad still looked okay, although he must have been totally exhausted having looked after us all weekend, so you can imagine the relief on our faces when we got to the front door of “Forber”. All we wanted to do, was to go to bed and get some sleep, ready for the ensuing celebrations of that day, but in our selfishness, we’d all forgotten one thing. We opened the door to find Joyce, fast asleep in a chair, which was just typical of her, for she'd purposely stayed up, unwilling to go to bed until she knew in her own mind, that we were all home safely.

By the time we'd got to bed it was about four o'clock, but that didn't stop us getting up a few hours later, in order to do our swanking and gloating with all the local "Reds".

After making those calls, we enjoyed the rest of the day celebrating, as we watched the telly and read the multitude of papers we'd already bought, specially. We made sure that those celebrations lasted a long time, mainly because we had waited so long for success, but little did we know then, that the supremacy of Manchester would be ours for a long time to come, a period of time, which took me through my own adolescence. Those pains of growing up started to arrive shortly after, as my new found confidence was getting stronger and stronger, unfortunately for me, my character and general nature started to change, but not for the better.

Chapter Three

Adolescence

During the next twelve months I started to become disobedient at school, by sometimes answering back whenever I was being disciplined, something that I'd never dared to do before, I also began to skive off and wag school, something which at one time would of been unthinkable. It was now that I started my own school rebellion against authority.

Physically there didn't seem much change, but mentally I was becoming uncontrolable, and consequently, it wasn't long before I got into my first serious trouble at school.

It was during the Easter holidays of 1970, and the school was running a week of daily trips to various resorts. Linda, Eddie and I were all on the same excursion and in hindsight, we should of known from the start that there was going to be trouble. The first two days had gone alright, they were a little boring, but it was better than hanging around the streets, however by the end of the third day we were getting restless and needing more excitement. I can't remember exactly where we went to, but I do recall us being in trouble right from the very start, all the way there we were getting up to all sorts of mischief, swearing and throwing obscenities at the other drivers, urinating in plastic bags then throwing them out of the window and even doing "moonies", so it was only a matter of time before we hit trouble.

That time came on the return journey home, as the coach pulled into a picnic area, somewhere near Shrewsbury, which had a collection of shops on site. Originally, the owners must have thought that it was their lucky day, as about fifty school children descended on them, "How wrong they were!". Within seconds everyone had converged around the counter, to be met with the owner rubbing his greasy palms with glee, "What a mistake!". A few moments later the display was completely empty, for amongst the organised chaos we had methodically decimated all his stock and display.

The coach passed the shop as it pulled away from the parking area, with us lot on the back row gesticulating through the window to the owner and seconds later we were on our way, swopping our stolen loot. That was until some twenty minutes later, when the Police suddenly flagged down the driver and made him pull over into a lay by. Only seconds earlier we had all been laughing and joking about our actions, but that joviality soon turned to gloom with the appearance of "The Feds". They boarded the coach with the owner of the shop and picked out the culprits, which led to us all being taken off in order to give a statement to the Police and return any stolen goods, which hadn't already been devoured. We were there for about an hour before we eventually got going again to complete our journey home and that last part of the journey was something I'll never forget. A sombre silence hung over the whole coach as everyone sat there reflecting on their behaviour, although Eddie and I were more interested in what we had to face at home, ie Joyce and Dad, especially Dad.

A teacher who I didn't know, called Miss Nolan, kept coming to the back of the coach, reminding us of the disgrace we'd brought on ourselves and the school, but that didn't really matter now, for we had far more important things to worry about.

That evening Dad was on nights, so it was left to Linda to come down from "33" to tell Joyce the bad news whilst she was on her own, making sure she came down later, when we were in bed. We lay there petrified, waiting to hear the sound of the back door as it opened, which would signal Linda's arrival and when it did, we silently listened to her telling Joyce the whole story of what had happened. We hadn't slept all night and at about four o'clock decided there was no other option, but to run away, because we hadn't heard from Joyce at all, so it was obvious that even she was disgusted with us, so we started to creep down-stairs and make our getaway. "Eddie, Paul what are you doing?, where do you think you're going?", Joyce said, she informed us that Linda had told her everything, and that we hadn't to worry. We were told to go back to bed and that she'd sort Dad out in the morning, "But how ?", we asked "He'll kill us", but she insisted we'd be alright, and once again told us to go back to bed. We had a discussion under the covers, but we couldn't figure out how she would do it, still we had to trust her, we had no other option. That night seemed like a lifetime, in fact we hardly slept a wink, and so, by the time we were supposed to be getting up refreshed, we were absolutely shattered. At about six o'clock we heard Joyce getting herself ready for work, listening to her every move, as we once again waited to hear the back door go.

At seven o'clock it did !, he was home, spot on time, we just froze there and then, "When would she tell him?, straight away?, or would she let him have a drink first?, would she leave it until later on when she got home?". We waited for an hour and a half, by which time Joyce had gone, so we didn't know what to think, then, as usual Dad called us, "Paul, Eddie, are you getting up?", so we got up, had a wash, then together sheepishly went downstairs, where we sat in silence, not knowing what to expect. Suddenly he broke the ice "If it hadn't been for your mother, you'd have got a good hiding this morning, but like she says, I can't punish you for something I've done!", then he proceeded to tell us about a similar incident which had happened to him, when he was a lad, but warned us, "Never ever, even think about stealing again".

Within a few days things had calmed down again and were back to normal, but Joyce was still unhappy in herself, she was ashamed of what we'd done and wanted to apologise to Mr Thorpe, the Headmaster, who she and Dad knew personally, as he taught both of them at the same school. The next day, she rang him up at home and was told by Mr Thorpe that he knew nothing of the incident, because the teacher involved hadn't reported it.

That was typical of Joyce's character, she was totally honest and couldn't tell a lie to save her life. In fact it was her honesty which led to the school holding an internal inquiry, which ended up with Eddie and I, like all the rest, banned from taking part in any more school trips, until further notice.

So with that saga behind me, I carried on in my present manner at school, getting ever more defiant and rebellious as time passed. However the work I was producing was still good, so there were no alarm bells ringing just yet and I completed that school year with a definite ease and confidence.

I enjoyed the next summer holidays, even though I was going to the upper school when we returned after the break and although still slightly apprehensive, I didn't experience the usual fears and projections as much as I'd normally done before, which gave me a good start to my third year studies.

When we returned back, not for the first time in my life, God was to move in the most mysterious of ways, for my new form teacher was none other than Miss Nolan, the teacher who was on the trips, when we got caught stealing, so to put it in a nut shell she just warned me, "Keep your nose clean", which I did.

Those first few months went well and once again I was applying myself in a positive manner, to anything put before me, when suddenly in the late November of that year an announcement was made in school. There was going to be a skiing trip to Austria in the following year, and any boys who were interested had to give their names to the games masters. Of course Eddie and I didn't bother, because of our earlier problems and so it came as quite a surprise when the games teachers asked us why?, especially, when as far as they were concerned our parents were quite affluent. In response we told them that we'd been banned from all types of trips because of the escapade when we were caught stealing, and so we didn't think we'd be allowed to go. However, within a few days we'd been given the all clear and were booked down on the trip, thanks to Joyce and Dad, oh and of course the two teachers.

It seemed as if 1970 was to be the year of the thief, because in the same year Nanna Williams was also caught stealing from her employers, Marks and Spencer's, where she'd worked for over sixteen years, so with only a few months to go before she was due to retire, the woman was sacked, and told that she'd be taken to court for prosecution. I remember that evening very well, for Nanna came down to our house, as she often did, to get out of the way of Grandad and have a gossip with Joyce, only this time it was to break the bad news to her. She broke down in tears as she came in, which immediately prompted my own Mother to question her, "Mum, what on earth's the matter, Kids, go and play", which was always the signal for us lot to disappear, but being the kids we were, we tried to listen, although all we could hear was the muffled mumbling sound of their voices through the wall, and the clear sound of Nanna crying.

It was one of those times that I really resented our Linda, because by now, she knew everything that was going on, whilst we were still being kept in the dark, and so yet again we couldn't understand why at the tender age of fourteen she should even be involved at all. Never the less, at the end of a two hour meeting, Joyce, Dad and Nanna, with Linda in tow all left the kitchen, but it was only then, when Nanna and Linda had gone back home to "33" that we were told what had gone on.

Joyce was heartbroken, as any daughter would be, but in her case there were more far reaching implications, because as I have already explained, Joyce also worked at Marks and Spencer but in another store in Stockport. It obviously put her in a very vulnerable, awkward and embarrassing position and so the next morning, without any hesitation she walked straight into work, saw the manager and handed in her notice. Obviously in a terrible state, she told him of her thoughts and feelings, saying that it would be very difficult for her to carry on working there, especially after what had happened, however the manager refused to accept her resignation and to this day she still works there. With that problem solved, Joyce only had one other immediate task left to complete, which was to tell her Dad, and that was something which was never going to be easy, because Grandad had suffered for quite some time with serious heart trouble, so it was a very delicate situation to say the least. Joyce knew in her own mind that she had to tell him about Nanna, but she didn't think he would be able to cope with any ensuing court trial or press coverage which would certainly follow, so she knew that somehow, someway she had to solve the problem. As a result the whole family agreed that Joyce and Dad should tell Grandad about the offence, but nothing else! It was decided that they would try to keep everything else a secret, by telling him no further action was being taken, which meant that it was now down to Joyce and Dad.

I will never forget that night either, because Joyce loved her Dad very much, so much in fact that her loyalty to him, sometimes caused problems in our house, with Joyce sometimes putting her Dad before our own, so there was one thing we all knew for sure and that was, she was going to get hurt.

Grandad very rarely came down to our house, even though it was only at the other end of the road, so an excuse was fabricated in order to get him to come. I can't remember what it was, but needless to say he turned up and when he did we just disappeared as previously instructed, until the dirty deed had been done. When he'd gone, Joyce as predicted, was in a right state, although even Dad who was quite a hard bastard and disliked Grandad immensely, felt sorry for him, but there was nothing more they could do, except wait.

Some six months later the consequences of Nanna's actions were still all around to be seen. Grandad was still feeling the personal pain and hadn't forgiven her, whilst Edith, Joyce's sister who had worked with Nanna, had also suddenly and mysteriously left the company, amidst further accusations and innuendo.

Joyce meanwhile, was still feeling very ashamed whilst having to face the obvious gossip at Stockport and to top it all she'd just received notification from the courts that her mother was due to appear to face charges. It meant that the whole shameful affair was to rear its ugly head again, and with it, long awaited problems for Joyce to try and tackle. Company policy meant that Marks's had every intention of making an example out of Nanna, in order to deter any other would be criminals and so thinking of her Dad's health, Joyce started making efforts to insure that the case wouldn't be made public.

Thanks to the kindness and understanding of the Marks and Spencer company, her appeals and requests were granted, which meant that all my Mothers efforts had paid off.

However, despite all the pain that Nanna had caused, she got a job at a fire station as a cook, slaving over a hot cooker all day and totally dismissed everything she'd done in the past with ease. It was only as a result of this whole episode that her real problems surfaced, which was a gambling addiction. The experience of Nanna's addiction brought about a variety of remarks and criticism from many different quarters, none of which surprised me, except one. That was my own Dad, talk about "Let him without sin cast the first stone", there he was condemning the old girl for getting herself into a right mess and ruining the lives of loved ones around her, whilst at the same time, he was in and out of the bookies like a bleeding yo yo, forgetting that he too was causing just as much pain and suffering in our home, with his own problems.

Meanwhile none of these "behind the scenes" developments were helping either Eddie, Carol or myself, as we started to form our characters and attitudes to life, but there again this was nothing new to us, while on the other hand, the same couldn't be said for Linda, who until now, had been spared this type of pain.

Just for once she was experiencing the suffering at the hands of the family illness that we were already used to, but needles to say, everybody carried on regardless, thinking this sort of behaviour was normal.

After much anticipation and excitement, February brought our school ski trip to Austria, our party numbered about twenty or so pupils, with two teachers and the bus which was taking us down to Luton Airport due to leave at nine o'clock, on a typically dark and cold night. Obviously all the proud, hard working parents were present, who had grafted to make it all possible for their kids, none more so than Joyce and Dad, who had managed to send both Eddie and myself, so with tears of joy they waved us all off.

During that next eight days I was to discover a whole variety of new and wonderful experiences, which ranged from spending my very first night away from my parents to flying on a aeroplane for the first time. Taking in the sights of the snow capped mountains from a cable car was dramatic enough, but to actually learn to ski down there in the thick, white powdery snow, was exhilarating. We even got the opportunity to toboggan down through the wooded mountains at midnight, whilst carrying a flamed torch, after spending a typically Tyrolean evening on the summit. Yet none of these things that I have mentioned could compare with, what to me was the most enlightening and enriching experience of all. "My first ever drink of alcohol".

From the very minute I had taken that first drink, I was a different person altogether, gone was the shy, inadequate and inferior thinking Paul, "This was the new me!". It was as if I had donned a mask and gown and transformed myself into the greatest, most talented actor in the world. For the first time in my whole life, I had the most fascinating ease about me.

I laughed and joked all night, holding court as I did, with everyone around finding me both amusing and interesting, but that's it, that's all I can remember, for after that first drink, I just carried on, not knowing when to stop. Predictably I blacked out and found myself waking up at lunchtime the following day, obviously feeling the worse for wear. I was in a right mess and no wonder, apparently I'd been sick all night, I believe the teachers and the lads who shared the same room as me, were so worried at one point, that they were contemplating ringing for an ambulance. Needless to say I recovered the next day feeling very fragile after my first encounter with alcohol, yet despite that first disastrous attempt at drinking, I wasn't put off, I went back for more, in fact it was the very start of what was to eventually become the longest relationship of my whole life.

"A marriage to the bottle!".

We returned from that holiday to the anticipating crowd of parents who had made it all possible for us, we were all in one piece, and despite my little encounter with booze and a few other minor mishaps, all had gone well, so we returned to school the following week, to an accolade of compliments from the staff for "flying the flag for Spurley".

There were no other really spectacular moments attached to that school year, in fact, by my standards it was quite a placid period. My own life seemed to have some balance and pattern to it at last, albeit downward and home life thanks to Dad's gambling and suspected womanising was as volatile as ever, but it was all reasonably predictable, without surprises, so there really wasn't all that much to shout about.

Which actually takes my story forward to the end of the following Summer holidays and my return to School in the fourth year.

I'm fourteen years old, showing great ability in all subjects and I'm being liked, admired and respected from many different quarters.

I have a teacher wanting me to play for the school rugby team, "A game that I don't like", another one wanting me to carry on playing for the football team, of which by now I was captain, whilst also being pestered to play for the basketball side, something that I'm not in the slightest bit interested in. At the same time various teachers are trying to persuade me to take their lessons and courses and on top of all that Dad's still knocking holes out of Joyce in between his womanising. So to put it rather mildly by now I'm a little bit pissed off. Adolescence was also "having a go" by bringing me physical problems, something which was very hurtful and personal at the time, something that I needed to discuss, "But couldn't".

One day during a P.E lesson, we were playing basketball in the gym, when it suddenly occurred to me that I was getting the odd funny look and stare, from one or two of the other lads, at first I couldn't understand it, so I just carried on playing. However, later on as I watched from the wall bars I discovered what was wrong, I was absolutely horrified and devastated, when I realised that I wasn't like any of the other lads, because I was developing a bust, rather like a girl, I just wanted to die there and then, for at that moment I had some idea of what it felt like to be a circus freak. My immediate thought was, "Why?, why me?", after all the pain I've already suffered in my life, "Why if there is such a thing as a real God, has he done this to me?". I just went back to the dressing rooms and got changed, crying as I did, I was heartbroken. When I'd got changed I made my way home, wanting to hide away, forever. I was supposed to be at one of the happiest times of my life, yet I was actually one of the saddest, loneliest people you could ever wish to meet, I was totally confused and needing answers to my many questions, but who could I get these from. Who could I talk to in my desperation, I needed help, but where could I get it from.

It was the very first time in my life that I contemplated suicide, because I couldn't envisage any other way out, all I could see ahead of me for the future, was a life spent hiding away from other people, a life of unhappiness. "I was desperate!".

It was an earth shattering blow, which was made ten times worse by the fact that I was so good at sports, if I hadn't been, it wouldn't have been so bad, because nobody would have seen me without my clothes on and there would have been far less for me to worry about. Almost immediately I was projecting, I started imagining myself with an enormous pair of breasts, it was a bit like Pinnochio, only instead of his nose getting bigger, it was my chest and I didn't even have to tell lies. Whenever it was P.E or Games lessons it was a nightmare, because I would sit there before we got changed, praying that we wouldn't be doing something like basketball, where one of teams were in "skins" (Topless), but in the end it was too much and I just stopped taking part altogether.

This unhappiness got so bad that it was mirrored in my performances for the school team, so much so, that I quit playing for the side. Even as I write this, the whole situation which involved lots of pain and sadness still hurts me, perhaps it was my growing resilience to pain which eventually produced the survivor instinct in me, that got me through, "I don't know". Needless to say I never said anything to anyone, I just let it fester inside me for the rest of my life,

"That is until now",

which is one of the main reasons for me writing this book. Despite these problems and the fact that I'd stopped taking part in sport I did start playing football for another team which quite aptly leads into a much more light hearted story altogether, which once again revolves around my Dad.

If you remember, he was a real tight sod when it came to giving anything away, never mind money and the next story just about summed up his general outlook on life, of "It'll do", or "They'll do".

Like all children we looked up to our heroes when it came to styles and fashion and for a long time Eddie and I had wanted a pair of football boots, just like the real soccer stars wore, but obviously they were very expensive, so therefore we had to wait patiently for Dad to fulfil his never ending promise. "As soon as your playing for a proper team lads, you can both have a pair". Well by this time, Eddie and I had played for various school teams and local boys clubs, I'd even played for a Manchester School Boys selection side and by now we were beginning to wonder what sort of team he originally meant, because as far as we were concerned we were running out of time as well as teams. "Well our questions were soon to be answered".

Like most fourteen year olds, we had become fashion conscious and fully aware of the modern styles, mainly due to the fact that most of the other lads we knew, were already wearing famous brand names, such as George Best and Alan Ball, "You name it, they had 'em". Which meant that it wasn't long before we started to feel a little silly, as we paraded up and down the local football pitches, modelling our "Timpson's Toebungers", so we knew that we had to say something, because we were due a new pair. The problem was, how could we tell him? We knew he'd go mad and have a fit, we could even recite the speech that he'd come out with, "Ya don't know ya bleedin born!", or "You ungrateful pair of bastards!, I'd have given my right arm for a pair of boots like that". It was always the same record, so how were we going to get around this one. After a long, lengthy discussion, we opted to leave it and see what would happen next.

"Perhaps he was going to change, you don't know".

The major stumbling block was that in the next few weeks, we had a couple of big games coming up, where we'd be on show, for all to see, so we needed to put our request in early, which we did and Dad responded by saying that he would get us our new boots in time for those matches, so all we had to do was, wait. By this time, all talk amongst our team mates revolved around the ensuing fixtures and the excitement that was building up. Most of the lads had either bought, or were buying new boots, especially for the occasion, so there was a lot of comparing being done. "Are you getting any new boots?" was a typical and regular question asked amongst the discussions, if you answered "Yes", then more often than not, the following question would usually be "What kind are you getting?". These two questions always put both Eddie and myself in a funny position, so we usually responded in an evasive manner, "Oh Yeah", then "Don't know our Dad's getting them, it's a surprise", which really was the truth.

With just over a week to go before the first match, no new boots were anywhere to be seen and we were starting to panic, that was until the Saturday morning before. Joyce was at work and Dad was just going out on his window cleaning round, as he left he shouted, "When I come back this afternoon lads, I'll have your new boots". Eddie and I just looked at each other in our normal manner, "Ha, I'll believe it when I see it". We both had two games that day, so we were well and truly pre occupied, but there was no way it was going to stop us thinking about our new surprise, even more so in the afternoon, because we were both playing on the same side and that was when we were at our funniest and best. I met Eddie and the rest of the team at the pitch, where we played and from that moment on, we just had the giggles, "Well Paul, he should of bought em by now", Eddie said,

"Yep, I wonder what he's got us".

Suddenly Eddie pointed to a lad, who was proudly carrying his new expensive pair of Adidas football boots,

"Do you think he's got us some of them", well I just burst out laughing, "You must be fuckin joking".

From then on, the joke got worse, each time we saw a pair,

"Perhaps it's them",

"No, it's them over there",

"No it's these here", by the time we'd got onto the pitch, we were hysterical with laughter. The manager had never seen us like this before, as normally we would listen intently to his every word and instruction, but not today. We gathered around him, for the team talk, but by now we were uncontrolable, suddenly Eddie tapped me on the shoulder and whispered, as he pointed to the ref, "Is it them?". Well I couldn't contain myself, I just burst out laughing, I ended up rolling around on the grass, crying as I did, and by the time the manager had finished his team talk, nobody was listening because they were all laughing too.

The reason was simple, the ref was stood there in the centre of the pitch wearing the most stupid looking boots that I'd ever clapped eyes on, in fact I'd never seen an uglier, more odd looking pair in my life, even worse they were tied up with the longest white laces you could buy, which were wrapped at least three times around the outside of his boots, "He looked a real wally!".

Anyway the game finally kicked off and eventually we won, despite our, for once, lack of interest, after which we then went home to wait, in deep anticipation for our loving Dad. We waited about an hour for him to return, in which time we made guesses, as to what type of boot he was going to get us, would it be Nike, Puma, Adidas or would it be Gola. Then the back door opened and we both looked up simultaneously awaiting his appearance with baited breath, because we knew we would be able to tell straight away from looking at the fancy box that they came in, so we were breathless with excitement.

"Well, here ya are!!", we couldn't speak, we were dumb struck, we just looked up at him, gazing motionlessly. There was a deathly silence which hung in the air, then, "Thanks Dad", "Yeah, Thanks Dad",

"What d'ya think of em?",

"Oh great, brilliant".

What more could we say other than, "Thank you very much you tight bastard", we couldn't even say that, because he would have fucking killed us there and then.

"Well, aren't you gonna try em on",

"Oh yeah", Eddie replied, "We'll go on the field for a kick about, come on Paul". With that we went out on to the field, after all, we couldn't talk properly in the house with him there.

Although I'm writing about my childhood and even though I swear, I couldn't repeat or even put into words the following discussion that took place between Eddie and myself, because like many others, it was just one swear word after another, as we called Dad all the names under the sun. After we'd calmed down, our anger turned to laughter, as we started to see the funnier side of the whole affair, the jokes just rolled off our tongues, one after the other, as we laced up the monstrous objects and in turn modelled them for each other. They were bloody awful, more like diving boots than football boots. They were black, with a white trimming, bright red laces and at least twenty studs on each boot, the looks were just about bad enough, but wearing them finished us off. "We can't show up in these!, we'll get laughed off the field", Eddie responded by saying "I'd sooner I never played again than wear these". We knew there and then, that we couldn't accept Dad's thoughtful and generous gift, so we decided to carry on and secretly wear our old ones, which all worked okay, until a few days later, when Dad told us that he'd be off work on the Saturday and would be able to watch us. This meant we had a bit of a problem, "How on earth could we play in our old ones without him noticing". In the end we were left with no other option, we had to tell Joyce and when we did she was fabulous, "Never mind lads, I'll get you a pair, we'll go tonight after school". It was that simple to her, she knew what he was like, so after school we went and returned with the nicest, smartest pair of boots we'd ever had, the exact kind we'd always wanted. For weeks we'd stood outside the sports shop ogling at them, but now we were the proud owners of our own pair of "Adidas Santiago", just like the real footballers.

"Are you pleased", Joyce asked, "Ya kidding!, Fabulous!" we both replied, "Ooh thanks Joyce they're lovely, but what will Dad say?",

"You leave ya Dad to me".

I don't know how or when she broke the news to him, all I do remember was the lecture he gave us after, on how and when to clean them and the threats of what he'd do to us, if we didn't look after them, after all it was Joyce who'd spent all the money on us.

With that, our performances continually improved, game after game we got better and as a direct result of our new footwear it wasn't long before I was spotted by a scout from Everton Football Club. That was one of the few occasions in my life that Dad had to accept that I was better than Eddie at something and although I wasn't interested in Everton's approach, due to my lack of confidence, it was nice to find myself in the position of having Dad and his "favourite son" looking up to me, for a change.

For quite sometime during this period, Dad had been coming home from work constantly talking about a bloke whose son was playing for Oldham Athletic, he went on and on about how good he was and how exciting it was playing for a big club, "I wouldn't mind, but he'd never even seen him play". Consequently it wasn't long before he came out with the obvious, "Eh lads, ya don't fancy going to Oldham d'ya".

By now you should be getting the picture, it wasn't long before he was running us both up to Boundary Park and we were being forced into something that I wasn't personally interested in. We turned up to the ground for the very first time and followed him in, I resented him there and then, as I heard him say, "I'm Eddie Davies, Stan's expecting me, I've brought my lads, they fancy a game", for the first time in my life I saw him as a crawler and a creep, grovelling and suck-holing to get us a game.

It was awful, within the space of six or seven training sessions I knew it wasn't for me, it was just a clique that contained a bunch of United supporters and from what I saw of it, team selection depended on who your Dad was. I stuck with it for about eight weeks, but I'd had enough, so I told Dad that I wasn't going again. This was right up his street, Eddie's big chance, the chance to show "big brother" how it's done, "What a joke". Eddie couldn't stand it either, but he was too frightened to say anything, so he stuck it out, I think he lasted about a season, but I'm not sure. It was pathetic, everywhere Dad went, "Oh my son plays for Oldham", I felt sorry for Eddie because I knew he wasn't happy, he wasn't even playing well and to me his selection was only down to "big gob" being there, railroading him along, but it wasn't any of my business, so I just let them get on with it.

By the time I was fifteen years old, both Eddie and myself had stopped playing football altogether and Dad was beginning to get suspicious, as the alarm bells started to ring. All the hopes and dreams that he and Joyce had long held for us all were just beginning to fade away, as they saw dramatic changes taking place in our lives and more importantly in our personalities and outlooks.

Linda had already started the ball rolling a year earlier, when despite all of her gifts and talents she suddenly decided to leave school, once promising to be a Doctor, Lawyer or Brain Surgeon, she ended up working in a laundry. So it came as no surprise when she brought the devastating news, that at the ripe old age of sixteen she was pregnant to Eric, a bloke much older than herself, whom she'd met at Maine Road of all places. It was a relationship that Dad had disagreed with from the start, because in his and Joyce's eyes, he was just a fat, boozy football thug. Dad's views though weren't heeded, in fact they were totally dismissed, so they had both a shotgun wedding and a baby Eric to look forward to.

That was only the start, by now I was just beginning to take an interest in the female gender of the species, as well as dabbling with alcohol from the Off License, so my interest in academic qualifications was waning by the day. Eddie was already going wayward before me and Carol was just starting to realise that there was much more to life, so things on the home front weren't looking good.

Linda got married in the Summer which gave me a great opportunity to experience the delights of proper lager from a pint pot in a real pub. I'd spent the past few months walking the streets with cans, so it was something that I'd looked forward to for quite some time.

Watching Linda get married was something that I can hardly recall, the church, the ceremony and the photo session are all a blur, but the reception, now that was a story. I can see myself sat there as I write this now, a crowd of people talking and dancing the night away, taking the odd break to pay a visit to the buffet, before taking to the dance floor again. I watched as people constantly made their way to the bar or the toilet, knocking glasses over as they went and the pockets of people kissing and groping each other as they sat dotted around the room.

> "This was my scene and for the first time in my life I felt at home, comfortable in the surroundings!".

I spent the whole night sat in a corner, just watching everybody else enjoying themselves, whilst relatives kept bringing me fresh glasses of beer as fast as I was emptying them. I felt like a King in his castle, surrounded by court jesters, as they performed in front of me.

I watched the women, fantasizing over them as I did and the more that night wore on, with the help of Carlsberg, the more my inner strength and confidence grew. I finished up "Chatting up a bit of skirt", even though she was old enough to be my mother, but it didn't matter, because for the first time in my life, "I could do it!".

At about one o'clock in the morning Eddie and I were stood outside the pub where the function had been held, with a few of our Linda's mates from school. It was then that with the help of Eddie, I pulled off the first rotten stroke of my sordid "drinking career".

We were waiting for our taxi, when all of a sudden Linda's best friend joined us with her boyfriend, we knew Pamela from school, so we automatically started talking to her. The girl concerned was a bit of a flirt and so it wasn't long before Eddie and I were throwing around insinuating, sexist remarks, to see how she'd react. We soon gathered that her boyfriend was a bit of a "dickhead", which only prompted the two of us to start taking the mickey. A long drunken debate ended up with Eddie and me telling the lad to "piss off or we'd smack his head in", so he did, leaving us to grope and fondle Pamela in the doorway.

That incident brought about a whole new awareness and meaning to my life, which ignited and aroused a number of new and as yet, untapped emotions and resources. "Girls", not women, Mothers or Grannies, but "Girls", my own age. All of a sudden I was into navy socks, navy knickers and the young white flesh of school girls. From nowhere I got the urge to masturbate and once I had, I couldn't stop, I started to take an interest in girls that I'd known for years, but noticing them in a way that I had never done before. Linda's old school friends, Eddie's, even Carol's mates, I couldn't stop thinking about them, wherever I turned they were there, it seemed as though I was walking around with a permanent erection. There was only one problem, "What would I do if I ever eventually got a girl?", until now all I had ever done was kiss the girls and women I'd met on the cheek, . . "Oh well, I'll just have to play it by ear".

I didn't have to wait long, because the answer lay in one of Carol's friends, who only lived over the road, for years she'd played with our Carol and been in the same class as our Eddie, but until now, I'd never noticed anything special about her.

It happened at a funny time in my life, but there again there was nothing new in that, suddenly for no apparent reason I shouted to her as she passed our bedroom, going to Carol's, "Jane, can you just come here a minute?", as soon as she came in I grabbed hold of her and planted the first kiss. With tons of courage and effort, I'd done it, "Paul, do you mind!", there wasn't one ounce of rejection in her voice and very little struggle to ward off my attempt, so I took that as the "Green light".

Over a period of weeks and months I'd progressed from kisses and fondles to my very first contact, with that most intimate part of a female's anatomy.

How could any man forget that experience?, my natural instincts told me that I wanted to go for it, so I did, but I didn't have clue what to expect as I slid my hand down her panties. I'll never forget that day as long as I live, the very first time I touched pubic hair, I'd never been that far before and as I carried on I can remember thinking, "It's not too late to turn back, but what if I get my hand stuck?".

Obviously having gone that far and playing the part of Doctor Davies, I carried on with my internal investigation, but that was as far as it went, yet despite my age and the knowledge that one is expected to have, I spent the next few days worrying that I may have made Jane pregnant.

That initiation ended up with me permanently perched at the bedroom window. I would sit there and ogle the hours away, like a dog with two dicks, in the hope that she'd be coming over to play records with our Carol, giving me the excuse to further my education. We never went any further than intimate caressing, but that didn't matter, because with Jane's friendship over the next few months and the passing of that school year came great changes.

I suddenly discovered my own real hero, to me he was the greatest, he was everything and he completely changed my whole outlook on life.

That man was David Bowie and strange as it may seem, I still admire him to this day. I remember the very first time I saw him, I was utterly gob-smacked as he stood there performing a song called "Starman", he wore clothes, the likes of which I'd never seen before and had bright red hair, which stuck out at all angles, his skin was snow white and he sang with a piercing tone, not to dissimilar to that of a cat which is in pain, but it didn't matter, for this was something new, different and out of the ordinary. The following night after school I went straight to the record shop and bought my first ever L P, it was called "Ziggy Stardust and the Spider's from Mars", I must have played it at least ten times that night, because by the next day I knew all the words, even worse I related to them!

Looking back, I honestly think that this is where I really started to change in my outlook to life and adopted my rebellious attitude, where I subconsciously decided that enough was enough.

In the August, Joyce and Dad changed the car again, only this time buying their first ever brand new one, which was another "Morris Oxford" and a couple of weeks later it was followed by a large five man camping tent. Between them they'd decided that it would be a good idea to go camping, an idea that initially didn't go down that well, but with a little patience and persuasion, we all eventually came round to their way of thinking, especially when Spain was mentioned as a destination.

It was the last week in August and we were off, the car was loaded up to the roof and the Davies's were making their assault on Europe, first the "Froggies" and then the "Spicks".

Despite the constant never ending flow of troubles within the Davies's and Williams's, this was one of those occasions when we were a happy family unit with, Joyce, Dad, Eddie, Carol and myself, altogether and sharing a new holiday adventure.

It took us about thirty hours altogether to reach the East coast of Spain, but despite both Joyce and Dad sharing the driving it wasn't all that bad, I don't know how, but just for once they didn't row and we were all well behaved, so it was quite a pleasant journey. It was a trip literally full of excitement, our first ever time on a boat as we crossed the channel on the ferry, driving on the other side of the road and especially the sights, the scenery was magnificent, miles of straight road, through beautiful fields, then up hill and then down dale, as we crossed the Pryanees and that was probably the most exciting bit of all because we had to stop overnight at Perpignan.

Tourist were warned not to try crossing the mountains at night, for fear of bandits, so there was a mass of cars, caravans and mobile homes all parked up, awaiting the early sunrise. We arrived there at about midnight, with both Joyce and Dad feeling shattered so Eddie and I decided to sleep outside in the open air, under the stars. We were all too tired to try and erect the tent, especially as it was only for a few hours, so we let Joyce Dad and Carol have the comfort of the car, as they needed some proper sleep.

With that we got out, to camp "Cowboy Style", knowing full well that the ground was literally riddled with ants, but we didn't mind because "It was our way of doing our bit, for the joint family effort". Some four or five hours later we started off on the next leg of our journey, over the Pyranees and that was an amazing experience, it was a miracle how anything could survive there, let alone people, "But they did!".

I suppose one of the strangest experiences of that holiday was when both Eddie and I had to speak in the French and Spanish that we'd learnt at school, with both Joyce and Dad looking on, because just for once they were dependant on us.

We finally arrived at our destination in the warm, early hours of the morning, at a camp site which was situated between the two towns of Canet and Arenys De Mar. We couldn't enter until eight o'clock, so once again Eddie and I slept outside, enabling Joyce, Dad and Carol the well deserved luxury of a few more decent hours sleep.

We stayed on that camp for the whole two weeks and enjoyed every minute of it. It was clean, spacious and offered various amenities, but it wasn't any of those things that made it a memorable stay. It was the friends we made and the things we did, which made it all magic. In those days there were a variety of nationalities, German, Dutch, French and of course Spanish, but there were very few, in fact hardly any English, so we immediately became noticeable and it was that notoriety that made us many friends. Shop and bar owners, pool attendants, even the local Police got to know Eddie and I, but there were two people in particular who we could never forget.

Our first encounter with Maria and Anna occurred halfway through the holiday, as we were walking to the beach. The coastline where we were staying ran adjacent to a railway line, which separated the beach from the countryside and any other form of civilisation and it was crossing the lines where we met the two sisters.

They were both stood there by the side of the track in hysterics, as they tried to scratch the tar off their flip flops, when suddenly Eddie and I passed. Their screams of laughter were so contagious, that we both started as well, but because of our shyness and reluctance to come forward, we just carried on walking, without trying to develop the situation. "Bloody hell Eddie, I'd give both of them one!", "Yeah, which one d'ya want?". In my fantasy world I chose Maria, the older and bigger of the two girls, she had tinted red hair and beautiful large breasts, leaving Eddie with Anna, the smaller, dark one, but that was it, as far as we were concerned they were both too nice looking and mature for us, after all "They wouldn't be interested in us!", so we just dismissed the whole incident and carried on walking towards the beach.

"Well, it just goes to show, dreams do sometimes become reality". About two hours later, Eddie and I were messing about in the sea with a lilo, when out from nowhere popped the girls, "Hola, Alemania", we couldn't believe it, they were interested in us! Instinctively we responded by using our knowledge of the Spanish language, telling them that we were in fact English, which only increased their interest in us. That day we spent at least an hour and a half in the water with them and by the time we were making our way back to Joyce, Dad and Carol, we were on cloud nine and looking forward to the nights entertainment. Evenings were normally spent around the pool and bar area of the camp, drinking larger and watching the foreigners, as they tried to sing along to the English speaking records being played, songs like "American Pie" and "Vincent", but that night was different, we had far more important things to do, such as talk about our new found friends and the possibilities that lay ahead.

The next day we were down on the beach early and we'd taken the large double bed size lilo with us, so that the two girls and us could all sunbathe in the sea together, but we couldn't find them, which left both Eddie and I slightly disillusioned for the rest of the morning.

However that disappointment soon turned to joy after dinner, for whilst we were both sunbathing, Maria and Anna had themselves arrived at the beach and were in the sea, suddenly they started shouting, "Hola Pablo, Edwardo!" trying to attract our attention, but in doing so they also woke up most of the people who were taking their afternoon siesta's.

"Eh Kids !, who the bleedin ell are these two birds, are they shoutin you?", with that we immediately picked up the lilo and made a beeline for the sea, in hot pursuit of our friends.

By now the girls only had a couple of days left before the end of their holiday, so we needed to make the best out of the what time was left, but how? The answer was simple, with the help of our double bed size lilo, we spent two hot, long days, floating around in the "Med", kissing, cuddling and drinking beer, knowing we were the envy of many other, sometimes much older men at the resort.

We only had two extra days ourselves and although we were disappointed when the girls had gone, we still had more fun to enjoy and it wasn't until the very last night that we really excelled ourselves. Dad's last words after tea were, "Make sure you're not late lads, because we've an early start tomorrow, we're leaving at four".

With only good intentions we set off for our last night out, "Okay, we'll see you later". That was at about eight o'clock, at approximately eleven o'clock, Eddie and I were absolutely pissed out of our heads, serving drinks at one of the local Bodega's. It was a bar that we'd frequented quite a lot during our stay, consequently we'd got to know all of the locals and most of the passing holiday makers and so the owner had decided to have a party for us.

At four o'clock in the morning, we were only just getting back, you should have heard us, I don't know what we looked like, but it can't have been good! Arm in arm and swaying from side to side we sang a Spanish song that we'd been learning all night, it was called "Quando es una nino", which roughly translated means "When I was a kid". Years later I found out that it was actually written by Demis Roussos, but at the time we didn't give a shit, for all we cared it could have been written by Jesus himself.

Eventually, with half the camp already awake, we reached our tent, to find Joyce, Dad and Carol packing up.

"What the bleedin! . . . where the hell ave you two bin?", Dad asked,

"I told you we were avin an early start!".

"We got delayed", I said

"You what, you got delayed" Dad repeated,

"Yep "Eddie replied,

"Are you two drunk?" that was when Joyce came in,

"They better bloody not be!"

"I thought you were supposed to be givin me a lift to take the tent down?", Dad inquired.

Well, that's when Eddie gave the game away and Dad blew his top.

"We are, we're ere aren't we"

"You're bleedin pissed, the pair of you!"

"No we're not, come on, what d'ya want us to do?", I said

"Don't fuckin bother, I'll do it myself!".

Due to our drunken state, we'd adopted an "I don't care" attitude to the whole situation, so we just sat there and watched them packing up.

By now we were at our giddiest, taking no notice of the remarks being made and each time they passed us, they would come out with some statement along the lines of "You should be ashamed of yourselves!" or "Just a bleedin let down, the pair of you!", but all were to no avail. We just sat there humming the tune that we'd been singing all night and that in itself was getting Dad even more annoyed, he was just about to start taking the tent down, when he realised that he'd need us to give him a hand. "Well, are ya gonna giv us a lift or what?", with that we pulled ourselves together, got up and prepared to complete the delicate task of dismantling the tent. Dad had hold of one corner, Eddie grabbed another and I stood inside at the centre, ready to take the weight, while Joyce and Carol watched. I was alright until I heard Eddie whisper to me from outside "Eh Paul . . . When I was a kid . . ." then he proceeded to start mumbling that bloody song again.

I immediately lost every ounce of self control, my strength suddenly seemed to disappear, as I burst out laughing and within seconds I'd lost it, the tent had collapsed, with me underneath it.

By now the whole camp must have been awake, but if they weren't, they were soon going to be. Dad started to do his Indian dance around the demolished structure, with me still underneath grinning away in a drunken stupor. "Fuckin ell Joyce, give us a hand these two are fuckin useless", but it was no good, even Joyce and Carol were laughing, as they too, started to see the funny side of the whole affair, which meant that Dad had no other option, but to join in.

It was a comical end to a great holiday, which made a good start to our long, hard tedious journey home, but as we left Arenys De Mar we all agreed to do it again, the following year.

Having the experience of the outward journey behind them, Joyce and Dad made good time getting us home, where both Eddie and I took great delight in telling our mates about the holiday and the adventures that went with it, but unlike Eddie, that holiday had a very profound effect on me, a long awaited boost that I'd needed for quite some time and it wasn't until I'd got home that I realised it.

Apart from Maria, no other girl had ever shown any interest in me whatsoever and as far as I was concerned it was the first time that I had ever been "fancied", which was a lovely feeling, one that made me believe, "Perhaps the ugly duckling, wasn't so ugly after all".

Yet another missing piece to the jigsaw of my life.

I was now feeling strong, stronger than I'd ever felt, I was care free, rebellious, quite clever academically and with the help of my mentor, I was "Free", free to be anything or anyone I wanted, free to say what I thought and to do as I please. When I drank, albeit a little, I had all of these beliefs and more, "I felt confident".

It was that confidence that brought about my first boy/girl friend relationship and once again, by God's design and not my own, it was an older girl.

I met Elaine at my mate's house where I used to go after school, more often than not she'd be there, having called after work to see his sister. This meant that most of the time, we would all be in the same company. Rather characteristically, I'd never previously noticed her interest in me, until some three or four weeks later, as we were walking home, when she suddenly stopped, put her arms around me and proceeded to give me the biggest French kiss imaginable, so I obliged by returning the compliment.

You see that was the difference between the old and the new Paul, the old Paul would have been shocked, wondering if it was all a set up or a joke, but the new Paul, especially after my holiday, just thought, "I'll have some of this, definitely!". That friendship lasted maybe another three or four weeks and it was good while it did, we would walk home together kissing and cuddling and we'd talk about a wide variety of subjects, but as soon as she started making noises about going out I started to worry as "I didn't have a clue!". I'd never been to the pictures, the disco's or the bowling alley, in fact I didn't know how to socialise full stop, so I panicked.

Beside these problems, I wanted to know just what it was she saw in me. After all she was working, whilst I was still at school, which meant she had money and I didn't. Even worse, I was convinced that she could do much better than me, even feeling as good as I did, but despite her constant assurances that everything was okay, I was still suspicious. In the end after going out with her for four weeks, I was bored, but I didn't know how to tell her, so at the back of my already twisted mind, I set her a test. It was simple, so far in our relationship, she'd let me fondle her tits and get my hand stuck in her pussy and we'd kissed in every way there was possible, so to pass the test she had to let me screw her on the back of the field, in order to take me further than I'd ever been before, but if she didn't, she was out.

Well Elaine was a nice girl when I met her and still was on the night of her test. Needless to say she failed, which gave me the excuse that I'd deviously wanted, so I told her that we were finished. In hindsight it was a very sad, callous and cruel thing to do, but I didn't know any different, it felt natural.

The end of that year also brought an opportunity for me to take the biggest step of my life so far and once again it concerned my own home life. It was another fight between Joyce and Dad, only this time I personally, had just about seen and heard more than enough, I was sick to the back teeth of it all, so I did something about it.

I can't remember exactly what the row was about because there were so many, but I do know it was around the same time that accusations were being made, saying that Dad was having it off with some other women.

For weeks we'd all been suffering terribly, under a wave of abuse and violence which had lasted longer than on any other occasion, but it was the sight of Dad strangling Joyce which made me act.

For years I'd heard the same cries of "Kids help, please!", or

"Phone the Police!", it was terrifying, listening to her cry and scream out every time he hit her, even worse when he was shouting at the top of his voice as he laid into her, but on the day in question it was too much, I looked at Eddie and Carol, as we heard it all going off. I'll never forget our Carol's face as she looked at me pleading, "Paul do something, he's gonna kill her, do something!". I then looked at Eddie, "Come on Eddie, we can't let him get away with it", but he wouldn't, so I stood up once again, as I had done on countless times before, hoping that it would stop, but it didn't.

It was then that I snapped, "Oh Fuck it, I'll kill the bastard!", I ran upstairs looking to the top as I did. I could hear him pounding in to her with each punch, then Joyce "Please Eddie no, No Eddie", while behind me downstairs I could hear Carol, "Eddie for fuck's sake, go and help our Paul!, I'll phone the Police".

It seemed like a lifetime as I climbed those stairs, it was similar to watching the Cup Final, as the winners climb up to receive the FA Cup, but this was no joyous occasion, it was more like "Poltergeist" or "The Entity", the nearer to the top of the stairs I got the more frightening it all became, suddenly I could no longer hear Carol and Eddie downstairs, "Just them!".

I didn't know what to expect as I barged through the bedroom door, I just did it. Dad was straddling Joyce on top of the bed, with his hands clasped around her throat, but it was as if he was having a fit because he wasn't even aware of my presence. Joyce stared up at me pleading through the expression of her eyes, as if she was both embarrassed and ashamed, whilst at the same time begging for help.

I had to act, "You bastard !, leave her alone", so I dragged him off and pushed him to the floor and at that moment in time I didn't give a fuck about the consequences "Just Joyce, that's all I cared about, Joyce, my Mother".

Surprisingly, against all odds he didn't retaliate, in fact, for once he appeared quite pathetic, as he looked up at me from the floor, it was a good job, because at that exact moment in time, I could have killed him, there and then, but there was no need.

That was the very first and last time I ever laid a finger on my Dad, not that I didn't come near to it mind, but as you will read, it was the last time I got directly involved in my Mother and Father's disputes.

I was battle fatigued and didn't give a shit any more what they did from now on, because between them, they'd already hurt me enough and I wasn't having any more of it. From that very moment, I decided that I would never ever be frightened of any man, ever again.

REFLECTIONS

Looking back, especially after writing this first chapter, there is much for me to puzzle and ponder over and there are many questions, as yet unanswered, but perhaps far more importantly for me, I have already learnt quite a lot.

It was my original intention to include a family tree with these reflecting thoughts, but unfortunately due to the high level of immorality within the family it will not be possible.

Adultery it seems has been a favourite pastime for years, alongside a few other vices, such as thieving, gambling and boozing, add to this a mixture of lies, deceit, violence and aggression and one is left with what I choose to call a perfect example of . . . "The Family illness!!".

However the things that I have mentioned above are merely a facet of what is a much deeper and larger problem amongst the member's of both the Davies's and the Williams's and that is a large Psychiatric problem.

I have seen and heard some terrible things in my life, things that no child should ever have to be subjected to, but it seems that it's all part and parcel of the whole confused package, which sadly my family still think is normal. Despite three suicides added to an even larger number of attempts, including two of my own they're all still oblivious to the fact that something is very seriously wrong.

Looking closer to home, I'm more confused than ever, on the one hand I had Joyce, who was probably the most loving, caring and hardworking Mother anyone could wish to have. Then on the other there was Dad, a man with a violent temper, who frequently used bad, often vulgar language, accompanied with violence to rule our lives.

Dad was both tight and mean, whilst Joyce was generous to a fault. Yet both were grafters and always tried their damnedest to give us the best. Despite the unpredictability of his mental state and his general behaviour, he was a loving Dad, who was always loyal to us, his direct family. In contrast, Joyce caused quite a lot of problems at home, as a result of her mis-placed loyalty to her own Mother and Father, which was something that I eventually grew to despise her for. More often than not she would put them before our own Dad and that really annoyed me, especially as she constantly took shit from her own Mum, Dad and family, whilst at the same time looking after them. Having said that she was probably one of the most devoted Mums and Wife that God has ever created.

So why?, why am I still so confused and why do I still feel that something is missing in my life? At sixteen years of age I have become so callous and hard in my views and so quickly. One day I was meek and mild, then the next I was like the Incredible Hulk and I didn't give a toss about anyone. Why is it that I was so close to committing incest with Linda? and it still didn't feel abnormal, yet still to this day, I don't believe she is my "full sister", or what about my cousin Helen and the countless times we played Doctor's 'n' Nurses together, enjoying every minute of it, even more puzzling, my attraction to her Mother Edith "My own Auntie", who I've always found attractive. The secrets and mysteries within the family are countless and these are but a few of my own skeletons that I still had in the back of the cupboard, but what have I learnt? . . .

THE SICKNESS DEVELOPS

Chapter Four

Rebellion

The February of '73 brought my mock o'levels, but unlike other exams that I'd previously taken, I didn't give a shit about them. I couldn't have cared less whether I did good or bad, which meant that there really wasn't any pressure on me. With my new adopted attitude to life I was both fearless and impulsive and it was that impulsiveness which prompted me to walk out half way through one of the tests. As I sat there in the main hall, I watched some of my mates from the other classes playing football on the field, then suddenly I paused, thinking to myself, "What on earth am I doing here?", with that I got up and started to leave the hall, "Excuse me Davies, but where do you think you're going?, it's against the regulations to even move, never mind leave without permission, now sit down"!, I then turned around with everyone sat motionlessly gazing at me, all awaiting my response. "Well one, I'm going out there for a game of football with my mates, two, stuff your rules! and three, I don't need to ask you for anything!", with that I left the building, which by now was in utter mayhem and went off onto the field.

Although I stuffed that exam, I did manage to complete the rest and with some quite surprising results, not only to me, but also to my teachers. That was the first real sign that I was ready to leave school, so without any hesitation I went home, told Joyce and Dad how I was feeling and immediately started to send off for job application forms and interviews.

The first contact I made was to a very large building company called "John Laings", you see, even back to my very first lessons and throughout my schooling, woodwork was a subject at which I truly excelled and felt comfortable in, so I believed that joinery would be my best option.

Laings responded by sending me a four or five page form to fill in, followed by an appointment for an interview a couple of weeks later and it was in those interviews that I realised the depth and strength of my own ability and potential.

There were about one hundred and fifty lads there altogether, all applying for just thirty various apprentice positions and it was an experience that the old Paul couldn't have handled, "But not me, I loved it, no I thrived on it".

The atmosphere was so tense, the air could have been cut with a knife, as a deadly silence hung over the room, I looked around at the mass of strained faces as everyone waited nervously in anticipation, not knowing what to expect. I remember looking at them all, thinking how pathetic they appeared, yet despite wanting to do well, I thought, "So what if I don't get the job, it's not the end of the world".

Suddenly a well dressed office type of bloke stood up at the front of the hall and started to give out his spiel on how good the company was and how they cared about their staff, "What a load of crap"!. After about an hour of waffle, he suddenly added a bit of spice to the whole affair by informing everyone that they were now going to sit an exam which would take about an hour and a half to complete, "Talk about surprise"!, well that just about finished off most of the others, they didn't even have to say anything, as their expression did it all for them. Most just sat there gob-smacked looking around the room at each other with that "Help!" look on their faces, whilst I just sat there, still treating it all as if it was some sort of a joke.

After about an hour the test was halted, with an announcement that a list of names was going to be called and that anybody whose name was read out had to go to the front, taking their test papers with them. This immediately aroused suspicion throughout the whole room and left the twelve people called slightly apprehensive and embarrassed, one of which was me. Having been called to the front, I was asked if I was the person who had filled in the original application form, to which I replied "Yes", the chap in charge then checked my exam paper, which only confirmed my claims, so I returned to my place, feeling even more relaxed than before. It was an exercise which immediately dismissed several of the other lads from the reckoning because it was actually their parents who had filled in their forms for them, so by now I'd already realised that I was in with a good chance.

Despite my self belief and confidence I applied for another vacancy with a different company and after the interview accepted their offer of a job, so I knew that I would definitely be leaving school at Easter and so it wasn't long before I found myself saying goodbye to my school friends as I started off on what was to become a very eventful journey.

What a change!, early mornings and going to work for the very first time, not frightened but apprehensive and thoughtful as I made that very first walk to the bus stop. It was a strange feeling as I acknowledged other people who I knew, old and young alike, who I'd seen going to work over the years, I really felt like a grown up and a man of the world. I'd never been up at that time in my life, I didn't know that a half past six in the morning existed, but never the less it was a nice feeling and so with the early morning sun in my eyes and butties in hand, I went to work.

The company was called "Mobile Site Units" and was situated amongst a nest of mills in an Industrial part of the Stockport area and as I got off the bus I disappeared in a sea of people all rushing to their own places of work, it was chaos and I was part of it all, but in spite of all my apprehensions I was happy, after all, this is what I'd wanted. As I approached the main doors for the very first time I just looked up to the sky and said, "Oh well, here goes"!.

I walked in and by detection made a beeline for the "brew room", I could hear the voices of the work-force, so I followed the sound of their discussion until I met up with them all.

Top show, full of false confidence and dead cocky I just sat down and waited with them all, as if I'd been working there years.

I settled in quite quickly and in a very short space of time I found myself carrying out all sorts of tasks, which I really didn't expect to be doing so soon, which meant that the company could take on another apprentice, meaning that I was now no longer the "new boy".

Whilst I was getting settled in to my new lifestyle, Joyce and Dad were making changes of their own, by collecting newspaper from houses and yet again it was another example of Joyce's enterprise. It started off with her going door to door with a shopping trolley and then in the car, but in a matter of weeks she'd got Dad interested despite his initial scepticism and so they bought a blue Bedford van together, which was the start of a whole new saga in our lives. For those next few months the Davies household was reasonably calm in its temperament, I was happy at work and just beginning to feel the benefits from it, while Joyce and Dad were busy making extra money out of collecting paper.

Meanwhile, Eddie was purporting to be busy studying and Carol was doing okay as well, so things were temporarily subdued.

It was also a period in which I really enjoyed myself more than ever before, because I found myself in a position where I could go out with money in my pocket and show off my new found independence to all my friends, most of which were still at school.

Two evenings a week were spent at Spurley Hey where they had evening or night school and these nights gave me the opportunity to flaunt the new Paul, who was forever getting stronger and more confident by the day. The rest of the week I would go out for a few pints with a couple of the lads from school, but as yet, I really hadn't drank to any excess. Most of my money was saved apart from money spent on David Bowie records, that was until I discovered my second hero "Lou Reed", until now I'd never even heard of the fella, but as soon as I did, I was knocked out. As with my other mentor he was outrageous, an odd ball and a total misfit of the highest nature, but it didn't matter for I immediately identified with him, because he was different.

This was bad news to Joyce and Dad, after all, they were only just getting over the shock of my discovery of Bowie and I'd already been accused of giving our Eddie and Carol daft ideas, so to put it mildly, they weren't impressed.

Within a month I had donned my own chosen style of clothes, a beautiful black bomber jacket, that had cost about fifty pounds, a pair of black leather pants, in the region of about seventy pounds and a plain black tea shirt from the "Army and Navy" stores. For footwear I wore a pair of black fifty pence plimsolls which were also from the "Army and Navy" stores and to round off my new look I got some really expensive looking welding glasses which had chrome frames and very dark small lenses. The first time Dad saw me he went berserk, "Ya fuckin tapped!, you'll get bleedin locked up lookin like that"!, but I didn't care, as far as I was concerned, I felt brilliant, "Just the way I wanted to be, I was my own man".

This whole change prompted Joyce to say something that she's always regretted to this day, "You'll be going in that bleedin Mersey Tavern next"!, well my ears immediately pricked up, "The Tavern " I thought, "Now where's that?".

The very next day I went to work and asked a couple of the blokes if they knew where it was, only to be met with a variety of off putting remarks. From what I could gather it was a pub which had a different sort of clientele and the reputation to go with it, so I immediately decided that it would be for me and that I would find it.

After work that Monday night I walked into Stockport town centre with the rest of the lads as normal, usually they would leave me outside Marks and Spencer, where I waited for Joyce to finish work, but not this evening, for with their help I made a beeline for the so called den of iniquity.

Before entering I stood outside and paused for a moment, looking at the awesome building and in doing so, I recalled a few of the comments that had been passed about the place, "The're all druggies in there", "It's a brothel", "You don't go there do you? " and my Dad's was the best "There are murderers and all sorts of cut throats in that place", but none deterred me, this was it, I'd finally found it, "The Mersey Tavern".

I'd previously been told, there was a sort of a ground floor to the pub, like a cave and that was my ultimate destination, but for my first visit, I settled for just getting in and out of the place in one piece. As soon as I walked through the door the mystic of "THE TAVERN" hit me head on, I found myself in a totally new, yet fascinating environment, which was steeped in the weirdest atmosphere imaginable. A strange distinctive odour, unknown to me hung in the air as I stood at the bar observing both the decor and the customers, I looked on in amazement each time somebody entered or left the building, because there were all types of weird and wonderful looking folk, all total odd balls like myself.

I usually had to wait about three quarters of an hour for Joyce and by the time I'd left the pub after my first visit, I was totally hooked, not by the smell of the drugs, or by the taste of the beer, but by the whole atmosphere of the place, I knew from the very minute I left, after that first visit, that I would be back!

For two or three weeks I became I regular visitor to the Tavern, but only after work and only for the odd pint, whilst I waited for Joyce.

I used that period of time to get to know some of the staff and get my feet under the table, "basically to do my own recce", but as yet I hadn't been in when the pub was full or gone downstairs, where it was all "supposed to happen".

After about four or five weeks of being a "regular after work tippler, in working gear", I decided to don my own clothes and chance my arm by going downstairs on a Saturday afternoon.

I bought my first pint upstairs off Gladys, my favourite barmaid then having already made my mind up to go down after that one, swallowed the last gulps and turned around to make my way down, "You're not going down there are you Paul?", Gladys asked, "I've often wondered what it's like, so I thought I'd give it a try".

The steep, twisting stairs which led to the cellar were fitted with dirty, red carpet and the walls were decorated in a manky dark green coloured paper. For the first time I could see the entrance at the bottom of the obscure staircase and the sign above the door, informing everyone that it was "The Guilded Cage". As I got nearer, the blackness downstairs overpowered the diminishing light from above with the strong smell of various drugs floating over that of the tobacco and alcohol fumes. Once inside, it was as if I'd been transported into another world, a fantasy world, where it seemed "anything goes". There were hippys, greasers, skinheads and queers, even lesbo's, with the number of different hair do's limitless, short, long, spiky and curly, it didn't matter and the colours, well I'd never seen anything like it.

The different fashions just freaked me out altogether, there were Afghan coats, jeans, leathers, even suits, so like a chameleon, wearing my new attire, I just slowly slid into the background of the surroundings, fitting in perfectly.

From that moment on I frequently went down into the cage, usually at weekends and although I never really spoke to anyone, it was just nice being able to hide away from the rest of the world, knowing nobody knew or had a clue where I was.

In the September of that year I was called into the office by the management of the company where I worked and told that the new courses at the Technical College would be starting in the next fortnight.

In order to fulfil my contract I was required to go on day release once a week, which meant that I would have a day off work with pay, but that didn't impress me one bit. I'd enjoyed every minute of my work up until then and just the thought of sitting in college made me feel sick, so I decided to stand my ground, knowing that I could learn far more at work. The company responded by telling me that they may have to terminate my employment and so I showed them a contract which I'd only received that week from Laing's. In view of that letter and the fact that I was so useful on the production line, it was agreed that it would be much more beneficial to both them and myself if the company returned the grant, cancelled my tuition and I returned back to normal work, "Which I gladly did"!.

Within a week of that decision I went on holiday with the rest of the family and once again we went back to Arenys and Canet De Mar.

A year older and much, much wiser we had a very enjoyable time, but despite our rapid mental and physical development and our increased tolerance levels to alcohol, by our standards it was a quiet trip, although there were a couple of incidents, each involving older females that do spring to mind. Both resulted in the said girls or should I say young women, being lured into the mountains by Eddie and myself as we desperately tried to break our duck, but the nearest we actually got to fulfilling our ambitions was ripping the knickers of both pairs of unsuspecting victims.

The only other highlight to that holiday was the sudden appearance of our cousin Valerie, Edith's eldest daughter, she was beautiful, but unlike her younger sister Helen, neither of us had been lucky enough to lay our dirty hands on her and so there was a lot of fantasizing done on our part. We purposely used to call around to their tent because Val wore really skimpy bikinis and each time she opened the entrance we'd find ourselves looking down at her beautiful brown tits. Unfortunately her German husband to be, Ronald was with her, so that's as far as it went, having said that I don't know what I'd have done if she'd been alone or unattached.

That holiday although enjoyable couldn't stop me missing the atmosphere of the Tavern, which meant that returning home wasn't so depressing, but we weren't back long when destiny and fate struck at the heart of the family.

Whilst on nights Dad had a really bad, near fatal accident, which left him with a severed main artery and the packing line where he worked full of blood flavoured cornflakes, it was the very start of what was to become another great change in the Davies' household and one which affected each and every one of us for a very long time to come. Dad's injury meant that he was unable to work for months, which immediately resulted in the two window cleaning rounds going, but undeterred Joyce carried on collecting the newspapers alone, whilst at the same time working at Marks's.

It was a good job because Dad never returned to Kelloggs, he officially left about six or seven months later with a privately settled claim, which comprised of a decent pay off and an agreement that he wouldn't be going back, but by this time a lot of groundwork had already been done and they'd already established themselves as waste paper collectors, so it didn't matter.

In that twelve months after leaving school many changes took place within the family, however none were more surprising than Eddie's sudden decision to follow my example and leave school earlier than expected. It was a great disappointment to Joyce and Dad as they really thought Eddie would "Show me how it should be done!" and instil some rather flagging confidence and belief in themselves, but unfortunately he had different ideas, ideas which they always blamed me for. In their eyes I was corrupting his mind and brain with my attitude and interests, but to me Eddie and I were so close that he had no option, but to follow me in my lifestyle.

Once again it was Joyce to the rescue, only this time she got Eddie a job at a screen printers and just by coincidence it was for a company who shared the same mill where I worked. Eddie was only there for a few months before being transferred to the company shop in the town centre and that was yet another one of God's mysterious ways of moving because it was situated right opposite "Yes, you've guessed it, The Mersey Tavern!!".

For a few months and a variety of reasons we didn't mix, mainly due to the fact that he was so intent on impressing both Joyce, Dad and his boss Reg, but that keenness soon evaporated with the arrival of the long summer nights. Seeing me going out most evenings proved too much for Eddie, which meant that soon enough I had a regular drinking partner and in no time at all we were going straight into the pub after work.

It was the beginning of a slow but gradual disappearance on our part, which eventually led to our regular absence from home, something that upset Joyce and Dad very much. Unfortunately for them, there was nothing they could do, after all it was the home environment of "Forber" that we were glad to get away from and they were the main culprits, so despite their constant objections, we carried on doing our own thing.

Within the short period of a few weeks our ties to the Stockport area had grown and we were spending most of our time in and around the place, new friendships had been made and so Eddie and I were seen actively taking part in what was "the norm" for the type of person who frequented the "Tavern".

More often than not during closing time, like all other regulars Eddie and I could be seen hanging around the band stand in the middle of the shopping precinct, either boozing from the bottle or sleeping it off and it was there that we caused Joyce most of her embarrassment. The band stand was situated opposite the main door of Marks and Spencer and without fail, at least one of her so called friends would return to work after their dinner hour "Oh Joyce, I've seen your Paul out there, with all those weirdos". It was statements like that, which severely dented her pride as she would be forced to listen to the other women as they boasted and bragged about how well their own children were doing with their degrees and their effort to do this and that. When she got the chance Joyce would repeat the same words for the benefit of our ears, but our response was different "So what, we'll see how they've done in a few years time"!. I remember once saying to Joyce "It's amazing, your friends never ever tell you anything bad about themselves, you never hear when things are going wrong for them", but she never understood that.

Looking back my Dad was half correct in his earlier accusations of one up manship and by now we were beginning to realise that there was definitely a "keeping up with the Jones's" ring about the place, but we really didn't care.

The final straw came when after many months of talking and deliberation I finally decided to have my hair cut and dyed red, "Bowie style", Eddie didn't believe I'd do it because as far as Dad was concerned it was a no go area, "You come home with bleedin dyed hair and you're out!!".

One Saturday afternoon in the middle of the Summer, having spent two hours in the pub "I did it"!, I was absolutely carefree, happy with the world and as pissed as a fart, but it was the missing piece as far as I was concerned to my own personal make up and once I'd done it I finally felt complete. There was only one problem, I now had nowhere to live and due to Dad's stubborn ways there was no way he'd change his mind and let me stay at "Forber", so I made my way home, still quite inebriated to pick up my belongings.

By the time I had got there Joyce was already home and as I walked through the back door both of them were stood together in the living room. I just walked in "Hi", and carried on through the hall and upstairs to our bedroom, Joyce and Dad stood there speechless at the sight of their son and the only real response that I heard was Dad's "What the?", but Joyce must have tugged at him because those were his only words.

I quickly gathered up all of my worldly possessions, about ten or twelve LP'S in all and made my way downstairs. Just as I passed Carol's room she popped her head around the door, "Eh Paul, that looks fantastic, quick Jane come and have a look at this", but although appreciated, her comments didn't help me in my efforts to defuse the situation and save aggro, as it was my intention to just bid farewell leaving as quickly as possible, without fuss. I came face to face with Joyce and Dad in the living room, but without even a pause I carried on walking as planned giving them both the briefest of farewells "Tara" and then disappeared into the kitchen. Just as I was about to grab the back door handle I heard Joyce's voice, "Where ya going luv?, you've not had anything to eat", but she knew full well what I was up to. "Well Dad said that if I got my hair done, I couldn't stay under his roof, so I'm off!!". Joyce just looked up at Dad with that "Oh Eddie luv", expression "Oh bleedin ell, ya can stay, but I'm warnin ya, if any fuckin make up or jewellery appears, you're definitely out, in fact don't bother comin home"!.

There was only one other problem with Dad's acceptance of the new me and that came when Eddie clapped eyes on me for the first time.

"Fuckin hell, what's he said to that"!,

"D'ya like it? "

"It looks brilliant, but what's he said? "

"He said I can stay as long as there's no make up or jewellery". Without giving it a second thought Eddie wanted his the same, but he couldn't afford it, so he decided there and then that he would start saving up and he would get his done as soon as possible. However due to my generosity and a tendency to feel guilty he didn't have to wait long, the following week I gave him the money which meant that Dad, in his own mind had lost two sons and gained two "Fuckin queers"!, all within seven days, but there were now't queer about us.

All our actions whatever they were, always seemed rather impulsive to everyone else, but nothing could have been more further from the truth and this escapade was no exception. This wild and outrageous behaviour coincided with a couple of concerts that were to be staged in Manchester a month later, where the artists appearing just happened to be both my mentors and yet again I was blamed for being a bad influence, only this time over Carol.

By now through sheer chance and not design she too had become a Bowie fan, but because she was quite a few years younger, Dad was more protective and sceptical, however in the end, after many fights and disagreements he allowed her to go to the concert, but only if I took her and only for the first performance.

Well, how could I refuse!, after all, it was because of me that she started listening to him in the first place and anyway it was another opportunity for me to get back at Joyce and Dad, whilst at the same time treat Carol to a night out with me, so I gladly obliged.

The night itself was a great experience, one which Carol thoroughly enjoyed, but more importantly for me, it was one of the few occasions in my life that I really got to look after her, but although Carol enjoyed the Bowie concert, she wasn't allowed to go to the Lou Reed gig. Dad knew that he would be far more of a bad and dangerous long term influence on her, so he put the block on the idea straight away, as far as he was concerned, Bowie was acceptable but Lou Reed was definitely out.

That decision immediately gave Eddie and I the total freedom to enjoy ourselves at this next concert even more. I met Eddie at the print shop straight after work and it was there that we got changed into our already secretly prepared gear.

To look the part, we wore blue knee length, three inch platform boots, that were studded with silver and gold stars, these were accompanied by black leather trousers, tucked in at the knees and to complete our ensemble we donned bright yellow v neck pullovers with the name of Lou Reed emblazoned in glitter on both front and back. Our facials were done with the help of a couple of the barmaids in the Tavern and once they'd finished their bit for the cause, even Danny La Rue would have envied us, so with image complete, we made our way to the Free Trade Hall in Manchester.

My hair was bright red at the time, a similar colour to that of a traffic light and it was stuck out at every angle imaginable, Eddie's was in the same style but black with green streaks making him look just as outrageous. We thought we looked odd, until we arrived at the venue and saw the mass of people gathered outside waiting to get in, even to this day I've never seen as much coloured hair in one place, or at one time, but never mind colour, the hairdo's themselves were so outrageous, the whole event could quite easily have been mistaken for a Coiffures conference.

Every odd ball and nutter from within a radius of fifty miles must have been there that night, in fact looking back it should have been called the "Cuckoo's Convention", never mind a Lou Reed gig. There were queers, lesbians and bi-sexuals all performing in the street, who in turn were surrounded by a mass of druggies, drop outs and other assorted degenerates. Just to round off this compilation of misfits there were a few psychos, schizo's and manic depressives hanging around, "Oh and of course us". I can't remember very much about that night, but it must have been good because both Eddie and I looked and felt shit the morning after, which was a sort of yardstick or barometer we used for many a year to come.

Dressing up for that occasion did at least achieve one thing and that was to introduce us to new friends in the Tavern. Until now we had only been on nodding terms with most of the regulars, but as a result of our efforts it became a major topic of discussion within the pub, which in turn brought about a touch of notoriety. That added to the fact that I had managed to appear on stage at both concerts and succeeded in getting my picture in one of the papers, meant that we were sort of nearly in with the "in crowd". I couldn't believe it, after spending nearly eight months hanging around the scene of the place, things started to gel, as I even found myself with a girlfriend.

Yvonne was a nice, well brought up girl, who came from a good, religious, old fashioned background, her parents were nearer sixty than fifty, but despite their age, they did seem to have some eccentricity about them. They lived in a large Victorian type house in the more affluent part of Bramhall, a house which was also home to a giant church size organ.

Right from the start of the relationship, I found both her and the family to be weird and after about three weeks of groping, fondling and manking about in shop doorways, precincts and passages, I started to get a little apprehensive, as I couldn't suss out the whole situation. Things were okay, but in my own mind I couldn't put the jigsaw together and so it was yet another example of the "new user friendly" me.

By about the fourth week, the going was getting a little tough and I was no nearer to "getting my oats" than three weeks earlier, so the old suspicious alarm bells started to ring and I knew I would have to do something. It all finally ended at a party, when I got her upstairs into one of the bedrooms. After about ten generous minutes of fore play it was looking like I was in with a chance and I was actually going to make it, when she suddenly went cold on me, "What the fuck's up now?, is it me?, or av you got V.D or something?".

After spending about a quarter of an hour consoling her and calming her down, I found myself feeling very guilty, thinking of how I'd upset her, but that guilt was soon replaced with anger, when she told me that just before meeting me she'd actually been into hospital for an abortion.

"Oh fuckin ell, I've heard it all now"!, with that I got up and stormed downstairs, leaving her weeping in the bedroom. About twenty minutes later one of the lads came up to me in the kitchen "Eh Paul, there's a bird upstairs asking for you, I think she's pissed, cos she's hysterical, an all she keeps sayin is where's Paul?, I want Paul".

I told him she was stone cold sober, she was just a nutter and I wasn't interested anyway and with that I got up to leave, but just as I'd got to the front door, she appeared at the top of the landing. Dressed in stockings and suspenders, she suddenly started screaming down at me,

"Paul, Paul, please don't leave me?, please!, I'll do anything for you, please", I just looked up at her and said, "It's a bit too late for that". I put my hand on the front door to open it when she started again, "Paul, come up now, fuck me if that's what you want, screw me, but don't go, please!!!". By now I'd lost all of my original respect for her, so with everybody listening and a few other more fortunate lads watching, I turned and left. As I made my way down the front path a lad who I didn't know at the time, stared in amazement and said "Who d'ya think you are, Paul Newman, only he leaves birds in that style, she's fuckin gorgeous man!!". I just carried on walking regardless of the situation with only one message for him, "Nearly right, Paul Davies actually, an if you or anyone else wants her, she's yours, ya can av her"!.

Not surprisingly that was the last occasion Yvonne and I met because after that she just disappeared from the scene altogether, but whilst it was the end of a very short relationship, it did prove to be the start of what developed into a very eventful couple of years in my life. During the time I went out with Yvonne, I also made friends with a few other faces within the Mersey Tavern and it was with those people, who I then automatically started to hang around with, as I was now once again a spare part.

By now my drinking activities and consumption had increased even more and so too had my encounters with the opposite sex, which all went to make life that little more enjoyable and interesting, for quickly following on from Yvonne came Carol and she was an absolute corker.

Carol came from Zimbabwe and had been visiting for the summer but it was time to return home and so we had a party for her. Needless to say it was a case of drinks flying all over the place and that's where my fun began. During these celebrations I got the biggest, most unexpected shock of my life, as half way through the proceedings Carol came over to me, "Have you got a minute Paul?, I'd like a word", "Yeah sure". I walked over to the bar with her, trying to work out what was wrong, "No not here, somewhere more private".

By this time I'm wondering what on earth's going on and as we climbed the stairs, making our way to the bar above, I became even more suspicious. Once we'd got to the top and in the middle of the main entrance, she dragged me even further by the hand, leading me up the extra flight of stairs, which in turn led to the top bar. Suddenly once we were out of everybody's sight she just stopped dead in the middle of the twisting staircase and placed a beautifully wrapped gift into my hands, "I want you to have this before I leave". Giving me no time to pause for thought, she put her arms around me and proceeded to give me the sexiest tongue job I'd ever had and by now, not only am I over the moon, but I've also got the biggest, hardest erection that I'd had to date. Minutes later and after the longest kiss I'd ever experienced, I pulled away and broke the deathly silence . . . "I see."

Desperately in need of more I told her we couldn't stay there because staff were coming and going all the time, as they went to and from the landlords private quarters, but there was no need to worry because I had a plan. Unlike most of the others, I'd spent many a night listening to the live bands on the very top floor, it was a place the others didn't now existed and so I led her upstairs. I knew there was a very secluded corner in that top bar and it was there that I spent the next hour with her, however yet again there was no leg over on offer. Plenty of intimate kissing and fondling took place and I even tasted her sweet sexy juices, but no leg over, still I couldn't complain, after all I'd already had far more than even I could have imagined, so we said farewell and that was one hell of a way to say goodbye!!

What a turn around, here I am, with all these females showing an interest and paying attention to me, I have money in my pocket, most of which I now spend on drink and boy can I drink! The "in crowd" of the Tavern actually like my company and even find me amusing and to top it all I'm doing exceptionally well in my job. The only drawback is that "I'm still a virgin", but so what. You'd think that by now, I would at last be happy, after all I have nearly everything I always wanted and desired, acclaim, respect, admiration and even a certain independence, but no, you would be wrong. Even though all these things had come my way and all as a result of my new found confidence you would be incorrect in your beliefs.

In the late July of that year Eddie and I were sat in the garden at home, with a couple of our local mates, it was a sunny Sunday afternoon at about five o'clock and we were bored and fed up. It may sound crazy but I needed more excitement to my life, a new challenge, something different, Eddie felt the same way, after all, he'd shared in a lot of my past experiences and a few others of his own, but how would this come about we asked? The other two lads were just as bored but they hadn't seen or done half as much as us, so we had to find a way of bringing more adventure to our lives. It was agreed by all that we needed a change of scenery and a bit of a break, but the problem was where, we all had different ideas Blackpool, Southend, Torquay, but we couldn't agree. To resolve the dispute each one of us secretly wrote down our chosen resort on a slip of paper, then one of the other lads, James, was nominated to pick out what would be the agreed destination. I will never forget his face, or his reaction when he read out the chosen place. We all sat there in silence as he stuck his hand in and then slowly withdrew it, amongst an atmosphere which was similar to that of a major lottery with thousands of pounds at stake.

We waited with baited breath as he unfolded the crumpled mess and watched his lips as he announced the result, "Fuckin where?, Spain!!, I can't go to Spain"! the other lad Phil just sat there as if he was in a trance,

"Yes!" said Eddie,

"Right that'll do for me!" I shouted, poor Phil still hadn't said a word. Once again James chipped in,

"But I can't go to Spain, me Mam n Dad'll kill me". Eddie and I both responded at the same time,

"But we all agreed that wherever it was, we'd all go",

"That's right"! suddenly Phil emerged from his shocked state,

"No way, you're both mad you two, you can't be serious"! he was both right and wrong, indeed we were mad and just to prove it we meticulously planned our getaway whilst at the same time proving him wrong, for we were "Deadly serious"!

The plan was simple we would sell off all our clothes and records in the pub and I would sell my tools at work, we would then both withdraw our monies from the Post Office which hopefully would leave us with enough funds to get to Spain.

However we never stuck to the original date because only a couple of days later Eddie and I met in the Tavern for a lunchtime drink and it was there that he told me he was more pissed off than ever before.

Reg, his boss had gone into work in a real temper, causing them both to have words, leaving "our kid "both angry and unhappy. "Fuck him!" I said, "Fuck em all for that matter, we'll go today"!

Eddie looked at me with a questioning expression,

"Ya joking?, what about your holiday pay?",

"Oh stuff the holiday pay, what the hell"! With that decision finally made, I ordered another couple of pints and we set about working out our new strategy.

It wasn't difficult, all we needed was the rest of our belongings, such as sleeping bags, Afghan coats and a few other things, so we rang Carol up at home and asked her if she would bring them.

We already had our passports and money so all we had to do was sell off some of our belongings to raise extra cash. Whilst Eddie did four or five trips bringing our stuff over from the shop, I went back to work to hand in my notice and sell my tools. Unfortunately I can't remember very much else, apart from asking the bloke who'd bought my saw to tell my Mum and Dad where I'd gone when he went round to pick it up.

So with cash in hand I made my way back to the pub, leaving both my employers and work mates shocked and stunned in disbelief. Once I was back with Eddie in the Tavern it was a case of "I'll have another one"! as we both stood centre stage offering a wide selection of our personal belongings. It was reminiscent of Dad's performance a few years earlier, only we were getting paid, whilst at the same time enjoying every minute of it. We sold records, tapes, clothes, everything, the more we sold the more we drank, in fact we got that pissed we even sold our sleeping bags that Carol had brought down for us. I have quite a few claims to fame in my life and despite eventually spending time with the rich and famous, I think one of my favourites was the day we turned the Mersey Tavern into a giant second hand market hall . . . "The day we set off for Spain!!".

To this very day I still don't know how we even got out of Stockport, never mind the United Kingdom, but we did. I don't even remember the ferry crossing for that matter, however I do recall being detained and locked up as we got off the boat, even worse being sent back on the next ferry and locked up once again on board ship.

We were so pissed, we were considered un-admitable, "Even for the froggies"!

Within twenty four hours we'd gone from Stockport to Dover, cross channel to Calais and then back to Dover, yet I was still pissed, we had no money and we were both starving. Talk about around the world in eighty days, "our kid" and I would have murdered it, no problem, but the question now was "Where to from here?".

We really didn't have any options, other than to make our way home and that was actually a lot easier than it sounds. Not surprisingly, nobody would give us a lift, so we had to walk all the way from Dover to London, but once in the centre of the capital it got even better. We were approached by all sorts of nutters, queers, Jehovahs witnesses, Sally army reps, you name it we attracted them, but we weren't that desperate yet for their help, so we carried on marching.

By the time we had reached the M1 motorway we hadn't even had a drink of water since our outward bound journey, some eight hours earlier and it was then than we began to pray. For all we cared or anybody else did for that matter it could of been the middle of the Sahara Desert, as not one shopkeeper responded to our pleas for a drink, in fact I'd never met a bigger, tighter bunch of bastards in my life, but despite these obstacles we carried on.

We were just about to give up when we realised that our prayers had been answered, "I don't know by who, but they had", for there on a bench were some old, cold chips in a sticky mud like gravy that some gang of kids had obviously left, and on the floor sat a cola can, "Was it empty, or did it have some left in it?". As soon as Eddie lifted it up and smiled, I knew we were going to have a party, no a feast! and that's exactly what we did.

At that moment in time we didn't give a shit whether they'd spat in the chips or pissed in the cola, it made no difference to us, for we were desperate and that meal was going to be fantastic, whatever the odds, so like a couple of tramps we devoured that dish and once we had, we were on our way again, back on the road.

I honestly have no idea how long it took us to get back, but I do know that we came back separately in order to make it easier to hitch a lift, but once home, Eddie and I had completely different ideas. Going home with your tail between your legs was an easy thing for Eddie to do, but no so for me. Unlike my younger brother, I was proud, very proud and so desperate not to let Dad see that he was right. To give him that satisfaction, as well as the last laugh would prove to painful for me, so I didn't return.

Instead I made my way to Linda's in Middleton where I spent all afternoon drinking tea and talking about all manner of things, her, me, the family and of course this latest episode. It was a strange thing, yet again I never saw her as my sister, only as a friend, but even as a friend I couldn't ask for help, which meant once again I was putting on a brave un-caring face. Despite being penniless I had no intention of asking her for cash, after all it wasn't fair on her, so instead I asked her if she would give me all her unwanted tablets, which I could then sell in the pub.

Like all the Davies's and the Williams's, Linda loved gossip and the fact that I was involved in drugs was pretty dramatic, so having a drug dealer within the family was both unique and exciting. Fully armed and ready to do business I set off on my way, "Oh Paul, just hang on a minute, I've got something for you", she came running after me and pushed a five pound note in my pocket "Take care, I love you"! with that I skipped off and made for the Tavern.

The journey from Middleton to Stockport was long enough, but sat on the top deck of the bus gave me time to think and it was whilst I was deep in thought, I realised what a cock up I'd made of everything. For the sake of a bit of excitement I'd ruined the lot, my job, home and now I had to go back to the mickey taking. I looked out at the rest of the world, all seeming at peace with itself, whilst I was running back from nowhere and then onto nowhere.

It was at that moment that I started to swallow my pills, one by one in a chain reaction, with my arm similar to that of a mechanical crane at the fair, the one where you never win anything, they always drop the goodies just in time, but not me, I was popping pills as if they were smarties going out of fashion.

When I arrived at Mersey Square I was still feeling okay, but rather surprisingly I didn't make for my usual hide-out, instead I went to a pub down the road called the White Lion, a stark contrast to my normal watering hole and it was there that I met Peggy for the first time.

Peggy was a rather attractive barmaid in the mould of Gina Llolabrigida only with long thick curly red hair, I was attracted to her from the start, she was

friendly and interesting, but in my hour of need and my fantasy world I thought God was going to give me a reprieve and despite her being old enough to be my Mother, she was going to invite me home.
"No such luck!!", at eight o'clock she left the bar to take a coffee break and that is where I departed, not from the White Lion, but from a state of consciousness.

The pills I'd taken were obviously taking effect and subconsciously I must have got lost in a blackout. The next three and a half hours or so, are a void in my life, but it was my next recollections that have stayed with me to this day.

I came around on the railway embankment, gazing up at the clear, dark sky, with the stars seeming so near, I felt that I could have touched them as they flickered, pitted against the blackness of the endless space. It was as if it was a black curtain stippled with pearls, dotted in any old fashion, which was an entrance to somewhere secret, then all of a sudden the silence was broken by the noise of a landing jet, as it made it's approach to the airport.

It seemed as if I was directly underneath it, but it carried on regardless of my presence, then in an instance it had gone, and with the returning of silence came an awesome feeling of inadequacy and loneliness, I screamed "Please, please, if you do exist and you are real, then take me, take me away from all this misery"!

Once again I faded into oblivion, I don't know for how long, but I did, it seemed like a second, although in reality it was hours, however my return to reality brought a different attitude, for this time I begged for forgiveness and the chance to live. "Please God, please I don't know what I want, but let me live", it was a brief return for I faded once again, however my third and final resurrection took place a few hundred yards away in the precinct, behind the shops.

It seemed as though I wasn't actually there in a physical form, more invisible than anything else, or in another dimension would be more apt, I felt as if I was in between places, on some sort of journey, but it was nothing normal. I stood motionless as a Police car turned into the loading bay with his headlights on full beam, I never even flinched as they shone directly into my eyes and pulled up along side of me.

Then as the two Policemen got out, I realised this was indeed an exceptional experience. Their movements were similar to those of people in a disco when there is a strobe light in use, only I was spared the discomfort of the flashing light effect, for me it was different.

I was part of another source of energy, for it seemed as though I was on the other side of a giant television screen comprising of millions of coloured hexagonal shapes and although a powerful barrier, it was invisible by it's nature.

I experienced those feelings throughout my interrogation in the Police station and to my surprise I was released over an hour later and left to make my own way home on foot, but it wasn't possible, so like a fatally injured cat I made my way to the nearest field and bedded down under a secluded tree, waiting to die.

With day break and the noise from the early morning rush hour traffic I woke up to the realisation that I was a total failure, jobless, penniless and for all I knew homeless, I was a dead loss, I couldn't even kill myself, "What a mess!!".

By now I knew that I had to swallow my pride and like an injured chick get back to the nest, where, hopefully I could repair the badly damaged ego, which is exactly what I did.

With much less of a cocky attitude and more in the fashion of a snake, I slithered into the kitchen only to be greeted by Joyce, Dad and Carol,

"Where've ya been?, we've been worried to death about you"! That was it, the weakest, mildest response I could have been given, it was certainly the most surprising and one which left me thinking "Oh well, homes not that bad after all." I didn't say very much, I didn't have to, my dishevelled appearance said it all for me, which gave me the excuse to make straight for my desperately needed bed.

Still unaware that I'd taken a load of tablets, they let me come around in my own time, but after three or four days of just loafing around the house in a daze, the subject of work was broached, "What are you both going to do for a job?".

A couple of weeks later both Eddie and I were once again at our irresponsible best, we'd overcome the shame and anger that we'd brought upon Joyce and Dad whilst at the same time we'd enjoyed the funnier side of our expedition. We both signed on the dole, immediately ensuring us of some money at least, but of course that all went on boozing and unfortunately a job search only succeeded in bringing out the worst in us.

Whilst drinking in the pub, we decided to hold a job quitting contest, with the winner being the person who quit his job the fastest. Looking back it was a shame, poor Joyce and Dad thought we were really keen to find work, sadly little did they know, what we were really up to. The first opportunity came when Eddie got a job at a plastics factory in Openshaw, of course Dad had his ten penny's worth, "What about you?, why don't you get a job there?", "It's not my scene", but there again he didn't know the half of it.

Fully aware of the situation I accompanied Eddie to his first mornings work and as we got off the bus he turned around with a massive grin on his face. Mimicking Joyce and Dad, I wished him well and good luck in his new job, "See you in about twenty minutes our kid"!

Twenty minutes later and bang on time as promised he came skipping through the main gates, "You should have seen em all in there, like a load of Robots, it's pathetic, the morons will do that for the rest of their lives if they have to, wankers!, all of em", so now it was my turn, I had to find a job and beat twenty minutes.

My first employment was part time and came via the Coop, once again in Stockport, but far better situated than Eddie's was, because it was right next door to our favourite watering hole. As per usual I got the job with ease, in fact the manager who interviewed me wasn't to far removed from Reg of Betterbuys in "Coronation Street" and in his own mind he had a budding Curly Watts.

What a shock he had coming, I walked in, stood there on show for all to see and waited patiently as he allocated work to all the staff, he then turned to me, "Right you, go with him". Well fifteen minutes had gone by now and it was time to act, so I told him, "Do it yourself, ya short, fat arsed little tosser". Everybody stood there gasping in amazement, like naughty children in school, giggling and tittering as they held hands to mouths, whispering "Did you hear that?". I just turned, walked away, well pleased with myself, I'd lasted eighteen minutes, so it was out of there and straight into next door.

Eddie sat waiting for me with a pint, he knew full well that I'd do it, so we sat down and had a bloody good laugh, knowing full well that once again, it was his turn. We changed the rules this time, as we thought we could make it a little bit more competitive and interesting, and we did this by both starting our new jobs on the same date, at the same time and more importantly at the same place.

Once again it was in a store, although I can't remember which one, but as usual the manager saw us both as having well above average intelligence and both being future management material, "Wrong"!

We weren't in the shop five minutes when I found myself behind the butcher's counter "This'll be good" I thought, while Eddie found himself serving veg and it was then he shouted over to me, "Some good bargains going today our kid!!". What a scream, you've never seen anything like it in your life, there we were thrown behind a counter, without any knowledge or ideas of prices, weights and quantities, and we were expected to serve straight away, so we did!

We weren't even shown how to use the scales properly, but we didn't mind and neither did the customers, "I'll have a pound a sausages please luv, four of those chops and two pound of liver". That woman thought it was Christmas, "Here ya are luv, special offer on today", she walked away with nearly three pound of sausages, eight chops and four pound of liver, "Here ya are, I'll throw these in as well", I threw two chicken breast in on top.

Over on the grocery stall Eddie was doing just as well, old women could hardly walk, as they were laden down with weight, sometimes ten or fifteen pounds all told, and if any of our customers were attractive then they hit the jackpot. One nice looking piece came over to join the now bustling crowd,

"Yes luv?",

"I'll have two pound of this, three pound of that and a packet of those please, oh and steak please",

"How much luv? "

"Two pound please", I stopped and looked at her,

"Listen, you're a fit piece of woman, so never mind pounds, how many pieces d'ya want?, tell me when to stop?".

By this time the store was buzzing with the news that Robin Hood had come to town and fights were beginning to break out all over the place, they were like vultures around a freshly rotting carcass, pushing and shoving to get served. Meanwhile I'm still chatting up my bit of skirt and Eddie's doing the same.

While all of this was going on, the manager being the dick head type he was, stood in the corner with his arms folded as he admired our ability. In his own stupid mind he really believed that it was our sale's patter bringing in the custom, but what he didn't know was that apart from serving them with twice as much as they wanted, we weren't even charging them anything for it. Had it not been for one old girl going over to thank him, I think we'd still be stood there now, but in the end, when he realised what we were up to, he raced over with his head in his hands screaming " What on earth are you doing?", only to be met at our sarcastic best, "Well if you don't like it, stuff it"! At that point we took off our aprons, upped and left, leaving one pathetic, confused manager, surrounded by a large crowd of disappointed, angry women.

I eventually won the competition by quitting a job in less than five minutes, but unfortunately that victory proved very embarrassing for Dad. By this time both he and Joyce were becoming frustrated by our antics and so in an effort to "stop the rot "he got me a job at a Cash n Carry where he collected cardboard from. I was to start at eight thirty in the morning, so being keen to impress I got there a quarter of an hour early, where everybody in the place did their best to make me feel at home, but I had no illusions of any lengthy stay there.

The bell went at eight thirty and one lad who was particularly friendly offered to take my coat,

"Here you are, give us your coat",

"No it's okay, I'm not staying", he looked confused

"Pardon?",

"I'm off, see you". With that I made my way into the town centre and waited for the pubs to open, where I could relax and do what I liked best, "Drink".

That very same week Eddie got a greenkeeper's job on a golf course, which finally brought him some interest, contentment and stability, while I had no interest in anything at all, other than drinking, so Dad suggested that I go out with him in the van, collecting waste paper and cardboard.

The business was doing alright, Joyce had got him some work with one of the Marks's stores and he had a regular early morning run, delivering newspapers to newsagents, he had other ideas as well, which I liked the sound of, so I went with him.

That was the start of a closeness, a trust and a bond that I'd never experienced before with my Dad and it lasted for nearly eight months, but what a time, it was a spell that I enjoyed more than most others in my life because the things we got up to were incredible. I'd never realised before what a rogue my Dad really was, in fact it was the first time that I ever actually saw the close resemblance and similarities between him and the rest of his family in their outlook.

Originally he started off just collecting cardboard and paper, but with my help we were able to do far more and diversify at the same time. During the course of a week Dad had regular pick ups, which are commonly known as "drops" and some of the places we went to were unbelievable. One local food store called "Wallmans" threw all their cardboard in with the rubbish in a corner outside of the yard and Dad spent weeks warning him that kids would one day set fire to it, but he wouldn't listen. Eventually after an arson attack the manager had a couple of out houses constructed and with the new sheds built we thought at last we may start getting really clean cardboard . . . "No chance".

There were all sorts in it, split bags of sugar, flour, broken bottles of washing up liquid, even mouldy bread which still had the mice fighting over it. It was a thankless task, but once we'd finished there it was onto a local pork pie and sausage factory and if you think mice on bread was bad, you should have seen this place. "Ravenoaks Foods" used to employ backward people and boy could you tell. We never ever knew what to expect, but when it was bad, it was really bad, one thing about Dad though, he would always get stuck in and that was something I was really grateful for, because more often than not, we would both wade through the stacks of cardboard until we got to the bottom and that was where the real shit lay. Amongst the old meat pies and sausages, floating around in blood, would be my all time pet hate . . . "Maggots"! There were literally thousands of them and I hated the buggers, Dad wasn't so keen either, but he was too proud to let me see his distastes, never the less, undeterred we carried on collecting from there.

Our next port of call was Mersey Shopping Precinct, which was a giant maze of surface and underground loading bays and it was there that I got christened in the art of "skip foreging". Anybody reading this now who has worked in either the scrap metal or paper games will smile in acknowledgment, as they will know full well what I mean. Like Gypsies or tinkers, scrap dealers are indeed a breed on their own, they have to be, for nobody else would even think about doing the job, but for all the dirt, the aches, pains, cuts and bruises, there was so much fun to be had.

Waste disposal skips came in one of either two categories, they were either good and clean or bad and dirty and in the latter I would never know what I was going to come across, for it could be anything ranging from a dirty old tampax or durex to a bucket full of canteen kitchen food. On the other hand, the opposite could occur, with an abundance of clothes, toys, perfumes and records to be found, as pilfering staff would hide stolen stock from their employees in the bins, with the idea of returning after work. Unfortunately and rather disappointingly they would discover that their own loot had been nicked by somebody else . . . us!".

It didn't take me long to get the hang of it, or to get addicted to it for that matter, which meant that Dad accompanied by his enthusiastic son could work even longer and much, much harder, it was simple "The more we weighed in, the more money we got".

That addiction had us both getting up at four o'clock in the morning, delivering the newspapers to all the newsagents in Cheshire and it was during those early hours that I experienced probably my most frightening moment of all. Whilst Dad reversed the van up to the containers, it was my job to go and check how much was in them, by opening the large side door. If it was full I would jump in through the top and start throwing the cardboard out onto the floor.

On the morning in question, I enthusiastically raced to the skip and opened the side panel, "Shiny shit!!", I jumped ten feet in the air, if I didn't, it certainly felt like it, I was speechless. Suddenly there in front of me stood Jesus himself, or so I thought,

"What are you doing here?, what time is it? " he asked, I stood there, shaking with fear, as he casually rubbed his eyes and climbed out. At that moment I half expected Mary and The Three Wise Men to follow, but they didn't, instead the tramp turned and walked off,

"A good morning to you, I'm sorry if I've inconvenienced you", leaving me still trembling and Dad doubled up in hysterics. What the dirty bastard kindly forgot to tell me, was that he'd pissed all over the cardboard that was in the skip during the night, which I now found myself crawling in.

My other main claim to fame took place in another bin on the same precinct, but on that occasion I ended up being the laughing stock of the day. There I stood in the middle of this container, as happy as a rat in a dustbin, throwing cardboard out at an almighty rate, I was working at my best, so much so that a chap from one of the shops said "Eh, that lad can work, can't he"!, when suddenly I found myself covered in tea bags, food waste, old dinners, you name it and I was covered in it.

What I didn't realise at the time, was that there was a chute above the skip, which was used by the cafe above and I just happened to be stood underneath it at the wrong time. Dad and all the lorry drivers were in hysterics as I stood there dripping wet, with tea running down my face, "D'ya want a brew? " one of the drivers said, I just looked up, totally disgusted and un-amused, "Very Funny"!

If the cardboard was quiet then we switched to scrap metal, which was just as comical, Dad and I nicked scrap from all over the place, his motto was "If it moves, take it!" and that's exactly what we did!

On one occasion we found ourselves stood in the centre of an old pig farm, in the middle of nowhere, but our eyes shone with glee at the sight of cast iron grids embedded in concrete.

Obviously we dug them out and on the van they went, our only mistake was that contrary to our beliefs, the farm was still in use, for as we were loading the very last grid, we were stopped in our tracks by a couple of grunts and snorts, "What was that?", Dad looked at me with that supercilious grin and said "Come on lets get out of ere". As we pulled away we both checked the mirrors and guess what we saw? . .

"Pigs"! which meant that we had inadvertently done a demolition job on some unsuspecting sole's property. But I think that our greatest achievement, without any shadow of doubt, took place slap bang in the middle of Altrincham town centre.

It was one of those many days we swore to ourselves, that we wouldn't return home empty handed. It was rather like the T.V serial "Bread", because for our own piece of mind, whatever happened "We had to earn something". We'd been out all morning, we were tired, hungry, piss wet through and just about getting fed up, there was no cardboard or scrap anywhere to be seen, because we'd "cleaned the place out", when suddenly . . . "Stop the van Dad!!, look over there", "We can't take them our Paul"! Whilst on look out duty I'd spotted some really big old cast iron gates that lay embedded in a wild overgrowth of grass, the question was, "Could we prise them free? " and if so, "Were we strong enough to lift them?".

In a manner similar to that of a pair of council workmen, we set about dislodging and loading the gates, but they wouldn't budge, which made me start to laugh. The reason was simple, what I've failed to tell you is that these were no ordinary gates, they did in fact belong to a church and just the sight of Dad and me struggling like two drowned rats set me off in hysterics, for there we were as hard faced as you like and in the middle of broad day light, confiscating "the holy gates" of "Saint what ever it was".

Weighing in was just as funny because all scrap yards had a foreman who graded the materials being brought in and they were there as a result of their honesty, but more often than not they could be "bought" to upgrade the load. It was a weak part of a system which should of been infallible, but not to a Davies, Dad wanted more, so he used his enterprising initiative to come up with a great idea.

Each time we weighed in a load of scrap, we would carry a few dustbins, which would be filled with either water, bricks or soil, consequently Dad would be getting paid for metal that he hadn't even brought.

During that period of time Dad taught me well and although I learnt so much, it was the enjoyment and closeness we shared together that made it even more worthwhile, so a few years later when I went into the game myself, I was what is commonly known as "a dab hand".

At that moment in our lives the Davies household had experienced another decently long period, Eddie was happy with his greenkeeping job, Joyce and Dad were content in themselves, I was enjoying the work with Dad and Carol wasn't causing any trouble at all, but as usual the boat was soon about to be rocked.

Chapter Five

Out Of Control

It was a typical Saturday evening, a packed Mersey Tavern, with the added disco types in sightseeing and observing the natives, as they waited for the club over the road to open. One minute everything was normal, the Cage was smoky, calm and generally being it's inoffensive self, then the next it was like a cock fighting arena, cramped with onlookers baying for blood.

A disco type, the worse for drink, had knocked over a regulars pint, sending beer all over him, which led to a debate, followed by a scuffle. It ended up with a gang of the smoothies leaving for the club over the road, threatening to be back later, but that was it, they left with idle threats, or so everyone thought. The regular concerned, was a drop out type who was obviously well known to most, but as I wasn't really "in" yet, I only knew him from a distance, "That was until about a quarter to midnight".

Both Eddie and I were stood outside talking to a leather clad biker, who we'd never met before, the taxi rank opposite was full of revellers awaiting transport home and a crowd of people were leaving the Tavern. Suddenly without warning, a fight broke out, the smoothies from the club must have been waiting for the same lad to leave the pub and with his appearance they proceeded to attack him.

For a brief moment we stood in silence, then the realisation of the situation hit us, "That's not on is it!, eight onto one, come on let's get stuck in!". With that we instinctively charged into the pack, grabbing a couple of them apiece.

I could hear onlookers cheering in the background as I laid into my victims, one of which had already seen enough with a couple of blows, so he was off, which left me with just the one and that was the initial culprit, the ringleader, "Trust me!". I just kept on punching holes out of his face, regardless of his pleas for mercy, "So you think yer hard d'ya!!". Then as if history was repeating itself, I felt somebody clasp a hold of my shoulder, only on this occasion somebody else cuffed my hands at the same time, you see in our keenness to be Good Samaritans we failed to see the three Police vans parked up down the road, accompanied by dog handlers. As I was being dragged off my prey and towards the Police van I saw Eddie making his getaway, as the others still scuffled and rolled around on the ground, "Run Eddie!, Run". Everybody who was stood at the taxi rank cheered, with staff and regulars alike jeering and clapping as I was frogmarched away, "Well done Paul!, leave em alone, they only helped". Although first to be thrown in the van, I was quickly followed by about five of the others, but Eddie got away, so I could at least breathe a sigh of relief there. The funny part about the journey to the station was that not one of us knew each other, I recognized Steve, the original victim and Phil the biker, but I didn't know them. The ringleader and two of the guilty gang got arrested, but we were all more or less strangers to each other, which proved both funny and confusing to the Police, as they questioned us in the station.

After lining up and emptying our pockets the desk sergeant proceeded with his enquiries. Pointing to one of the others he damanded to know what all the trouble was about and who had started it.

"Well him there, I knocked his drink over", the sergeant interrupted,

"Who are you with? " the lad then responded by pointing to the ringleader and then to his other mate.

The sergeant then looked towards Steve, "Where do you come in then?",

"I'm the victim" he replied, "These lot jumped me and . . " the sergeant butted in, "Hang on!, what about you two?", Phil looked at me and we just smirked, "You're mates aren't you?",

"No" I said, "I don't know any of these lot". By now the sergeant was getting a little pissed off to say the least because he thought we were all taking the mickey out of him, so we were all locked up for wasting Police time.

Eventually at about four o'clock in the morning everybody concerned was charged then released and it was then that I first got to know Phil properly. It wasn't until the next day in the Tavern, that I realised the full implications of my action, for unknowingly, I had finally achieved my sole ambition, "I was now a well respected hero in the Cage!", truly "in" with the crowd.

That admiration brought me acclaim from many people, people who I'd never had any dealings with before, "The big boys" of the scene, but in hindsight accompanied with their respect came something far more sinister, something that had been lurking inside me for quite some time. Their appraisal of my behaviour aroused me and the more I got, the more I wanted. It was as if I was an actor on stage whose never had enough applause, he keeps coming back for another encore and so, I too wanted more. My irrational thoughts and mad behaviour were by now on the increase as I ventured into the drug scene and by the time I'd finished my normal course of a day's drinking, mixed with the nights pill popping, I couldn't see beyond my own nose.

I was now the centre of attraction, Mr Big, Mr Funny, in fact I was the Paul Gascoigne of my day, for in other peoples eyes I was a "great guy" and it was as a result of that demand on my company, that I got invited to what was for me, a very important party, which took place in the most significant of weekends.

It was a Saturday afternoon and closing time in the pub, which meant that the next stop would be the bandstand in the precinct, via the off license. There was quite a crowd on the day, more than usual, which for some unknown reason prompted a few of the lads to go and play football for a change and it was only in the park that I noticed and paid attention to a certain girl watching called Francesca, who had been in our company all afternoon. After the kick about she asked me if I would be attending the party being held in the evening, but at that moment and thinking nothing more about her question I told her I wouldn't.

At nine o'clock that evening I soon changed my mind, actually Francesca and a few of the other girls changed it for me, as their requests for my attention became too promising to refuse, not of a sexual nature, but on the sheer guarantee, that there would be plenty to drink.

Actually getting to the party was a laugh in itself, as twelve of us made our way to Poynton on the bus. It was rather similar to Cliff Richard and the gang in "Summer Holiday", with all of us having a sing song from start to finish and guess who found himself leading with main vocals? There I was slap bang in the middle of everyone, doing my best party piece amidst four or five very attractive girls, although at the time they did seem more like women. Once we got to the house it was a case of me making a beeline straight for the kitchen, where all the booze was, so like a greyhound out of a trap, I was off.

After "topping up" with the help of a party five, I made my way into the living room, "Where's Fran?", it was then that one of the girls told me she'd gone upstairs for a lie down, as she had a bad head.

Without giving it a second thought I went upstairs following the directions of Sharon, who lived there and tentatively entered the room "Are you alright Fran?", she was lay on the bed and at first I thought asleep. "Hi, I could do with a cold drink", still not thinking, I went downstairs and returned with a glass, her first words upon my return were "Oh stuff the glass, it's you I want"

"Bingo!!", I'd finally hit the jackpot and with that news it took me all of about fifteen seconds to rip off every ounce of clothing. Jeans, bomber jacket, tea shirt, even my most prized possession, the plimsolls, all lay in a heap as I dived into bed with this very attractive, classy bird.

Within seconds the stallion was in action, as if I'd done it a thousand times before and at that very moment, I couldn't have given a shit if she was enjoying it or not. I must have done okay because the only time either of us left the bedroom was to go to the loo, apart from the morning after when we eventually surfaced, which actually proved to be a slightly embarrassing moment.

Unbeknown to us, anyone downstairs who'd managed to stay in any sort of conscious state had the dubious pleasure of listening to the added noise coming from our squeaky bed and floor boards above, needless to say our sudden appearance downstairs was met with a chorus of jeers, cheers and applause. A quick exit was in order, so Fran and I got a lift off one of the revellers down to Stockport, where I left her at the bus stop. It was funny because I remember the very first record I over heard on the radio that morning, it was "I shot the sheriff" by Eric Clapton, what a laugh, I didn't shoot the sheriff, but I'd shot something else and it was far more important, so just for that morning, I called myself "pistol packing Pete!!".

As was the norm everyone re-united in the Tavern for "afternoon drinks" and it was then that I really noticed Sara for the very first time.

Whilst everybody conferred notes, talking about what a good party it turned about to be, I just sat there inwardly grinning to myself, like a Cheshire cat, as I relived my first real night of passion and my initial conquest and it was because of that selfish, self centredness, that I didn't take much notice of Sara, well at least not until the evening anyway.

It was as the Cage opened for the night's gathering that Sara and I really started to get to know each other. I'd arrived downstairs in my usual fashion, with bottle or glass already in hand from upstairs, so I didn't need to buy a drink, but it was when I went for a refill that I got, yet another one of the many shocks in my life. As I stood up, I turned to her, "Would you like a drink?", she refused at first, but I persuaded her to have one and with that I went to the bar. Whilst being served, she came over to me and clasped my hand, pushing a piece of paper into it. I didn't read it until I'd returned to my seat, but in hindsight and in view of it's contents I'm glad I didn't, for I'm sure I would have probably dropped the glasses I was carrying there and then.

The note read . . . "Dear Paul, you turn me on you randy bastard, I want you". Can you imagine how I felt?, having just lost my virginity only the night before. At first I thought it was a joke, but as soon as she returned from the toilet, I knew that it wasn't, so like an ice skating judge I said "Well!, I've got to give you ten out of ten for style!!". It was the start of a relationship which brought even more changes to my life, physically, mentally and geographically. In a similar style to the evening before, that first night and the early hours were once again spent in bed and boy, by the end of the weekend could I tell.

First there was Fran and now I found myself with Sara, both had screwed the arse off me and by now my prick was throbbing and feeling very sore, but I knew right from the offset, "This girl was different, something special" and that she was.

Only the second woman that I'd been to bed with and just less than twelve hours after my inaugural attempt, she screwed me whilst on her period, which was one hell of an introduction to sex, "Talk about the Good Sex Guide". From the very start, she fucked me and made me laugh, which at the time, was all I needed, but there was no way that things could possibly stay like that, it would have been too boring, so we progressed together.

Between us, we made friendships and acquaintances, using them all as we went along our way, as the need to feed growing habits gradually became more of a problem. For the first time my drinking and pill taking was now causing me problems and I was now becoming unreliable, as I started to let Dad and other people down more and more. The majority of people blamed Sara as the bad influence, "But what did they know?".

By the time a few months had passed, I was in a real mess, I'd left home, living here and there with her, borrowing this and that to get by, she'd fucked me in every way imaginable, so there was nothing left to do there and to top it all she'd screwed me to the wall financially, so I was now basically skint.

It took some time for me to realise that I'd served my purpose as far as she was concerned, but even with that awareness, it was both hard and very painful to accept that I had to let go of her.

Once I'd realised that mistakes had been made, I should have been wise and courageous enough to do something about them, "But how could I?", after all, I really knew very little, probably nothing. At that moment in time I needed love, understanding and care, I needed my family, but I daren't go back and say "Oh well, I cocked up again!!"

Instead I dealt with it in the only manner I knew or understood . . "Violence". My automatic reaction, was to lay into her, in a wild frenzy and with an ever increasing occurrence, the ferocity of the attacks got worse.

There were times, I felt as though I actually had my fathers spirit inside me, as I seemed to emulate his past behaviour, but unlike Joyce, Sara reacted differently, her response was to go out, get another much older bloke, take him back to the flat and dive into bed with him. By the time I'd returned home, boozed and pilled up to the eyeballs, it didn't matter, for in that state all I could do was go and cry in the other rooms, weeping as I heard her making love.

The ending of that relationship brought about a very "pathetic Paul", the old

Paul and with it returned some "old ghosts", to haunt me from the past. On one occasion, I stood on the balcony, some twelve or thirteen floors up, desperately wanting to jump, but I was neither brave or desperate enough to do it.

After a few weeks of pain, suffering and degradation I somehow ended up back at home, I had to, for I needed to once again heal, from my wounds and scars of life and start again. The rebuilding process took longer and cost more than any other I'd undergone before, because far more drinking was done in the name of therapy and as a direct result I started to become a frequent visitor to many other various establishments. This was mainly due to my fast gathering reputation for being a trouble causer, as I was now becoming quite a character and it wasn't uncommon for me to be barred from two or three pubs at the same time.

Quite often I would be seen turning up tables and throwing glasses around after a good drinking session and more often than not, I'd end up in a fight or scuffle somewhere, but it was all part and parcel of my recovery. Eventually it worked and having done so I promised myself there and then, "Never again will a woman ever hurt me like that" The only consolation I could pull from all of the wreckage at the time, was that I doubted if I would ever meet another dirtier, sexier, kinkier woman then Sara in my life, so not all was lost, for as inexperienced as I was, she was the nearest thing I could have imagined to a prostitute. That relationship with Sara brought about the first of a few breakups between Eddie and myself, until then we'd been inseparable but at the time it seemed as if he was jealous, not of me, but of her. The fact that I'd led him along so far, supplying a social life and finding him new friends was too much to take and of course when he saw me changing for the worse, like everybody else, he blamed her.

During my absence he'd passed his driving test, which meant that on many occasions he would drive down to Stockport to meet the lads and it was then, that with his conning methods, he "bought" his way in with my original mates, which meant that with my return came bitterness between us.

It was the first time that I ever saw the other side of Eddie, the cruel, nasty, evil, deceitful side and it hurt, but I had to see it and learn, despite the pain. On many occasions unknown to Joyce and Dad he would pass me at the bus stop as he made his way to the same destination, if they'd known, he wouldn't have been allowed to drive in their vehicle at all, but typical of me, I said nothing.

By now the atmosphere between us had got so tense that something had to give and it was me. An almighty row erupted in the Tavern, with him calling me and visa versa, in the end I could take no more. With one fell swoop every glass on the table went, I then lifted it, threw it aside and went for him. That was my last visit downstairs and as a result of a ban, I never went back again, giving me a new problem to think about, "Where would I hide now?". The answer came in the shape of a pub called "The Manchester Arms" and it was there, that I spent my eighteenth birthday, "Alone!!"

For three or four months I sat in there, quite happy in my own company, but it wasn't much longer before I was joined by a few of the other faces and things started to get back to normal.

Looking back now, even though I felt happy with my own company, I really was a sad person, the things I'd done to all of those around me were terrible, but on the other hand the things that had been done to me were just as bad, unfortunately I was confused and left with only one answer to suppress my emotions . . . "Alcohol".

By now my fleeting interest with drugs had waned and only drink could give me the laughter and warmth that I demanded, so I consumed more. Luckily for me, the crowd I now found myself mixing with again, were all heavy drinkers, that was their only interest, so I was in good company. One of the lads, was the same guy Eddie and I helped in the fight and it was because of that night, we both became good friends with all this new crowd.

The format for the next couple of years was simple, drink, drink and even more drink, with plenty of laughs along the way and if any one of us was lucky enough to pull a woman on the trip, good luck to him, he'd need it, for the state we intended to get in, it could prove to be both a thankless and impossible task.

Whenever the pub was open and we weren't working, we were there, each night, midweek, Saturdays, Sunday afternoons and nights, we lived for it, it was the best therapy I could have had to cure my depressions and the things we got up to were even more therapeutic.

By this time even Eddie and I had heeled our differences, so everything was "Hunky Dory" as they say. Visually the seven of us resembled a cross between "Status Quo" and "Spinal Tap", gone was my red hair for the more natural long shoulder length, thick, curly look and out were the leather pants, bomber jacket, and plimsolls, instead it was jeans, jacket, Afghan and clogs.

More often than not at weekends Eddie, "By choice" would drive us all off to Blackpool or somewhere and it was on those trips that we performed best, as a band. I say that because on one occasion by sheer accident, we were mistook for a rock group in a country pub in Blackburn, which happened only as a bi-product of our imitation of "Alright Now" by Free. The young locals really believed we were a band, so we "did the business" and performed, mimicking to the music on the juke box. By the end of the night we'd really lived the part and had our beer paid for in the process, we even signed autographs for the six or seven "well to do groupies", we'd managed to take in with our facade, so from then on, that became our "anthem".

It wasn't uncommon for one or two of us to be left in the middle of a strange town and usually it was an impulsive decision made by the majority, which more often than not came about as a result of the "pissed up" state of the person(s) being abandoned. We all thought it was funny to get into such a condition, yet looking back it was both irresponsible and dangerous.

There was another favourite party piece, which always took place at weekends and once again the basis of the action revolved around the scenario of a wealthy rock group, only this time the targets were restaurants.

Each weekend, with or without "wheels" we would systematically pick out a place to eat. It didn't matter what they were, Chinks, Pakis or Indians, it made no difference they still got, "the treatment". The "band" would enter the chosen restaurant and immediately request pints and pints of beer, an enormous order, the size of which they'd probably never seen before. Then as the waiter came to take the order, we would offer to pay, which was where the real fun began.

Before going into the restaurant we all pooled our money together, which made it look like we had a giant wad, then as the waiter took our food order we would all argue over who's paying,

"I'm paying tonight",

"No . . . its my turn!", then someone else on the other side of the table would join in by standing up. Reaching towards his pocket, pointing towards one of the others he would suddenly make a statement along the lines of "Look, you paid last night, so its my turn". It was well manufactured chaos and it worked, because the one ordering everything under the sun would then pull out this enormous looking stack of money, "Shall I pay now or later?".

With our un-caring, irresponsible behaviour and the added incentive of seeing lots of real hard cash, the suckers would not only refuse payment, but they would then proceed to give us the "star studded" treatment, which was always the "green light" for action.

When it came to acting like a bunch of slobs, we didn't have to try very hard and drinking gallons of lager proved no problem either, but by the time we'd eventually got around to eating the meal itself, we were only capable of eating half of the dish and that was always the signal for our impending, pre-planned action. The group would gradually disband in maybe two's or three's, making a fuss as they left,

"Are you okay with the bill?",

"Yeah sure, see ya", with an acknowledging wave to the owners and the staff, they would then depart. Still unsuspecting and smiling with their false pleasantness the victims would continue to be nice and it was at that point that the last one, whoever he was, made "the great getaway".

The style and manner of the escapes varied, depending on circumstances, usually via the front door and into the back of the awaiting van, although on one occasion, it was necessary for one of the lads to vacate the premises by leaping through the main front window.

It was all a very dicey game to play, but it added that little touch of excitement to our weekends. Sometimes, when we had no van, we could be seen "legging it" down the road, laughing and joking, doing our war dance, like a bunch of Indians leaving the site of a burning waggon train.

Earlier on in my story, I told you how both Eddie and I deemed what was a good previous night out, with the help of our bad heads, well this was one of those periods where we did it quite a lot, however mistakes were sometimes made.

On the night in question I and at least two of the others were well and truly "out of it", Eddie was driving and joined in the front of the van by a couple of the others, which is how we got home. As usual I got up mid Sunday morning looking like something from the film "The day of the living dead". "Bloody ell our kid, that must have been one ell of a night, I've got a stormer of an ed!". Eddie paused for a second or two as he looked at me, "You and Bob are lucky to av an ed at all!, never mind a bad un", I just looked at him confused,

"What d'ya mean?". Pointing to the mirror, he told me,

"Take a look!", following his advice I discovered bruising, cuts and scratches to my forehead and it was while I surveyed the damage Eddie explained how Bob and I had slid out of the swing open doors at a set of traffic lights. Eddie had pulled away as the lights changed to green, whilst we were both pewking up out of the back, which left us on the bonnet of the car behind, totally oblivious to everything that was going on.

The fact that Eddie was driving did keep him out of quite a lot of trouble for most of the time, however there were times when he made up for it and boy did he!

One such occasion was the night we all bet him that he wouldn't hitch-hike down to London wearing cricket whites, of course the bet was made when we were all pissed, but never the less, he took us on . .

We were all smashed out of our brains by about seven o'clock, but there was no sign of our kid. The idea was that we would all meet and await his appearance, but by about half past seven he hadn't shown, leaving us all thinking we'd won the bet.

At eight o'clock he turned up and I swear I've never laughed so much in my life. The darkness of the room suddenly lit up with a vision, "No not of Christ or even The Virgin Mary, but Eddie, Eddie Davies wearing all white". Every piece of clothing was white, he even pulled his trousers down to expose his white underpants and just to round off his performance, he donned a pair of white sun-glasses.

On the stroke of midnight he was supposed to leave, setting off on his long, "through the night journey", but that original time had to be delayed as there was more beer to drink. However at a half past midnight, Eddie wasn't the only one going off globe-trotting, for in our drunken stupor and as a result of Eddie's manipulative ways the bet was changed, with the winner being the person who could get the furthest away from Stockport.

The next thing I recall was waking up at about four o'clock in the morning at Knutsford/Pickmere roundabout on the M6, with the realisation that I then had to make my way back home. At about half past five, fully clothed I climbed into bed feeling really crap, yet despite my delicate state brought on by boozing, I was more annoyed with myself for not winning the bet, convinced that Eddie had gone onto win . . . "Not on your life!".

About half an hour later I was awoken by the dulcet tones of Joyce and Dad screaming at our kid in the back garden. I couldn't decipher what was being said and I didn't really want to know because it didn't sound all that good, so I stayed hidden under the covers and went back to sleep. I didn't surface until approximately ten thirty, but having done so, I immediately wished I hadn't, I'd only got to the bottom of the stairs to be confronted with "An don't you say a fuckin word to me either!", just in case you hadn't guessed, that was Dad. I looked at Joyce, hoping she'd give me some sort of clue or support, but she was no better, "Look at the bleedin state of ya, half past ten on a Sunday morning and you get up looking like that, you want to be bloody ashamed of yourself!". I knew straight away there was big trouble, so without any hesitation, I bailed out and headed for Stockport.

My arrival at the Manchester Arms was met with a variety of chuckles and grins from the other lads and with acknowledging smiles, when I signalled to them from the bar "What d'ya want, lager?". Once I'd got the round in, I marched over to them,

"Well how far did you get?"

"Knutsford, what about you?", that question was met with an outburst of laughter from all three, "What's so funny?". The lads then explained that one of them had got as far as Didsbury, a mere two miles away, another went straight home and the one with the biggest grin hadn't even got out of Mersey Square. Pulling his arm out from under his coat he explained how in trying to catch the last bus, he missed the platform and inadvertently ended up in hospital with a plaster cast on his arm, "Where's your kid?", one of them asked "Now that's a bit of a mystery" and with that I started to tell them about the goings on at home. This in turn ended up with me asking about the others, to which they replied, "Don't know, not seen them yet".

It wasn't until that evening that I found out exactly what had gone on, but when I did, I was just grateful not to be involved.

At approximately four o'clock in the morning Joyce and Dad had received a telephone call from the police, saying that Eddie had earlier been found on the platform at Altrincham railway station.

You may be thinking so what?, big deal, what's the fuss?, it's simple Eddie had shit himself in his best "cricket whites" and they'd found him slumped against the wall, but because of the state he was in, nobody wanted to move him. That task was left to his loving Mother and Father, who were none to pleased at being given the job.

Later on when I quizzed him about the ranting and raving in the garden in the early hours of the morning, he told me that it occurred when Dad was burning all his clothes, he said he was alright until Dad told him to take off his trainers and that for some unknown reason, in his totally blitzed state, was too much for him to take, so apparently he stood there stark naked shouting "No, not my trainers, anything but my trainers!". Once again it was a case of the Davies's using enterprise and initiative by going into the "early morning call" business,
"Although I don't think BT could have competed with this, fire and all!".

Although we got into many a state, I always made sure I was fit for work especially after Dad had given me so much support, but in the March of that year I for once, felt guilty, as Dad was going through a bit of a quiet patch. I knew in my own mind that he was struggling to make his own wages, never mind mine, so I suggested that it was about time I left to get a job elsewhere. The relief on his face said it all, but still being the loving Dad he was, his reluctance came through with the question "Are you sure you don't mind?",

"No problem, I'll ask Ted if he has any vacancies?"

Ted owned the paper mill where we weighed in, called Jeffries, it was ten minutes away from home, I knew everyone there and I understood the paper game, so it was an obvious choice. I started the very next day, settling in immediately and it was fun right from the start. The characters that worked there, were all individuals in their own right, but they all had one thing in common, they were all receiving money from the social security.

Signing on days were hilarious, as we all piled into Ted's big jag and systematically called to our various unemployment offices to register, after which we would all return back to the factory. If we were a driver's mate on the road, then we'd roll up to the dole office in either a giant box waggon or a forty foot, heavy goods lorry, but as far as we were concerned, it didn't matter as long as we got our money. Like most waste paper factories Jeffries was a dirty, dusty, scruffy place, that employed a sort of a "waif and stray" type of character, most of which seemed to have more than their fair share of problems, consequently I didn't feel out of place. Yet despite this crazy assortment of what I look back on as "Sad types", there was always a sort of happy atmosphere about, which seemed to focus around lots of laughter and frivolity.

I worked there for about eight months, without getting caught by the social security spies, but it wasn't easy. Quite often in the early hours of the morning I could be seen doing my impression of Chris Bonnington or Lynford Christie as I either scaled garden sheds and trees or hurdled the fences in-between. That Krypton Factor course, sometimes became a regular feature of my working day, but I had to do it, because just the sight of a strange car parked with someone in it, brought the threat of being caught and quite often, those spies could be keen little beggars. Most of the lads were boozers, but unlike myself they spent every single penny on the stuff and that's where I was different.

As a result, in the June of that year I went to Benidorm for a couple of weeks holiday, I went alone, but nearly didn't make it. At about ten o'clock on the morning of my departure date, I went to have my hair cut at my local barbers, taking with me a few cans of lager, which in hindsight was a good, clear indicator of my intentions.

Unfortunately that's all I can remember, the next thing I knew, it was about a quarter to four in the afternoon and I was supposed to be at the airport. My flight was due to take off at approximately half past, but because of my inebriated state I'd totally forgotten and it was only because of my mate's inquisitiveness that I remembered at all, "Eh Paul, aren't you supposed to be going somewhere today?". In all honesty I looked at him baffled and confused, "Me, No . . . I don't think so", he then responded by saying, "I knew this trip was a wind up". I just stood in silence, holding a pool cue, trying to work out what on earth he was going on about, then a few seconds later, I remembered,

"Oh shit, Cliff I wasn't joking, I'm supposed to be at the airport", still disbelieving he approached the table to take his shot, "And when should you be there for this phantom flight?". Putting my hand inside my jacket to feel for my passport, tickets and money, I let out one almighty yell, "Now!!!".

Memories of that journey are very vague indeed, I remember jumping into a taxi, shouting at the driver, "Get me to the airport in fifteen minutes!!". The next minute I was stood at the foot of the stairs, waiting for the doors of the plane to be reopened and finally the hostess handing me my only luggage, which Dad had kindly dropped off for me, but that's it. In my next bout of consciousness, I woke up in the reception of the hotel where I was staying.

With my revival came an abundance of very negative feelings, which centred mainly around loneliness and guilt, obviously brought about by my behaviour, but even worse I was confused and left asking myself, "What am I really doing here?".

My room had already been sorted out by some caring sole, I don't know who or why because I was obviously in one hell of a state, but they had and what little hand luggage I'd taken, had been put in, so there was really only one thing to do, "No, not bed, but the bar!!". Once I'd had that "hair of the dog", I knew I would be okay and sure enough I was, I went off, only this time with a mission in mind.

My Mother's sister, Edith, was working in a bar at the time, slap bang in the centre of old Benidorm and it was my intention to find her, which surprisingly, I did with ease. I expected to see my favourite Auntie laughing, joking and looking happier than I'd ever done before, but what a shock, she did look well in her appearance as she displayed her quite tasty sun tanned body, but in her eyes she was both sad and discontented, it was obvious that she was in fact a kitchen slave, which at that moment prompted me to think, "Perhaps I'm not the only unhappy, lonely person in this town".

I can't remember leaving her that night, in fact the only thing I do recall is my sad, pathetic state as I walked back to the hotel and the weeping, crying state I was left in. I never saw her again, even though I desperately wanted to, although on reflection I remember wanting to do more than see her. I actually wanted to go to bed with her, to see if she was as sexy as she'd always previously appeared to me.

Sadly, once again in my life, it was a case of me desperately wanting something, yet at the same time, not being exactly sure of what it was, but at my resilient best I bounced back and during the course of my stay I made quite a number of acquaintances.

They ranged from single people of both sexes to courting and married couples of all ages and "Boy did I have some fun!".

During the course of the next ten days I constantly drank and with my friend "King alcohol", inside me, I became a "redcoat type" character throughout the hotel. Due to the fact that I was alone, the drinks kept flowing, paid for from all directions, which meant that the more I drank, the better my performance got and sure enough, towards the end of that first week the bonuses started to fly in.

A few of the families who had been staying in the hotel were due to leave and as usual in those circumstances, they'd been forced to vacate their rooms early, so like a flock of sheep they'd gathered at the reception much sooner than necessary awaiting the arrival of their coach.

In the event, their downfall proved to be my good fortune, for as I made my way to the bar from the lift I heard someone calling me, "Paul, Paul, yoo hoo!!". One of the women came over to me, "I'm glad we've not missed you, you've been such good fun". I couldn't see her husband and the kids, so I asked her where they were. "Oh they've gone down to the beach for the last time".

Automatically the brain slipped into gear, "Really", I wasn't prepared to waste any time so I instinctively asked her to follow me. I led her down one flight of stairs into the darkness and seclusion of the closed disco bar and with little opposition or reluctance, she followed, "What d'ya think your doing?, where are we going?". Once we were downstairs and out of sight, I started to kiss and fondle her and within seconds we both wanted more.

"What time does your old fella get back, with the kids?",

"I don't know", it was one of those most inopportune moments that any woman could have picked to be gormless or dilatory.

"What d'ya mean ya don't know, well what time is the coach due?", she didn't know the answer to that question either, so I knew I had to take matters into my own hands. "Oh fuck it, come on", so I took her up to my room and gave her a real good "shagging".

An hour later the bus pulled away, with me stood on my balcony looking down and her with the rest of the families waving up to me, "If only they'd all known what we'd just been doing!".

One effort that didn't go according to plan was my surprise seduction of a blonde piece, who I found drinking alone at the bar. I'd watched her for about a couple of hours, but there was no male companion to be seen, so with the time approaching nearly two o'clock in the morning and despite the fact that I was pissed out of my brains, I made my play.

I gave her my best spiel and she fell for it so without much of a fuss we made our way upstairs.

We started as soon as we got in the lift and by the time we'd got to her room on the top floor we'd already given each other a good hand job. Stood outside as she put the key in the door, I was already firing on all four cylinders, the adrenalin was pumping and I was all geared up and ready for action, but due to past experiences, I already knew that in life, "You never know what is coming next", and this was certainly one of those occasions. As she opened the door I couldn't believe my luck, I remember thinking to myself, "God this is easy!".

Then the luck changed, the silly pissed up cow had only forgotten to tell me she had a husband, who'd been in bed suffering with the "shits" for three days. It wasn't even as if you could forget him that easily, especially as he was about six foot something and at least fifteen stone. The only course of action left open, was to "Leg it", which I did.

Thankfully they were leaving the day after, but God knows what I'd have done otherwise, needless to say it was a close shave, but I'd got away with it by the skin of my teeth.

With only five days left of my holiday and already a few successes under my belt, God once again moved in one of his many wondrous and mysterious ways.

Whilst stood at the bar in my favourite "pissed up "state, I overheard a couple of women sat next to me, they were having a real good time and in doing so, giving everybody else pleasure. One was much older than the other, with the younger being about my age, but once again it was a case of, "When you're not looking for anything, something usually smacks you in the face".

By the end of the night we'd arranged to meet the day after, although I didn't give it a second thought, as I presumed they'd probably forget. I was wrong, for the next day they were both sat there as I arrived and from the very first moment we got on, so for the rest of that trip, they became my best drinking buddies.

Although Millie and Josie were related, no onlooker or outsider would have been able to tell that they were in fact Auntie and niece. They got on so well together, one would automatically think of them as mates, especially as Millie was so youthful in both her looks and attitude. That afternoon we all got to know each other and by the time the drinking session had finished I felt that I'd known them both for years, so it was prearranged that we would meet later on in the evening. However when that time arrived only Millie turned up, so undeterred we sat, drank, talked and basically carried on from where we'd left off in the afternoon.

Looking back it seems that although I thought of myself as "street wise", I was never the less, pretty naive and Millie with her thirty six years of age certainly proved that.

At some point, midway through the evening, she asked me what the rooms were like, I think I must have said something like, "They're ok, it's just a room to me". Immediately following up and in a blatant fashion she posed the million dollar question, "Well are you going to show me?".

What a plonker!, I took her up, marched her in and proceeded to give her a viewing, "Well here's the bathroom, toilet, and here's the balcony". There wasn't much to show her actually and writing this makes me laugh, just thinking of how pathetic I must have looked as I did my best impression of a "Barratt show house girl".

Of course she only wanted to see one thing and when she grabbed a hold of me, I knew that it wasn't the room. Unromantically and unceremoniously the clothes came off and we got down to it, but it wasn't until after we'd made love, that I asked her a question, which seemed to have been missed amongst all of the others, "Where's your husband?". When she answered, I was convinced she was taking the piss, "He's dead", I responded in disbelief, "Come on, stop taking the mickey". The problem was that we'd laughed so much in each others company and she was such a rum bugger, that I didn't believe a word she said, "Okay, well when did he die then?". The next answer was even more unbelievable, "Three months ago", well it was always an ambition of mine to " Stuff a widow", but never in my wildest dreams, could I have envisaged doing it so early on in my sexual career.

After our "bonk", I took her back to their hotel over the road and whilst over there, we spent some time with Josie in the room, she was supposed to have sunstroke and sure enough when we got there she was in bed, so we rounded the night off with a cup of tea.

Walking back to my room, I looked up to the sky thinking,

"What a fucking day"

Well as if it couldn't have got any better, the day after, Josie had made a remarkable recovery, so she too decided to pay me a visit . . . "Alone", only this time I cut out the guided tour.

It was only a matter of weeks after the holiday, that I had desires to go and see the two girls, but unfortunately it was a long way to Tillicoultry. However the problem was soon solved one Thursday afternoon at work, in the shape of a lorry driver who I was loading up, his destination was Aberdeen and by sheer coincidence, he was intending to pass through the region of Alva, so there was, at last, a chance of me getting there.

Thursday was pay day, with the ritual of collecting your wages being carried out at finishing time, but due to my excessive drinking, more often than not, my wage packet was just thrown in the middle of the floor, where everybody else took out what I owed them. Whatever was left was mine and so with just fifteen pounds to my name, I asked the driver if he fancied having a pint with us all. As he wasn't leaving until about four o'clock in the morning, he accepted and it was whilst we drank together, I propositioned him for a lift, he responded by saying

"You be here at four in the morn, and ya can gladly hav a ride" . . I was and I went. Without telling anybody I disappeared and stayed up in Scotland for four days. The faces of all concerned were a picture, as I rolled up at St. Johnstone's Crescent, I only went the once, but it was a very memorable weekend and one that I've never forgotten.

Once I was back home, it was the same old song and chorus again,

"You're irresponsible, I honestly don't know what you think about, half the time". When I got into work it was no different there, Ted was great, he always said, "I was well out of my tree", but even he was left nearly speechless, "You can't just leave everyone in the lurch"

Expecting words pleading for forgiveness he awaited my response and in my usual manner I had no intention of disappointing him,

"Ted, can I have a sub?, I'm a bit skint!".

For a short period of time, Eddie and I started to cover Joyce and Dad's market stall, but once again it didn't last. In their own minds they were trying to do their best, but yet again, we abused both their faith and trust. Our drinking habits were insidiously getting worse and with that progression came more selfish and un-caring behaviour.

We used to take it in turns to dive over to the local boozer and by the time we'd done a couple of hours, we were in no fit state to deal with the public. Other traders would cringe as we told potential customers to, "Piss Off!". If somebody came to the stall stating that the bloke on the other side of the market was cheaper, the answer was simple, "Well go and bleedin buy it from him then!".

Any market trader worth his salt will tell you that, without fear, whenever you're packing up, people will always come around wanting this or that and as the customer is always right, you should oblige. Not us!, in our case it was always something like, "Av you just got out a bleedin bed or somethin!", sometimes they wouldn't get the message, so it had to be made clearer, "Look luv, the pubs shut in ten minutes, were packin up, now fuck off!!".

We were on a short enough rein as it was, without any other distractions, but when I spotted a decent looking piece of fluff on the stall opposite, that was it. It wasn't long before I was sniffing around her and in a very short space of time, I was actually in her. At first I thought it was going to be hard going, because she had a baby which was only a few months old, but I soon learnt different, she screwed me everywhere, her Dad's, her mate's, at home, we even managed it in her red Mazda and then it was full of the second hand clothes that she sold, but wherever we did it, it was always good.

Kath as usual, was a good few years older than me and once again, with age came experience, she always knew what and how she wanted it and it was my job to supply the goods. I can remember the very last time we went to bed together, she was lay there with me slapping her around, while she screamed "Hurt me!, hurt me for God's sake!", I think at the time she was trying to tell me she liked it rough and everything was going well, until baby James started crying. Suddenly slap bang in the middle of my performance as an SS interrogation officer, she let out an almighty scream . . . "James!, fuckin shut it will ya!", that response didn't put me off my stride, but I do recall thinking somehow it didn't seem to be like that on the telly.

Once we'd been removed from the market I never saw Kath again, which was a shame because she did bring a new dimension to my life, but it wasn't until some time after, that Eddie admitted to "doing "her as well, so I supposed one could say on that occasion the Davies's really left their mark!

My next adventure came in the May of '76 in the shape of a holiday to Menorca. I stayed at a place called Sa Paise in Cala 'n' Porter and once again it was a solo effort. I went on the recommendation of Joyce and Dad as they'd been the year before and I wasn't disappointed.

The lady who owned the place at the time was called Joyce, like my mother and although I was welcomed with open arms, I was an exception to the rule because normally Joyce only catered for the Germans.

Most of that trip was obviously spent boozing and as a result it introduced me to new friends and acquaintances, yet having said that, my consumption and intake of alcohol had risen dramatically, so I was heading for trouble. It came in the shape of four women from Oldham and a German girl from Koln and once again it was a combination of my constant inebriation coupled with naivety.

In the first incident I found myself going to take a shower in the communal bathroom opposite my room, it was a scorcher of an afternoon and I needed to sober up, so off I went. As I opened the door this beautiful German girl walked past "Halo" and with that I just smiled and said hello back. Instead of carrying on, she stopped and started asking me a million and one questions. Ten minutes later and we were still stood talking, me with just a towel around my waist and her in a bikini, clutching a beach towel. "Look Christina, you'll have to excuse me, because I have to go, I'm running late".

Another fifteen minutes later and feeling much better for a cold shower, I'd gone back to my room and I was just about to zip up my jeans, when there was a knock at the door. She stood there looking absolutely gorgeous, modeling a beautiful tanned body, topped off with a thick mass of wet black hair. "Excuse me Paul, could you possibly change this?", she held out something like the equivalent of a twenty pound note, I don't remember exactly what, but I know it was for some stupid amount. Like the fool I obviously was, I said "Sure" and instinctively turned, making my way towards my bedside drawer. Having got the money, I turned around to find she'd entered the room, closed the door and let her hair down. By the time I was stood directly in front of her, I was for once, stuck for words and all I could do was take in the truly awesome sight facing me. With her long wet hair draped over her shoulders and her firm sun tanned breasts trying to jump out of her skimpy bikini, she was the epitome of beauty and I couldn't believe that this was really happening to me. With her hands behind her back, she stood there clasping the door handle, with a mixture of water, sun oil and perspiration trickling down from her hair and face onto her breasts. It was just like a scene from the film "Nine and a half weeks", but unlike Mickey Rourke, I had a different approach. "Here you are Christina!", holding out my hand, I offered her the money.

Basically I'd dropped the biggest bollock of my life, although I hadn't realised it yet, she took my pesetas, gave me hers, turned around and left the room and it was only a few seconds later that it dawned on me.

"What on earth have I just done!, that girl was begging for it", I scrambled to the door in a mad panic and ran into the corridor, but as if by magic, she'd disappeared, which left me wondering whether or not it was all a dream. The next day I discovered that it was all real, for tucked under the door was a note from her, it read, "Dear Paul, sorry if I offended you, I didn't think for one minute that you were homosexual". What a wanker!, there I was with one of the most beautiful girls I'd ever seen and she thought I was queer, still it was too late to do anything because she'd left that day, for Germany. The other incident revolved around four barmaids from a pub on Broadway in Oldham, they were all having a drink in the bar downstairs and that was where we met. After a good hours drinking and getting to know each other, the eldest who was in her late thirties asked me if she could use the toilet in my room as the ones in the bar were grotty.

I had no objections, so I took her up, let her in and waited outside, a few minutes later the noise from the cistern, signalled that she'd finished, so I went in. The first words spoken were "Ooh Ta!, I was just getting desperate, I can't stand dirty loos", she then paused for a minute and went outside onto the balcony, where she took in the view. It was then that I, thinking of the ice cold Pernod waiting for me at the bar came out with a peach of a line . . . "Ok, should we get back to the others?". I never thought any more of it and she certainly never said anything or showed any sort of reaction, so we went back downstairs.

Unfortunately for me, once again I'd got it wrong, for a couple of nights later when everybody was just about to finish for the night, she came out with the question, "Well who's going to walk me home?". Sober and eager enough to want to screw her, I immediately volunteered, "I'll take you!", to which she replied, "Oh no you wont, you had your chance the other afternoon".

Those two separate incidents only gave me cause to drink even more, for they'd both ended up with me being in a sort of way "rejected" and that was always a desperate state for me to be in, so in the knowledge that my drinking was helping me to be a reject, I did the only thing I could . . . "I celebrated!" and oh boy did I!

After that holiday I came home to an empty house at "Forber", because Joyce, Dad and Carol were on holiday and Eddie was living with some bird, so I was on my own.

It was the first time I'd ever experienced delirium tremens and it was horrendous. They started midway through the flight, which proved to be a nightmare and by the time I'd got home, I just wanted to die. Talk about Bill Hailey, shake, rattle and roll wasn't even in it, my teeth seemed to be chattering at least fifty times a minute, as I shivered and retched at the sink. It carried on all weekend as I constantly made efforts to consume the softest and lightest of drinks such as lemonade, but all were to no avail.

On the Monday I returned to work in much the same state, but by the Wednesday I was back to normal and back in the pub.

For the past few years despite my absence, Eddie had carried on watching City, but with the appearance of this new tart in his life and the fact that they lived together, his own interest had also waned, which prompted me to take up following the blues again. I joined the supporters travel club, became a member at the Social club and with a mate, took off on the road again watching City.

Like everything else in my life, there were no half measures and so out went my friends in Stockport, as it was now going to be football, drinking and football. That's how it started and to all intent and purpose, that was how it was supposed to carry on, but as with most other things in my life God had different ideas. For not long after whilst following my team, I inadvertently and unintentionally met another older woman.

Chapter Six

Marriage . . . An Olive Branch?

My first sighting of her came as we were all fleeing for our lives from West Ham football club. Their fans were throwing all sorts at our coach, bricks, bottles, cans even dustbins, as we made our way home, so everybody on board had to duck for cover. I had no intention whatsoever of getting involved with anybody else, whether they be male or female, because I just wanted to be alone for a while, so I stuck with Phil if we bumped into each other, other than that I stayed on my own.

Actually being on that coach was a million to one chance in itself, because my usual mode of transport came by the way of hitch hiking, so the fact that she appeared to be both attractive and sexy didn't really matter at that time, as I probably wouldn't see her again.

I couldn't have been more further from the truth if I'd tried, as three or four weeks later, there I was stood in the middle of Newark bus station, thumbing a lift, when suddenly the club coaches pulled in. As the first one passed I saw her again, sitting on the back row and it was then at that very moment, I knew I wanted her. Frustratingly I chased amongst the dozens of cars, coaches and hundreds of people, looking for her so that I could "break the ice", but it was no good, there was too much chaos. I'd given up all hope of seeing her, when all of a sudden the coach that she was on slowly pulled passed me.

Like a scene from a film we communicated through the thick glass,

"I'll see you at Norwich",

"Yes, okay", but disappointingly I didn't, so the long journey home was hard work to say the least, but as luck would have it and rather unusually, we had another away fixture the week after and once again it was in East Anglia, only this time, Ipswich. Throughout the journey down and during the whole of the match I could think of nothing else but Jean, the only problem was I hadn't seen her, although that was soon about to change.

I hovered around the coach park after the game and sure enough she was there, "Hi, how are you?", I felt as if the old shy Paul had come back to haunt me, "Okay thanks, I'm hitching as usual", that was it, the limit to our conversation because the steward proceeded to usher her and the others onto the coach. Desperately I shouted to her as she disappeared, "If I get back to the club in time I'll buy you a drink". Thankfully she acknowledged my parting statement, so with everything to play for I started off on the long journey home.

For weeks I kept sending drinks over for her in the other bar, but she played hard to get, mind you what decent woman wouldn't, especially looking as I did, but in the end after lots of coaxing and persuasion she came around, which meant that once again, I'd got what I wanted . . . "My own way".

Our mutual interest in football meant that we had quite a lot in common and it was over in the Social club that we made all of our rendezvouses. It suited Jean because she only lived over the road, but she didn't let me know that for quite some time and so it was only after a good few weeks and much socialising that I got my first of a few invites over for coffee.

Jean was fourteen years older than I, single and a career woman, she owned a two bedroomed terrace house and drove a nice, neat, tidy, little Fiat and she was independent, but despite all of that, it was her and her body that I wanted from the start.

At last I had found what I'd been wanting and looking for . . "I was in love!".

In a matter of months, we were spending most of our time together as I was going straight to her home from work, yet despite the length and time the journey took, it was worth it, so it wasn't long before the inevitable happened and I moved in.

I was so happy with her and she seemed happy with me, it was as if we were always meant for each other, I was getting involved in the house doing D.I.Y and generally playing "the married man", while she was enjoying the benefit of having extra money in her purse and things were looking good for the future. Although predictably as always in my life that was too simple a thing to ask, "I mean a good run for Christ sake".

The company she'd worked most of her life for had "gone bump", leaving Jean right in the shit, so I came home from work one night to find her in a real old state, "Oh Paul love, what on earth are we going to do do?".

For the first time in my life I really felt like a mature man of the world, Jean actually needed and wanted me and although I was unsure at the time I think she loved me as well. It was a time for action on my part, a time to "stand up and be counted" and a time to prove that I was a real man, despite the fact that I was only nineteen years old.

At that moment, I knew Jean desperately needed my love, support and loyalty and I had no hesitation in holding back on any.

We sat down, talked and it was agreed that I would do as much overtime as I could, despite the low wages, but typical of her that wasn't enough, because like me, she was a born grafter as well, she couldn't bare to see me putting in all the hours of work I was doing, so without me knowing she went over to Maine Road Football ground for a cleaning job, earning a mere fifty pence an hour. "What a way to convince a man that you love him".

That girl was prepared to wade through four and five inches of human piss, as she wire wooled the copper pipes in the male toilets of the ground on a Monday morning. On her hands and knees she scrubbed seats and benches and walked miles as she pushed a brush or mop up and down miles of terracing, then hours would be spent sweeping up dog and cat shit on the outside of the ground.

Not surprisingly just the thought of her doing these jobs severely dented our pride, especially mine, but things weren't getting any better. Due to her age it was proving a difficult task for Jean to even get an interview for a job and financially we were struggling, so I knew I had to do something. I decided that my best option would be a job at Kelloggs, so following Dad's example, I applied and thankfully they accepted me. That eased a lot of the pressure off us both and took away the necessity for Jean to work at the ground, so without any second thoughts she left to look for a proper job.

I really was at my happiest now, knowing that in a few weeks I would be earning really good money, I'd finally shown that I was capable of being both responsible and reliable and to round things off, I was madly in love. The best part was knowing that Jean truly loved me, so why?, why o why?, did I have to once again "Screw everything up!".

One night during the week, we'd been over the road to the club and I must have had a fair few pints because in the middle of the night, I'd wet the bed.

I hadn't realised what I'd done until I woke up the following morning, but the guilt and the pain afterwards made sure I never forgot. Jean must have slept in the back bedroom, but hearing me getting ready for work, she'd got up and appeared at the door near the bottom of the stairs. I sat there with my head buried between my hands, as she pleaded with me, "Paul, why?, why have you done this to me?", I couldn't even look at her, never mind speak, so I just sat there, looking a right pathetic little mess. Once again she asked, only this time with more anger in the tone of her voice, but it was when she broke down in tears that the pain became to unbearable and I had to look up. Normally she had large, lovely, clear brown eyes, but on this occasion they were sad with disappointment and the whites had turned red through the tears she'd shed during the night. For the first time she had bags under them through lack of sleep and her nightie was crumpled where she'd obviously been snuggled up as if she'd been cowering. It was a dreadful sight, the one and only person who I'd ever really loved, I was about to lose and in such a terrible way, even worse she'd loved me and I'd done this to her, "What a way to say thanks!".

Now full of guilt, despair and self disgust, I finally stood up with the intention of speaking, but I couldn't, for I was choking as I tried to hold back the tears. Instead I finally caved in, started to cry and made my way off to work, waving my hand behind me as I left.

Work that day was horrendous, as time and time again I relived the nightmare of seeing her in the morning, but regardless of what had gone on, I returned that evening, where we talked about the whole incident, which resulted in apologies being made and accepted, then I was left with a hair dryer and the task of cleaning up the mattress.

Once we'd put that incident behind us, we returned back to our normal selves and in the May of that year, I started working at Kelloggs.

It was only for the Summer, but because of Dad I got on days, knowing full well that after six months there was the possibility of further work, so I knew I had to impress. We were both fully aware that if I was taken on full time, then it would be on continental shifts, so it was going to be necessary for me to learn to drive.

It was something that had never interested me before, but now because my circumstances had changed it was needed and I went for it.

After seven lessons the instructor put me in for my test, "No problem, you'll walk it!", well that's what he thought anyway. The day of the test, I was a bag of nerves and needless to say I failed miserably, but that failure was made ten times worse by the fact that against all expectations, Carol passed first time and on the same day. With that news there was only one thing left to do.

"Once again I was a failure", so off I went to the pub, where I got absolutely well and truly arseholed. That action and the state I'd got in did nothing for Jean's confidence, as it followed on with relatively quick succession from my last hiccup, but regardless of that fact we patched things up and so yet again I got my head down to face responsibilities and act like a man.

The November brought two major hurdles for me, which I knew deep down I had to get over, although none would be easy. The first was the retake of my driving test and the second the change over to shifts at Kelloggs, but both had just as much importance, as they went "hand in glove" so to speak.

I desperately needed to pass that driving exam because the shift systems were on a continental basis and so I would find myself going to work at all sorts of God unearthly hours.

Having said that, even settling in on a totally different job with new rosters and getting to know a million new faces and places would be a "killer" to me, but I knew it had to be done.

Despite being tremendously unhappy and against all the odds, I succeeded in getting over both problems, but it was only done out of necessity and my love of Jean.

At around the same period of time she got a job working at a local garage. The advertisement originally asked for a clerical office type, but having done a morning she returned home for dinner totally distraught and disillusioned. When I asked her how she'd gone on, she broke down in tears, "Oh it's awful, I'm brewing up like some old tea lady, I'd have been better off staying at the ground", she couldn't say any more she was too upset. Sat there clasping a cup of tea, it was as if she felt embarrassed, ashamed and utterly dejected, but after a brief pause she continued,

"They talked to me as if I was a kid or slut, they were so rude!"

"Right, what's the number?, come on, what's the number?", she sat there looking up at me, tears welling up in her sad eyes, "Why, what are you going to do?".

In typical Davies fashion I turned to her and said "I'll show ya!!" and she gave me the number. I picked up the phone and spoke to the owner in a very elegant manner, "Listen hear you ya twat, nobody speaks to my lady the way you have this morning, so I think it's best that you shove ya cheap job up ya big fat arse!!" and with that I slammed the phone down. "There ya are, its easy, nothing's worth being unhappy for", she looked at me, stood up and put her arms around me, "Oh I do love you".

A month later she got the shock of her life, for against the stiffest odds imaginable, she'd been given a high position at Manchester University, so in the end, for once things had worked out okay.

As we were now in a much better financial position, we decided that it would be a good time to take our first holiday together, so care of Joyce and one of her contacts, we had the opportunity to go to Benidorm. We were both really tired and in need of some sunshine, so off we went for a cheap, relaxing late Winter break.

Well if there's one thing that my Mother has always been very good at, it's exaggerating and with regards to that holiday she certainly didn't let us down.

"Oh you'll love it our Paul, it's right in the centre of the town and dead handy for the shops, the road goes straight down to the beach, the apartments are lovely and the coaches and buses stop right opposite". If she'd have been in a holiday company, she would have been sued ten times over with that description.

There we were, just getting off the coach in over seventy degrees of sunshine, absolutely shattered and ready for a long, cool drink, but I couldn't see our block, "Excuse me luv, can you tell me where 'New Life Three' is please?", the rep turned acknowledging my question by pointing up this bloody long dirt track road, "Yes Sir, up there".

I couldn't believe it, it was at least half a mile away and cross country at that, "That bloody Mother of mine, I'll kill her!".

We couldn't even get into the place when we eventually got to it because everywhere was locked up, the bar, the shop, even the tiny so called reception. By this time we were really pissed off, "Come on luv, let's go and sit around the pool", as we walked towards it a horrible thought occurred to me, "If there's no water in it, I'll go absolutely spare!", there was, but it was one of the funniest things I'd ever seen.

As we turned the final corner we were confronted by a whole host of people frolicking about in a soap sudded pool, as they all seemed to be having a communal wash. The reason was simple, Benidorm had been suffering from a severe water shortage due to a drought, all bottled water had run out and it was the only means of a wash available, barring the sea.

It was all a great start to a long, hard earned rest, but there was even worse to come. Having waited over two hours for entry to our room we finally got in and when we did, there was only one thing on our minds . . . "Sex!".

It took us a few minutes to realise that something was wrong, "That's funny", Jean said, "Where's the bed?", considering we were supposed to be two quite intelligent people, at that moment in time, we must have looked pretty thick. Soon enough, we discovered that there were actually folding beds concealed in the wall, so naturally we did what any other normal couple would do and pulled one down. We had only been making love about a minute or so, when suddenly there was an almighty crashing noise, screams of laughter and jeers could be heard coming from all over the place, as people from all floors appeared on their balconies clapping. We were both doubled up crying whilst at the same time trying to cope with a bout of uncontrolable laughter, so like everybody else we made our way onto the balcony to be met with a large chorus of people shouting "Welcome to New Life Three!".

What we couldn't possibly have known, was that each newly arrived couple did exactly the same, which always ended with the identical result . .

"The folding bed had collapsed", needless to say that evening our first appearance in the bar was greeted with "Oh you're the new arrivals then!".

Beds seemed to be the main theme for that first holiday because it was due to us sleeping separately whilst we were away, that we discussed swapping the double at home for two singles. Due to my excessive sweating and constant turning Jean was missing out on her own sleep and as uncomfortable as they were, the fold ups were by far a great improvement for her personally, which meant that on our return we bought two new single beds, so we left 1977 sleeping separately.

The year of 1978 kicked off with a real bang, Dad was in hospital having his first heart attack, whilst at the same time I was having a pretend one of my own.

Just before Christmas Dad collapsed and was rushed into Manchester Royal Infirmary, I'd received a call from Jean and so I met her at the hospital, she'd never really believed half the stories I'd told her about my family, but she was soon going to see the truth for herself. There we were in the waiting room when all of a sudden Dad was wheeled through past us into Intensive Care, Joyce had been quite calm until then, but she suddenly started shouting at him "If you think you're going to skive in here for a while then you'd better think again, we've got a business to run!".

It was incredible, there was Dad being wheeled into a possible operation and all Joyce could do was think about work, because I didn't have much communication with them, I didn't know the full circumstances, but if my memory serves me correctly, once again the atmosphere at home was bad and as usual they were rowing.

My scare was more of an embarrassment than anything else, but once again it was all down to alcohol and my inability to drink like a gentleman.

Due to my contentment at being with Jean and the added satisfaction of being able to fulfil my commitments with responsibility and maturity, bouts of heavy drinking were not as common place, but as a result of having her Auntie Barbara around with her two sons over Christmas and New Year all that changed.

Once again when in the company of other people, I needed drink to enable me to mix and although we had a really good enjoyable festive season, by New Year's day morning, I was dead from the ankles up.

Going to work that morning even I couldn't believe how ill I felt, but never the less, I went, retching and pewking in between bus journeys.

Trafford Park was so quiet, I thought there must have been only me working . . . Surprisingly enough I wasn't wrong, but it was only as I opened my locker and proceeded to put my overalls on, that the penny dropped . . . I was so pissed I'd travelled over six miles by bus feeling absolutely shite, only to go back on a Bank holiday, a day early, "What a plonker!".

With the departure of Jean's family I once again returned back to some normality and a couple of weeks later enjoyed a very quiet but private twenty first birthday party. It was a total surprise and once again Jean with the help of her younger sister and my best mate Phil, managed to make me feel so wanted. It wasn't like a normal twenty first as I felt much older, like a real mature man of the world, but I was so happy, I remember thinking "Why can't life always be like this?".

With the passing of that birthday came the great news that there was a job vacancy on my old department and that better still it was for permanent days, so without a second thought I applied.

I couldn't stand shifts, I didn't like the hours, hated the work and despised the foreman, having said that Ronnie couldn't stand me either, all of which made for a jolly nice working relationship.

Sadly, despite all my efforts, deep down I hadn't changed all that much and so after six months of chasing me around the factory he had to concede defeat and admit that I was unmanageable.

What a shock Peter my old foreman got when Ronnie went down and requested that he take me back off his hands, "You're joking, Paul, he's a great lad!, I'll have him back tomorrow". I don't think I have to say much more, his wish and my desires were granted and so I went back on days, which meant that both Jean and I were at our happiest.

In the July of that year I became ill and absent from work for the very first time, I had a very bad virus, I wasn't feeling so good and so unnaturally for me I was quiet, very lethargic and desperately in need of a "non alcoholic pick me up".
It came from Jean as we both strolled around the park, when she suddenly asked me if I would marry her. For the past twelve months I had repeatedly asked her, but without success, so it came like a bolt out of the blue when she suggested it, so while I was off we went down to the Registry Office and put the bands in.

At 11.30 am on the 6th October 1978 we were married at Jackson Row Registry Office in Manchester, it was a small ceremony with very few guests, but that was just the way we wanted it. My bride looked lovely and I was as "Proud as hell" as we stood there making our promises to each other and just for once in my life I actually knew I was doing the right thing.

For the very first time I found myself experiencing what I considered to be the nearest possible thing to Utopia, as I stood there looking at "One hell of a lovely woman", who I was so proud to say was mine.

As soon as the ceremony was over we returned home, where we'd already prepared a buffet, the front door was left wide open and the celebrations began. The first thing I did was go over to the Social club and down a quick couple of pints to celebrate, I didn't stay long, maybe a half hour at the most, but then I didn't need to, I had a house full of booze.

With my track record one would expect me to have been blotto by about three o'clock, but uncharacteristically of me I stayed sober all afternoon, in fact I was still sober at eleven o'clock that evening, as we checked in to the hotel reception in Ibiza.

Unlike today in the seventies it was frowned upon when unmarried people shared a room and because our passports were in different names the receptionist questioned our status, where I was forced to tell him the truth and the fact that we were actually just starting our honeymoon. It was really embarrassing, you've never seen such a fuss or palaver in your life, first they sat us down, then they brought us champagne, they even carried our bags to the room while we sat in the reception drinking. I wouldn't have minded, but all of this was going on whilst the rest of the guest were still patiently waiting to check in, all totally dumb struck, wondering who we were.

Eventually having finished our drinks we were escorted to our room, the head receptionist opened the door and led us in, proudly showing us the honeymoon suite. We couldn't believe it, I looked at Jean and she looked at me, as our host turned to leave us alone, "Compliments of the hotel, Mr and Mrs Davies". As soon as he'd shut the door we burst into laughter, "Shit Jean, what are we going to do now?", she looked at me in amazement, "There's not much we can do". There slap bang in the middle of the room was a double bed, the only problem was, we couldn't sleep in it as we were used to our single ones.

After being asleep for an hour Jean woke me up, "Paul, Paul it's no good, I can't sleep like this love, we'll have to do something".

We needed separating, but how, barring me moving onto the balcony it was going to be difficult, near impossible, then suddenly I had an idea, "Hang on a minute", walking over to a low, long coffee table I said "If I put this under my half of the bed, I'll be higher than you and as long as I don't roll over, we should be alright".

It worked, but I'd love to know what the chamber maid thought each morning when she came in to clean and found this little table under one half of the bed, she must have wondered what was going on because each time she pulled it out, I shoved it back in. Anyway there can't be many men who can lay claim to sleeping on a coffee table on their honeymoon.

Once we'd returned from our holiday, things returned back to normal, Jean at the University and me back at Kelloggs, however it wasn't long before I started getting itchy feet.

I was beginning to get fed up and bored at work, so I started toying with the idea of self employment, I had desires to go back into the paper game and as usual, I ended up doing just what I wanted.

The idea was that I would buy a cheap tatty van, do the cardboard part time and leave Kelloggs when I knew I was going to be busy enough. With the help of Bob and Dave, Jean's brothers I got a van, but within a couple of weeks we both realised that I had a better future working for myself, so in the March of '79 I left.

I set off with that much enthusiasm, vigour and effort, there was no way I could fail and within a couple of months the money was rolling in. There I was in my first van, like the king of the road, collecting every ounce of cardboard I could find and for all I cared my tatty pride and joy could have been a Rolls Royce.

I couldn't have been faulted by anyone on enthusiasm and it was because of my success that Joyce and Dad asked me if I would like to take over their paper collecting round.

Eddie had been doing it for the past year or so whilst reaping the rewards in at the same time, but predictably he was now getting fed up, so as a second thought and a kind of saviour, I was asked.

With the promise of good earnings, we struck a deal, I would buy Dad's big box van accompanied with as he put it, "the goodwill of the business" and then pay him off by letting him keep the income I'd earned doing deliveries for Marks and Spencer.

At the time because of Dads heart trouble and ensuing illness, I thought no more of it, he couldn't work which meant that Joyce, like a mule was carrying the heavy burden. Working at Marks's, looking after the market stall and taking care of Dad at the same time, would be a tall order for anyone, so I thought that six hundred pounds was a fair deal.

My very first trip out was a total disaster, but it could have been far worse. My keenness to succeed straight from the offset caused me to have a near catastrophic accident, as I'd overloaded the van.

It was packed to the roof with heavy bales and due to my inexperience I unknowingly ended up with my nearside wheels in the camber of the road. The consequences were frightening, one minute I was bombing along, as happy as Larry, the next I was in a Police station giving a statement.

Due to the weight of the load, the van was tilting to one side and as I passed a bus shelter, I took half of it with me. There were quite a few children stood inside it and to this day it's a mystery to me, how nobody got hurt, but at that time they weren't my first consideration, you see I'd been drinking.

How I got away with it I'll never know, but there again at that time I didn't know what was coming, perhaps if I had, I would never have driven again.

Knowing full well that I'd collected the van that afternoon, Jean waited in anticipation for my arrival home, but when I eventually got in she was disgusted, "That's terrible, your own Mother and Father will charge you six hundred pounds for a van with a hole in it!". Without knowing about the accident she thought my sudden ownership of their work, the damage to the van and Eddie's sudden disappearance were all tied together, I even kept the Police charges a secret from her, so for years she innocently blamed everyone else for my own stupid and senseless down fall.

That accident prompted me to make a huge promise to myself with regards to drink driving and it was simple . . . "I'll never drink more than two pints if I'm on the road". Once again I'd escaped by the skin of my teeth, so it was a case of knuckling down straight away, because I was to busy to wallow in shit.

Sadly I forgot that episode rather too quickly and it wasn't long before my "weighing in" times at the mill revolved around their dinner times, when all the lads from Jeffries could be found in the pub. As you know my relationship with Jean brought me lots of contentment and with it my bouts of heavy drinking subsided, but unfortunately the freedom of being on the road with nobody ordering me about, gave me plenty of time and opportunity to further my drinking career, whilst at the same time abuse the love, trust and loyalty of the one person I was fond of.

I couldn't see that I was doing anything wrong, after all I worked hard enough, so in my mind I was entitled to a little pleasure, but unaware that I was sick and suffering from a very sad illness, I knew no better, so I carried on.

In a matter of months I'd gone from drinking only a couple of pints during the day to no less than four or five, having said that I wouldn't need any more until I was safely home, having finished work. Once I did get home, the usual routine would be tea and then a doze on the couch while Jean watched telly, which was always acceptable especially after I'd worked hard all day.

However in the September of that year we discovered the real reason for my constant need to lie down and sleep. Following the appearance of an eye infection and subsequently a visit to the hospital, we were told that I had an illness called "Ankylosing spondilitis", my back ache was a direct result of the disease and so I was prescribed a mixture of pain killers and anti inflammatory drugs.

Inadvertently those Doctors only succeeded in giving me one hell of an excuse to drink, as I increased my intake of booze to ease the pain. In my own opinion it was the best cure and better than any tablet they could give me, so I used it as a bloody good excuse.

There was more good news as well, Dad told me that I'd finished paying him for the business and that in future I would be invoicing Marks and Spencer myself.

I couldn't have wished for more, there I was with a licence to drink more and now I also had the money to pay for it.

By now, subconsciously I was beginning to pull in a different direction to Jean as all my deep thoughts and ideas revolved around alcohol. Whilst she was still solely interested in us, the home and the two dogs we had, without knowing, I was becoming more tied to the bottle and as each day passed I was becoming a much sicker and sadder Paul.

It seemed to be a sort of cycle where I had both good and bad patches, but sadly 1980 brought the very last good one as my ties to the bottle grew stronger.

My only real recollections of that year revolve around an Adriatic holiday we took in Italy at a place called Cattolica.

At that time although I was drinking heavily it didn't actually show in my behaviour, I didn't take much interest in other women as I was still wrapped up in Jean, so on the surface, things didn't appear too bad, we still both took great interest in football, especially City so not all was lost . . . yet.

Just by chance the Italians were hosting the European Championships which is probably one of the reasons why I even remember the break at all. I'd never been to Italy before so it was really something to look forward to and actually going to see any of the football matches was an idea we hadn't even thought of, so to find ourselves in Turin watching the final was a surprise in itself. That experience alone was probably the highlight of the holiday for both of us, especially hearing the last post being bugled at midnight outside the barracks.

The trip home through the night arriving in the early hours of the morning as the sun rose over the Adriatic sea was another spectacular sight and so to was St. Marks square in Venice, which we saw on a totally separate trip, but none of these sights were finer than San Marino.

Although I said earlier that my interest in other women was minimal, there was one lady who I couldn't fail to notice and that was the rep who gave us our guided tour of the tiny republic.

As soon as we got off the coach on our arrival, I'd seen all I needed to, because all I had to do for the rest of that day in order to keep happy was follow her around.

The lady in question was English, in her late thirties or early forties, attractive, well spoken and gave off the impression that she was some sort of school teacher type, she wore a light blouse with no bra underneath and a Summer wrap around skirt. I was happy enough with what I'd already seen, but when she stopped for that first sight and turned around to face us all and explain it to us, I just flipped. I don't know what any of the other men were thinking, but I was in another town . . . country . . . planet even.

It was a breezy day and with the first gust of wind we were treated to a far better sight than anything San Marino could offer. Like on most tours everybody followed her up hill and down dale, it was a typical comedy sketch, "Now here's the castle and on your left you can see the town itself, over there is the Palace and over here . . ". The woman went on like guides do, with everyone following her every word, or at least purporting to and typical of a guided tour there's always the doughnut at the front with the camera, guide book, pad and pen . .

"Not this time!", I was there and like the dirty little sod I was, I watched intently but I wasn't looking at her lips as she explained the sights, I was more interested in her breasts, nipples, thighs and . . . well I don't think I need to say any more.

Despite my keen interest in the woman, that was as far as it went because at that stage in my life I wasn't easily tempted by such delights and to prove the point there was another example on the same holiday.

The two women concerned were staying in our hotel, one was about Jean's age, in her late thirties and the other woman was my age, twenty three. Throughout the best part of the holiday their main topic of discussion was fellas and the desperate need for both of them to get one.

As far as I knew, for all their concerted effort they were unsuccessful and from all accounts they really did try with every married man in the hotel, including myself, but for once and in a sober state I consciously refused their advances despite many an opportunity and the full knowledge of what was on offer.

At one point whilst Jean was alone on the beach they offered me the chance to go to bed with both of them, at the same time!, but due to my "Still in tact values", I declined to take them up on their offer, even though it would have proved very enlightening and I'm sure, educational.

Chapter 7

Rock Bottom!

We returned home from Italy, both with me morally in tact and the two of us in love, but sadly that was the last time I was able to boast the fact, for the next three years of my life were to take me into the deepest, murkiest depths of a disease called "Alcoholism" To write in detail about every affair or as I prefer to call it, "sordid relationship" would be impossible for I could produce a second book alone on that subject, so I think it's best that I deal with only maybe three or four of my acquantancies in the last part of this chapter.

By now I was drinking in a manner the likes I'd never done before, my days started continued and ended with it as my dependency on booze grew. I couldn't even sleep during the night without the taste of liquor passing my lips, as more often than not I needed to creep downstairs, like a grave robber to get to my secret supply which was hidden beneath the soil in the back garden.

At that same time I was just starting out on a new apprenticeship, that of a magician!, because with my increased appetite for the stuff came the added problem of feeding the habit and that needed funding.

My earnings alone couldn't cope with the demand, so I had to find new ways of obtaining the necessary funds. Typical of a drunk, I immediately turned to immoral, illegal and deceitful methods of earning money, which unfortunately all revolved around breaking the law.

In desperation I turned to crime, an abundance of which ranged from theft to fraud and in the blink of an eye, I suddenly found myself on a "merry go round of hell".

It was a vicious circle, I couldn't keep away from pubs, whether it be day or night and obviously the more I was in them, the less work I was doing and so it wasn't long before I started missing on the repayments of the van and other responsibilities, such as loans etc.

I couldn't keep friendships either and it wasn't because of my personality. Although constantly and totally steamed out of my brains I could still amuse any gathering crowd or people in my company. The problem was that anyone who was unfortunate enough to get the slightest bit involved with me ended up "steamboat" and usually found themselves in some sort of embarrassing state as well.

Consequently it wasn't that long before I entered into another stage of my illness and that was "the loneliness of the long distance drinker", where I would either stand alone at a bar or hide away in some dark corner.

I honestly don't know how I managed to keep the business running at all, but I did, I had to in order to maintain my lifestyle, whilst at the same time feed my habit and it was only as a result of my strong constitution that I maintained an element of freedom and more importantly contact with women, which proved to be a very significant factor at the time.

Understandably by now Jean was beginning to feel affected by my drinking, with the ever present dirty, foul smell of second hand beer, a real "turn off", so the next victim and casualty to booze, was our relationship. The situation surrounding our already abnormal sleeping arrangements and our nearly none existent sex life got worse, making the act of intercourse a very rare, empty and unfulfilling experience.

Our social life had always revolved around the City Social club, with it's handiness of being over the road, it was both sensible and economical to stick to it, so most of our "friends?" came from there, but Jean did have the one or two old bonds and ties and it was with a couple of them that we experienced our first "shared" holiday.

They were a nice couple, Dave worked on the stock exchange, was a bit staid in his ways and a fair bit older then me, while Helen was a very down to earth type, with a wild streak to her and just that little bit younger.

From the very first time I met them both we got on, especially as they were staunch City fans and it was because of our immediate and natural compatibility that we agreed to a "joint holiday".

On the 11 June 1981 we set off for Almeria, "the frying pan of Europe" down in the South East corner of Spain, none of us had been there before, so we were all excited and determined to have a good holiday. We lined up at the airport waiting to check in and whilst the other three talked amongst themselves, I weighed up the "cracker" in the queue, looking for possible, potential leg overs.

Disappointingly, there was only one decent looking piece in the whole line out, she had a good pair of "knockers", thick blonde hair and no husband with her, there was one slight draw back, she had a kid of about nine or ten years old, but still there were possibilities!.

Having checked out the whole flight compliment I set about my favourite pastime and with the passing of a few hours we were there, "The Zorraida Park Hotel". We arrived in the early evening and it was whilst we stood waiting to go into the dinning room for the first time that I somehow knew that it was going to be one hell of a holiday.

With a sudden nudge of my shoulder, Helen turned to me, "Eh, have you seen that German girl over there, weighing you up?, you don't know her do you?", in response I turned to have a look and couldn't believe my luck. I didn't actually know the girl, but you would have been forgiven for thinking I did, for right in front of Jean, Helen and Dave she made no secret of her intentions, despite having her own bloke stood next to her. For the next couple of days that girl couldn't keep her eyes off me, it got that bad Helen kept swearing to go over and have a word with her, "Dirty Crout!, I'll go and tell her in a minute Jean", I would then chip in and say something like "Oh leave her, she's doing no harm", little did they know I really wanted to have a dabble.

On the third day things got even better, because by sheer chance we met the blonde piece I'd clocked at the airport, she was sun-bathing near the pool, however she did have her husband with her, but they didn't seem to happy together. It was then that Dave came out of his shell and not for the only time on that holiday surprised me by secretly whispering "Bloody ell Paul she's alright!, I noticed her at the airport", I couldn't believe my ears, old fashioned, Victorian Dave fancying a bit of skirt, "Mind you, lay there topless as she was, even a Priest or Monk couldn't have failed to notice her!".

That was the last time I saw Jenifer because the day after Jean took ill and was confined to bed, she'd suddenly been struck down by a bad throat infection which meant that I found myself on my own in the company of Dave and Helen.

My initial reaction was a desire to return home as I couldn't see her getting any better otherwise, but not wanting to spoil anyones holiday, she persevered, which left me a "free – single agent", well it should have done . . . Cue, my German friend!

Being such a caring person as I was, my only thoughts revolved around looking after my poor, loving wife . . . "Not on your nelly!".

My first instinctive reaction was to go downstairs, get "canned" and look for my mystery Fraulein, so that we could arrange a secret rendezvous . . . "Ha!, what a joke!".

It was an exercise that turned out to be both near impossible and comical, everywhere I went guess who was with me?, yes correct, Dave!. If Helen was up in the room with Jean, he'd be there keeping me company, that bloke never let me out of his sights, not once while she was ill!

They were even supposed to be going on a trip to Granada, something which Helen had been looking forward to for weeks and right up to the very morning I was asked, "Are you sure you'll be alright on your own?", I don't think I need to tell you what my answer was.

There I was convinced that they'd gone and just about to make my way to the very quiet T.V room, where I'd prearranged to meet Olga, when I heard those dreaded, deep, boring tones, "Paul mate, how's Jean?", I just didn't know what to say, he stood there in his khaki coloured shorts with a lumber jack type shirt on and his thick rimmed black glasses crossing over the bridge of his nose, but as much as I liked the fella, I wanted to punch his eyes in there and then.

I wanted to tell him what an over weight, ugly looking idiot he was, but I couldn't even do that, so I went over to the bar, ordered some drinks and frustratingly sat in a corner, with one eye on the pool and the other on the T.V room.

A few minutes later the prick turned round to me and said "Eh Paul, there's that German bird, she's a bit of alright her!". I could have fucking killed him and probably would have, if I'd had the means at my disposal, because I knew that was my last chance to get to grips with Olga.

Once Jean had recovered, things got much better and they left us a bit more to do our own thing, but I never got over missing that golden opportunity, as it was truly "a chance of a lifetime".

After that, the nearest I came to being immoral was a bit of arse groping and flirting with the blonde and that was only when I helped find her daughter who was missing, but by then even a handful of sexy arse was better than nothing at all, especially when I got a positive response and definitely when I could follow up the situation when I got home.

The rest of that holiday passed quickly and I'm ashamed to admit it, but without any more problems especially misbehaviour on my part, so a majority of the talk on the journey home revolved around the next forthcoming holiday, some twelve months hence.

Due to my contracts with Marks and Spencer I always dived straight into my work, usually as soon as I'd got in and that holiday was no exception.

Eddie had covered the job for me whilst I was away and kindly got me doing some "free" charity work for one of the managers at Marks's immediately upon my return, so without even having time for a cup of tea, off I went.

I never liked charities, charity work or the people that took part in them, so I was pissed off to start with, I'd not had the best of holidays with Jean being ill and even worse, I didn't get a leg over, which meant that I was in the wrong frame of mind from the beginning.

It was a long way, the journey took ages, the place wasn't on the map and I wasn't even getting paid, but somehow I knew that my luck just had to change, after all "It was for charity!".

Due to the van being low on petrol I needed to fill up, I was lost and desperately needed a cold drink, so I pulled into the nearest garage.

That was the smartest move I'd made in ages, for there stood behind the counter was this stunning looking woman, who despite her uniform, reeked of sheer class. Whilst serving me she passed a comment on my nice sun tan, which in turn led to her questioning me further about my holiday, because I was running late my reply was both brief and sketchy, but as I left her, I parted with these words, "I'll tell you one thing luv, during the whole two weeks I didn't see one woman that could touch you and I'll be honest, right now I could just do with you!".

That job went from bad to worse, in fact the woman in the garage was the only thing that had gone right, so two hours later, full of anger and gasping for a pint, I made my way back home.

By this time I was "gunning" for our kid, because I was convinced he'd arranged it all in his sick sense of humour on purpose, but that aggression soon vanished and a smile appeared on my face as I once again passed that ill fated garage . .

"Ah bollocks to it, what the hell!".

I pulled into the forecourt, raced straight into the shop to be met with a really soft, warm smile "Hi!", she didn't get chance to say anything else because I butted in "Listen, what are the possibilities of you meeting me for a drink this week?", without giving her the opportunity to answer in fear of her saying no, I said "Wednesday or maybe Thursday, what's the best for you?", once again she smiled,

"Oh Thursday then", making it look as if I was in a rush, I headed for the door, "I'll see you in that pub over there, what's it called?, the Bamford?". By now her smile had turned to a full bout of laughter, as I asked her what time was suitable,

"Oh one o'clock, I don't even know your name!",

"Paul, what's yours?",

"Julie",

"Okay Julie, I'll see you Thursday at one!".

I drove off and left that garage "on cloud nine", "Thank you God, thank you!", knowing that whatever else happened, Thursday couldn't possibly come around fast enough.

At a quarter to one I sat there wondering whether or not she was going to turn up and at a quarter past, I was disillusioned, believing that my original suspicions were correct, then all of a sudden she strolled through the main doors of the hotel/pub in one hell of a nonchalant fashion and I knew there and then, that the girl had definitely done this sort of thing before. I will never forget the sight of her sexy thighs and hips as they sort of swayed from side to side, for she was the kind of woman who made very male turn his head when she entered a room.

That relationship only lasted about six weeks, but in that time I had the pleasure of experiencing some wonderful delights, mainly of a sexual nature and the one memory I will always cherish was the very first time I touched her intimately.

Over the years I'd made love with literally hundreds of women, but none had the class of Julie, and it was after an afternoon's drinking that I first realised what sort of a woman I was really dealing with. We sat in her posh sports car in a country lane and started kissing, I'd already been seduced by the fragrance of her expensive and erotic perfume, so I didn't need a great deal of encouragement. Initially I undid her blouse, intent on caressing her breasts, which were beautiful, but what made her different from the rest of the women I'd been with, was her bra, it could have been made of satin or silk it was so fine. After minutes of kissing, petting and fondling she took a hold of my hand, placing it between her knees, I knew full well what she wanted and there was no way I was going to disappoint her, so I slowly slid my hand up her legs and skirt towards her thighs, where I suddenly found myself touching bare flesh. For the first time as a man and old enough to appreciate it, I had a woman who was wearing stockings and once again I was to experience the pleasure of touching soft, silky, sensual lingerie, the more she moaned the more I wanted to tease her, then suddenly she made her move for me. I'd never experienced anything like it in my life and from that moment, I was addicted to her, for she was the other end of a spectrum, the stark contrast and total opposite to Sara.

I enjoyed every minute of that friendship, the laughter, the excitement, the drinking, oh and of course the sex, but the one thing I will always remember about Julie was a statement she made one afternoon whilst parked up at Marks and Spencer in Macclesfield, as she made me feel very proud and special.

Very profoundly she said "Paul darling, would you still like me if I came around that corner in a battered old mini instead of this?".

The answer to Julie then was yes and still to this day, many years later, nothing has changed.

Once Julie had given me the old "Heave Ho" the temporary reduction in my intake of alcohol, if I can call it that, had ceased and I found myself returning to my normal levels of consumption.

Back were a whole host of negative feelings, such as disillusionment, fear, un-wantedness and despair to name but a few, all rekindled as a bi- product of her rejection of me, so after a brief period of release I was back on "the road to hell".

Somehow despite my pile of secret debts, I still managed to buy a brand new van, foolishly thinking that the extra responsibility would help "stop the rot", but it was a very naive and desperate attempt, which in the end proved as futile as all the others.

If I wanted any identification to help me see where some of my problems lay, then looking back, there was a golden opportunity which cropped up in the August of 1981.

Nanna Williams was eighty years old and so Joyce had secretly prepared a party. For any other family that wouldn't have been such a big deal, but not in our case. As I said in my earlier reflections the whole history of the Williams's and Davies's is steeped in sad innuendo and getting everyone together under the same roof, at the same time was an impossibility, but never the less, still undeterred Joyce, God bless her, tried.

It wasn't a full turn out, but in hindsight that was a blessing, for there was enough trouble with those that were present.

Each member who intended going, swore an oath that just for once they would keep their "usual" big mouths shut and it worked, but rather disappointingly for Joyce and Dad it was our kid who spoilt the celebrations.

I don't know how it came about, but I ended up in the kitchen as barman and straight from the start I was giving out measures, the likes of which only I normally drank.

The party started at a half past seven and was in full swing by eight o'clock. Jean and her Dad were there and at that moment, I think she was quite proud of me in a way, so all was looking good.

At about nine o'clock things changed, when Eddie and Linda's husband, Eric returned absolutely "ten sheets to the wind", there had been some sort of a fight at the pub so they'd already experienced trouble. At that time I wasn't involved because I'd been far to busy running the bar, whilst secretly drinking half of it, but just the sight of Eddie goaded Jean, so expecting trouble her and Harry, her Dad, made a rapid exit.

That was when I, in my totally annihilated state, unconsciously got dragged into the whole mess, but due to the fact I had personally polished off nearly a full bottle of Pernod, I can't remember very much at all, as I was going through what was to become a regular feature in my life, "a blackout".

Apparently I and a few of the others had joined in by going off and getting involved in a bit of a brawl, we'd come back to get on with the party, when there was a sudden knock on the front door. One of the newer neighbours, who obviously didn't know us all, had come over to ask if we could turn the noise down a bit. That action resulted in him returning home with an earful of abuse from someone and obviously thinking it was a total waste of time.

A few minutes later Eddie, who by now was really well out of it, heard about this invasion of our privacy and decided to take matters into his own hands. Within a few minutes he had stormed over to the house on the other side of the road, kicked the door in and set about attacking the occupant, who by now was obviously both terrified and bewildered.

Apparently it was like some sort of scene from an American cop series, but unfortunately for Eddie he'd made one very big mistake . . .

"It was the wrong house!". His actions brought complaints and the involvement of the Police, which eventually drew the curtain down on the whole episode, bringing it to a sad end, with the finale resembling something from the "Key stone cops".

Four Police vans, one dog handler, a couple of cars and us lot rolling around fighting on the garden, whilst Nanna and Grandad sat there,

"Oh Joyce thanks love, it's a lovely surprise!".

I can't remember getting home, although I do recall the morning after and Jeans face of disgust as she read out the riot act,

"You're pathetic, you should be ashamed of yourself!".

I was in no mood for that, especially considering my suffering state, so displaying the scars of battle, a really bad shiner and a cut head where a brick had hit me, I proudly marched straight over to the club, to hold court and "proudly" tell my funny? story. . . how sad?!!

Although by this time I was in a desperate state, like most alcoholics, I had a pretty strong constitution, which very often prompted me to still try and defy all normal logic. In doing so I continued to take part in sport, especially football, I'd played in the amateur leagues for years, gaining both respect and admiration from players and refs alike, but my persona had now changed so much, that I had the new reputation of being a mad psychotic animal, a bad bastard !, which courtesy of Harry, Jean's Dad, led to my then famous nickname, "Bad Bascombe".

To round off my defiance of others I even completed the first Piccadilly marathon and several others after, all pissed!!

The year of 1982 was a total blur, with my only recollections revolving around a holiday to Matalascanas, although they too are indeed vague, so my story leap-frogs into the following year and what I now consider was the final part of my descent into a most enormous dark pit of despair.

I'd now found myself in a hopeless situation, as all my past resources were dropping off one by one, there was no money in the Access or Barclay card accounts, so they were cut up, I'd run out of people to borrow off, so that avenue was closed, I found myself in real trouble at the bank, as the overdraft was by now enormous and even Dad had given up on me, so I couldn't lend money off him.

Even the thieving of goods from factories had stopped because I hadn't paid off my partners in crime and I was no longer able to obtain phenomenal numbers of free tickets from Maine Road to spiv off, so basically I was "knee deep in shit". My addiction was now getting worse by the minute, not the day, but my major problem was "How could I feed this animal?", with the eventual answer coming in the shape of all things . . "food".

It was part of my verbal contract with Marks's that I destroyed all the remains of their fresh food, once their staff had been given the opportunity to buy it, so I immediately started using it to pay for my beer.

It was the beginning of a new relationship that lasted the final course of my drinking career, giving me yet another place to hide away and the very last chance to once again enjoy being "Mr nice guy" and "Mr big".

The Sandpiper in Didsbury/Northernden was to become both my saviour and safe haven, as Max the manager was more than happy with the food and I was in heaven, "Drinking as much as I possibly could".

In those last twelve or fifteen months, I ate, slept and drank in The Sandpiper as I gradually lost interest in everything and everyone around me. Some people even assumed that I was staff, due to the time I spent in the place, but sadly even though I do have lots of good memories, it does remind me of probably my worst action while under the influence of booze.

For years I had fancied a certain manageress at Marks and Spencer, constantly asking her for a date, but for years she'd refused, then all of a sudden, to my surprise, she agreed and subsequently turned up.

It was arranged that we'd meet for an afternoon drink at the Sandpiper and true to her word, she rolled up. With her arrival I was both pleased and disappointed because although I was initially happy to see her, I was unhappy to see that she'd brought her daughter with her, never the less we still had a good afternoon.

Margaret was a flirt by nature and in typical style she didn't disappoint me on this occasion, but unfortunately for her, I and my drinking friend took her suggestive remarks about threesomes seriously, so we all ended up at our other house which was, by now, up for sale.

With her daughter present we had to think of an excuse to pre occupy her, with "hide and seek" being the obvious choice, so off she went with Barry in pursuit. Margaret and I then found ourselves alone, in the bathroom upstairs, enjoying a brief "kiss and grope" session, but the daughter, who by now was proving to be an utter pain in the arse, seemed determined to spoil my fun, so with her re appearance we all went downstairs. Next it was my turn to chase the little horror so with a nod and a smile, I left Barry and Margaret alone in the kitchen, saying "Enjoy yourself!" before leaving to chase after her daughter.

That child was a little shit, for I just couldn't keep her apart from her Mother and the most frustrating part for me was that I could hear the other two mumbling in the kitchen.

Once more the daughter returned, yet again putting a dampner on the affair, so for the third and final time we went through the rigmarole of counting from one to ten.

By this time Barry and I were getting a little desperate, so as soon as the girl had disappeared I grabbed a hold of Margaret's hand whilst at the same time telling Barry to do likewise. With her pinned helpless against the wall I grabbed hold of her right breast, "So you fancy a threesome eh Margaret?", she just looked without saying a word,

"Go on Bas, give it to her, she wants it!", at that point, her pain in the arse daughter was coming down the stairs again, so I shouted out

"Where are you little girl?". I then left the other two in order to keep the daughter at bay, with the parting words "Make sure she enjoys it".

Viewing from the hallway I could see them struggling, but Margaret was strong and making a fight of it, I'd never realised until then what a good pair of legs she had, mind you it was the first time I'd seen so much of them. Then just for a moment it seemed as if things were getting a little too much out of control, so I ordered him to leave her alone.

With that she got up collected her daughter and took off at high speed in her car.

At first we both laughed, but shortly afterwards we realised the seriousness of the whole situation, so I went off in hot pursuit of her in the van, she was nearly home by the time I caught up with her, but it wasn't until I rolled up alongside her car at a set of traffic lights, that I truly realised what a cruel and heartless thing I'd done.

Poor Margaret, her face and expression of fear was a picture I'll never forget, for it was at that moment, I first realised where alcohol was actually taking me to.

Despite the awareness of that situation and the fact that for the first time in my life, it had occurred to me where I might end up, I carried on drinking, after all I didn't want to stop, so why should I?

Well a bloody good reason was because I couldn't keep a hold of any sort of relationship and a good swift hard lesson if ever there was one, was just about to occur.

I was called by one of the manageresses who I dealt with at a Travel agents, who asked me if I could do her a favour, "Yeah sure, what is it?". I was to pick up a three piece suite from her friend's house and deliver it to her own home in the same night, so with address in hand I made my way to Sale.

The area had a lot of old faggots living there and so me with my rather cynical, sceptical head on, projected that the job was definitely going to be a pain in the backside.

What a surprise I got, I rolled up, reversed the van up the path and jumped out in my usual fashion, expecting to be met by some "old girl", but this was no old girl, this was yet another tasty piece of stuff. Maria was in her thirties, had two daughters and best of all, no husband, but probably the biggest impact she made upon me that night was when she asked me if I would like a drink?,

"No thanks, I'm ok"

It was a cold Winter's night and I knew that the quicker I got the job finished, the sooner I'd be in the club, so my main objective originally, was to get away as quick as possible.

That was when she really put the "cat amongst the pigeons",

"Well would you like something stronger?, I've only got brandy", my mind was already made up and I certainly didn't need asking twice,

"Ooh yes, that'll be lovely!".

Never mind her looks, with questions like that, this girl had a friend for life, whether she wanted one or not, but she didn't stop there, for as if to pour fuel on the fire when it's already burning, she asked me for my number and suggested that she made dinner for me one day, so not for the first time in my life, I went off with plenty to look forward to in the near future.

A week later the phone went in the van as I was driving home and when I discovered it was her, I immediately felt over the moon, we had a brief conversation which resulted in us both making a date for the Wednesday afternoon, where she suggested I went straight around to her home so that she could prepare a chilli for me. Unfortunately because she was so attractive I knew that I would have no self control if I found myself alone with her, so very reluctantly I declined her offer, preferring to meet her at a pub.

That date wasn't only everything I'd hoped for, it was more, because sat in her car afterwards she quite openly and bluntly confronted me with a profound statement, "Look Paul, let's cut the bullshit, I want to go to bed with you and you want to sleep with me!". I couldn't believe how forward she was, "Yes, I think I'd agree with that", but that was it, we never made it.

Despite me pestering her for ages, the nearest I ever got to sex with her after that was when I forcibly parted her legs and fingered her, which at the time confused me even more, for on the one hand she was getting rid of me and on the other she was wet with excitement.

All of which at the time, left me totally baffled, wondering

"What the bloody ell is she playing at?".

Only a few weeks earlier the same woman was opening her arms, her home in fact her whole independence to me, as I was flavour of the month, then with a blink of the eye, I was out!

Once again I'd built something up with an initial meeting and my own personality, only to see it fall apart, but still I couldn't understand it all, leaving me with the same old question, "Why?".

It took me a long time to recover from Maria's rejection, only this time it was a much more painful process than on the last occasion, as I was now a very sick and lonely person, with my only comfort . . . "Alcohol".

The June of 1983 brought my last drinking holiday and with it the knowledge for me personally, that I wasn't really going anywhere with this life. I knew in my own heart that I couldn't carry on in the same fashion and that I was, "rapidly coming to the end of the line".

The holiday itself gave me the opportunity to escape the sad reality of my life, the chance to live a fantasy for a couple of weeks and the time to take stock of my whole situation, the mess I'd got in and finally a conclusion.

At the end of the fortnight, on the very last day, I took a long walk of at least three maybe four miles in order to give myself the space and time I needed to make up my mind and decide what I was going to do next, which not surprisingly ended up with me in tears.

Stood silently and totally alone on a golden beach I looked out to the ocean and the crashing surf like waves as they came thundering in, feeling very small, weak and vulnerable.

I then looked up to the sky and started to talk to myself,

"Please God, why has all this happened to me?, how on earth am I possibly going to get out of this horrendous nightmare?".

I don't know how I had the nerve to say such a thing, because I was a total disbeliever at that point of time in my life and the only time I ever said anything remotely like a prayer, was when I was on the cadge.

Not surprisingly I heard no voices, crashing thunder or saw any flashing lights, so I made my way back to the others, just as depressed, making one last plea to whoever, "Please God make that plane go down so that I can finally get out of this shit I'm in, then I may at least die a hero".

Well the bloody silver bird landed in one piece, with me on it, thinking "Well you couldn't even do that for me, you lousy bastard", and so I found myself a mere one hour away from another nightmare . . . the mail!

I had a secret arrangement with our postman, whereby any shitty, crappy looking mail, especially brown envelopes, were kept until he saw me alone but the problem with us being away so long, was that there could be anything from a bank statement to a bailiffs letter, lying behind the front door when we got home. Not for the first time, I was lucky, as there wasn't anything really bad for Jean to discover, which meant that once again, like a black cat I'd had a lucky escape, but of course I'd used up yet another life. However it was only a small respite because in my eyes, God had badly let me down and so I now had to put plan B into action, which comprised of a basic format . . "I would simply drink myself to death!!".

Most alcoholics despite their many weaknesses do have the constitution of an ox, they have to, in order for them to take so much self – inflicted punishment, it's just a shame that they don't actually realise it.

I say that because some five months later, I was still drinking myself silly, averaging no less than twenty pints a day with whisky on top, but I still kept going like a punch drunk boxer, who doesn't know when he's had enough.

In the December of '83 I was glad because whilst doing a shop clearance on the outskirts of Stockport, I bumped into a ghost from my very eventful past.

There stood looking as sexy as she did some ten years earlier was Sara and she didn't appear a year older in looks. It was like going back in time as we reminisced in the pub, about times gone by and what we'd done in between then and now. I still loved her in a daft sort of way and of course I wanted to make love with her but I was now a much older Paul and of course more experienced.

By the time we'd left the pub she was well out of her tree and I was ready to make my play, so I drove her to our previous home, which was still empty and up for sale.

As soon as we'd got through the door I grabbed a hold of her, dragging her through to the bare floor-boarded living room, "Right you, I've waited ten years for this!!". I gave her the biggest, roughest, hardest fucking, I guarantee she'd ever had and I enjoyed every single minute of it, then I took her off on my rounds with me, stuffing her another three times during the course of the afternoon. By the time it had got to five o' clock in the evening she was well and truly knackered and so just to round off the events, I bought another four bottles of lager for our very last session. At six o'clock that evening, we were parked up in a field and we'd just finished the last of the booze, when she suddenly started giving me her best spiel. It may have worked ten years earlier, but not now and so I responded to her tears and bullshit of "I still love yous", by telling her that she hadn't changed one little bit.

Just to prove a point, I grabbed a hold of one of the beer bottles, started pummelling her vagina with it and she still came!!.

Once I'd finished with her, I dumped her off and drove away as pleased as punch, that after all those years I'd finally got my own back . . . "At last!"

That questionable "victory" proved to be my very last because on the 15th January 1984, at a quarter past five in the evening I purchased a bottle of Bell's whisky and some Paracetomol tablets, knowing full well that I was now incapable of carrying on.

I could now no longer look Jean in the eye, especially as I was also causing her so much pain. I neither loved or cared about her, the dogs or myself for that matter and I could see no feasible way out, other than suicide.

Just by sheer coincidence, it was my birthday the next day, but I could only envisage sadness, not joy and the celebrations that one would normally expect. I knew only too well that like the hounds of a pack hunting the fox, it was only a brief matter of time, before all my creditors would be onto me, then like a flock of starving vultures, they would pick my bits off, down to the bare bone.

For the first time in years, I slept well, waking up early as usual, only on this occasion without the need of my early morning drink, so I lay there under the bed clothes, secretly listening to Jean's every move. By this time we were experiencing a total breakdown of communication, although I wasn't sleeping in the front bedroom just yet, so I waited until I'd heard her car engine start up and I was sure she'd gone. Once she was out of sight, I got up and started taking the tablets, whilst at the same time washing them down with the whisky.

As I took each pill, my mind fluttered about like a butterfly, recalling all different manner of times, people and faces and soon there were tears as I begged for God to relieve me of my pain and agony.

As the birds sang outside, I hated their every whistle and call for they were happy, whilst I was sad and alone, crying in my bed.

It wasn't long before I'd sunk into a coma, but despite the mixture of Paracetomol, whisky, time release pain killers and the anti inflammatorys, I'd taken, I was still alive at six o'clock that evening. That was the first time I gained consciousness and it happened as a result of my Dad calling around to see me. It was the first time I'd set eyes on him in over six months, a split, which yet again was caused by an argument over booze and my drinking habits. Sonia, Ted's daughter, from the paper mill had called him because she was worried by my recent behaviour, so he wanted to know what was wrong as after all, when all's said and done, he was my father and he did love me.

At that moment I cried, for it was the first time in my life, I'd ever heard him speak those words. Having told him the full story of my debts and worries, he assured me of his help and support and within the space of a couple of weeks, I was once again back on my feet armed with yet another guarantee, that I would never drink again.

It was a promise that I kept for over several weeks but towards the end of that last week I caved in, by calling into a totally unknown pub and getting plastered. My only recollections of the event are the barmaid's parting words to me as I left, "Do you know luv, you've had ten pints in less than three hours and you still seem sober". Those comments had no effect on me whatsoever until I'd got into the van and prepared to drive off, for it was then at that exact second that I, for the very first time in my whole life, actually needed and more importantly, desperately wanted to stop drinking!!

It seemed that at last, I was stood at the "crossroads of my life" and my own personal "turning point" . .

REFLECTIONS

I don't really know where to start, for it seems so much has happened to me and in such a short space of time, that even I am surprised and saddened by my "achievements", as it would appear that from the minute I left school, I set off on a sort of suicide mission in life, where by I was to spend nearly a decade of time running through life like a hurricane or tornado.

I've never been totally happy with my lot and in hindsight I didn't really stand any chance of being so either, for whenever I have managed to build anything decent, whether it be a relationship, based on trust, love and respect, or a home, even a job, I then pressed the self-destruct button, only to break up what ever it was into tiny bits, leaving even more casualties behind and sadly, others the task of either repairing the damage or picking up the tab.

I finished my last page of Reflections with the question "So what have I learnt?", well obviously not very much, for if I had I wouldn't have carried on in the manner I did.

I left my childhood to enter my teen years, thinking I'd left most of my pain behind me, but looking back I couldn't have been more further from the truth.

My first "true love", Sara, left me high, dry, skint and in pain, thinking I could never meet a sexier woman in my life, I was right!, for as yet I haven't, but the long term effect of that relationship was devastating, for my prime goal in life since, has been to make sure that I never get hurt like that again.

Sadly as a result, I in turn made dammed sure that I used, abused then dumped most of the people I came across, especially women, treating most of them as whores, slags and no better than a dirty old dish cloth, with the ideology that "once in tatters, then discard it".

My constant search for something, "whilst not knowing exactly what?" has been fruitless to say the least, but what else can I expect?, after all I still haven't got a clue, as I'm totally lost in life, yet even in my present pathetic state I'm still wondering is there something that I've missed out on?

How can I feel so upset at hurting so many who have loved me?, my Mother and Father, Jean, her family and many others, yet I still carry on causing them all pain with my drinking, behaviour and finally my debts.

Is there a solution to all of my problems?, is there any way out from the mess I now find myself in?, if so where and how?

It seems that I am destined to share this prison cell of constant, uneasy turmoil in my head, with no glimmer of hope, chance of escape or release to freedom, so where do I go from here? . . .

THE JOY OF SOBRIETY

Chapter Eight

The Turning Point

That sudden realisation prompted me to drive straight to my Doctors in Gorton, where without shame, guilt or a second thought I came out with the words, "I think I've got a drink problem Doctor Levy, I need help". What I really meant was, I know I have a drink problem and I think I'm an alcoholic, but at that exact moment it would have been a far too painful thing to say especially with its ramifications, so I left it there.

Having asked me a few questions he made an appointment for me at the local hospital, then wished me good luck as I left his surgery to make my way home.

Instead of going straight home though I called in at a local pub to celebrate the admission of my problems, which just goes to show the power booze had over me at the time, for having literally wept buckets as I drove from Stockport to the Doctors, then "come clean" as it was, I returned straight back to the very poison which was causing all the damage.

I never told Jean about my visit to Doctor Levys, but there again by this period we didn't talk much anyway, so it came as both a total shock and surprise to her when I eventually received a letter from the hospital giving me notice of my first appointment.

On the morning in question the postman had, as usual retained all of the bad/serious looking envelopes, meaning that I with a certain amount of confidence could let Jean set about opening what letters there were.

Imagine my reaction when she suddenly called out to me, "Paul, what's this?, it's from Withington hospital and it's for you", by the time I'd arrived in the living room from the kitchen she'd already read it.

I will never ever forget the sight of her stood there, dressed ready for work, trembling with one hand clasping hold of the note and the other touching her chin, as if in pensive thought.

Then with my appearance at the door, a tear or two rolled down her face as she looked towards me, "I can't believe you're doing something about your drinking at last, at long last, Oh God, thank God!!", with that I held her in my arms as we both broke down in tears. For a good five or six minutes we clung tight to each other as we tried to force words of comfort out, but the constant weeping, sobbing and tears of joy with our relief forced us to abandon all attempts.

Eventually once we'd calmed down I answered her every question, "But when did you decide to do something?, when did you go to the Doctors?, why didn't you tell me?", although her final question only succeeded in starting me off again, when she said "What's suddenly made you stop after all this time?". I was unable to reply, for at that moment I didn't know the true reason, so with a shrug of my shoulders and a raising of the arms I once again moved towards her for even more comfort, gesticulating "Why?, I don't know!". It was then, as we once again held each other, that she proclaimed her love for me, as we stood together looking out of the window, "Oh I do love you Paul, I'm so happy!".

For the first morning in probably twelve months, or even a couple of years, that girl was able to go to work feeling on top of the world, but it was only once she'd left the house that I took a second look at the note from the hospital to read it properly. I started off feeling quite good and pleased with myself, but that pride soon turned to shame and anger as I read on . . . only to discover that my appointment was with a Psychiatrist.

Furiously I stormed around the room muttering to myself, "Loony bin, psychiatrist, what do I want one of them for, there's nothing wrong with me!!". I screwed the paper up in one hand, throwing it into the paper bin as I did, then made my way out, off to work.

Once I was out in the van, alone on the road, I had the time to calm down and take stock of the whole situation and so with the added help of a few cans of lager I came to the conclusion that in view of Jean's apparent contentment, it would be best if I at least appeared to be doing something about my drinking, ie keeping my appointment, so I returned home to take the paper out of the bin and put it away upstairs.

It worked! . . . and so for the next nine days I carried on in the same sort of fashion as I had previously done, only this time it seemed with her blessing, believing that finally there was now a glimmer of light at the end of this long, dark tunnel.

Jean rather typically offered to come with me for the first appointment, but her offer was rejected by me in my own rather arrogant manner, "Na, yar alright luv, I got myself in this mess, I'll get myself out of it!", so on Friday 23rd March 1984, I set off for Withington Psychiatric Unit.

As I drove to the hospital my mind raced all over the place, projecting the worst scenarios possible, padded cells, strait jackets and electric shock treatment even though I knew, in my own mind that this was going to be a "lie on the couch" session, so by the time I'd got to the main doors I was already drained. My first real doubts about the whole exercise hit me as I sat parked up in the van outside, as per usual for me I was early, so I had time to think, which led me to the question, "What the fuck am I doing here?".

The truth of the matter was, that for the first time in my life I really knew that I wanted to stop drinking, despite the self doubts that it would be possible, therefore by turning up I could satisfy both Jean and myself that I was at least, trying. I looked at my watch, which said ten minutes to ten, then stared in the mirror at myself and those bloody sad eyes, "Well ere goes!, I've got nothing to lose " and with that I made my way in.

The only thing I knew about nut houses was what I'd seen on the film, "One flew over the cuckoo's nest", which basically meant that I had very little to go on with this new un-chartered territory I was about to enter, so unarmed for combat, feeling very naked and vulnerable I went in.

It took me all of about five seconds to realise that the depths and depravity of my problems lay within the walls of the building in which I was stood, it was dirty, smoky and had the air of sadness hanging around the place, but even as low as I was feeling, my initial response was "I don't belong here, I'm not that bad". It got worse, the lady at the reception who was protected by a screen, directed me to what was called the "day room", "Just wait in there please, you'll be called when it's your turn".

My own loneliness struck me as I waited in that awesomely depressing room, with the stale smell of yesterday's smoke lingering in the air.

A tatty looking table stood in the corner facing me, littered with dirty, chipped, un-washed cups, ash laden saucers full of cigarette dimps and a manky, steel tea pot. Used tea bags lay everywhere as if they'd been thoughtlessly dumped and the walls paid testimony to the fact that both children and dirty adults alike frequently used the place, as a result of hand, finger and footprints.

Then suddenly I was joined by two young girls with a baby who confirmed all of this by letting the child run wild, mauling everything in sight. Shortly after that, I met my first co patient of Withington Hospital's "Alcoholic Treatment Unit" (A.T.U), a scruffily dressed man, simply called Fred, who immediately made an impact on me with the first words he spoke, "Are ya alright cock, is it ya first time ere", sheepishly I replied "Yes", to which he wittingly replied, "Don't worry ya'll soon get used to it".

By the time it had got to ten o'clock, a few other odd looking types had joined him and it was then, that they all set about cleaning up the table and the surrounding mess. As each new "regular" arrived the more sickened, disillusioned and shamed I became, as I found myself surrounded by what I could only describe as a bunch of tramps, vagrants and layabouts, all of which left me thinking, "Well if this is what I've come to, then I'm really in the shit".

By this time I must have stood out like a sore thumb as I sat there, the only person in the room who even resembled a normal human being, consequently I was just beginning to feel uncomfortable, when my saviour, or so I thought!, appeared at the door, "Mr Davies?".

A tall looking, prominent type of character stood there, who's aura boasted an abundance of confidence and superiority, whose appearance at the door brought a natural instinctive silence to the whole room and an abrupt end to the on going conversation between the others.

As I left the day room to follow him, Fred called out, "Good luck cock!", with one of the others also butting in, "Yeah you'll need it".

I went with the Doctor into his office fully expecting to have to lie down on a posh leather couch or something similar . . . "Not on your life!", "Sit down Mr Davies, now I'm going to ask you a few questions, which I want you answering to, with either a yes, no or a figure, understood?", to which I obviously replied "Yes".

The man then set off with a quick fire, none stop, relentless barrage of questions, ranging from how old was I?, to how much did I drink?. I was doing well until he'd got to that million dollar one and it was then that I tried to return to "type", my normal bullshitting self, by answering, "Well erm, drinking er . . ".

Suddenly and abruptly he reminded me of his earlier statement, "Number of pints only, please!" and by the time we'd finished, which was a mere five minutes later, I hated his guts, he was an arrogant bastard and there was no way on this earth that I could see him or his stupid hospital getting me well, so I left with a massive chip on my shoulder and the knowledge that I had to go back for a course of alcohol education sessions.

Obviously Jean had spent all morning at work wondering and worrying as to how I'd got on, so having already pre-arranged to have our lunch together, we met, where I told her of my experiences that morning, the following course of events and the future treatment available.

That news in itself seemed to bring a smile to her face, the fact that there was help available and to all intent and purpose I was now taking the offer of it, so with that in mind I went to the sessions provided. Those groups consisted of all types of people, young, old, men, women, rich, poor and even the famous, all struggling as I was, with drink and their lives in general.

We were asked questions, given answers, provided with information and advice, but more importantly at the end of the five weeks given options, options on how to try and get well and it was whilst we were choosing those options that I made my own personal firm commitment to getting sober.

There were all sorts of courses on offer, various daily support group meetings, programmes which took place within the hospital, controlled drinking programmes where those taking part lived in for six weeks and even day courses, but the one I chose was a very strong non drinking group which took place twice a week. The meetings apparently had the reputation of being very aggressive, they consisted of people with quite long lengths of abstinence, so it was a straight talking session and one that most newcomers found "off putting", but of course it sounded just right for me.

I'd only attended two of the meetings when suddenly "the penny dropped" and I'd got the message and it was whilst I was on my way to that third meeting that I bought my last pint of lager.

I say that for as I write this now, by sheer coincidence and God's will, it's five minutes to seven in the evening of the 2nd May 1993, some nine years to the minute from my very last drink . .

I'm afraid that I had to stop writing for a while at this point, as my emotions were temporarily upside down, I cried as I tried to recollect every thought, feeling, phobia and memory from that very night.

As was the norm in those days, in typical cavalier style I stormed into the Mauldeth Arms on Kingsway and ordered two pints of lager, I always ordered two because by the time I'd drunk the first one, the bar maid would just be placing the second ready for consumption, but for some strange reason on this occasion I didn't start drinking until I had both in front of me.

Everything seemed normal, the juke box was playing in the back ground, there was the odd nice looking bird in and of course the "office type", quiche men who'd gone straight from work. However on this occasion something was missing, somehow different, as the normal smelly, smoky atmosphere of a pub that had always attracted me, started to have the opposite effect. I don't know why but I suddenly felt nervous, small and very vulnerable in a place where I'd always felt secure, safe and above all else "as large as life", I then became weak as my whole body started to tremble as if from lack of food or suffering the D.T 's, but what was most frightening at the time, was the fact that I knew full well that these experiences were nothing to do with either, as this was due to something more sinister. In fear I tried to lift the glass once more thinking that perhaps one more drink would cure me, but I couldn't even make that, instead I grabbed hold of the bar rail with both hands gripping tightly, as if I was holding on to it for my life. By now everyone in the pub must have been looking on in both amazement and curiosity, not that it mattered, for at this point I really didn't feel a part of their world, for I was somewhere else, lost in no man's land. Suddenly I felt an awful, eery presence of a grotesque, powerful nature and I was losing, in some sort of inner fight.

It seemed as if there was some form of violent turmoil and action actually taking place within me, a struggle between good and evil, then at that exact moment I could take no more pain, I started to sob whilst shaking and trembling at the same time, but soon that sobbing changed to weeping as my own personal fear grew. Something was definitely inside me, fighting like hell to get out, but I in my innocence didn't have a clue what was going on, I cried out in panic, pleading for help,

"Please God help me, please I'm begging you, I can't go on any longer like this, please give me my life back!", but it was no good, for there was nobody listening.

I was now just beginning to feel desperate and as all desperate men and women do when all hope is lost, I knelt down and begged for both mercy and forgiveness. "Please God if you do exist, I need you now, more than I ever have done before, forgive me for all the wrongs I've done in the past, have mercy on me, please, I'll do anything you ask".

It is almost impossible to try and convey on paper my next experience, for it was truly the most unreal occurrence of my whole life, but never the less something which to this day, I have always cherished, for as if by some miracle I felt the strongest presence, in the form of a good spirit enter my body and slowly cleanse my inside, as if it were too strong and powerful for the evil, which had previously lived there rent free for so long.

Once again the strong internal battle raged on, only this time the good seemed to be winning as it gradually pushed the evil presence to the outer walls of my body. By now I truly believed that I was about to physically explode, when all of a sudden everything calmed down. Seconds later every ounce of badness lifted from my soul as it was sucked up through my head in a swirling white light and with it my long ill fated desire to drink, but with that departure came the arrival of a new energy and a new power, which brought with it my second chance, a chance which I instinctively knew would be filled with eternal hope and promise for the future.

A future which I knew there and then would guarantee an abundance of new wonderful feelings and emotions that would revolve around caring, love and kindness.

As I said earlier, since that day nine years ago, not a drop of alcohol has passed my lips, but even more importantly I have not even had the desire or thought of a drink, as just for once I'd kept my side of the deal I'd made with God.

Having left the pub I made my way straight to the hospital group meeting, where I just sat there in silence as I had done on the two other previous visits, but once again this was to be no normal night, for my new found God had one other trick up his sleeve.

It came in the shape of a small, chubby, barrel shaped man called Colin, an arrogant self righteous person, whose guts I hated from the very minute I first set eyes on him.

Those support group meetings were a fascinating experience from the start and it was because they were so weird that I decided to take along a newspaper to read in them. They started at seven o'clock on the dot, but not one word was ever spoken for at least ten or fifteen minutes as everybody in the room just sat there in silence. Some would look up at the ceiling, others down at the floor, some would just stare through one of the many windows in the room, with the odd few like me, who didn't give a shit just looking at everyone else. It was absolutely pathetic, in fact I can remember thinking " Well if this is supposed to get me sober, then I'll show my arse in Piccadilly", so because of this morgue like atmosphere I decided to take the day's edition of the Daily Express word game with me and that's when we had our first words.

During the Summer months I always wore shorts, football shirts and fancy trainers, especially if it was hot and in the May of that year we had some beautiful weather, so fully dressed in my "posers attire", I ponsed into the meeting, sat down, minding my own business and proceeded to do the word game.

We didn't need to speak, for just the sight of him made me sick, so when he did, it was like showing a red rag to a bull, especially in the tone in which he came out with it, "I'll tell you what, you'll never get sober in these rooms, coming in dressed like Kevin Keegan, sitting there doing crosswords ".

As we'd already had ten minutes or so of deathly silence everybody in the room reacted in some way or other, a percentage of them sniggered or grinned whilst others looked totally gob smacked, the rest of them who I now know today, were the more sober and experienced, just sat there all awaiting my own reaction and response.

Well I didn't disappoint them because the one thing that they never anticipated was my aggressive and volatile, "couldn't give a shit" reply, when I turned to Colin in answer to his statement, "Listen you, ya fat cunt, you lose some weight and then perhaps you might be in a better position to come and tell me how to stop drinking, an yer know what, then I might just listen to ya!".

I thought I'd done well, especially as most of the room were in stitches laughing, but I'd got it wrong because in answer to my tantrum he smiled wryly and said "Well chum, I'll not die of being overweight, but you will from drinking".

From that moment on and for the next few weeks after, that bloke and I had a love, hate relationship that could have bettered anything produced by "Burton and Taylor" for he loved me from the start even though I despised him.

The idea of the groups were, that people would generally share their problems with each other, in an honest way, so that they could obtain other views and sometimes advice, with the main accent being on staying sober.

Unfortunately, because of the ferocity of some attacks, members were often reluctant to come forward for fear of an assault, by the rest of the group.

In my case, mainly because of my personality and basic instincts, instead of cowering in a corner, I came out fighting which in my own personal opinion, despite the ignorance and stupidity of what I said, did do me more good than harm for the future.

Having made that initial impact on the group, I then quite purposely sat back and slipped into the background for a good period of time, so that I could watch, listen and learn, without being harassed any further.

After a few weeks of regular meetings and effort being shown on my part, the atmosphere at home got slightly better with Jean showing just as much enthusiasm, after all, we now had exactly what we'd always wanted, so what more could we wish for?

In our own naivety and innocence, both Jean and I believed that all of our problems would just up and away, leaving us two to live happily ever after, but unfortunately we were wrong, for like most other folk little did we know just what getting sober really involved.

After four weeks of attending meetings I began to get the full picture of what all this was about and it was then that I started listening to the one man I initially hated, for sat amongst those twenty five or thirty people, he was the one who stood out like a rose amongst a bed of weeds. Both Colin and another bloke, called Roy had something really special, I didn't know at the time, exactly what it was, but I knew that I desired it.

Most of the time they would just sit there, full of confidence, smiling in response to other peoples moans and complaints about how life was doing them down, they had an air of certainty about them which oozed out, but above all else, I discovered that these two guys knew perfectly well what they were talking about, for rather embarrassingly for me, they had both been sober for a fair while.

After my debut performance the only thing Colin ever said to me was "Have you been to A.A yet?" and so after four weeks, I was just about getting a little pissed off with his repetitiveness, so at my usual "I'll show you best", I toddled off to my first Alcoholics Anonymous meeting.

I wanted no fuss being made, so I went off on my own to the Monday evening gathering held at the unit, I knew that there would be others present from the support group and various other hospital programmes, so there was little chance of me feeling strange.

I went with the sole intention of being able to say "Yes" the next time Colin asked me his favourite question, but there was no way I was going to enjoy it, as I wasn't like them, a tramp or a dosser, but as always in my life, if there was a point to be proved, then I was the man to prove it, so off I went.

Once again my pre-conceived notions and ideas were totally wrong, for as I entered the recreation room where the meeting took place, I got one hell of a surprise because gathered together was a wide spectrum of "normal" looking people, from all walks of life, there was the odd down and out character, but for the main part they were just as normal as myself. I didn't have much time to look around properly for I needed to get sat down somewhere and so my natural instinct took me to the furthest, tucked away, hidden corner, where I'd have less chance of being spotted.

The second shock came as the meeting started, when I suddenly recognized the voice of the chair person, I lifted my head up to check and there he was . . . "Colin!", seemingly pleased that I was there, for as our eyes met across the smoke filled room, he smiled with a warm and caring acknowledgment, as if to say "Nice to see you, welcome home!".

By the time that first meeting had finished I knew I was in the right place because I'd realised where Colin got "it" from and how he kept "it".

The "it" was a package of things called Sobriety, which is why I have so aptly named this last part of the book "The Joy Of Sobriety", for it was as a direct result of A.A's example in Colin and others like Roy, that I grasped the tools which enabled me to go forward for the rest of my life, able and willing to cope with I, self, ME!!

I soon realised that this was no picnic trip that I was embarking on, that it was in fact, a great whole new experience, an adventure and that for me personally there was going to be, no turning back.

With those ideas firmly set in my mind, I then proceeded in typical "addictive" Davies style, committed to one thing and one thing only . . . Sobriety!! and no matter what the cost, it was going to be worth it.

I then set off on a personal course which took me to near enough ninety meetings in ninety days, whilst at the same time, worked twice as hard as I had done in the previous three or four years put together.

For the first time in my life I was actually happy, I was paying off debts from my drinking, instead of boozing my earnings away, I'd started to make a new circle of friends in A.A and most important of all I wasn't drinking, "At last I was truly alive!".

Sadly I'd forgotten one very important thing and that was the one person who'd stood by me through the years of unhappiness, the evening and early morning retching, the wet beds, the sick and the verbal violence.

The one woman who had stayed with me through thick and thin, who'd forgiven me on so many previous occasions, yes Jean, the only woman who had ever really loved me.

With everybody else's interest and attention focused on me and the constant questions such as "How's Paul doing?", she was understandably feeling both bitter and slightly jealous. I wasn't improving matters either by spending so much time away from her, despite the fact that I was doing it for both of us, so consequently the atmosphere at home eventually returned to "the old drinking days" state.

For the first time in our relationship I ended up sleeping in a different bedroom, but we'd already spent years in separate beds, so in my mind it wasn't that devastating. However once again I was proved wrong, for it was in fact the first of many actions which eventually led to the total and final breakup of our marriage.

It was suggested after about six or seven weeks that Jean herself went to hospital for counselling and support, an idea which she first treated with contempt, but having thought about the proposal for a while she did change her mind.

That first appointment was a joint one which we shared together, which was both made and held by my regular staff nurse at the unit. It was supposed to be a very frank, open discussion, where we had the opportunity to talk honestly to each other about our true feelings, with regard to our marriage, but of course as usual I held back on the "honesty bit".

Joan the nurse, ended the proceedings by pointing out the most important questions, which really needed answering at that time, which were as follows, "Do you have a lot in common with each other? and if so, what?, Do you still like each other?" and finally "Do you still love each other and want to make a go of it?".

Then with those questions in mind we left, with a lot to think about and depending on the answers, a lot more work, in the form of "bridge building" to do.

It was a shame in a way, for there we were, two people who obviously cared a lot about each other, both trying to achieve the same goal, yet because of the circumstances surrounding our situation, in hindsight, it was never really on.

Although I was doing well as a person, I was very raw, I didn't know, understand or even care about other peoples feelings and emotions, for I was "fresh" and didn't even know my own.

I was as confused as I'd always been, yet this new Paul wasn't threatened by that fact, for I was just glad to be alive and "free" from the curse that had hounded me for so many years and just to prove the fact, for the first time in my life, I couldn't even cry.

After a couple of months without drink I found myself totally lost, in a world where I understood nothing, I had no emotions whatsoever and became confused by others who were lucky enough to have them.

I became unaffected by other people's tears or bouts of anger, their worries or apprehensions, even their joy and happiness, as everything in my world was either one or the other, either "black or white".

In my mind life was simple, "I was sober and that's all that mattered", as I seemed to adopt even more selfishness than I had in my drinking days, after all, I had enough to cope with just trying to learn to live again, so I carried on regardless, soaking myself in both A.A and hospital group meetings.

Chapter Nine

My Inspiration

However on the 12th July, God, once again had other plans and in his own wisdom decided to change the whole course of my life, a course which was to eventually fulfil every promise of A.A, with a guarantee that "things will happen beyond your wildest dreams" and they did. Although at the time, if any living sole would have told me, what was going to occur in the future course of my life, neither I nor anyone else would have believed them, as the rest of my story, although factual is an account of one of God's true miracles.

On the morning in question I'd been up as usual, very early, where the singing of the birds, the milkman delivering and the sunrise, were things which in the past had always haunted me, but not sober, now it was different, for more often than not, I would be up at the most ridiculous times with those very same past pains of my life. There were good reasons and motives for this action, as it was helping me to pay off some of my debts, you see although I was, at the time, being taught to "get honest", I found it difficult, near impossible to immediately let go of all my old traits, especially if they could still be used to my own purpose or advantage.

Dealing in stolen factory goods was one such flaw in my character and at the time I did have an on going arrangement which was proving to be a big help with my "honest" intentions.

The Kelloggs company where I used to work, had a relatively new printing factory in Irlam, so the idea was that in the early hours of the morning, depending on what shifts the lads were on, I would reverse the van into the plant, where they would then load me up with a full pallet of unused, unwrapped, white coated card. Each pallet was worth about six hundred pounds retail, but as they were stolen, I only received three hundred cash, giving the two lads sixty pounds each. I must have taken twenty or thirty at least over a period of time and to this day I still find it hard to believe we never got caught, never the less we didn't and so once again God must have been on my side, helping me to battle on. That morning after I'd once again successfully weighed in, I returned home for a cuppa and a read of the mail, which surprisingly enough wasn't to devastating, so after a few very brief words with Jean, or should I say, more of an acknowledgement, I set off once again this time heading in the direction of Tyldesley, on the other side of Manchester.

Despite having a good day up until this point, I wasn't looking forward to my next pick up, for it was at the Coop store in Tyldesley town centre, where the cardboard was always a mess, I never got a brew and the manager was a real twit, which all meant that I needed a good talk with myself, in typical A.A fashion. "Self lectures" were by now, a common occurrence in my life which usually took place whilst I was alone in the van, they were always necessary whenever patience and tolerance were going to be required and this was certainly going to be one such occasion.

There I was bombing along the East Lancs road with not a real care in the world, having a good chat with myself as I prepared for the ensuing encounter, when all of a sudden I found myself distracted . .

On a duel carriageway, doing no less than seventy miles an hour, with the radio on full blast and every single window open on the van, I needed to overtake a car, enabling me to get to the inside lane, so I indicated in order to let the other driver know of my intentions and proceeded to pass. Any van or lorry driver will tell you that it is a normal, sometimes instinctive reaction, to look over in these same circumstances, which is exactly what I did, but on this occasion I couldn't leave it at that for I immediately became transfixed, even sort of hypnotised by the sheer beauty and sexuality of the woman driving the car. The proud owner of a thick, black mass of hair and wearing the classiest pair of blue sun-glasses I'd ever seen, she looked absolutely fantastic and even though there was distance between us, I couldn't help notice her sexy "hot" lips that paid testimony to her outright beauty.

From the very split second I saw her, something once again incredible happened inside me, something not to dissimilar to my own spiritual awakening, which told me she was the most beautiful thing I'd ever seen in this new world, I now found myself in. I'd already learnt that I was a good manipulator and that it was wrong of me to use the "gift or ability" for one's own end when trying to stay sober, so reluctantly I felt that I had to leave it at that and carry on regardless.

With soley good intentions at the fore of my mind, I put my foot down on the old accelerator and reluctantly raced off to meet Mr Twit at the Coop and collect my crummy, dirty cardboard.

By this time, because I was abiding by the "rules of the game" when staying sober, the man suddenly returned to being a boy, as poor Paul, "couldn't have his rattle back". In a matter of seconds the cardboard was crap, the manager was a twat, not a twit and despite the lovely blazing sunshine, it was a pretty shitty day where it could have been pissing down for all I cared . . . For the first time in sobriety I couldn't have what I wanted and I didn't like it one bit, then as I approached the next set of traffic lights they changed and so did my luck. Normally I dived through lights whether they were on green, amber or red, "But not today mate!", I slammed my brakes on, screeched to a halt and in seconds, God was good, so was the cardboard, the day was once again beautiful and even the manager wasn't that bad either, for I was going to get a second chance to see that bloody "turn on" of a woman.

I sat there looking at the lights, checking the rear view mirror and watching the other traffic, "Come on, where are you?", can't she drive any faster?, then in a panic I lent over thinking she may have turned off somewhere, by now my heart was thumping and racing away, I was that keyed up you'd think I'd just made love with the woman, never mind just seen her for the first time. Then she suddenly appeared and rolled up a few cars behind, "Thank God, she's here!". In my own mind I had to have a second glimpse of her, at least, but I couldn't see her from where I was, so I dived out of the van and just stood there, leaving everyone behind me with the impression that I'd just broken down, but unfortunately the lights changed, which meant that I had to get back in and drive off.

Talk about split personality, Doctor Jeckyl and Mr Hyde weren't in it, for I immediately returned back to my "Mr Bad" mode as I realised that I wanted this woman, whether it be right or wrong.

The next set of lights were a couple of miles up the road, which prompted me to slow down, in the hope of catching her at the next junction, which was my last chance of making any headway, for it was there that I turned off for horrible Tyldesley. It was a road which in comparison was rarely used by most traffic and it was that fact alone, which made my mind up for me, it was simple, if fate were to deal me a vicious blow, then she would carry on down the Lancs to Liverpool, totally unaware of my interest and presence. However if on the other hand, God was really on my side and by some million to one chance she took the same route as I, then there was no way on this earth, that I was going to let the opportunity of a lifetime pass.

I approached those lights in the most untypical fashion possible for me, as I slowly and patiently rolled up, coming to a smooth, calm stop, I even put my handbrake on, which was totally out of character as I stared through the rear view mirror, in anticipation of her arrival, then as she slowly approached the same lights my heart beat increased, accompanied by a stronger pulse, as I became hot and flushed through excitement, thinking "Which way will she go?, what lane will she choose?". My questions and prayers were answered, for against all odds she pulled into the same lane, some two or three cars behind my van and at that moment I knew that I had to act in order to make something happen, so once again I jumped out of the van, only this time I signalled to her, in an effort to attract her attention.

My emotions were by now totally upside down and I was confused enough without God interfering once more, when he decided to change the traffic lights from red to green, so once again only this time accompanied by the tooting of horns and the odd "Come on, get out of the way!", I climbed into my "passion waggon" to turn off the main A580 road.

I knew in my own mind that there were neither chances or time to waste, I had to do something there and then, or live to regret no action on my part, for the rest of my life, so as soon as I'd cleared the lights, I stopped the van for the last time and got out with the sole intention of stopping that lady, even if I had to lie down in the road to do so.

As if some sort of traffic cop, I stood in the middle of the road with one arm raised instructing the lady concerned into the side of the kerb, which was when I really got nervous, for this was a "first" and totally unique experience for the "new me".

Slowly she lowered her driver's window, only a few inches, but it gave her enough space to feel safe and secure and me enough to take in her beauty, whilst I muscled up the courage to come out with my well meaning but nervous words. Those few seconds as she lowered her window seemed like minutes, as I stood there thinking to myself "God I can't even do this now!". The realisation that I couldn't even do what I used to be best at, "chatting up a bit of skirt" left me feeling very vulnerable, especially as this was "one hell of a lady".

Despite looking very feminine, classy and sexy, she had a hard tone about her features which not only enhanced her looks, but also made me aware that she was independent and quite capable of looking after herself, leaving me very worried as to how she was going to react.

Realising all this, only served to make me even more nervous and by this time the leg muscles at the back of my calfs and thighs were twitching.

I stood there very sheepishly and "schoolboy" like, ". . . Excuse me, I hope you don't mind me stopping you like this, but I thought you looked absolutely gorgeous as I passed you on the Lancs", she looked suspicious by my rather odd advance, so I tried to reassure her that everything was okay, "There's no need to worry, it's just that I thought and hoped that you might like to come for a drink?".

At that moment it was as if she purposely leant on the door catch to gain comfort and reassurance from the knowledge that it was locked, but at that point I myself became upset for she looked so worried, when answering my request "Pardon?, Oh no I don't think so, I'm busy, but thanks all the same".

I was so disappointed, but I had no intention whatsoever of giving up the ghost that easy, so in begging fashion I once again pleaded with her, "Well what about tomorrow then?", with a shake of her head she once again implied "No" and by now I was both desperate and even more keen for her company.

"Look I don't go out into pubs and clubs or anything like that, but if I did and I saw you in one, I would certainly ask you then".

Once again she politely refused my pleas by telling me that she was actually in a rush, "Look I'd better be going, but thanks all the same", she was just about to start winding her window up when I gave it my last and best shot,

"Look just jot your phone number down and I'll give you a ring in a few days time".

Then for the first time she smiled and I could see there was a glimmer of a chance, a breakthrough perhaps?,

"Oh alright then, here you are", she then started to scribble her number down on a scrap of paper, whilst I furthered my interrogation,

"What's your name, I don't even know your name?",

"Jeannette",

"Hi, I'm Paul", by now I was over the moon, on what I call a roll, I wasn't "full of it " or anything like my old self, but I did eventually ask her, "Are you married?". I don't know why I asked such a stupid, ridiculous question, as it wouldn't have made one ounce of difference, but I did, perhaps it was nerves or something, anyway the answer was "No", so with her number securely grasped in my hand I skipped off, absolutely "full of the joys of spring", well and truly prepared to meet Mr Twit.

No other encounter had ever affected me in the same way, having said that it couldn't have done, for this was the first time I'd ever had such strong, instantaneous feelings while being sober. It was a wonderful experience which left me overjoyed as I was full of happiness and looking forward to sharing that wonderful ladies company, totally believing in "love at first sight".

After that there was no chance of me being able to concentrate on anything else that day, other than Jeannette, I'd already made my mind up that I wasn't going to be affected by anyone, as all I wanted to do from the moment I'd left her, was ring her up at home, as soon as possible.

I had to wait until the day after for that pleasure, but when I eventually did, once again it was "unknown territory", for even though I'd done that sort of thing as a drunk, I'd never done it sober.

I stood at the phone for ten minutes, looking at it trying to pluck up the courage, whilst at the same time work out exactly what I was going to say and so after much rehearsal, I picked it up.

The sweat dripped off me, as the adrenalin pumped throughout my body, then a cold shiver swept down me from head to toe as someone at the other end of the line lifted the receiver, "Hello, could I possibly speak to Jeannette please?", then, there was a sudden silence.

My initial reaction was that she shared a house with somebody because the person answering didn't sound all that old, but that hypothesis was blown into pieces with the reply "I'm sorry there's nobody here of that name, you must have the wrong number, sorry, bye".

I couldn't believe it, having spent well over a day and a half projecting love, happiness and beautiful sex, with this, the most gorgeous of God's creatures, I suddenly found myself feeling as flat and drained as a dead car battery, on a cold, damp Winter's morning.

I wasn't angry, just disappointed because the lady in question despite the hard, independent touch to her appearance did seem to have a "very special warm glow" about her aura and I didn't in my wildest dreams, think that she'd even think about pulling such a fast stroke, however not all was lost because in typical "Davies alcoholic" fashion I'd already taken precautions.

Just in case this eventuality did occur, I'd taken her car registration number as she'd pulled away, meaning that I still had a remote chance of tracking her down. That lady was so enigmatic that I'd already prepared myself for this outcome, I desperately needed to try and win the ladies attention, so with that thinking firmly in mind, I contacted a friend in the Police force, in order to set about finding this very, very special lady.

Those next two days were incredible, I could neither eat or sleep, I was incapable of any sort of communication with anybody else and I had no concentration whatsoever, work was also right out of the window as I lived in a sort of dream world, hopefully awaiting and praying for good news.

My friend in the Police force did originally tell me, that it would take him about twenty four hours to get any sort of a result, but he never called, so you can imagine the state I'd got in after nearly forty eight hours.

When he did eventually ring me, I once again experienced new feelings and emotions as he told me her full name and address. With each word he spoke I became more excited and by the time he'd finished and I'd put the phone down, I was tired, no knackered, as I nervously fumbled through the A-Z of Manchester to find out exactly where she lived.

By the time I'd found her number in the phone book I was in a right old state, I was wet with sweat, hot with flushes and covered from head to toe in goose bumps from excitement . . ." At last, I've found her!".

Having spent days in pursuit of this lady and sleepless nights thinking about her, one would have expected me to pick up the phone straight away to contact her. Probably the old Paul would have done, but not on this occasion, because I found myself feeling unsure, with not as much confidence and just for once thinking about the other person for a change, "What will she say?, how will she react?, will she be frightened, after all I don't want to scare her off".

For days I wondered what the hell I should do, although I was sure of one thing, I knew that if she was available, I wanted her, but how was I to go about it? . . . I didn't have a clue!

In the end, after nearly a week of inconsistency, unsurety, doubt and unknowingness the whole situation became too much for me, even if there was no chance, at least just speaking to her once again would be a truly beautiful experience in itself, so I decided to act by giving her a call.

Making that phone call proved to be ten times harder than any other I'd ever made in my life, which with my track record is really saying something. Especially when one considers the number of times I'd called the bank from the pubs and clubs in the afternoons, as I desperately tried to stop cheques being bounced, whilst at the same time being fully loaded and canned out of my brains.

Even harder than when I phoned A.A in the middle of one of my benders, or the countless "morning after" calls to Jean, from places where I shouldn't really have been, such as other women's houses, sometimes even beds. After all the creeping and bullshitting I'd done on the phone in the past, this should have been easy, but it wasn't, for I'd never made a call that had so much importance at stake, depending on it's response.

Nervously picking up the hand-set I remembered thinking "I haven't got a clue what I'm doing!", but if I'm to have any chance at all of getting to know her, then I've got to do it.

The minute she answered I recognized her voice, I'd relived our only previous conversation time and time again, so I knew it was her, but despite my awareness I still needed confirmation to save myself from looking and sounding a prat,

"Hello, could I possibly speak to Jeannette please?",

"Jeannette speaking", then very sheepishly and embarrassingly I began,

"I don't know whether or not you'll remember me, but I'm the chap in the van, who stopped you on the road the other day", she replied in a rather suspicious tone, "Yes I think so, after all it's not every day I get accosted in the middle of the road like that and in such a manner".

Instinctively I wanted to reassure her that everything was okay,

"Look, please don't take offence at me ringing you like this, but I only want a second chance, so that I can meet you properly, say take you for a drink?", she responded rather quickly by asking me how I'd got the number, so in the form of bait or a proposal I said,

"That's for me to know and for you to find out, I'll tell you what, you meet me for a drink and I'll reveal all, it was difficult but I'll tell you how I did it".

Once again the ladies warm, caring and thoughtful nature came through, when she refused saying that she was off to Colwyn Bay for her holidays in just over a week, but even though she was rejecting my offer she didn't do it in a rude, abrasive manner, for it was as if she was still Christian enough to consider my feelings, even in the uncomfortable, weird position she found herself in.

I didn't really want to put any pressure on her, especially as she was single, but at the same time I knew in my own mind that I had to give it my best shot, there and then, as I couldn't forsee me getting a second attempt, so once again I pleaded with her, only this time from a different angle.

"Well do you work during the day?", she replied with a very evasive, "hard to get"... "Sometimes", so undeterred I followed that question up with "What about a lunchtime then?, there can't be any harm in that", thinking she was frightened, I then continued to lead the conversation, "Bring somebody with you, a mate or someone, then you'll know you're safe".

At that point, I could feel myself instinctively reaching into my hidden psychological box of secret tools, to pull out my most useful implement . . . "manipulation".

"Look, how about if I meet you at the Ellesmere on the Lancs, go on, it'll not do you any harm", once again she refused,

"No thanks, you've been very kind all the same, but no I don't think so".

In sheer desperation I immediately replied, by telling her that she'd be under no obligation whatsoever and that if she wasn't enjoying herself she could just up and leave any time she wanted, but once again she rejected my offer, "Oh I don't know".

The minute I heard the questionable, "don't know", I wasted no time at all in latching on to her "second thoughts", "Look let's say Thursday, I'll be waiting there for you, say one o'clock, whether you're coming or not, but if you can make it please try, I'd love to see you". I knew at that point that there maybe a chance, so once again I emphasized that whatever she chose to do, I was going to be there, "I'll just turn up in hope, but please try if you can, because if you do, I'll be chuffed to bits, I'm dying to meet you properly".

I'd made my mind up that whatever she said in response, that this was definitely going to be my last plea, so I wasn't totally disheartened when she ended the call by saying " I'll think about it okay, look I'll have to go now, bye".

Those next few days I might as well have been living on the planet Mars because wherever I was going or whatever I was doing, I really didn't know which was coming first, "my head or my arse". They do have a saying in America for this type of psychotic obsession that I was suffering with, although there, victims are usually the famous film stars who are being hounded by some sort of weird nutter, well this lady was definitely a star "of the most spectacular kind" and I certainly qualified for the part of the nutter, so I suppose there were similarities.

During those few days of what I prefer to call "build up", I once again used my conniving head and ever-present friendly asset called "manipulation", to try and ensure in the nicest but craftiest way possible, that the beautiful lady did at least, turn up. In order to do so, I purchased a gift voucher from Marks and Spencer, bought a nice greetings card and then wrote a simple but caring message, telling her how much I really wanted to see her on our date. The message was brief but hopefully effective saying, "Just a small token of my appreciation for the kindness that you've already shown, whether you turn up or not it's still been a pleasure to have met you, if I don't see you again, good luck for the future".

The next day I was sat there in the van at twelve o'clock on the dot, talk about keen and early, I was so keyed up, I was just a complete bag of nerves, all fingers and thumbs as I tried to tidy myself up a bit. Once I'd put on some talc and deodorant, brushed my hair and had a quick run around the facials with a Bic razor, I sat there with my crazy mind playing its usual funny tricks, as it took me everywhere, trying to telepathically read her mind, thinking, "What will she be doing now at this exact moment?, will she be at work?, I wonder if she has any real intention of coming?", then I started to panic, wondering if my "back up" system had worked, "Suppose she didn't get the card and voucher?", after a little negative thought, I once again became positive, "Well, there's one thing, if she still has any reservations when she does open the mail, at least that might make her think again".

Once I'd cleared up that little problem inside my head, I immediately started on something else, "I wonder if she is coming, what will she be wearing?", I then started to fantasize about her actually getting changed, but in the end I came to the conclusion that it didn't really matter.

"As long as she's got those sun-glasses on and looking as sexy as last time, who cares?".

By about five minutes to one, she could have come in a bubble car for all I cared, because I just needed to see her . . . "Oh I wanted her so badly!".

At ten minutes past one she hadn't shown and I was down, I was pissed off, angry with myself for getting in such a state and I felt a right dickhead, I wasn't impressed, life was a shit and God was a two faced lying little twat, for even making me think that I had a chance, the only real thing in my favour, was that I was still glad and happy to be sober.

I'd all but given up any hope of her showing, when she suddenly entered the car park, pulled up and wound her window down, only this time fully!!. Once again, God was good, life was great, the sun was shining and she looked absolutely stunning, "I didn't think you'd come, I really didn't think you'd turn up, so all I can say is thanks", I was like a kid on Christmas morning, or a man who'd just won the pools, I could have climbed Everest, because that was the awesome, powerful effect this lady had over me, then she spoke her first words . .

"I've just called out of politeness, I can't stay, but I didn't want you stood about waiting for me, I have to go into work and I don't like letting you down, but I just wanted to say thanks for the card and gift, although you shouldn't have bothered, it really wasn't necessary, but thanks again".

Talk about ego deflation and low self esteem, at that exact second, you could have physically shit on me from the tallest skyscraper in the land, as it was without doubt, the most disappointing moment of my life, feelings which must have shown clearly in my expression, as I replied in answer to her statement.

"Oh no!, you're joking, aren't you?, you've got to be, I've so looked forward to this moment, please tell me you're joking?".

Whether or not it was my pathetic, sad, "little boy lost" look, I don't know, but whatever it was, she suddenly changed her mind, "Oh well, ten minutes then, maybe just one drink". That was it! . . . a posse of wild horses couldn't have stopped me from then on, "Great, I'll just lock my van up".

When she got out of her car, I was dumb struck, wearing a black and white summer skirt and a black blouse, she automatically "bowled me over", "God you look absolutely lovely!, having said that, I must apologise for my own attire, but I've not been back home, since I left this morning".

With introductions completed, I then found myself in the most embarrassing of situations imaginable, especially when one considers I was desperately trying to impress, "Look, I'm really sorry about this, but we can't go in there because there's a sign on the door stating, no jeans or trainers."

I then shrugged my shoulders, lifted one leg and pointed to it proclaiming my apology, "Sorry", where upon she looked as if to say, "What the bloody hell am I doing here?".

I don't know what possessed this lady of class to stay, for I looked a real old mess, I'd been up since four o' clock that morning, I'd had a "make do" shave in the van, I wore tatty jeans with holes in and a football shirt and just to round me off, my dirty, hard worn, running shoes. It's a miracle that she didn't just get back into her car and drive off as fast as she could because I wasn't far short of looking like a tramp, but she didn't, she stayed and I'm forever grateful to God that she did, for it was the start of a long, caring and lasting relationship.

It was a friendship which took us along the strangest, rockiest road imaginable, on a kind of "mystery tour of life", that eventually taught me how to do the one thing I'd always thought I was incapable of . . . "LOVE!!!".

Once we had found another pub that would accept my attire, we sat down outside in the sunshine, shared with each other about our lives and discussed everything, we got on so well, it was like a dream or fantasy come true, as we both talked openly and honestly of our own personal situations.

Looking back it's a miracle we got a second chance, for that first, "ten minute, one drink", lasted at least a couple of hours, after which, no bookie would have given us odds of making it a second time.

The reason was quite simple, I had told Jeannette that I was married, she informed me that she was divorced and off men forever, I hated kids, but she had a boy of ten, then I was a non religious, alcoholic, yet, she played bingo and went to church, so on the surface, there really wasn't all that much going for us.

It was strange because having said that, we never stopped laughing, joking and smiling all afternoon and from the very start, I knew that this lady was something really special, she even "copped off" with some other bloke, who was weighing her up, which brought her even more attention from me, when I said, "Look at that cheeky bugger over there, giving you the 'come on', when you're obviously with me".

It was a perfect example of the woman, for she was both very attractive and imposing at the same time, even more magnetic than many a celebrity and certainly, "a woman to turn men's heads", whose mere presence made me feel very proud, even powerful to be in her company. We parted with the agreement that I would ring her up once she'd returned from the trip to Colwyn Bay, so with that, I kissed her on the hand, wished her a safe and enjoyable break and expressed my hopes of seeing her on her return.

I left totally wrapped up and besotted in the lady and now that I'd met her properly, I knew that I was in love, I couldn't wait to see her again and I was only just driving away from the pub where we'd met, so knowing that she was going away and where she was going to, I immediately started to scheme.

The day after, work became secondary, as I had much more important things to do, so instead of whizzing around Greater Manchester collecting cardboard in my van, I stayed at home and made telephone calls.

After spending over an hour on the phone, ringing hotels in Colwyn Bay, I discovered where she was going to be staying and promptly arranged a surprise, by having the owners of the hotel purchase a large bouquet of flowers and a magnum of champagne for her, on my behalf. I wrote her a greetings card, care of the owners and posted it on, accompanying it with the payment and then I waited, desperately waited! . . . in hope and anticipation of her return.

Whilst she was away, I felt that my attentions may, by some million to one chance, return back to Jean, after all nearly everything in my life at the time was totally upside down, as I once again found myself in unknown territory, but I had no idea just how strong the power of true love really was, in the end the answer was "No" and so I couldn't wait for "the lady" to come home.

The day she was due back, I made a point of calling around to her house, I'd never been before but I didn't go for that reason, I went to drop her off some groceries, obviously stuff I'd got from Marks's life-saving waste. I thought that with her being a single one parent family, it may be handy and save her going out shopping when she got home, it also gave me an ideal opportunity to leave a card, enabling me to keep up the momentum I needed in my pursuit of her.

I purposely left ringing her until the Monday morning, even though she actually got home on the Saturday afternoon, because although excited by her return I was never the less lacking in confidence, especially as I didn't know how she'd react to the stroke I'd pulled with the flowers etc.

On the Monday morning at about a quarter past nine I had eventually raised enough courage to pick up the phone and give her a call, with her reacting in exactly the manner I'd prayed for.

"Hi it's Paul, did you have a nice holiday?", she immediately replied by thanking me for the flowers, champagne and card, telling me how lovely it was prepared and what a surprise it proved to be,

"It must have cost you a fortune". I told her that it was all worth it if she'd got pleasure from it and no embarrassment or harm was caused, "Well I can't say I wasn't embarrassed, but I certainly wasn't offended by them at all". We then spoke about the holiday in general, the weather, the hotel, the place itself and of course her sister and the kids they'd taken.

Following that topic of conversation she then asked me, how I'd managed to track down which hotel they were stopping in, which was my cue to "sell myself", by explaining the extraordinary lengths I'd gone to in my pursuit of her. I then rounded off that story by asking her my most important question of all, "Look Jeannette, I hope you don't think I'm pressing you, but is there any chance of us seeing each other again?, maybe this week sometime?".

My basic character defects hadn't changed all that much since I'd stopped drinking and as a result, I "hung on" to her every word, especially then!!, as she said, "Well I suppose I don't have much choice do I, not when you've gone to so much effort and trouble".

At that point my lips started to quiver with nerves, excitement, "I don't know what!", so we made a date for that Wednesday, at the same time, but a different pub.

The pub was called the Bridgewater, it was situated slap bang in the centre of the small village of Worsley and it was a "posers paradise". I was determined to improve on my last performance, so I made sure that I had a proper shave, "With less blood running down my neck", I wore a nice, clean, white shirt, neat, black trousers and my customary shiny black shoes, "that you could see your face in".

At one o'clock I sat there in the blazing sunshine, looking more like a lazy, bone-idle waiter than anything else and I'd chosen to sit at the table nearest to the kerb, in order to make sure that she didn't miss me, as by now I was hungry for the ladies company. When she did arrive it was as if I'd known her for years, for gone were the fears, apprehensions and doubts as we once again seemed to have some sort of a bond and interest in most of the topics of our conversation.

On this occasion however I did "come clean" with reference to the work I did, by telling her what a "bent sod" I was, with regard to being dishonest and making money, I explained about the abundance of wide ranging fresh food I got from good old Marks and Spencer and the other "freebies" I came across on my travels.

Once again, at about a quarter past three she had to leave, to pick up her son from school, although this time there was no question or doubt about us seeing each other again, so in my own inimitable way I parted in real "Davies style",

"Listen Jeannette, would you like some food now?, only I've got some in the van, there's not that much choice, mainly veg, but you can have a look if you want?".

Straight away I saw the resemblance to Jean and my Mother when her eyes lit up as if to say, "Ooh Bargains!!", she followed me to the van, I opened the doors, then just at that moment her eyes nearly popped out of her head, "Oh my God, I've never seen as much veg in my life!, I thought you were only talking about a little amount".

Not really giving it a second thought I proceeded to fill a wooden orange box with a variety of food, "Tomatoes, d'ya like them?",

"Please, if you don't mind",

"What about potatoes?", I then went into my market trader's act,

"Ere ya are take them, oh what about carrots?, have you got some of them?", she then told me that she felt awful, cheeky even, saying,

"Are you sure you don't mind?".

Did I bloody hell, I loved every minute of it because I actually had the pleasure of seeing the lady enjoy herself and by the time I'd nearly filled her boot, she herself got cheeky, "Do you mind if I have a colly", meaning cauliflower.

Well that was it!, all systems go at that point, the green light!,

"You're joking!, how many d'ya want?". At last I'd found this hard, independent ladies weak spot!, which meant that when I had finished, she was piled up to the roof and I knew that no matter what else she thought of me, she certainly liked my "mixed vegetables '.

I closed the boot, followed her around to the driver's door and took a hold of her hand, "Jeannette thanks for coming, you've made my day", at that point I thought "Oh shit to it, if she slaps me, so what!" and gave her the slightest, most delicate, gentlemanly kiss imaginable and with that I drove off knowing "I'd done it", believing that finally "she may be mine!".

It was really the start of our courtship, for after that I frequently met her at various pubs and at different times of the day, during a "getting to know you" period.

I had to fit our rendezvouses in and around my own A.A and hospital meetings, but obviously I was more than happy to do so. It meant that Jean, started to see even less of me, which made the already sour atmosphere at home even worse, as we continued to go our own separate ways, more or less as a couple of strangers.

I knew from my very first visit to the A.T.U that life was going to take on a whole new meaning and that changes would take place, but like every other person who ends up at clinics and A.A, I didn't understand just what was involved.

When they informed me that I was lucky to still have a wife, I breathed a sigh of relief, then the next minute they told me that once I'd been sober a while, we may not like each other.

Jealousy, joy, hate, love and any other emotion you care to mention was strange and confusing, previously in my writing I said that for the first time in my life I couldn't cry, I couldn't sleep either, as I started to suffer from insomnia and panic attacks. By the time I'd eventually closed my eyes and got to sleep I would be shattered, only to wake a few hours later to face another new horror . . . "anxiety!".

As I also said earlier those first few months were great, the early morning sun, the singing of the birds, even the milk and the postman were a "newly discovered" delight, but even that changed in sobriety as I found myself lying in the fetus position, curtains closed, too frightened to get out of bed.

At first, despite my knowledge of the illness I blamed it all on my love for Jeannette, thinking God was paying me back in his own way, for not committing my all, to my wife, although A.A soon put pay to that notion as I got identification from others in the fellowship suffering in just the same way.

My "honeymoon" period of "So what, it doesn't matter, it's not important" attitude was over, as I realised that despite my "wonderful achievement?", in staying sober for a few months, the real world hadn't changed all that much and even despite my efforts, everybody still carried on in the same way, regardless.

It was a large, hard pill to swallow, the fact that I thought I was somebody special as a drunk, I'd done well sober, thinking I was even greater, only to find out that really I was a "nothing", small, just as inadequate and "Definitely not the centre of the universe!".

It was the most complicated and confusing time of my life, as everybody close to me enthused over my effort and the typically "full blooded" first attempt that I was making.

For years I craved, no demanded attention, but it hardly ever came, then sober I had everybodys, but at that time I didn't know how to handle the situation.

My relationship with Jean constantly became more strained, yet Jeannette and I were getting closer in the most innocent way, with sex having no part. Even her child and I got on, yet I couldn't stand kids, but extra effort in that area on my part, proved no problem, after all I knew to have her, I had to take on her son!

For the first time in my life I really began to question both things and people, yet having spent nearly three months being prepared to imitate a "door mat", I started to adopt a mind of my own, as things once again "did matter". I began to realise that I actually loved and hated Jean at the same time, I loved her Dad, whilst at the same time despised my own parents more than ever before.

My fellow A.A members warned me, as they do with every newcomer,

"Do not make any major decisions for at least a couple of years", but I already had, when I'd decided that Jeannette was the one person I wanted to spend the rest of my life with.

The hospital staff at Withington constantly questioned me, "Why don't you come in for six weeks, do the programme, then see how you feel?", what a joke that was, a few weeks earlier they'd been telling Jean that I'd substituted my drinking with A.A. Well I'm glad they did get one thing right, for it was that substitution that I firmly believe saved my life, because it was at that point the message of Alcoholics Anonymous really started to sink in to my "thick, arrogant" head.

I'd already started making effort to learn about A.A but after nearly a meeting a day I was now beginning to realise that staying away from drink, was a daily "life or death" situation, so I grasped a hold of the programme and vigourously set about working it.

In hindsight it was a good job, for the next few months seemed to just flash by as I suddenly found myself facing my first Christmas . . .

"Hopefully without booze!".

It's a time of the year that a lot of alcoholics fear, especially the new ones, with work's do's, pubs, clubs, private parties all no go areas for anyone trying to stop or stay off the drink, but not me, for I had other, far more important problems. Oh Yes, I resented Christmas and New Year alright, only because, I being sober was forced to watch everybody else "playing at it", by that I mean playing the fool and I didn't like it one bit.

My main concern was "Where should I be?", should I have Christmas dinner with Jean, her mum and Dad and the rest of her family?, or should I be with Jeannette and her son?, never mind Christmas day, what about Christmas Eve? and a week later at New Year?

By the time I had finished projecting my mind was in utter turmoil, not knowing which way to turn or who to hurt.

Having done much self searching and reasoning I came to the conclusion that it would be best for all if I tried to split my loyalties in two ways, one to Jean, the other to Jeannette, but of course that hypothesis led me straight into trouble.

Arrangements for Christmas dinner had already been made by Jean, which meant that we had to be at her Mothers for three o'clock, so in the morning I spent a couple of hours at the hospital "day room", called to see Jeannette and then went to a lunchtime A.A meeting. After that I made my way to Jean's Mum and Dad's for the usual festive turkey dinner, but unfortunately I wasn't there long enough to taste it.

Everything was okay until we'd sat down at the table to eat, when I discovered that there was no booze, none of them were, what I would have termed as "big drinkers", but even the smallest tippler in the world has a sherry on Christmas day. I immediately made an issue out of it, resenting the fact that they weren't drinking in an effort to help me, it was kind, but I didn't want to affect their normal routine, especially as I'd done that enough in my drinking days.

Sadly it ended up with Jean and I having a stand up row, which resulted in me unceremoniously and childishly storming off in a tantrum. It was a shame because, as on many other occasions, I spoilt the party, yet only now, as I write, do I feel guilty when I look back and think of how good her Dad and brothers were to me.

I always found her brothers very friendly, sarcastic, but friendly and whenever I had any sort of problem with my vans they would always be there, "no questions asked", if I was on the look-out to buy a new one, once again they were always on hand to help, so I was eternally grateful to them whilst respecting them at the same time.

Their Dad, Harry, was brilliant, like Ted who I wrote about earlier, he too was a "one off", a real "odd ball" as Jean used to say, but I always loved him in a way that I always wanted to love my own father. If I had a fiver for each occasion we walked the dogs outside Maine Road football ground, calling the two women and putting the world to right I'd be "well off", or even a tenner for the number of times we'd be out under the bonnet of my van or Jean's car when they wouldn't start.

If I had a twenty pound note for the number of times I've called "foreigners" and Man City with him, I'd be a millionaire by now, but that was Harry and me, forever moaning, just like Victor Meldrew.

Harry always said I was mad and he was right, Jean's brothers would often repeat his words when I was at their garage in Stockport, "You know what our Dad says Paul . . . You can never tell what "Bascombes" thinking, or what he's going to do next, can you?".

That unpredictability seemed to amuse Harry, my irrational, odd behaviour and defiance of Jean's domineering attitude was always something he envied, as he saw me care less and less, the more she went on. When I think of the hours he spent telling me how he'd wished that he'd stood up to his own missus years earlier, instead of taking it all and how he was delighted when he saw me in the "dog house", but sadly that year Jean's Mum died and so they all celebrated the fact by having their first holiday abroad!

I refused to go on the trip because I felt unsure of myself, my strength in sober terms and a holiday with them wouldn't have interested me anyway, so Jean left me at home. Even that caused a row, most women would be glad to get away on their own for a week or two, but not her, she couldn't stand me, yet still wanted me to go.

It was a subject or should I say issue which had been dying to rear it's ugly head for quite sometime and this was an ideal opportunity for it to do so, whilst giving her the chance to bring a few of her gripes and resentments out into the open and up for debate.

I discovered that she resented being told that it may take at least a couple of years for my head to clear, she didn't understand the necessity for me to do as many meetings as I was and also hated the fact that we did nothing together and that we had nothing in common. The worst thing she found hard to accept was this "new person" she lived with, this stranger, whom she couldn't control or manipulate, as he was sober.

On the contrary instead of being predictably unpredictable, I was now being "totally" unpredictable and self supporting at the same time, for seemingly to her "the boy had become a man" overnight, sadly leaving her feeling used, abused and well passed her "sell by date" saying "But what about me?"

That detachment from my wife meant that I had more time to spend with Jeannette, the woman who I really wanted to be with and so my visits to her home during the day time increased. In the mornings she worked for herself, running a leaflet distribution team, finished at twelve o'clock midday, then in the afternoons worked from home as a comptometer operator, but of course as soon as I found out that she had "free time" after one o'clock, it didn't take me long to decide where I was going to be.

With a little reorganising and shuffling about of work, I always made sure that I was somewhere in the region of Worsley for about one o'clock in order to have lunch with her. I would call her from the van, "Hi, is it alright if I come round and bring my chips with me?", she never once said "No" and so I charged in to see her, where she would be sat on the patio in the garden, with a cup of tea ready and waiting for me.

During the second month the "chip butties" had gone, as she was buying me my barm cakes with hers and after three months I was calling in for morning coffee at half past eight before she went off posting leaflets.

By this time I was accepted and known as her boyfriend, I'd got to know all her family, her work mates and even some of the neighbours, so far, I'd got on with her son and I was doing well in the business and continuing to work hard, despite spending so much time with Jeannette, so "everything in the garden was rosy" as they say.

Obviously the more time I spent with Jeannette, the more I saw of her family and so with the growth of our friendship, came more closeness between her sister, brother in law, their children and myself.

Jim, her sister's husband, had been in the Police Force for over twenty seven years but had been forced to retire on health grounds, he suffered from agoraphobia and couldn't travel "step in Doctor Davies" please.

In my caring Samaritan attitude to life and feeling very dutiful to Jeannette, I started to take him out on the road with me collecting cardboard, only locally, but enough to start getting him out of the house and to my surprise he enjoyed it.

Within a couple of weeks he'd been bitten by the "cardboard and paper collecting bug", he loved it and more importantly it did him good, so we started off in the mornings with set destinations in mind, but if he didn't think that he could make them, then he just said and we changed the routine.

The hilarities and fun of working in the scrap game soon took over and with a little encouragement from myself we were getting him to places that he'd never even thought possible a couple of months earlier.

Jim's only problem was that he smoked a pipe, but in view of his mental state I had to consolidate by being a little considerate to his feelings and emotions, so reluctantly I let him smoke in the van, which automatically gave me the idea of nicknaming him "Popeye".

We got on extremely well, with me bending over backwards to "please", but after a while I realised that I was obliging far too much and doing what is commonly known in A.A as "people pleasing", which eventually ended up with me saying "Well what shall we do today?".

Whatever he wanted to do, or wherever he preferred to go, we did it his way, regardless of it being my business and livelihood and despite the fact that I had times, pick-ups and deadlines to keep. Unfortunately because of this, I knew I couldn't carry on succumbing to his whims and fancies indefinitely, so a parting of the ways was imminent.

Jim fancied having a go himself for quite sometime, but never wanted to commit himself, however when I ordered and bought my own brand new van, his real interest was aroused, he loved cars, vans, in fact anything to do with motoring and the thoughts of driving around in such a fashion impressed him, so for the first time in his life he ended up working for himself.

My reasons for buying a new van were totally different and far less extravagant than his, I needed one out of necessity, as mine was dying by the day, but the initial thoughts of doing such a thing were prompted by what I considered were rude, thoughtless and arrogant comments dished out by the manager of Marks and Spencer in Macclesfield when he said, "D'ya not think it's time you got a new van, that's looking a bit tatty now and it's bad for the companies image".

I was deeply hurt by his comments and observations, especially as it was mine and paid for, unlike his "firms" family car, so I answered his claims by telling him that I had neither regular or ample enough work to cover the cost of a new van, especially as I had no contract or guarantees from the company, with regard to the services I offered.

I questioned all the managers concerned as to the possibility of more work if I bought a new one, which prompted a good, positive response from them all. That rude man was more enthusiastic than any other, "You can get a new one and I'll give you more work carrying stock", which meant that I would be given work carrying clothes, foods and equipment to and from the warehouse in Stockport.

Over the years I'd done my fair share of what they call "transfers" but they did seem to have dropped off in numbers over those previous twelve months, but they were good money earners, the only problem was that they weren't regular and I never knew when the company would ring with them. The loads could be anything from a van full of velvet skirts and jackets, worth about seventy thousand pounds, to dumping enormous amounts of food at the local tip, because the freezers in the stores had broken down, either way the work was easier than collecting a ton of cardboard in it's place.

Chapter Ten

A Dose Of Reality

In buying a new van and especially in view of the reaction from the managers, I generally anticipated much more cleaner, better "transfer" work, such as clothes, food and equipment, so based on trust, I went ahead with the purchase.

Unfortunately the exercise back fired on me leaving me struggling to make ends meet, the work load didn't increase and to make matters worse I lost the verbal contract with the very first Marks and Spencer store my Dad had took on. Losing it was painful enough, but the manner in which it was done, like many other strokes that the company eventually pulled, still hurts me today.

Joyce, my Mother had always brought us all up totally believing in Marks's faith, honesty and integrity, so with those thoughts in mind, I always gave them my utmost loyalty, never letting them down, or ever saying "No" to any request. My Mother also brought me up to believe that "you get out of life what you put in" and that "you get your just rewards in the end". Sadly as I write this I have to disagree with her, for my earlier loyalty was now "not beginning to pay off!". I never did get an official explanation or apology and to this day I'm still awaiting, the only information I ever received was given by a "two bit" precinct council worker, who told me "You're not allowed on here any more, you don't do Marks's now!" . . . and that was over nine years ago!

That start in itself was bad enough, but believe it or not it did get worse, as I shortly discovered that the company were soon to start implementing new plans and ideas on waste removal.

Suddenly echoes of my Mother's advice once again started to ring through my ears, "Keep your prices down Paul, you never know where you'll end up with Marks's", was one good one, but her favourite one was" Marks's will always look after you", well Joyce I'm afraid all of your talk and belief about waiting for the big day, the commitment, the big contract, "the loyal little guy gets big" dreams never flourished. Instead it was a case of who knows who? and sod him over there, as other, already large concerns were earmarked for the big prize, but if I still had any doubts then they were dispelled in 1985.

Whilst loading the van up, a lorry driver from a company called "Christian Salvesan" came out with a real sarcastic remark, "You'll not be taking much of that stuff soon, will ya?".

When I asked him exactly what he meant, he told me of his companies future plans, with reference to a new warehouse in Warrington and explained that they were already taking back numbers of clean bales, which were supposed to be mine. I was gutted when he told me, but felt ten times worse when I'd made some of my own enquiries, for I discovered that once again my past loyalties, faith and belief in Marks and Spencer had been totally shattered.

Some four or five years earlier Jean was at home alone one evening, when she received a threatening telephone call from the company servicing the St. Helens store, who were wrongly informed by a warehousman that I had been poaching work.

After carrying out my own investigation, I found out that the waste paper company concerned had rather cleverly obtained my number from the manager at one of the stores that I covered, on the pretence of offering me more work. The next morning I rang the manager of the St. Helens store and explained the situation, telling him how frightened and distressed we both were as a result of the whole situation, "Look Mr Davies, I'm appalled at the things you're telling me, but I must ask could you give me sometime today to look into the matter, before you decide to go to the Police?". I had no objections whatsoever and in the afternoon he did return my call, he was quite apologetic and obviously upset by the whole affair and ended our conversation by asking me to go to his store to meet him personally.

When I did go, he offered me the work there and then, but believing in the things I'd been taught by my Mother, I didn't think it would be right to accept the work. I refused it, fully expecting the incident to be registered in the hope that I could be looked after by Marks's at a later date. "What an idiot!".

Not only did I find out that my cardboard was being "snuck out" to their new warehouse at Warrington, but guess who was actually weighing in?, "Well!, surprise surprise, it was my friends from St. Helens".

Talk about angry, it wasn't even in it, I was absolutely fuming, thinking of what a bloody doughnut I'd been. Five years earlier I had the opportunity of having them thrown out altogether, but because I didn't feel it was right of me to take bread from somebody else's mouth, I now found myself actually begging to survive.

For months I'd struggled with dirty bales that I couldn't sell, which were contaminated with polythene, carrying all the shit away from the stores and doing a good job at that, only to find these bastards were officially having my bales taken, delivered and sorted, all with Marks's blessing.

Well I know one thing, that incident with Marks and Spencer brought a new meaning to the words "hard work, honesty, loyalty, oh and especially commitment!", their actions also gave me quite a lot to think about, including my future.

I couldn't believe a company like that could work in such a way, especially after all my service, but what hurt even more was that I'd done it the A.A way, the proper way and still been shit on.

Suddenly I became angry when I realised and thought about some of the major scrapes and near misses I'd helped get them out of. The times I'd driven van loads of fresh food from store to store, mixed in with dirty, smelly cardboard, or the Christmas and New Year periods, where I carried van loads of frozen chickens and turkeys in my "tatty, dirty heap" as Mr Harrison put it, to get the goods on the shelves for four o'clock in the morning. They didn't mind my service then, or charging the general public for food which had been thrown around in a van full of shite and unrefrigerated at that.

I recalled the order "cock ups" which meant that I would race from say, Liverpool to Manchester with a van, full to bursting of expensive garments and the managers parting statement, "Just get everything in Paul, just get it all in, the girls can iron and press it all when it's unloaded, before it goes on display".

The way Marks and Spencer used to finally "get rid" of any old, out of date, damaged or returned stock was always an amazing experience and one which meant that I would never know just exactly what I was carrying home. I've already written about my mother getting food from the "waste trolley" but I've not yet explained how the system worked.

At the end of each day, when the store had closed, all staff would line up at the check out, where they would be given the opportunity to buy anything on display, they would get the goods at ridiculously low prices which obviously meant that they would generally leave the store laden down with shopping bags. Now because of my pick-up system, the Macclesfield store was always my final collection point, which meant that I had to be outside the store for closing time and that was the most amusing part of the day.

Apart from the fact that it was a good "picking up" spot for a lot of my past "legovers", it was also fun watching the staff leaving with this abundance of food, because anything left after they had their opportunity was automatically mine. My verbal contracts stated that at the discretion of each branch, the manager could either give the stock to a good worthy cause, such as a home or a charity or just dump it, via me, but of course whoever had the bonus of getting the stuff, had a field day.

Over the years I had some of the most amusing, comical and hysterical experiences of my life, which were all as a result of the vast enormous amounts of good, decent quality food, plants and pottery I would end up taking home with me. Apart from my present home, wherever else I've lived, it was never any different, I always had a kitchen littered with food filled, bin liners, with a dining room or sometimes even the living room, just the same, being a regular feature. On many an occasion, the hall would also be filled, with the widest range of fresh produce imaginable, such as turkeys, chickens, legs of lamb and joints of beef. We ate like kings and were never short of anything from chops, steaks, pies and sausage to cakes, biscuits even trifles.

It didn't only stop at food, for plants, flowers and pottery were also a regular item as quite often the warehouse men would break perfectly good stock up, in a sick attempt to make sure that the rest of the food was non-resellable, even more pathetically, some of them even enjoyed doing it. I remember going home many an evening, wondering if they'd thrown out any of their "new lines", such as cosmetics, household toiletries and home furnishings. It was crazy you could always tell if I'd been to someone's house for there would be "tell tale" signs all over the place. At home and in Jeannettes' there would be deodorant, air fresheners, cosmetics, even toiletries, with "tester" labels on them and millions of quality ceramic plant pots making the rooms they were in, look like the household goods departments of Marks and Spencer themselves.

The only difference was, our pots had cracks in them, but they'd all been cleverly stuck together by the women in my life, in fact they were both so good at it, that I'm convinced they would have made good renovators. The hours we spent cleaning up bin liners full of food with either broken eggs, yoghurt or cream poured over them were countless, but never the less funny and enjoyable. However the real pleasure for me, came when I watched either of them empty the bags, as they bent down and placed their heads, near enough fully inside. At times such as these, I would wait for those most repetitive of lines, "Ooh look what's in here!!", or "Oh bloody hell!!", followed by some declaration or other, "It's fresh salmon!" or "Oh look prawns!!".

Right from the start of our relationship, Jeannette had some fascination, even addiction or something to cauliflowers and many a time today I can joke about it with her saying, "You only wanted me for my colly!!".

For years right up until this part of my story I'd always done quite well out of the waste, it brought me a lot of pleasure as I gave it to Jean, Jeannette and my Mum and Dad, whilst at the same time it gave them pleasure to give it to other friends, neighbours and work mates but I also got the chance to use it for business as well, yet not once in all those years did I sell one scrap of food to anyone. I may have used it to forge and sustain contact and relationships in both business and pleasure, but I never sold it to a soul, unfortunately the same however, could not be said of others, who weren't only taking better "unsoiled" goods than I, but far more in quantity and under a far more deceitful pretence, which brings me to yet another story relating to the branch at Macclesfield and my good friends who worked there.

I originally took the job over as a favour for the "then" warehouse manager of Stockport, a Mr Burt Harrison, who was a friend of my Mothers, he called me up one day, all of a panic, "Listen Paul, I've got a real problem at Macclesfield, the guy who normally collects the bales, rubbish and food etc, has had a heart attack and there's no one else capable of doing it, could you help?".

I told him he could rely on me, no matter how long it was for and that he wasn't to worry, however it did end up a permanent fixture, but throughout my whole experience at Macclesfield there were nothing but problems.

The first manager I dealt with was a Mr. Lee, a tall, balding, Jewish chap, who was as pompous as they come and a hard man to deal with, I knew from the minute we'd had our introductory meeting that it was going to be a tall order forging a "decent working relationship", but not impossible as long as I could find a way to get through to him, which I eventually did, by way of supplying him with tickets to Manchester City Football Club games, because both he and his son were "blues" and so I used that to my own advantage.

I had problems straight away, but couldn't do anything about them until I was totally sure of the facts, but thankfully I was proved correct in my assumption. I'd discovered that the foreman, who had been there years, was secretly supplying the "Pig farmer" who used to collect the stuff with most of the "waste food" that I should have been taking.

Gerry Lee, the manager was upset but cleared up the problem straight away, which meant that I enjoyed just a few of the rightful rewards and bonuses for my endeavour up until the present day, however it did make for a distant, untrusting relationship between me and his staff.

By the time the November of '85 had arrived, I hadn't been on holiday for over a couple of years, I'd been sober eighteen months and I was just starting to live and learn properly again.

I was beginning to see that stopping drinking, was in essence the easiest part and that living without booze under life's conditions and terms was now the real problem, as I had to start "growing up".

The fact that I couldn't play to everybody else's rules was the hardest thing in the world to accept, for I knew in my own heart of hearts that I couldn't get away with the tricks other non-alcoholics could.

Although I didn't like the way people spoke or treated me, it was irrelevant, for I was beginning to realise that I could do nothing to change anyone or anything if it was meant to be, at the same time I felt content that I was making Jeannette feel happy and wanted, whilst sad that my wife was quite unhappy.

There were days when I saw and heard things which infuriated me, but I had to learn to stand back and try to ignore situations, which brings me to what was another crossroads in the turmoil of my mind.

Over those past few months the distance between Jean and myself had grown, she had changed her lifestyle and like me, "gone her own way", she'd even started taking holidays abroad with her friends, as I wouldn't go, so "something" had to give.

It did and it was her, for upon my wife's arrival home after the second holiday of that year, she came in through the door, wasting no time at all, to come out with a real gem. Having been in the house all of five minutes, she gave me my present, a leather bomber jacket and gave me her thoughts and ideas for the future over our first cup of tea, "There you are luv, listen, I hope you didn't mind me saying this now, but I don't think there is a good time, I have enjoyed myself tremendously on these last couple of holidays, in fact so much so, that I don't really want to go away with you again". In a quite honest, unhurt, but saddened reply I said, "Oh it's okay, I fully understand and I can't blame you", it was as if she expected a row even at that early hour of the morning and after she'd just got in, but once again I surprised her with my reaction and response, which highlighted the real problem now facing us both,
"We didn't know each other!".

What actually happened next in my life and especially in relation to Jean and I, could only be put down to bad timing on God's part, for my next move in my wife's eyes could only be purported as "awkward".

Only a week or so after her return and the news that she'd brought, I was asked by one of my A.A friends and sponsors, how long it had been since I had taken a holiday? Having told him, he replied by stating that, "A good break would do you the world of good".

It was the news or should I say reassurance that I'd been awaiting for quite some time, which only confirmed my own thoughts and desires, so without further a do, my mind and concentration were focused solely on sunshine and a trip abroad.

I was so excited because I'd waited so long for that first vacation, but at the same time, I knew I had to be careful, thorough and prepare well, so in typical A.A fashion I sat down with pen and paper to plan the whole thing.

Choosing a destination was simple, it had to be somewhere that I hadn't been before or hadn't left my "trademark", company was another, as I didn't like many folk, but the when was simple, as "Any time!", was the answer to that one.

In the end I chose Portugal, I'd been with Jean on a day trip from Spain, knew no women there and had no bad memories of the place, company was just as easy, for I chose Harry, Jean's Dad, after all he'd been good to me over the years, so I felt that it would be a good way of paying him back. The man was as "odd" as I, we'd always got on and of course he'd only just returned himself, off his first holiday abroad with the family, so he was quite keen on the idea, especially, as I was paying for the trip and he could further his own foreign travel experiences at the same time.

On the 17th November 1985 we set off for Portugal from Manchester Airport, on an Air Europe flight, with no definite place to stay or destination in mind.

We must have looked something like "Laurel & Hardy" or "Abbott and Costello" that day as we set off, me in my typical "Gypsy Davies" style, with one piece of hand luggage and him, with his pre world war one looking case and shopping bag, to round off this picture of wealth and bachelor image we should of been portraying.

I already had an idea of where we should go, so on our arrival at Faro Airport we got a taxi to the East coast and the border of Spain and Portugal. Well "Haz" was an habitual moaner and I knew full well before we set off, that it was going to be pleasant, but not an easy holiday and so on our arrival he didn't disappoint me.

It certainly wasn't the hottest of days, sunny, but not boiling, we had nowhere to stay and we were both hungry, which all made for a bad start as it was, however nothing could have prepared us for what was to follow. We'd booked into a hotel, in a town called "Monte Gordo" which was nearly empty, so he wasn't over impressed with that, then in the same afternoon we'd gone swimming, where his next complaint was that despite the sun being hot and the sky clear, the sea and the wind were cold. To round things off that evening, he didn't fancy any of the local restaurants, which meant we needed a journey into Villa Real, a border town situated one mile away, which was where I had my first doubts and second thoughts about the whole trip.

It was a beautiful place, very scenic, lots of typically Portuguese shops selling junk, with an abundance of cafes, bars and restaurants lining the cobbled streets. There was only one major problem with this beautiful holiday setting, that most people would have given their right arm for, "Harry didn't have a filament to boil water, for a drink in the room".

I couldn't believe it, there we were supposedly, trying to enjoy ourselves and all he could think about was being able to have a cup of tea in the room, to have with his "Jacobs" water biscuits he'd taken, which he was addicted to. After nearly an hour of searching in every household and electrical shop, we eventually found one and he was happy at last, so with our first shopping expedition completed and the filament safely in our possession, we decided it was time to eat. Finding a suitable place to dine proved even harder than getting the tea making equipment, because unlike myself, Harry really wanted the nearest thing we could get to a "Wimpey" or burger bar, however yet another hour later we sat down to a meal, which surprise, surprise he didn't enjoy.

To round the night off Harry thought that it would be a nice evening to have a stroll back to the hotel, I was in two minds about the idea, because the one road to Monte Gordo was a mile long and had no street lighting whatsoever, but in order to please him, I rather unfortunately agreed.

About two thirds of the way down, in pitch darkness and still basically in the middle of nowhere, we passed a group of five maybe six Gypsy type lads, who asked us if we had any cigarettes, to which I replied, "No, no fumer". Seconds later I heard the sound of their "pacey" following footsteps, "Run Harry!, run!", I had no option but to stand my ground, so I turned to face them, as all manner of things ran through my mind.

My initial thought was "Oh shit, now were in it!", our first night and this has happened especially after I'd promised Jean and her family that I'd look after him as well. I turned around for a second glance to see "Haz" and his little old legs carrying him as fast as they could go, shuffling along like some "Chinese geisha".

Once again I shouted to him "Keep going Harry, never mind me, I'll sort these lot out!", then I turned to face the five or six aggressors, letting out one hell of a yell as I did, "Right come on then, you fuckin twats lets hav yer!", it seemed that my life was flashing before me, as though time had stood still on me, while I watched them get nearer and nearer, then all of a sudden, it was time.

I realised that the first action I took would, "without doubt" be my most important, especially as I was so outnumbered, but the muggers themselves helped my cause somewhat by making the first move, which inadvertently was their biggest mistake.

Instead of sticking together and all going for me, two of them ran straight past me in pursuit of Harry, which left me with the other four. Contrary to what they probably predicted, I immediately grabbed a couple of them and with some sort of extra human strength, threw them into a roadside ditch, then set about the other two, by smacking their heads together.

By this time the two, who were climbing out of the ditch had already seen enough, they'd obviously figured out that I was a madman and had decided to "give up the ghost" there and then. They shouted out to the others who had already caught up with Harry, but I couldn't understand what they were saying, although it was quite obvious that it was something along the lines of "let's leave it, it's not worth it", meanwhile I'd decided to get "my money's worth" out of the two that I had hold of and continued to clash their heads together.

Eventually I let go of them both, whilst at the same time telling them all to "Fuck off!", thanks to the British football hooligan it's a terminology and euphemism that even the "wogs" in the jungle comprehend, so they obliged with their tales tucked well and truly behind them, as they made a break for it, empty handed!

My immediate concern was for Harry, "Are you alright" Haz'?", but typical of him, whether it was nerves, relief or whatever, he just laughed, "Bloody hell Bascombe!, you did well then, you sent them scampering, eeh I was proud of you lad!", the grand bloke that he was, he was more interested in my performance, than his own, or the black eye that he'd obtained in the bargain. It was funny really looking back, because after all we'd been through, the very first thing we both seemed to worry about was, "what will they say at home, when they find out?". By the time we'd got back to the hotel, it was already agreed and decided that we would be moving out the following morning, heading off for some other resort, so as we went through the reception, I informed the staff that we'd be going the next day and to cancel our original plans.

At least once in the room, we could enjoy a fresh cup of tea and Harry his water biscuits, but it was whilst we sat on our beds making light of the whole situation that we got a knock on the door of the room, disrupting our "party".

One of the staff had been sent down to escort us both upstairs to the restaurant, for drinks with the manager, as an apology on behalf of the many kind, decent people of the Algarve.

To my surprise Harry had no hesitation in accepting the invite and so we both went upstairs to enjoy the hospitality of the hotel manager himself. Having discussed the whole affair in great detail, he was apologetic, understanding and more importantly helpful, for he gave us the address to a sort of hotel cum guest house that he owned, in a place many kilometres away, which was run by one of his family.

The next morning we were up at the crack of dawn and after a specially prepared breakfast by the hotel, we were once again, on the road and on our way.

After such a bad start to the holiday, I knew now, more than ever before that I had to make "doubly" sure Harry enjoyed himself and that even if I had to bend over backward, I would do so.

It was a good job as well, because as soon as we'd boarded the express bus, there was only one place he really wanted to try . . . yes, you've got it in one! . . . "Albufeira!".

Even though Louis, the manager of the hotel had been so kind, "Haz" still wanted to go there, so Albufeira it was.

Some two and a half hours later we arrived, tired, hungry and in Harry's case both bruised and slightly battered. It was dusty, busy and there were a million and one kids running all over the place, while we trudged along with our case and hand luggage. We'd only walked about thirty yards towards the town centre when he said, "What d'ya reckon Basc?", I just looked at him with dust on his glasses and shoes, his shirt opened up and the obvious displeasure in his face, fully aware of the fact that I knew what he wanted me to say. It was only then, that I realised just how much that kind "oldish" man was relying on me and it felt good, so I replied in the most fitting manner I could, "Not much, what about you?", which automatically brought contagious fits of laughter out of him, that started me off.

There we were, thirty yards at the most from the main bus station, we'd travelled since seven o'clock that morning, we'd been up since a half past five, we'd only just got off one bus and there were no more moving for another couple of hours at the earliest. It was time for a "board meeting", so we ordered coffee at a bar and discussed our next plan of action, although to me there really wasn't that much to debate.

Whilst I was ready and prepared to trust the guidance of the hotel manager, Harry in his older age wasn't, he was more suspicious than I, but realising that I had to take full control, I decided that we should find out exactly where this place was, then "go for it".

At five o'clock that afternoon we were dropped off the bus, at a hotel just outside the town, the town of Armacao de Pera, the hotel stood at the bottom of a steep hill and following the directions of the reception staff, we started our ascent.

By now we were both absolutely "shagged", we'd already got a sun-tan, lost pints of sweat, plus pounds of fat and desperately needed a bed, even I was having second thoughts, believing we'd been conned, when we suddenly found ourselves stood outside the place.

It was absolutely beautiful, the most enormous villa I'd ever seen, all newly constructed, but perfectly presented, with well looked after gardens at the front and side. The area it was situated in, was without doubt, probably one of, if not the classiest place on the Algarve, but that was nothing compared to our next surprise . .

Having rang the bell at the rather impressive front entrance, we were greeted by this quite attractive lady, who possessed the most innocent, warm aura imaginable, one that very few people have. In fact she probably would be the closest to Jeannette in terms of innocence and kindness and her name was "Ludy", Ludy Morgado, who with her friend Terressa made everything right from the very start.

From the minute she greeted me with a warm smile and a twinkle in her eye, I knew I'd done the right thing in taking us there, even though Harry still had his own doubts, but even he had to change his mind when he discovered our own tea pot, cups and saucers in the room.

This meant that he could enjoy his water biscuits in the plushiest surroundings possible, even though we did nearly get our heads beaten to a pulp in our search for a filament in the "cause of a brew".

For two weeks we were treated like Kings, with the two ladies catering for our every need, full, fresh, well cooked English breakfast each morning, our own proper English tea, provided in a nice matching service whenever we required a pot, they even offered to wash and iron the few clothes I had taken with me.

It was everything, "No more", than I could have ever wished for on my first trip and so I left them both as good friends, with the promise that I'd be back in the not to distant future.

The journey home on the plane gave me time to take stock, not just of the holiday, but of my life, I was dying to see my wife and Jeannette again, looking forward to my A.A, but more glad to be taking Harry home in one piece than anything else.

I felt quite proud of myself as I sat there watching him thumb through the duty free brochure, working out how much money he had left and what presents he was going to buy with it, he had a list already prepared, but despite the fact that the whole trip had hardly cost him anything, I knew that he was still struggling to "make ends meet", to cover everyone in his family. Yet again, the soft touch I was, I couldn't even say "No", or ignore the fact, so I gave him some of my money, whilst at the same time having a toast, me with orange, him with lager, "Cheers 'Haz', thanks for being a good mate and travelling partner".

We eventually got home carrying an abundance of presents and tall stories of our experiences, with him proclaiming me a hero and I my respect for the dear "oldish?" man, who I was proud to call my father in law.

Once home, it was back to reality, the sadness I was still causing my loving wife, the joy and happiness I was bringing my good friend Jeannette, my devotion to sobriety and Alcoholics Anonymous, then finally those other incidentals of life, my now greatly receded debt mountain from my drinking, the work which enabled me to pay it off and the major problem in that area . . . "People".

I came back "full of the joys of spring", felt proud at my achievements, I was coping with my problems quite well and life was looking good, however, whenever I felt so good, someone or something usually came along to "spoil the show", which is exactly what happened.

My second Christmas had passed without any real problems, as I learnt from my first one by keeping away from everyone, my twenty ninth birthday had gone as did my other birthday, sober, "without any self recognition" and I was ready for another holiday.

Remembering Jean's words the last time she came home from her own trip, I impulsively decided to go within a couple of days, by getting a cheap last minute seat, only this time "go alone".
I came home on the Friday evening as usual with her housekeeping and the "What I thought", would be my unimportant, uninteresting announcement, "By the way Jean, I'm going back to Portugal on Sunday", for a brief moment or two, not a sound could be heard, then she started, "You're joking aren't you?, you only just came back before Christmas!".

It erupted into one hell of a row, with her accusing me of being selfish, I told her she didn't understand, then she told me I didn't care about her or the two dogs, oh, it went on and on, she finally ended her long outburst with the best statement or question of the lot, "What about me?, I've not had a holiday with you in ages!".

Instead of calming matters the A.A way, I, with my big inconsiderable gob said, "Well, it's only for a week, it's not two, like the last time and anyway, you told me that you didn't want to go away with me again!". Well that was like pouring petrol, instead of water onto a raging fire, so she had another go, by which time even the two dogs had pissed off out of the way and into the garden.

At this point in the proceedings, my practising of the A.A programme was totally non existent, gone was any possible, remote chance of me rationally reasoning with her, so I became "Mr Hyde" again, only "dry" without drink, which is where most of the difficulties and self made problems come with sobriety.

Even without drink I could frighten that poor woman, I didn't have to rant or rave, just the swift change of personality was enough and so once again I stormed off leaving her with this parting statement, "Oh I see, it's alright to take your Dad, but it's different if I go on my own". This was a much more common scenario or picture of life at home by this time, one which was very sad indeed, particularly as we were still together after being through so much, but we neither had the knowledge, courage or deep seated desire to change it, so off I went to the surprise of everyone, especially Ludy and Terri.

My appearance was greeted with love, emotion and gratitude, as they hugged me tightly "Paul, you came back, we didn't think we'd see you again", it was as if

I'd known them all my life, but I hadn't seen them for years. "Why didn't you phone or write and let us know you were coming?, we thought you were like all the other English people and that you were all talk".

That greeting lasted all of a couple of hours, as they asked me how Jeannette was, how Harry was doing, all about myself and the business, I had to find out about them too, their families and the friends I'd made on my previous trip. By the time we'd finished comparing notes I knew in my own mind that Ludy, Terri and the Casa Bela Moura were going to be seeing much more of me.

Rather similarly to the trip with Harry, I was their only guest in the villa, it had room for another thirty people, but once again I was alone, which enabled me to find out even more about the house, the town, it's people, in fact the whole history of the place and as a result I had the great pleasure of meeting one of the kindest men I've ever come across.

The man in question was tall, well built, quite athletic looking despite his obvious age, he had short silvery crew cut hair, wore an old military trench coat over a lumber jacket and constantly donned a leather money satchel around his waist.

Each evening he would mysteriously come into the villa, use the phone then leave, bidding us a good evening as he did, he resembled some sort of "Eastern Block" hardliner, so Harry and I had already nicknamed him the "Hungarian Rhapsody", from our earlier visit, but I'd never got the chance to actually speak to the man.

I personally found him a fascinating character from the minute I first set eyes on him, mainly because of the strangest atmosphere that filled the room with his presence, so I was determined to "at least "get on nodding terms with him before I left, this time.

By the time my week there was over, I'd become spiritually attached to the place, my friendship with Terri and Ludy and many others had grown, I'd made even more new Portuguese friends and even got on acknowledging terms with the mystery man himself, "Senor Salvador Garcia", all of which once again told me "I'll be back soon!".

Whilst I'd been away Jean had obviously made up her own mind that she wasn't prepared to carry on in the manner we had been doing and promptly decided to tell me upon my arrival home, "Look Paul, I think it would be best if we had a temporary separation, I think it'll do us both good". In total agreement, thinking it would be best for all, I moved out and for the first time as an adult, went back to my Mothers and Fathers.

It wasn't far, only around the corner, but it was enough to give us both the time and space we needed apart, in an effort to see if there was still anything worth rebuilding on.

It was very difficult returning home, especially at the age of twenty nine years old, but my Mother and Father were once again there when I needed them both, only this time I was sober !

I felt strange and confused, even in the very same house I was brought up in, with all it's memories, good or bad, happy and sad, silly things that one never forgets, like putting a shilling in the meter in the dark, or the bathroom with "cold water only" in the early hours.

My Dad hadn't changed all that much either, he was still opening my mail, then apologising after, saying it was a mistake and bringing me tea and toast to make sure I was up.

Joyce, God bless her, hadn't altered either, as she tried her best to make me feel "at home "and as comfortable as possible, whilst at the same time being distressed to realise that yet another of her flock weren't entirely happy with life.

After a couple of weeks they'd hardly seen me at "Forber "and Jean hadn't seen me at all, as I was either at A.A or with my ever closer friend, Jeannette, so lots of questions such as " What does he do?, where does he go?, how does he spend his time?" were being asked.

I thought I was coping quite well with everything that was going on in my life, "Alright, so what!, I'm temporarily separated from my wife, the waste paper and cardboard's slack and I'm torn between two women, so, big deal!, I can handle it!".

The fact that I wasn't even thinking of a drink, never mind taking one, helped me to believe I was okay and that I was doing fine, but it just goes to show how wrong you can be, especially about oneself.

That Friday night I went to a usual group therapy meeting at Withington Psychiatric unit, where I was later accosted by the staff nurse,

"Paul, have you got a minute?".

I followed her into the office, where she asked me how I was feeling,

I was quite surprised really, because I never saw much cause to ask for help or waste their valuable time, as I thought others did enough of that. Anyway I thanked her for caring and asking, honestly believing that I was alright and made my way to Jeannettes' from the hospital.

However it wasn't until the next morning, that I first realised the staff at the hospital had far more awareness than I gave them credit for, because I ended up feeling really poorly.

It lasted all weekend and so on the Monday morning I headed straight for the Doctors surgery, feeling really "shitty".

My G.P informed me that I had contracted "Shingles", saying that it was a stress/

nervous related illness, which usually affected older people. The physical symptoms left me within a matter of weeks, however the real "root cause" to the problem, my nerve ends, suffered for over eighteen months, a period of time which brought many changes to my life and with it a whole new meaning.

In the April, Jean left a message at my Mothers, asking me to call round to see her, so I obliged and when I did, I got quite a surprise. Walking up the path of my own home, for the first time in ages, was an "eery" experience, one which certainly didn't do my nerves any good at all, but actually sitting in the place, having to face Jean was ten times worse. It seemed as though I loved her, felt guilty and sorry for her, yet at the same time I didn't really like the person sat opposite me. At the end of an hour's discussion, she'd told me that she wanted me back, she missed me, so did the dogs and that the house wasn't the same without me. I had to admit that, yes, I'd missed my own home, her and the animals, I missed my "home comforts" and most of all, my privacy, so I went back home, believing that I owed it to her, more than myself to try again.

After a week the discomfort and pain within my head was unbearable, I both loved and hated her, I loved her cooking, then all of a sudden, after all those years, I couldn't stand it. When I was at home, I wanted to be with Jeannette, yet whilst I was in Jeannette's company I'd be soaked in guilt, wondering what my wife was thinking, or whether she was hurting, it seemed as though I was constantly "torn between the devil and the deep blue sea", once again a misfit in society, not knowing where I should, or even wanted to be.

A couple of days later, I couldn't take any more. No, I didn't drink!, I didn't even think about one, but I experienced the being "lost and lonely" feelings that I'd done in my other life. I recalled all the good, wise advice I'd been given in A.A, "Don't make any important decisions and don't get involved in any new relationships", I sat there remembering the many experiences I'd heard shared in the hundreds of meetings I'd been to, of how people had their downfalls, hitting the bottle after taking "God's Will" back in their own hands and I was scared, "No terrified!".

Rather amazingly, I wasn't scared of drinking, it was more the consequences of my actions, the trouble, the tears and the pain that I was saddling on those around me, who actually cared.

At one point I remember thinking, "Well, I still manage to wreck peoples lives, sober!", the question was "Where do I go from here?".

After much to-ing and fro-ing with my conscience whilst my wife was at work, the bin liner was once again packed and I made off for my good, close friend Jeannettes'.

As usual she greeted me with a hug, kiss and a smile, but immediately realised that there was something wrong, "What's up?, you look worried to death", so I told her my bin liner was in the van, "I can't stand it at home any longer and I don't want to go pestering my Mum and Dad again, I just haven't got a clue what I want to do, or where I can go, I'm so confused".

I was really asking her, in a sly, crafty sort of a way, if I could lodge at her place, but she automatically put that thinking at bay, when straight off the bat, she said "Well you can't stop here, you must go back to Gorton and sort all your problems out, even if I wanted you to, I don't have a spare bed".

Reluctantly I returned home to our house at Sutton Road in Gorton, it was about ten o'clock in the evening and Jean had already realised my clothes had gone, but even despite all the uncertainty surrounding me and my actions, she still had a caring compassion for me.

"Oh Paul luv, where've you been?, what's wrong luv?, talk to me".

Once again, I couldn't "come totally clean "with my views, opinions, feelings and emotions, I just skated over the surface of them, saying I needed time.

I think she asked me if there was another woman, but I wasn't even capable of admitting that, despite the fact that Jeannette and I still hadn't made love.

What a position I found myself in, lovemaking had been a thing of the past for so long, but all of a sudden my wife wanted to "do it".

In the most unnatural of circumstances I lay there as she "writhed and thrutched" on top of me, then changed position, as if it was several years earlier when we'd first met. I just couldn't believe it, especially after the few pathetic love making sessions we'd had over the last few years, which ended up with her interrupting my ejaculation with some sort of statement like, "Would you like a lemon meringue making for tea tomorrow ?", or the times I was coming, having sweat buckets on top of her, obviously in a world of my own, only for the woman to say,

"Eh, have you seen that crack in the ceiling?". The saddest and most embarrassing level that we'd sank to in relation to sex, were the many times I had to pester her to make love, only to be told "Oh bloody ell, you can have a backward one then, but don't take all night!!", yet there we were, like a couple of newly weds on their first night.

Unfortunately for me, her interest, activity and keenness were all far too late, because just for once it was me pretending to enjoy it, even though I felt sick in the pit of my stomach.

Perhaps the most disgusting thing of all, was the love bite she gave me on the neck, something else she'd never done before in our relationship, which accompanied by her "false" sexual moans and groans of pleasure made me for once, feel used, abused and even sort of "raped".

The morning after I felt sick, as I looked in the bathroom mirror to discover the results of her false passion and the state of my neck, realising that there was now a real chance that once Jeannette saw me, she may finally call it a day.

I feared then I would be left having to try and make something of my relationship with Jean, despite the fact that, I may have found out who I really loved "a little too late".

Due to the fact that I was so busy, I didn't get to see Jeannette until the evening, but that only made matters worse for me, as I had all day to wallow in the dustbin of my own head and fester.

All day I relived the happiness that she'd already brought me, the special feelings she always seemed to leave me with and the joy of looking forward to seeing her each "next time", in our string of rendezvouses, but not on this occasion, as I felt terribly guilty in the belief that I'd let her down.

I walked in and tried to speak to her, but couldn't, instead I just pitifully cried and sobbed as I seemingly pleaded with her, "Look, look what she's done to me, Jeannette!". The genuine, understanding person she was, she just put her arms around me in comfort, "Eh come on now, come on luv, calm down".

Eventually I did and having done so explained all the horrible, gory and sordid details to her, where by in her own loving example she showed empathy and understanding, the likes of which I'd never ever seen before, not even in A.A.

It took me a good couple of days to get over the whole sad experience, perhaps three, when the marks had eventually disappeared, but once they'd gone I had no hesitation whatsoever in booking a flight to Portugal and going back over to the Casa Bela Moura, for yet another weeks holiday, to escape.

It was the same old routine, a Saturday afternoon, I was fed up, working my bollocks off to keep afloat in the paper game and I wanted some sunshine, so I called up my regular seat only contact and booked a flight.

As on each previous occasion, I asked Jeannette if she'd come with me, but the answer once again was " No", so the day after, off I went for a week, alone, in the sunny Algarve, to get away from it all.

It worked a treat, as the break did me good, it gave me the chance to see my friends in Portugal, got me away from my problems in England and made me finally realise, once and for all, that my marriage was well and truly over, futher more I didn't mind and realised that I had much more to look forward to.

For the first time in well over a couple of years, I felt there was clarity in both my mind and soul, I knew where my heart belonged, I believed I was capable of facing the truth and more importantly not afraid to be "alone", so I returned home, yet again, quite "a different Paul".

It was a bloody good job too, because three days later Jean suddenly gave me the ultimatum, "I've had enough now, all of these stupid bloody trips to Portugal, I think you've got a woman over there, is it that Ludy or whatever she's called?", well I just laughed because Harry had obviously put two and two together and come out with five, so at my sarcastic best I responded, "It's a bloody long way to go for a leg over and expensive too!". Within seconds there was a "good old blazing row" going on which eventually ended with Jean once again, as if she was at work, laying down the law, "The next time you go back to Portugal we're finished, I mean it, because when you come back, I'll be gone and I'm not joking either!".

It was a surprising statement for her to make, especially as she knew me better than anyone else, whether I was drunk or sober. The fact that she even thought to goad or tempt me was astonishing, for I like most other alcoholics, will always rebel no matter who, what or where and this occasion was no exception, so on the 31st May I went back to the Algarve, only this time it was different.

As a result of my wife's threats, I made sure that I gave her good notice of my intentions, so, some four days after her ultimatum and three days before my departure I told her, "Listen, d'ya know what you were saying at weekend about my flying about?", she then looked at me with a keen, interested, but questionable eye "Yes", then I came out with it, "Well I'm going back on Sunday".

In the whole time that we'd been together, I don't think I'd ever seen her as mad, "Well you'd better decide what furniture you want, because like I said, you go again and I'll not be here when you return", but once again I rose to the bait, "Look you don't need to go, I'll move and you can have everything", she responded by saying the house had too many sad memories for her, even though we hadn't been there all that long, which was my cue to play "mister hero", "Look you've had enough shit over the last few years because of me, you keep the lot then we'll be even and I won't have to worry about you struggling with a move".

Seconds later it was "deflated ego time "again and who better to do it than my loving wife, "Ha!, you, worry about me, where've you been for the last six or seven years when I needed you?", then she moved towards her handbag, pulled out some estate agents papers and threw them on the coffee table, "I don't need this place, I've already got my own, so I suggest you make a list of the furniture you want, I'll have a look at it and we'll sort something out".

One of my biggest problems was that I always had to have the last say in matters, so in predictable style I left Jean with one final parting statement "Look!, it would make me feel much better if you had the lot, I don't need any of this anyway, so you have it, just leave me one phone and the video and I'll be happy because I can get a telly".

We didn't speak again, in fact we hardly saw each other, but in the early hours of the Sunday morning before my departure, despite believing every word she'd said, I really thought that she would at least get up to say "goodbye", after all, it was for the very last time.

"Not on your life!", not even a murmur, so once again I left for the airport, only this time with just a slight tinge of sadness and a tear in my eye, thinking we'd come to such a sad state of affairs, where we couldn't even say "Goodbye!".

I arrived at the Casa Bela Moura some seven hours later, but what a shock I got, for gone were Terri and Ludy, as a new manager had taken over in their place. The man concerned opened the door, then cuddled and embraced me, like some long, lost relative, "Ah mon dieu, mon dieu!, Pablo!", yes, it was none other than Senor Salvador Garcia, the "Hungarian Rhapsody", who didn't speak a word of English.

After several trips and the fact that I spoke Spanish, my Portuguese was now quite good, so he explained how relieved he was to see me, especially as he was running the place on his own, his cleaning staff and chamber maids only spoke their own tongue and to top it all, he was expecting a party of English tourists any minute.

I couldn't have wished for a better form of therapy to help me try and forget about my own problems, because from the very start, right through to the very end of that trip, it was nothing short of a "laugh a minute", hectic !, but a "laugh a minute!".

From the minute his first guests arrived, it was something like "Faulty Towers", as the silver haired, silver tongued, wise old man and I became like Father and son.

I couldn't stand Southerners, I always found them big-headed, loud mouthed and false, the nice part was that Salvador felt in exactly the same way, but he had his own way of dealing with them, one which I marvelled at the sight of.

Due to the fact that Mr Garcia couldn't speak any English, our only form of communication came via my quite good Spanish and "pigeon" Portuguese, consequently, as a result of my already dark tan from two weeks earlier, they didn't have a clue that I was English.

Being able to understand every word they spoke, whilst at the same time enjoying the pleasure of being "a fly on the wall" was an amazing experience, but sometimes in many instances, one doesn't need to comprehend the language or fully understand what a person is saying or thinking, as their rudeness, generally says it for them.

A flash of the eyes, a click of the fingers or a raising and wave of the arm was the "norm", but "Sal" was having none of that. The "cagey" old bugger would leave them all waiting at the bar, gasping for a drink, whilst he sat in front of them, watching the football on the television, quite often telling them to be quiet if they were making a noise. Another favourite trick of his, was to give them the wrong drinks on purpose, forcing them to have something they didn't initially want. Despite the man's age, he looked well and much younger than his actual years, he certainly had a twinkle in his eye for the ladies and used it to the best of his ability, by getting the odd bit of "bust or arse" off his female guests, but once again to me, it was yet another way of him getting his own back, on their pig ignorant, cocky men.

However his "piece de la resistance" over the whole week came one evening, when he invited all the guests down for dinner as a "thank you?" for their custom.

It was to be a typically Portuguese night, with a menu to match and it was definitely that, the only major problem was that if they didn't like fish . . . then it was tough luck!

In the morning, of the day in question, Salvador took me to the main fish market town of Portimao, where he purchased heaps of the poorest, tattiest, cheapest fish available from the fisherman, all of whom he knew. Then we strolled through the town centre itself, rooting in a whole variety of shops, as he bought some of the craziest, weirdest junk imaginable, things that only an eccentric would purchase, yet everywhere we went he was greeted with warmth, appreciation and respect. That observation prompted me to ask myself "Why is he so well known?, even important, what's so special about this man?, who is he?", which then set my inquisitive nature off, making me start to think and want to know.

Having returned back to the Casa Bela Moura, he explained that it was his intention to cook dinner for his guests and give them one hell of a night to remember, one they'd never forget.

For two hours he prepared the dishes, then they cooked for another three and by the time it had got to seven o'clock in the evening, all was ready.

The guests filtered down, all looking at their bests, a couple had even gone to the extreme length of wearing dinner jackets, but that just about summed up what they were like, in fact some of the women had gone to so much trouble, you'd have thought they were going to a ball or a banquet, never mind "dinner in!". Even though I say it myself, the hours of work we'd both put in, were all worth it, for the setting looked absolutely lovely, as the candles flickered in the dimly lit room, giving a romantic touch and feel to the whole place.

As each couple appeared they gave testimony to the fact, by coming out with something like "Ooh doesn't this look wonderful!", or "I can't wait to eat, if this is anything to go by!", whilst still totally unaware of the fact that I understood everything they were saying.

As soon as everybody was seated, I served drinks in my usual waiter stroke barman style, amidst a setting that resembled a Cointreau or Nescafe advert, whilst the visitors carried on being "millionaires for the day" as they waited for "Salvador's speciality".

At seven thirty it was soup time, so the "old man" poured, whilst I waited on, then the "bullshit" started.

"Oh darling, this looks wonderful!" one woman said, then another chipped in with her "ten penny's worth" These Portuguese people certainly know how to put a show on and make you feel good". Then it was the men's turn, "the golfing type", syndrome, "This should be good Charles, smells jolly smashing!", then ponsey Charles had a go himself, "Yes, fish soup old chap, I'll enjoy this!".

Once the bread was being "dunked "and the spoons were going "plate to gob", Salvador and I returned to the kitchen for our own starter, which was slightly different to their's, I must say.

Every now and then the "old man" went out to check his guests were all okay and enjoying themselves, as if to gain reassurance, they were!! and so after nearly half an hour the first course had all but gone.

Once again it was drinks time, so whilst I did the honours and tried not to laugh, as I listened to their "Oh it was gorgeous thank you's",

"Sal" put the finishing touches to their main course, which was a local delicacy, an extravaganza of "la cuisine", which by way of a change was . . . "Fish!".

Yet again, the noise of cutlery could be heard, above the noise of their horrible Southern accents, as they bullshitted and sometimes joked about the lovely meal they were devouring and the service being given.

The more "free wine" they gulped, the worse they became and within minutes, the tall stories were getting even bigger, as each one of them bettered the others job, career or profession.

By the time they'd got onto the third and final course, which incidently wasn't fish related, you couldn't breathe properly, for the bullshit flying around, which only brought "Sal" and I to tears, as I translated the, on going crap being talked in the lounge and he gesticulated, doing his own sarcastic impression of them all in response.

Once they'd finished the desert, followed by coffee, Salvador and I appeared to a rapturous round of applause and in a typically pathetic English tourist manner . . . "Three cheers, hip hip, hooray!".

We loved it, every minute of it, the ladies kissed us both and the men shook our hands, all still totally oblivious to the fact that I was in fact, one of them, then one of the big gobs, came out with the line "Sal" had been waiting all night to hear,

"Pablo, drinks all around!".

Doing my best imitation of "Manuel" I obliged, "Si Senor", making him point to each drink he required, whilst still trying to keep my own face straight.

Once the pigs were fed and continuing to be watered, we then had the task of cleaning up the pots and dishes in the kitchen, but it wasn't that easy, for we were both doubled up in hysterics, listening to them all going on, as our dirty deed had not yet been discovered, although it was only a brief matter of time and like two mischievous kids, we couldn't wait!

You see, for all our effort, time and presentation, plus their attempt at being "posh", pretending to be something they certainly weren't, it was a huge prank, a joke played by the silver fox himself, because I personally, couldn't have touched some of that fish and I've roughed it! In some cases it was the dregs of a trawler, stuff right from the bottom, crap that you wouldn't even give to the sharks.

That was nothing!, the wine they were gulping down by the barrel was some of the best Algarvian shite available, which I wouldn't have touched in my worst drinking state. All of which prompted Salvador to stand up and imitate a chain pulling action, where he pointed to his watch and said "Pablo, a tres hora, cuidado y escuchar!". Which basically translated means "Paul at three o'clock in the morning, watch out and listen!".

The man was spot on, for between two thirty and six o'clock there was chaos, as the noise of people moaning and groaning in pain, rang out all over the villa, some coughing, others being sick all to the accompaniment of toilet cistern's being flushed. Salvador said they'd have the shits and boy did they, although never in my wildest dreams did I expect such a phenomenal reaction, he didn't leave it at that either, for the next day he rubbed salt into their wounds by charging them for the wine, which had done most of the damage.

We carried on with the facade of me being Portuguese until the very last night, which coincidentally was there's too, I'd heard and seen enough that week to last me a lifetime, as I pampered to their every need, all in the name of fun, so I decided that "now" it was my turn to have a say and once again at their expense.

With their suitcases at the front door, they all ferried in for a last drink and to pay their bar bills, which proved one hell of a shock to each couple, for these "well to do" people, who had spent the last week bragging, about what they'd got and who they were, now found themselves having to "copper up". It was hilarious, listening to it and watching them in such an embarrassing situation, they were really all skint, desperate and panicking, until the only real "class" one amongst them all, came in to bail them out, after which he ordered drinks for everyone.

As I prepared the enormous order, I realised that it was going to be my very last opportunity to "screw" the ignorant bastards, so I gave them the shortest measures they'd ever seen in their lives, hoping that they'd "shoot off" with their big cockney mouths.

Well!, they didn't let me down, because no sooner had I taken their last escudos from them, when I heard someone say, "It's no wonder we've got no money left if he's been giving us measures like this all week, they must be rolling in it here, I wont be coming back!", I let the others agree and voice their own displeasure, before I finally dropped my bombshell of advice for them, "Do you know, I've listened to you lot going on all week, about what you've got, who you are and where you all come from, you've constantly treated the "old man's" efforts with sarcasm and arrogance, all of which makes me feel ashamed to be English".

At that moment you could have heard a pin drop in that bar, as they all sat and stood there gob-smacked, so whilst I had their attention and I was on a roll, I thought I'd really go for it and make their day.

"You're the biggest bunch of bullshitting wankers I've ever clapped eyes on! and as far as your women are concerned, both me and the old fella could have poked any one of them if we'd wanted, because you're all so fucking boring and they're a bunch of slags".

Whilst I gave my speech, Salvador just stood there, nodding his head in agreement and acknowledgment, as I'd already told him what I was going to say, having done so, they all made a quick, sharp exit, rowing amongst themselves, leaving us two with a true friendship, forever sealed and much to muse over, which we happily did.

I returned the next day with many of the mysteries and questions I'd previously had, answered, I'd discovered that Salvador was in fact a retired professional soccer referee, which meant that he was quite a celebrity and man of importance, especially as football played such an important part of their lives. I also discovered that he was quite wealthy as a result, that he did actually own the Casa Bela Moura alongside a second home in Estoril, where his wife lived.

Then there was the mystery of "La Baraca", the little white hut at the back of the villa, where he lived with his dog, "Pega", in preference to the luxury of Bela Moura. That little hut had always fascinated me, just as much as him living in it, with no electric or water, so on this trip, in view of our new found bond, I asked if I could see inside the place and I wasn't disappointed.

It was the real "hermits hideout" I'd always thought, only it's contents took my breath away on that first viewing, for it was any true football historian's dream, "a real aladin's cave", which boasted a collection of the most prized memorabilia anyone could ever wish to own.

There were countless framed pictures of the man himself in the company of various "greats", such as Pele, Eusabio, Puskas even De Stefano, all taken in different stadiums and assorted matches.

Lying all over the place were souvenirs, such as shirts and pennants, all from the great matches and occasions he'd been part of, then there were the trophies and medals he'd won, over what was obviously a long established and successful career.

Yet despite all that success, he was such an unassuming, generous, caring man, all of which left me saying, "If only I could be so humble in life".

Once again the flight home gave me the opportunity to look back and reminisce, whilst at the same time prepare for the always uncertain future. On the one hand I was sad to leave my new, close and genuine friend Salvador, yet pleased and looking forward to once again being with my good "lady friend" Jeannette. As ever, I was starved of my A.A and desperately looking forward to my meetings again, yet pensive, suspicious, wary and apprehensive of what might be awaiting me at home.

As I walked up the path to the front door, I felt really strange, I knew my wife wouldn't be there, but wondered how she'd left me, "Would there be a note, a card or something?, had she left me some flowers even, as a goodbye ?", I then realised how stupid it was of me to even think of such things, so I returned my thoughts to more realistic questions such as, "I wonder what she's taken?" or more to the point, "What's she left me ?".

I opened the door, walked in and immediately realised that she'd certainly not left me any plants, for gone were the full range of Marks's seconds and repair jobs from the hall. Already feeling a sort of emptiness, I turned back to look directly into the kitchen, which once again was empty, where, never mind plants, there wasn't even a knife and fork. By now I'd got the picture, so already prepared, I walked through into the living room to check and see if she'd left me my only two requests, the video and one of the many, new B.T phones we had.

At that point I thought "Surely even Jean can't be that hard?", so I tentatively pushed the door open, fully relieved to find a phone and video recorder sat in the corner.

In a crazy way, I sort of "patted myself on the back "as if to say "I told you so!", but stupidly I'd said it too soon, rather like "jumping the gun" a bit, for Jean definitely did have the "last laugh".

I'd been sat there for a few moments when I recalled a story I'd heard in A.A, where a member, who loved horse racing was sat watching the Grand National, his television then blew, so needless to say, he was angry, blew his own top and stormed down the road to buy a second hand set. The guy at the second hand shop said that he only had enough money for the stand, so in order to spend all his money, "thus take away the remotest chance of him going on the piss", he bought the stand, took it home and pretended to watch the race.

The action, as crazy as it sounds worked, for the man calmed down back to his normal sober self, from being a mad raging lunatic, without taking a drink, so with that in mind I went to plug the video in, "After all, at least I would have the flashing timer display". That's when I realised Jean had got the last laugh, for as I bent down, I discovered she'd even taken the plug off it, which automatically left me sad, not mad, thinking " Have I really hurt her so much?".

When life's like that, there's only one course of action to take, so without giving it a second thought, I picked up the phone to ring my sponsor. Even that action had a lesson in it for me, because it was only then, that I realised my wife had taken all the good, new phones, leaving me with the only old, crappy one.

Once my sponsor answered, I set off on one of my tantrums, cursing, swearing and basically just going on and on, with what we call in A.A "the poor me's", but being the wise knowledgeable chap he was, he just let me carry on until I stopped for breath or had a coronary.

In the end I stopped by choice, with the statement, "Well Colin, what d'ya think about that then?", rather naively expecting sympathy.

Fortunately Colin knew better and so he gave me a good dose of hard, honest truth, with the statement that carried quite a profound message to it. "You know Paul, do you not think she's trying to tell you something in a nice way?, quite politely in fact!".

In reply to his comments I said, "What do you mean?, she can't stand the sight of me!", his one word answer of "Exactly !!" said it all, he then asked me if I was alright, to which I replied "Yes", which led him onto his next piece of advice, when he told me to do the obvious and get my arse off to a meeting, before doing anything else. Without question, yet again, the countless years of A.A's experience and the members who'd walked the same path before me, had paid off, so without hesitation I made straight for a meeting to try and give something back, before I went to see Jeannette, the one person who I loved outside of the fellowship.

That kick up the arse couldn't have come at a better time in my life, for it served more than one purpose, especially as I'd just entered into my third year of sobriety. I was told by fellow members that "this is where real life begins chum" and they were right, for I could at last see with clear vision, the wreckage left, from the damage I caused to others with my drinking.

I knew from those experiences that my main attention and effort now had to be focused and directed at the three main and important things in my life, Sobriety, Jeannette and work. There was no questions on A.A and living sober, for that was always first, in fact a must, so the next item on the "sobriety" agenda was the "lady of my life".

For nearly two years we'd been really good friends, yet totally out of character for me we hadn't been to bed together, I'd spent literally hundreds, no thousands of hours fantasizing over her, even masturbating in the process, but never yet had the courage to make an intimate pass, for fear of rejection.

I can't speak for her, only myself, but whether the fact that I was now really well and truly single made any difference or not, I don't know, however by sheer coincidence and after much wanting, we made love for the very first time that week.

The numerous occasions I'd imagined unbuttoning her blouse and sliding my hand between her bra and breast, or daring to move my hand up her thigh, even kissing her in the most sensual and seductive way I could, were all fantasies about to come true, with me, at my finest hour, a bag of nerves. Throughout our whole courtship, from the very minute I first set eyes on her, I wondered, "Could she really be as sexy as she looks?". Well the answer was an emphatic "Yes!", but apart from that, there was one thing incredibly different about making love with this woman and it was simple. Unlike the hundreds of women before and the thousands of times I'd carried out the act of performing sex, this wasn't just a case of making up my score-card, for I really and truly loved the lady, in a way that I'd never loved anyone before, making it the most wonderful experience of my life . . "shared".

After so much agonising, apprehension even fear, it seemed the most natural thing in the world to do, meaning we'd finally lost the very worst of our inhibitions, which if you like, gave us the "green light" to go forward with our relationship.

Instinctively, I spent far more time at Jeannettes' than at my own house in Gorton, even though she had helped me with furnishings etc to start up a new home, but it wasn't long before I'd near enough moved in with her, apart from sleeping there. I'd never slept overnight for three reasons, one because she wouldn't let me, two because she had a young son and three, her very high morals were still in tact, despite the fact that she was associating with me, so each night cum early morning, I always returned home to sleep in my own bed.

I didn't mind the situation because just for once in my life, I hadn't placed the greatest of importance on sex, even though my character defects had always led me to crave warmth, touching and affectionate attention. I was still as dependant on touch as ever before, but there was always enough love in Jeannette anyway, to make up for staying alone at Gorton. It also served to give us our own independence, which was always handy, when we'd had a row, for I could always tear off in a rage, go home and sulk

By the time July had come, I'd enjoyed "a bit of a good run", my personal life and relationships had improved well beyond expectations, my sobriety was good and despite the quantities of cardboard available rapidly diminishing, I was doing okay in work too, so I knew something at some point had to give, for my God never seemed to allow me the luxury of good, sustained, balanced periods.

The answer came shortly after, with the "hick up" area being work and my lovely friends at Marks and Spencer in Macclesfield with problems, once again revolving around the "waste".

As I've briefly mentioned, the past twelve months had been a constant struggle on the cardboard, with the new company policies at Marks's biting hard into my profitability, the amount of good saleable cardboard was fast disappearing, so I ended up having to improvise to survive. Once again it was a case of me reluctantly having to draw on old resources, such as "fiddling" to make ends meet, but to do that I knew I would have to abuse the long standing, trust and friendship of the only friend I still had from my past.

Marvin Wood was a man who I'd first met nearly twelve years earlier, whilst I worked for Ted at Jeffries, he was a real "wide head", a well respected business man in the industry, who seemed to be quite a powerful character.

The man was a frequent visitor to the factory who often ended up rooting through cartons etc in the warehouse, despite the fact that he wore expensive suits and overcoats. Yet even though he had the power, presence and aura of a really important man, he always found time to come over, have a chat and be pleasant. The man was courteous and interested in whatever a person had to say, whether it was a managing director or a tea boy he was dealing with, all qualities which I immediately picked up on and never forgot.

The similarities between him, Ted and Ted's son in law, Roy, were uncanny, as if they were all "bred in the same stable" or went to the same "old school", so I suppose it's no surprise that with the sad death of Ted, I transferred my business to the company that he worked for.

The Davidson Group were and probably still are, one of the biggest "players" in the British waste paper industry, where they totally controlled the "local market" and consequently the "price".

Marvin was a "big wig" there, the "Marketing, Managing Director" and over the years we'd done some extraordinary deals outside of the "paper game". I was always just as entrepreneurial as he, brought up by my own Dad to believe "somebody always wants the rubbish others are throwing out", consequently with us both having the same train of thought and "ideas "on life, we struck up many good, sound, profitable deals, which in themselves gave us lots of pleasure, topped with plenty of laughs. It was a friendship that spanned years and which comprised of respect, trust, admiration and even love for the man on my part, as we swapped, bought, sold and more often than not, gave "freely" of ourselves to each other with many other "favours".

Sadly I had no other option available, which would bring a satisfactory answer or conclusion to my problems, so feeling both reluctant and guilty I preceded with my plan.

Instead of being in a position of the past, where I usually had two or three van loads of clean cardboard bales to weigh in, I found myself with two van loads of worthless rubbish, so I made a deal with the mill foreman, where by he'd upgrade my load, let me drive straight around the back, dump the crap in the companies rubbish skip, then weigh off again empty and disappear like "shit of a shovel".

A ton of good clean cardboard bales was worth about thirty pounds, but a van load of worthless rubbish bought me between thirty to one hundred and sixty pounds, depending on the grade one of the charge-hands gave me, so it was quite good business while it lasted.

The only thing that eased the pain of letting Marvin down, was the fact that the mill manager and his associate were "a pair of right pricks", who knew absolutely nothing about the industry and the people in it, they'd constantly harassed me since I'd started trading with the company, so I took great delight in "doing it" on them.

I know full well that Marvin was aware I fiddled a bit because in our book, it was all part of the "game", which typified the real genuine folk of the scrap industry, but the other two jerks didn't understand that and so despite the guilt of deceiving him, I carried on in typical rebellious style against their stupid "I'm in charge" attitude, which only added to the expenses of the company they "thought" they owned and were "saving".

Until now it had worked a treat, because even though there was the constant problem of getting rid of the rubbish, there was still the added bonus of the waste food, which did help considerably with the cost of living. However, even that was mysteriously cut back, which meant that I now had to do something, as I had done previously the last time this type of incident occurred.

Rather predictably it was my "wide boy" friend, the foreman of the store and yet again the food was going to the farmer, who'd had the contract before me. Only this time I learnt even more about the set up and the further connections between the farmer, his family, the store and another company, which did well out of the Macclesfield branch, who funnily enough were also related or connected in some way.

Whilst I'd been pulling my bollocks out over the last few years, the foreman had once again been constantly feeding the farmer with best, fresh produce, only not for his pigs, but for the family unit as a whole.

That was bad enough to swallow the first time around, however on this second occasion, a further discovery only served to make me feel ten times worse and fifty times more angry, for one of the most arrogant and ignorant men I'd ever met over the years of dealing with the store, was also involved in the scam, even though he already made a limitless "packet" out of the branch, a fact which he even had the cheek to openly brag about.

The man concerned, owned a family building business, which serviced three stores, Macclesfield, Stockport and Altrincham, I knew most of his staff, even his nephew, but what I didn't find out the last time I played "Inspector Clouseau" was that Jim, who owned Walters Brothers, was in fact the farmer's brother and that Ray the nephew who worked for him, was the same farmer's son.

Even with my track record, I don't think I'd ever felt so angry in my whole life, but more embarrassingly on the part of Marks and Spencer, as low and deceitful as I'd been, I never stooped to such a level and in such a sly, sneaky way.

There was only one thing for it, I had to go and see that horrible, little, insignificant manager, who I've never liked, inform him of the facts, then against my better judgement, trust him to act accordingly, in the hope that he may show me some loyalty in return.

Well, once again I have to quote my Mother, because Joyce always spoke of the honesty, open minded, loyalty, integrity and complete trust, that Marks's store managers had to have and do you know, on this occasion she was right!

Only twenty four hours after I'd been to see the man, everything had suddenly changed, there were literally dozens of trays, full to bursting with veg, meats, poultry, all sorts, there were even plants and flowers by the bag full, but there was only one problem . .

Just as I was about to load up the van, I was stopped by one of the warehousmen, "Oh no, they're not for you Paul, that lots for the nun's", I just stopped dead in the middle of my tracks, "Nuns, what nuns?", wearing a really cocky "pleased with himself" smile, he nodded his head as if to say over there. I couldn't believe it!, reversing up in a brand new car, as charitable organisations usually did, were two penguins, leaving me stood there totally shocked, embarrassed and gob-smacked. Once again good old Marks and Spencer had done it on me, only on this occasion I was struggling with tons of shit, knowing that my days of dealing with the store were now numbered, as it was quite obvious what the manager thought of my honesty!

By the time I'd got to Jeannette's I was in a really foul temper, but as always when I was upset, she calmed me down saying, "Don't worry, it'll be a 'one off', wait until Monday night, they wont be there then!", as if to reassure me she continued, "Look luv, the Nun's won't go like you, every night of the week, just on the off chance that they might get something".

Cum the Monday night they weren't there, which cheered me up no end, but unfortunately that joy was very short lived, as the numerous bags being brought out to the van, were systematically saturated in thick, dark blue dye. Though I'd never liked or trusted that manager, even I was shocked by his hurtful, petty and childish actions, I both knew and accepted the fact that he didn't like me, but never anticipated such a spiteful or vindictive reaction. I thought in terms of nastiness he'd done well, even by my own standards, but unknown to me at the time it was just the start of his own personal vendetta against me.

I felt angry, bitter, very resentful and wanted revenge, all commodities which any alcoholic intent on staying sober, can't afford to carry amongst the luggage in their head, but at the same time, I also knew that there was nothing I could do, other than accept his actions, so with Jeannette's love and the help and support of A.A, I got back down to the basics of life, by solving what problems I could, after all it was only food.

Once I'd sorted out that minor problem, it was rapidly replaced by another two or three altogether, only this time they were much closer to home and on a much more personal note, the first of which came in a loving letter from my own Mother.

My Father had been down at Harefield Hospital for a good six weeks, with Joyce there in support and they were supposed to have left Eddie and Carol in charge of the market, but whilst they were away there had been some sort of bust up, leaving them in a real mess.

At the time, thanks to good old Marks and Spencer, I found myself pulling my bollocks out just trying to survive, whilst at the same time also looking after their interest without them knowing. As if all that wasn't enough to cope with, my "quickie" divorce was due to be made final and Jeannette's son was giving her trouble, by kicking up a fuss, so I could well have done without, ill fated, bad timed letters from my Mother telling my how irresponsible I was. Whilst reading it I broke down in tears as I just couldn't belive my own eyes, for in her letter she also accused me of being immature, financially insecure and of having the wrong priorities in regard to my outlook on life. She couldn't understand why I'd neither contacted or enquired about my Dad or why I could never just sit down in silence and accept being told these things.

Unfortunately for her, little did she know just what effort I was putting in or how responsible I actually was being, but far worse than any of that, she rather profoundly praised Eddie for being mature and sensible as a direct result of him being married with a child and supporting his family on one wage, all of which made me feel utterly sick, especially as he was the last person in the world I wanted ramming down my throat. That letter hurt, especially as I already had a good idea where Eddie and Carol were eventually going to end up, as a consequence of their own drink problems, but it was nothing compared to the pain I felt on the 29th September . . . the day my divorce was made absolute.

For weeks I'd prepared for the day, yet despite the constant cries of "It's not easy" and "It's a painful experience", which came from Jeannette and my many friends in A.A, I still thought I knew better, "Oh give over, it's not that bad!". Sadly I was wrong, but thankfully I found myself in the good, caring company that I needed, because with that final "rubber stamp" came an emotion and feeling I'd long since forgotten . . "failure!".

What a crazy situation to find oneself in, there I was madly in love with probably the kindest, warmest, most caring person, one could ever wish to meet, yet I was ringing up the courts to see whether my wife had gone through with it, still in the hope of a "last minute reprieve".

A last minute reprieve for what I ask, more pain, more tears and more ever lasting sadness around, No!, I was asking to be "let off", admonished for making an enormous "cock up", a "balls of it", a real mess of something that started off as a beautiful thing, something which should have been a joyous adventure, which regrettably I turned into an unbelievable disaster of mega proportions and even worse, "I'd only just realised it!".

Once again with the love and support from both Jeannette and A.A, I came through yet another hurdle in my life, only this time with the briefest of respite for in the same month it was my turn to play "good Samaritan" . . . to my sister, Carol!

She'd been living down South for a good few years, which meant that we only ever saw each other when she came up here visiting, so I knew there was something seriously wrong when she returned home for good . . . "alone!". Because I'd never had all that much communication with my family, I knew very little of her circumstances and so putting the break up of the relationship down to normal matrimonial differences was my initial train of thought.

Carol moved in with me in the October, on the clear understanding that she covered the electric, gas and telephone bills as I was hardly ever there, plus she had a "free reign", which meant that she could go whenever she pleased. With regards to us both getting on well together, there was no problem, so just for once in my life, I actually had the opportunity to be of support to someone else, instead of me being on the receiving end. We were doing okay, apart from two slight problems, one, Carol smoked and two, she was quite scruffy in her sloppy attitude to housework, but considering I spent most of my time at Jeannettes', neither caused me too much concern.

As if to put the icing on the cake, Nicholas, Jeanette's twelve year old son decided he'd throw a tantrum or two, which was really the last thing I wanted at that moment in time. Most of his life had been spent alone with his Mum, which meant that he was quite a "spoilt and pampered" child, who constantly demanded attention, they were obviously very close, but in my opinion too close and so after a couple of years the inevitable happened, whereby he became both jealous and threatened by my presence.

Rather characteristically of myself, I'd given our friendship my "all" in terms of effort, with Nicholas receiving more than his fair share of attention, so when he did eventually "turn" having a "funny 'n'", I knew I'd done my best and that nobody else could have given more. Luckily, even though he meant everything in the world to her, Jeannette was honest enough to see straight through his behaviour, so we started off on yet another new course in our relationship, on what was already proving to be a bit of a journey.

One of the main reasons, despite my constant requests, that we hadn't, as yet been to Portugal together, was my reluctance to take Nicholas along on such a trip, for he was quite a moody, selfish and very manipulative child, with the latter of the three obviously being the one characteristic I despised more than any other. Over the past couple of years he'd pulled many fast strokes, in an effort to get his own way, all of which I'd considered "smart moves", so there wasn't any real love lost between us, especially as he'd tried it on with me. Consequently a difficult time was being had all around, as emotions, feelings and tempers were running at "high fever pitch", with each one of us, as individuals having to accommodate another person within our lives. It was hard for us all, but none more so than Jeannette, for it was now her turn to play "piggy in the middle" and so as a direct result and against my better judgement, I decided that if "the mountain won't come to Mohamed, then Mohamed must go to the mountain" by suggesting that we take our first trip to the Algarve . . . together.

The past five months had totally drained me and I was shattered, I also knew that Jeannette was, she had to be, especially after putting up with me, so with Carol at home and available to cover the job, there was no better time for me to go back to Portugal and so off we went, Jeannette, Nick and I, for our first holiday together.

Throughout our friendship, Jeannette herself, never mind my ex wife, had wondered why I had this fascination for the Casa Bela Moura and my friends on the Algarve, well after all of twelve months, seeing me coming and going like a yo yo, she was about to find out.

We sat there in her home, waiting for the taxi, armed with a full, brand new set of Gulliver suitcases, which I'd bought the night before, all packed, full to bursting. Jeannette as ever, looked beautiful, as she sat there posing for the first "snap" of the trip and I felt proud, proud that at last, after all her "giving" and my "taking", I was returning something back. She'd not travelled abroad much and not for a long time, so we were all looking forward to it, her and Nick the sheer excitement of it all and me the responsibility of taking care of them both, so with the arrival of the taxi, we all set off on yet another new adventure.

It was a good holiday, one which brought us even closer together, it gave us both the opportunity to learn even more about each other and more importantly the triangle we were part of, all of which enabled us to return home even more in love and inseparable than before we'd left the week earlier.

By the time mid December had arrived I needed yet another break, because I was doing near enough fourteen hours a day, constantly throwing two and three hundred bales around, as I tried to "keep my head above water". It was hard, painful work, but it had to be done, although it wasn't half as bad as the mental strain I was beginning to suffer through watching my sister Carol, slowly "go down" as she began to sink into a terrible mess of a young woman.

Due to the fact that over the past couple of months my visits home were very rare, I'd noticed the change and it wasn't nice, the house was a disgrace and she was just as bad, but I didn't know why?, so yet again I buggered off back to Portugal, to get away from it all, knowing full well that on my return home would bring Christmas and the end of what had proved to be a very difficult, trying year.

Chapter Eleven

Step Three – God's Will

Having gladly got '86 out of the way, 1987 started off with a real bang, which came in the shape of even more personal pain, as Carol once again was the cause, whilst I looked on as a recipient.

I'd gone home on one of my occasional visits to find the place resembling a bomb site, only to discover the yellow pages telephone directory left open at the "Hospitals" section, alongside an empty tablet bottle, so I instinctively pressed the redial button to find it connected through to the "Samaritans" number, which told me she'd probably attempted to take her own life. I immediately felt guilty, asking myself a million and one questions, "Why?, why has she done this?, why didn't I spend more time with her?", more importantly I couldn't understand why she couldn't even talk to me, knowing full well that I'd been through a similar crisis in my own life. There was a circle scribbled around the number of the Royal Infirmary and so having made a call to discover she was actually in casualty, I made my way there in the hope that I wasn't too late . . . too late to do anything at all, which could help my own lost and very lonely sister.

I arrived some twenty minutes later to discover her sat with a psychiatrist, who had been with her taking notes for over an hour, so I, in my most basic and tactless self, came out with my own piece of good, sound advice for Carol, whilst at the same time aired my views on where she should actually be. "I don't know what you're writing down Doctor, but you're wasting your time, because you'll not be able to do anything about her problems, until she's prepared and willing to do something herself", the Doctor looked confused, "I'm sorry, but who are you?", so I told her, which only prompted her to come out with a typical reaction, that only someone in my position would expect, "Look you may be her brother, but that doesn't mean that you know or understand what is wrong with your sister".

At that moment I decided that action was definitely going to be far better than words, so I threw my A.A book on the desk to shut the woman up once and for all, "That's why I understand Doctor, you see she's a 'piss pot' like me, only I'm sober and unless you're prepared to section her, then I can do far more for her than you can!". The Doctor agreed, so we left, I rang Jeannette up and with her permission made straight for Worsley to have a good long chat over a few cups of coffee.

By half past midnight Carol was in a real state, but I was no nearer getting the truth out of her than the Doctor at the Hospital was, she was just starting to feel the full effects of D.T's, so I knew from my own past experience that it was time. I knew she craved a drink, so I wasted no time, "You want a drink now Carol, don't ya?", a question which prompted the quickest response I'd had all night,

"Oh yeah, I could murder one, I'm sick of this coffee",

"Right then!" I replied, "I'll tell you what I'll do, I'll give you one of my drinks that I used to knock back, but it'll be the very last drink of booze I ever give you ok". There was never any question that she'd refuse my offer, so I poured her a full half pint of whisky into a tumbler, "There ya go!". Within a few seconds and after a few gulps, life and things generally had improved beyond compare, with the girl even breaking out into a smile,

"That's lovely our Paul, just what I needed, thanks Jeannette!". A quarter of an hour and half a glass later, she was a different lass altogether, who'd transformed herself from a weak, shivering wreck into a jolly, happy-go-lucky girl, who'd suddenly and miraculously adopted an "I couldn't care less attitude".

She was so funny that both Jeannette and I were in stitches laughing as we listened to her call everyone and everything under the sun, "He's a fuckin this and she's a fuckin that, Joyce and Dad are no fuckin better and what about our fuckin Eddie!". Not one person was spared her wrath, as she systematically ripped people to shreds with her anger, resentments and bitterness, all of which left Jeannette absolutely aghast as she'd never heard such language, with every alternate word being an F, C or B.

However by the time she'd finished the glass, Jeannette, God love her was shattered and more than ready for bed, whilst Carol was happy, pissed, but at least happy, so it was time for us to go and get her home to Gorton. Having sort of like "poured" her into the van, I said "goodnight" to my dearest lady and off we went, although we didn't get far because I needed petrol, so we called into a local garage some five minutes away, which in hindsight was a "good move".

As I opened the door to get out the cab-light automatically came on, enabling Carol to discover my numerous cassette tapes on the dashboard, which seemed to bring her back to life, "Can we have some music on Paul?", I didn't object, so I left her rummaging through whilst I filled up with juice, "No go ahead, put whatever you want on". I returned no more than five minutes later to find her absolutely heart broken in tears, of course I'd forgotten the one thing which is the scourge to all alcoholics . . . "death music", a time when most drunks wallow in their own shit, by listening to music of the past, a time to "get real", to reminisce. By the time we'd got home to Sutton Road she was unconscious, so we slept downstairs in armchairs, amongst the shittiest, dirtiest mess I'd ever seen, even in my own drinking days.

Carol fell asleep within seconds of sitting down, but not I, for I had a million and one thoughts, feelings and recollections to sort out, apart from helping my sister. I remember sitting there in the dark, with the gas fire on thinking "how at peace with herself and the world she seems", "I wonder if I ever looked so at ease", I muttered.

Sadly I also knew the discomfort and pain she'd feel in the early hours, once the effect of booze had worn off and that awful awakening which would bring with it guilt, shame, remorse and the begging for forgiveness. As I listened to her snoring, I recalled my own past experiences, whilst at the same time I counted my blessings, selfishly, but sadly thanking God that it was her and not me.

Then my train of thought took me to my family as a whole and the general mental sickness, which prevailed over all of us, such sadness, such despair and so much aggression. Once I'd covered that ground, my thoughts returned to me "Paul" and my own life, I looked out into the hall, then at Carol and the living room we were in, as the small light from the fire played tricks with shadows on the walls, thinking to myself "Yes Jean was right, this has been an unlucky, unhappy house".

Daylight brought the predictable four hideous horsemen we talk about in A.A and so I asked Carol if she wanted help, to which she replied "Yes!", so I drove her straight to Withington A.T.U, where they very kindly gave her a bed, in an effort to "dry her out".

Looking back I think that my staff nurse had more "my interests" at heart than Carol's, but it didn't matter because she did at least get admitted straight away, a procedure which normally took much longer, especially for new patients. In my own innocence, confusion and love for my sister, I immediately wanted to do anything and everything I could for her, even worse I actually believed that I would make a difference to her own outlook and that first real attempt at getting sober. But it was foolish of me to even contemplate such a thing, especially with my own sobriety and personal experience of the Unit, I already knew that I couldn't get anyone else sober, I also knew full well what the percentage rate for alcoholics going back drinking was, yet I still felt guilty when I shouldn't have, and continued to do all manner of other things despite knowing better.

I was Carol's only contact with the outside world and as such the only one entrusted with the secret of her exact circumstances, as it was yet another example of "what ever happens, don't let Joyce and Dad know", so I kept the whole occurrence "under wraps" whilst at the same time played, "Big, clever, sober brother" to my very inadequate sister.

In my own silly way, despite my self knowledge I was proud, proud to chair the A.A meeting held within the unit, one which all patients were forced to go to, I thought "Well, if Carol can't get it from me, she's no chance!".

On the 16th January, it was my thirtieth birthday, Carol needed some items of clothing and I needed to check the mail, so I returned home to find God had decided that in his eyes I didn't have enough to worry about. As I entered the house I discovered that there had been a burst, which had occurred in the loft, consequently an upstairs bedroom and the kitchen were both absolutely soaked in water, leaving me with yet another small headache and problem to sort out. For most other people whether alcoholic or not, the discovery of such devastation would have brought much despair, lots of discomfort and a whole host of other problems, apart from hard work. Not so in my case, for as I said earlier, with my wife's previous departure, went all the furniture we possessed, therefore apart from the decorating and structural damage, which were the responsibility of Suttons Estate, not too much was lost, so inadvertently there was an opportunity, a glimmer of hope that from such destruction, there maybe a chance of me giving Carol a whole new "fresh" start.

At the time the weather was very unpredictable, the insurance companies were snowed under with claims and so the loss adjusters were busy too, all circumstances which made it an ideal opportunity to make a strong well over the top claim and with the help of my good long time friend Norman Hill from Garner's Insurance Company that's just what I did. Norman and I went back a long way, in fact he even helped me track down where my ex wife had moved to, which meant that he was fully aware of my exact circumstances, so all that I had to do was follow his every guiding instruction.

Some two weeks later, Carol left the A.T.U with the staff still no nearer to finding anything out about her, as far as she was concerned she had no problems at all and her life on reflection wasn't all that bad, which left me with a "still very sick sister", plus a house that resembled a disaster area.

My original intention was to revamp the whole place whilst she was in hospital, but because the loss adjusters still hadn't been, I could do nothing to give her the "new beginning", I'd wrongly wanted to, mistakenly thinking that new surroundings may give her a better chance of recovery, so she returned home to find the very same depressing environment she'd left three weeks earlier.

Like most patients she left the Unit, thinking "I'm not that bad yet", but with a bit of gentle persuasion I managed to get her to A.A, however once she'd been to a couple of meetings I left her to her own devices and of course her own choice as to whether she carried on going.

Unfortunately as happens in most cases A.A was not for her, so she stopped going thinking she'd be alright and that it would be possible for her to stay sober without outside assistance, news which obviously saddened and disappointed me to say the least.

Knowing full well I had no other choice, I left Carol to sort herself out, in the everlasting hope that she may eventually see sense, however it wasn't to be and so in the first week of March I reluctantly had to ask her to leave.

The whole affair was sad, messy, even heart breaking as I stood there in the kitchen watching Linda, my older sister, help her leave with those most hated of travelling necessities . . . "bin liners".

In typical alcoholic fashion Carol was angry, bitter and resentful, believing I'd let her down badly, despite the fact that the place looked an absolute tip, there were Gin, Vodka and Bacardi bottles everywhere and no bills had been paid, leaving me "high 'n' dry" in arrears.

It was my own fault, for I should have known better, but funnily enough I wasn't angry with her, more at myself for being so gullible and stupid and for being "taken in".

Coincidently with Carol's departure came confirmation of a substantial settlement offer from the Insurance company, which allowed me to proceed with my originally intended plan, those of totally transforming the place.

For two weeks I worked incessantly, non stop around the clock, day night, mornings, in fact any time I could in-between collecting paper, meetings and my visits to Jeannettes'.

I wanted to wipe out any memories I had of the place, Carol, my ex wife, anything, so I set about re-decorating and painting every room, from top to bottom. Jeannette and others from A.A said "I would make myself ill", but at the time I was experiencing one of my "insomnia" periods, where I couldn't sleep, which meant I would have only been sat there festering in my own company as a result.

Two weeks after I'd started, at four o'clock in the morning my work was complete and the place looked absolutely beautiful, as well as unrecognisable from what was before. Each room bore snow white walls, all of which were surrounded by shiny, bright woodwork, brand new carpet graced the floor, with bright clean curtains, supplied by my own Jeannette rounding off each of the windows.

I sat drinking coffee in the living room, where it looked nicer than it had ever done before and I cried, for as nice as it looked, and as proud of the place as I was, I felt like a stranger on a brief visit, who wasn't intent on staying. Despite the work and effort I'd put in, I sat there thinking "Why have I done all this?, what is it all for?", then I once again recalled some of my many sad moments I'd had there, only to realise, "God, the pain of my past still lives here in these walls and nothing, whether it be paint, wallpaper, carpeting or anything else for that matter is going to get rid of it", so I did the only sensible and natural thing I could in such circumstances, which was to phone another A.A member to rid myself of the pain I was feeling.

With my project finished and me left knackered I once again decided to up and off to Portugal. I desperately wanted Jeannette to come in the hope that we could finally have some time alone together, but once again she refused to leave Nick, her son in the capable hands of her sister, so reluctantly I went alone.

I returned a week later, on the 8th March to discover that just for once the postman had been kind to me, as amongst the mail was a settlement cheque from the Insurance company for over six thousand pounds and so without hesitation I asked Jeannette if she'd like to get engaged.

She accepted my proposal and so on the 17th March we went arm in arm and totally in love to Preston's the Jewellers of Bolton, intending to spend about two hundred and eighty pounds on an engagement ring. We left having spent considerably more in what can only be described as my most unromantic and disappointing performance in our relationship, for rather unceremoniously, whilst sat in a dark, underground city centre car park I rounded the whole day off with these words "Ere ya are, you might as well wear it now as havit in the box", then "Come on, we'd better hurry up or you'll be late for work", all of which proved that I still had a lot to learn.

Four days later I was off, back to the Algarve and once again alone, I was basically pissed off with people, whose greed and selfishness did nothing for my own recovery, I despised the thoughtlessness I could see all around me and didn't want to be a part of it all.

In my own naivety and ignorance I stupidly thought it was me and that a week away may change my whole outlook, the head I carried and more importantly my own attitude to life seemed wrong, so I unknowingly tried to "escape", thinking things would be different on my return.

A week later they weren't, in fact they were ten times worse, only now it wasn't just I who was feeling a bit like a victim to society, as Jeannette herself started to experience problems with her job and the staff she employed, all of which just about finished me off.

It was a period of time in my life where it seemed everybody was "doing" it on either me or mine, as people, companies and policies from various directions all seemed to be doing their damnedest to chip away and destroy anything relating to me.

Earlier on in my story I spoke of a blonde piece that was a bit of a flirt, who I'd met on one of my drinking holidays, I said that although I'd only got a bit of tit and arse from the woman I wasn't too perturbed, as I could "follow it up" on my return home, well that's exactly what I did and as a consequence ended up taking food to the farm they owned in Astley for many a year after.

It had been a nice arrangement, for years I gave them Marks's waste, whether it was clean or soiled and in return they would allow me to stack my ever growing abundance of dirty contaminated bales on their land. Until now they had used the food to feed both the family and livestock on the farm, but due to the fact that most of my present waste was made "inedible" they got greedy and so a long friendship was sadly severed. Roy wanted more in return for his favour, so I suddenly found myself with the enormous problem of having nowhere to dump my vast amounts of rubbish, he ended up with a field full of useless bales and more friends had been lost due to Marks and Spencer's greed.

As if all that wasn't bad enough, Jeannette also found herself being messed about, only from two different angles, with her staff becoming both greedy and unreliable and the companies she'd worked for doing much the same. In a similar fashion to Marks and Spencer, both the standard and quantity of work she was being given was rapidly becoming less and less by the week, there were no "free samples" being delivered and the local free papers in the area, care of cheap "child labour" seemed to be doing the majority of the work she and other team owners should have been doing. Needless to say her income was rapidly shrinking, I was already struggling to make ends meet and things weren't looking good for either of us.

I've always believed that when a man's down, for God's sake don't kick him, but there have been many times in my life when I think God himself disagrees with that view and this was certainly one of them.

In desperation to solve my own problems, I made a deal with a "pig farmer", where by I supplied him with waste and he allowed me to store bales on a weekly basis, as long as they didn't mount up, it wasn't an ideal solution, but there again, "Beggars can't be choosers".

After a few weeks it suddenly occurred to me, just how much my own working lifestyle had changed and how in such a sort period of time I'd been driven to my present degradation.

Looking back it was sad and I don't say that with any self pity because it was, but even sadder was the fact that I didn't even realise it until the night Jeannette came with me, as I was working extra late and she witnessed it all for herself.

Being there and seeing it with her own eyes, only served to upset her, which became apparent as we left the farm having finished to drive home, "Oh Paul love, you can't go on like that, it's no wonder you need all these breaks away, you're going to be seriously ill if you're not careful". She was right and I knew it, but at that moment in time there was nothing I could do except carry on, even though my loyalty to Marks and Spencer was killing me both physically and mentally.

It meant that within a few weeks I was ready for yet another break, and so on the 26th April I was off again.

A week later I returned, with my passport by now looking like a used up ration book, displaying dozens of stamps on each and every page, it all payed testimony to my travels, but even so, there were more to come as I was innocently and unknowingly heading for a "breakdown", with my frequent visits to Portugal proving to be both an "escape" and a delay of the inevitable.

I arrived home on the 1st May feeling great, I'd topped up the by now, ever present tan, cleaned the head of every ounce of negativity and returned with numerous "self promises" and intentions, however as anyone reading this will know, "all roads to hell are paved with good intentions" and hell is exactly where I found myself blindly heading, for two days later whilst sat in Jeannette's house, I broke down in tears, weeping, "Oh luv, I feel so ill, what's wrong with me?, I wouldn't mind but I can't even say I want a drink, or I'm even thinking of one, I've just come back a few days ago and I still feel shattered". How thoughtless of me, there I was going on about all my problems, yet not once did I think of the woman opposite and the responsibilities which lay on her shoulders, without her having to tend to a "lame duck", such as I.

Looking back it was pathetic, but there again I was, for I couldn't cope, so the day after I ran away again, and yes you've guessed it, back to the Algarve.

By now my discussions with God, "my own higher power" were taking part on a regular daily basis, sometimes even on an "hourly basis", but I still found myself "none the wiser". I couldn't understand why he'd brought me from the depths of despair, only to suffer as I was in sobriety, or why he'd given me such honesty, love and beauty in Jeannette, only for her to also undergo her own separate pain.

I'd always been told "God was good", but at that point in my life I was just beginning to doubt whether he even existed at all, as I became even more confused than ever before, about this whole bloody facade, called . . . "life".

I returned on the 12th May, only this time more refreshed, clearer headed and prepared to tackle any problems that lay before me, whether they be Jeannette's or mine and so with a "new "lease of life, I got back into the real world, the one which I'd always found it very difficult to live in.

Although I came back in a totally different frame of mind, things despite my efforts still got progressively worse, as all manner of people seemed to be knocking nails into our coffin lid. What with Marks and Spencer's expecting me to work for nothing full stop and the leaflet marketing companies Jeannette dealt with, opting for the cheap "child labour" on the free papers, true caring and Christianity certainly did seem to be a scarce and sparse commodity. Even worse was the fact that due to the amount of paper being collected by charities, the price of waste had dropped dramatically, making survival in the industry even harder. Just to crown matters, Davidson's Paper had also stopped all books or magazines being taken from the mill, while nuns, priests and other "do gooders" were still taking what food was available from Marks and Spencer, leaving me the only constructive conclusion, that I could possibly come to, "Perhaps charity work is more profitable!".

Well by the time we'd got to mid June I'd had more than enough of "slogging out" to survive, but not all was doom and gloom, for on the 25th, Jeannette and I took our first holiday to Portugal . . . "Alone!".

Nick her son had gone on a school trip to France, giving us the ideal opportunity to have some well deserved time together.

Although it still wasn't without many a tear as my lovely lady still proved to be "a bit of a pain", finding it difficult to "let go", even though he was over a thousand miles away, being well looked after and in the company of his mates, all of whom were in just the same boat.

Despite the fact that she understandably missed Nick, we had a fantastic holiday, we hired a car for the very first time and I made the best of the opportunity to show her the whole of the Algarvian coast from East to West, even managing to cross over to Spain for a day. But the week soon passed and we were on our way back home, with me wondering if there was anything left of my crumbling empire and her looking very much forward to seeing her well loved son.

We weren't home all that long before I had yet another "nail knocked into my lid", for on the 8th July I was summoned to the manager's office at the Macclesfield store, to be told that my prices were too high and that I needed to find even more profitable, or should I say cheaper ways, to get rid of his rubbish. He told me that he'd been approached by another local company, who could save him money and that I had until the end of the month to come up with a better offer. I sat there absolutely amazed, I was so shocked that just for once, even I couldn't think of anything to say in response to his statement, so I took it on the chin and left his office secretly wanting to kill the bastard.

I spent the next nine days running around like a headless chicken, trying my hardest to reduce my charges, I had to, I had no other option, because although I really would have liked to have just told him "he could stick his shite up his arse "I wasn't in any position to and he knew it.

Talk about feelings and emotions being upside down, my whole life seemed to be crumbling around me, yet there was nothing I could do, I knew that, I now faced losing everything I'd worked for, all because of that sly worm at "Mac", "To think that my future is in his hands!".

On the 22nd July I went to see Mr Harrison, knowing full well that I could reduce my charges by the ten pounds per week he'd originally demanded, so I knocked on his door and entered fully confident, happy in fact, that I was going to keep my work, realising that after all the painful projecting and worrying I'd done over the past few days, not all was lost.

What a thick, stupid, blind fool I was to even think such a thing, an awareness that struck me from the very second I entered his office, because for the very first time in all the years I'd known him, he seemed genuinely polite, concerned and even respectful.

The man even came over as slightly caring and sincere in his manner, which really did "rattle" me, especially in view of my last two visits to his office, anyway I was there to give him the good news and that's what I did.

I explained how I'd chased around worrying, making every effort I could to oblige his wishes and requirements, then I told him just how much I needed to keep his store under my wing and finished by reminding him of my past commitment, good regular, reliable service and finally my unquestionable loyalty.

Some five or ten minutes later when I'd finished, he smiled, then looked down at his desk and proceeded to tell me how he'd appreciated all the work I'd put in, the loyalty I'd shown, especially when buying the new van and a whole host of other "incidentals". He then started talking about himself, the company and the company policies, at which point his ability to look me straight in the eye became conspicuous by it's absence, leaving me wondering, "What's coming next?".

Well I didn't have to wait long, because his next line said it all, "Look Paul, there's no easy way to say this, but I really don't require your services any longer, even though you've brought your charges down, I'd prefer it if you'd look elsewhere for work".

I was gob-smacked, I just couldn't believe my own ears, alright the bloke didn't like me, but there was still no need to have put me through so much pain, leading me on thinking I could actually do something about the situation. He finished by telling me that he didn't want to put me out of business or anything, but looking back it was an empty statement with no depth to it whatsoever, rather like the man himself.

We shook hands, I left him in his office, went downstairs and waited outside, as normal, for the rubbish to be brought out thinking, "What a fucking twat!".

Half an hour later, whilst I was still waiting to load up, he did something for the first time that he'd never done before in nearly seven years, he smiled, waved, said goodbye then drove off in his nice new family, company car and I could have killed the bastard.

I became disillusioned, disappointed and more confused then ever before, I had a million questions to ask in my head, another million problems to sort out in my life and only two real desires of prime importance, which were one, to stay sober, then two, get even with the worm.

By now I felt that I was swimming in an endless "sea of crap" as my whole life seemed to revolve around rubbish, not much cardboard, just rubbish and for the first time in my life I regretted ever getting involved in the scrap game.

It was a sad way to end up feeling, especially as I'd set off several years earlier full of hope, ambition and endeavour, but sadly dreams that loyalty, reliability and honesty would bring commitment, security and wealth were well and truly shattered, as all hope for the future was fast disappearing and so, not for the first time in sobriety, I secretly knelt down to pray . . . asking for guidance and a release from the mental torture I was suffering.

God must have heard my pleas because on the 25th July he finally acted, obviously having decided that I'd taken enough punishment, for he counted me out like a well hammered boxer, bringing my long shit collecting career to a very rapid end.

One minute I was making a cup of tea in Jeannettes', the next I found myself in agony on the floor with a very acute debilitating pain in my right leg. It felt as though I'd broken it, but knowing full well I hadn't Jeannette took me straight to the local hospital at Salford for a check up.

It couldn't have happened at a worse time because both Jeannette and Nick were in the process of packing ready for their first ever family trip abroad, which they were going on the next morning.

As I said earlier, the five of them had previously gone to Colwyn Bay, but because of our holidays together, Jeannette had only one destination in mind that Summer, which of course was the Algarve.

At eleven o'clock in the evening, the poor girl was stood with me, giving me badly needed support, when she should have been getting ready for bed, excited and looking forward to her early start.

At four o'clock in the morning, some five hours later we left the hospital none the wiser, with the pain I was enduring ten times worse, but I had to pretend and really put on a brave face, so that Jeannette could at least getaway for that first trip without worrying too much about leaving me alone.

Once again it was a case of pulling out a few of the "old tricks", this one being my acting ability, but it worked and so at seven thirty the next morning we set off in the van, heading for Tyldesley to pick up Jeannette's sister, Rita and her two children. There we were at the exact traffic lights where we first met, Jeannette, Nick and myself in a van that normally carried cardboard, only on this occasion loaded with suitcases, hand luggage and a cold box.

It was as if the whole trip was destined to be a disaster from the start, for as the lights changed we suddenly stopped, the engine had cut out and we'd broken down, a matter of yards away from her sister's. What a mess we were in, Jeannette and Nick a bag of nerves already because of their "first trip" alone, me near enough disabled suffering in terrible pain, whilst trying to act normal and a van that had never broken down before having it's first moody, leaving us all stuck in the middle of the East Lancs duel carriageway. I don't know how, but Jeannette, all dressed up in her best clothes pushed us around the corner, which eventually got us moving, although I must admit it was in "kangaroo style" never the less we jumped or should I say bounced around the corner to her sister's.

There was no other option, Jim, Rita's husband would have to take them instead of myself in his van, simple enough?, "Problem solved!".

"Not on your life!", of all the mornings to have an agoraphobia attack, he decided that this was it, "I can't make it to Manchester Airport Paul, you'll have to take them in my van", so as originally planned I ended up driving the five of them to Ringway.

By this time Jeannette herself was beginning to have doubts and second thoughts about the trip full stop, believing that the whole affair had what we call the "Indian sign" hanging over it.

First I was ill and as a result she'd had no sleep, then despite my acting she didn't want to leave me, believing I was worse than making out, she felt even more guilty as I was supposed to be looking after her leaflet team and to top it all the van had now broken down for the very first time, the morning they were going on the ill fated trip.

In the book I've spoken about similarities between the Davies's, Williams's and the "Beverley Hillibilies", but none of either could compare with this first Yates, Mackenzie attempt, which would without doubt, have graced any "Carry on Abroad" film.

Because of the amounts of luggage and the size of the full party of five, no family car would have been big enough, but there again in "normal" circumstances any two parties would have had two separate cars. However because of Jim's illness, my empty van was the only solution, until of course the breakdown. Others arrived at the airport in taxi's, minibuses, black cabs, even coaches, but not us, we rolled up in Jim's dirty looking van, full to bursting with cardboard and paper.

Jeannette and her sister Rita dismounted in similar fashion to the Queen as she vacates her horse drawn carriage, the only difference being the state of the transport provided, then as I opened the back door to the van Nick, Stuart and Kerry all sort of slid out down amongst flat sheets of cardboard, quickly followed by the abundance of cases, bags, cold boxes and even a sun brolly.

Saying "goodbye" was fifty times harder than I'd ever imagined, a duty made even worse knowing full well that Jeannette would be looking after everyone.

It took a lot of guts to take control of such a situation and to accept the responsibility for it, yet even though I'd pre-arranged the rent-a-car plus the accommodation at the other end and knew it would all be okay, I still worried because I loved her so much.

Anyway we said our weepy farewells and I left them all at the terminal knowing I was now going to miss her far more than I'd originally anticipated, especially considering how ill I was really feeling, so I took Jim's van back, got mine going again and made straight for the hospital, as previously arranged the night before.

It ended up being the longest four hours of my life, as the excruciating pain I was suffering got worse by the minute, where despite my pleas for help with the pain, I had to wait in casualty for well over an hour. Having seen one Doctor I was shoved off to another, where after that it was up to x-ray and then into some other department, with me finally ending up at the main doors to the Orthopedic ward, where I sat in a wheelchair for over three quarters of an hour, before even being spoken to. After spending a full morning being wheeled around from here to there, I felt both useless and frightened, I realised just how much Jeannette meant to me, how much I needed her and just how vulnerable I was without her mere presence, all feelings compounded with inadequacy when the ward sister walked up to me announcing my admittance to the hospital, "Right we'll soon have you in a bed Mr Davies".

I'd never been in a hospital, I didn't like the places and I certainly had no intention of making this a "first", so the matron's words were my cue to rapidly wheel myself out of the place in a mad frenzied panic. It must have taken me all of twenty minutes to find my way out, because anyone I stopped for directions either didn't know or couldn't be bothered, so by the time I did get to the van I'd reverted back to using my own crutches, with my faith and belief in human Christianity much the worse for my ordeal, in fact, nearly non existent.

When I did eventually get positioned in the van I wept with relief, relief because the comfort of sitting in the privacy of my own company brought an instant release from both the physical and mental pain. The last twelve or thirteen hours had been a total nightmare and all I wanted was the comfort of Jeannette's bed, hoping by some miracle or other, the pain would disappear with a good days sleeping, so I put the key in the ignition, turned it and . . . "nothing!".

Nothing happened, not even a click, for in my desperate rush to get help I'd left the lights on when I'd parked up, something that through sheer habit, I'd not done for years.

I became sort of hysterical, weeping uncontrollably with my head firmly buried in my hands, "Oh God please!, I need your help, I'm suffering terribly, there's no way I can push start this, help me please!". There was no way on this earth that I could see anyone giving me a lift, especially considering the amount of rude, un-caring, sorts I'd already come across that morning, but I was wrong, God did answer my prayers, with the solution coming in the shape of a little Irish man of all people, the very nationality I'd hated and called all my life.

The man God bless him, got me started and that in itself taught me one great lesson, which was, from that moment on I would never again "tar all people with the same brush "and so I made a beeline for Jeannettes' and the comfort of her bed.

By the time I'd got back and struggled upstairs I was distraught, as the incredible agony became unbearable, but even suffering as I was, my thoughts and worries were transferred over to the direction of Portugal and my lovely lady, "I wonder if the rent-a-car people were there to meet her?, God I hope they've not been let down with accommodation", then I got a little more pessimistic and questionable in my thoughts,

"Oh God I hope they've landed safe!".

For nearly twenty four hours I'd lay there suffering alone, accompanied by physical, mental and very hurtful, emotional pain, all of which were unwanted sleeping partners, with the latter being far worse to cope with. I hadn't heard from Jeannette and so my head immediately started to project all sorts of mishaps, cock ups, even disasters, as I lay there worrying whether she was alright or not, for despite my own predicament, my only concern at that moment was her safety, the fact that she enjoyed herself and that she was being well looked after. However not long after my mind was at ease, for I received her first call and the good news that everything was okay, so all I had to do was falsely convince her that I was much better and that everything at this end was alright.

I lay there on the bed like some Greek or Roman Emperor, supported by four or five cushions, all of which were strategically placed to stop any movement of my pain riddled body, with the only things missing to round off my impression of Ben Hur being grapes, wine and a couple of nice looking bikini clad girls, wearing veils.

I told her that I'd been worried to death, having not received a call, where upon she commenced to tell me about her experiences so far, with the change of accommodation, the picking up of the rent-a-car and the weather being just a few, I then informed her that as previously agreed before she left, I'd be giving Marks and Spencer notice that I'd finished, where we then discussed her work and my supervision of the team in her absence.

On the Monday morning through God's will I inadvertently got the chance to bugger Marks and Spencer off before they eventually did it to me and so I took great pleasure in ringing Mr Harrison up first to tell him that I wouldn't need until the end of the month as I'd already finished. With that step taken care of I only had one other immediate major worry, which was Jeannette's job, but God even had a hand in that a couple of days later when I miraculously recovered. It was great news especially for Jeannette because after such a difficult, trying start to their holiday, it meant that she could well and truly switch off to enjoy her well earned break, knowing full well that I was looking after everything as originally planned.

They returned on the 2nd August and it couldn't have come a day sooner, for I'd missed her so much that it hurt far more than any of the physical pain I'd endured whilst being ill. It seemed as if she'd been away for a year never mind a week, so needless to say I was hungry for her, no starving!

When she did eventually walk through passport control, she looked absolutely radiant and even though she always kept herself smart and tidy in her appearance, I swear she'd never looked finer, especially as she was now displaying the most beautiful of tans. We talked incessantly throughout the journey home, where she told me of their adventures and I told her of mine, of how I'd recovered in somewhat of a dramatic fashion, which had enabled me to look after her work, so with her return home things were looking good.

Two days later however, God decided to change the position of the goal posts because as if by some action replay I was once again struck down with the same acute debilitating pain, only on this occasion it had returned with an even more painful vengeance. For the second time in just over a week I ended up at Hope hospital in Salford, being poked and prodded as well as being shoved from here to there, the only difference this time was that I had the love and support of my inspiration alongside, but even that couldn't alter the fact that we left many hours later, once again, none the wiser.

The next couple of weeks were a nightmare, not just for me, but for Jeannette also, because she'd already had the sad experience of nursing both her parents through terminal illness, memories of which all returned with my sudden similar state. How swift those changes took place, one minute I was a fit, energetic, lively young man, the next I was a disabled, bed ridden cripple, spending most of the day or night tossing and turning, writhing in pain, with an easy chair, stool and pillows my only feasible method of gaining comfort. Getting upstairs did prove to be a thankless, impossible task, so that lounger and the view from the patio at Jeannettes', accompanied by her loving tender care and the pain killers I was on were my only aid or release from the pain and turmoil I was enduring.

I eventually ended up at the Manchester Royal Infirmary care of B.U.P.A, I was on the scheme and in hindsight should have opted for their care automatically, because on that first visit I was immediately relieved of my physical pain courtesy of two severely administered injections, on my second I was thoroughly examined and tested for everything from T.B to AIDS and on my third properly diagnosed, where after I was treated accordingly. The relief of knowing that it wasn't cancer or anything similar was unbelievable, even in spite of the fact that I still had quite a serious illness called "Soft Tissue Rheumatism" to contend with, one which the specialist informed me was a "warning "from my own body.

However despite Doctor Bernstein's objections I got my own way and was treated as an out patient, on the condition that I was well looked after and that I rested, as it was going to be a long arduous recovery, where at least one years treatment would be necessary.

He was right, it did take a long time, but in defiance I originally made a promise that I would be up and working again within that exact twelve months.

I wasn't stupid, I knew that it would be a trying time for both Jeannette and myself but in all honesty I didn't expect to be treated by the Social Security system in the manner I was.

For the first month of the illness I'd not even received a letter in response, never mind any benefit, despite the fact that all the required forms had been filled in accordingly, but I was far too ill to even worry about such things, so it really didn't matter at that moment.

However by the time six weeks had passed I was more mobile and in effect beginning to "wake up" to the predicament I now found myself in. I could see Jeannette going out to work whilst trying to look after me at the same time, but I knew she didn't earn enough to keep us both going, so I was worried. My inadequacy hurt me as I felt more like a hindrance to her than anything else because with the job went the food on the waste, so I couldn't even help in that department and I knew in my own sick mind, that we just couldn't carry on, "It'll be alright when the social pay up, they'll back date what they owe me!".

Well that was the next shock in store, for on the 2nd October I received a visit from a Social Security investigator, followed up by a letter informing me that I would receive no benefits whatsoever, as in their eyes we were living together as man and wife.

I was distraught, devastated, yet still Jeannette consoled me by putting on a brave face, "Eh luv, never mind God's good to gobins!", that was what she'd always said and she truly believed it.

I came to love her even more through that period, as she by her own example showed me yet another way of displaying her love and commitment.

There were days when she would set off, having loaded the car up with heavy boxes of leaflets whilst I looked on, totally helpless and unable to do anything, then with her exit I would cry, for I loved her so much, yet at the same time I felt so useless. I'd hit my first ever depression in sobriety and I knew it, as some days I would get up feeling great, believing that total recovery was just around the corner, then the next I would find myself down on the floor again full of negativity, once again sinking back into depression.

Extra love and comfort also came from another area, that of A.A, as countless members called around and rang, keeping a watchful eye over me, making sure that whatever physical state I was in, I kept my brain working, all of which reaffirmed my trust and total belief in the programme and the miracles it provided. I needed their help, guidance and knowledge more than I'd ever required it before, support that I knew would get me through the vast minefield of disastrous emotions that lay before me and there were many, which ranged from one of low self esteem to sheer joy and ecstasy.

My mind, however, the most powerful weapon I always possessed was well and truly kept pre occupied, with my appeal against the Social's decision, an appeal which I had to attend in order to do my bit for the cause.

It was eventually therapeutic, although a hell of an ordeal at the time, with the build up and preparation proving just as hard, as I was forced to advertise a full house clearance, then sadly watch the nice "new" home I'd only recently re – built in Gorton, literally be dismantled before my eyes.

I stood there on crutches whilst people came and went, as if viewing a "show house", some empty handed, others with more than they could carry, yet all were there for the same reason, to barter and wrangle, scavenging like a pack of vultures, all oblivious to my own apparent downfall.

With all my worldly possessions either given away or sold, it was time to prepare my case, we knew that the monies raised would see us through and so it was time to tap old, reliable, deceitful tricks from my imaginary magic box, then use them to get what should rightfully have been mine in the first place. In order to win my case, I made sure I was heavily armed with evidence to prove my innocence, taking with me a rent book from my home in Gorton, another covering Jeannette and myself, letters from my Doctors at both B.U.P.A and Withington ATU and a whole host of other receipts to prove I'd sold my own furnishings and personal goods to survive so far.

The odds were stacked against me from the start and I knew it, for both the Citizens Advice and the Welfare Rights warned me of the daunting task ahead, but despite their scepticism and pessimism I went for it, knowing full well that if I wasn't successful, Jeannette because of me, would also find herself in a financial crisis.

On the day in question, I was a complete bag of nerves, I'd never experienced such worry and emotion, especially as I was wanting to do well for someone else, not me!!, I cried as I said "Bye" to her, I cried in the van on the way, I even sobbed as I stood at the main doors of the building, but once I'd stepped in, that was it, the tears stopped!!, for the battle to save us was about to commence.

It was a bit of a sombre affair, where three people sat in judgement, a secretary took notes by shorthand, the Social Security were represented by one of their own officers and I represented myself.

The hearing lasted maybe twenty minutes, at which I presented my case and answered questions in the process, then sat there listening to the Department state theirs', which only took a matter of seconds.

They offered no evidence whatsoever, which took both myself and the appeal judges totally by surprise and so both the Social Security representative and myself were asked to leave, whilst the panel made their judgement.

Under normal circumstances the appellant, which in this case was myself, is usually told the outcome of the hearing a couple of weeks later, by letter but because of my efforts and the fact that I was so ill, they made an exception to the rule by informing me there and then, so I left the building absolutely drained, with only one real intention in mind, I needed a phone to tell Jeannette the news. As I stood in the phone box I shook like a leaf, trembling with a "cocktail" of different emotions churning over inside of me, I was so relieved that it was over, whilst at the same time fumbling, as I tried to press the numbers, wanting to give Jeannette the news, knowing that she'd painfully and patiently be waiting, whether it was good or bad.

The only words I got out after she'd lifted the receiver were "Hello luv" , because my immediate follow up was a breakdown of tears, accompanied by snivels, "Are you alright love, how have you gone on?". Once I'd managed to pull myself together, I told her the news, "I did it !, we're OK, I won the case, can you hear me?, I won, we're alright, Oh I do luv you Jeannette, I luv you so much!!".

I could feel the relief in the tone of her voice, so with that she went off to work, for her afternoon stint and I made my way home to her house, "my lodgings", praying thanks to God as I did.

Knowing that we finally had monies coming in did ease a lot of pressure, it meant that for all her love and care, I could at last give her something back in return, it also automatically brought about a great acceleration in my mental recovery, for it meant that I hadn't caused her the financial pain I'd first thought, the question now though was, "Would I have the monies owed to me by Christmas?".

All my life, even in my drinking, I'd always enjoyed giving more than receiving, so with Christmas around the corner, I dearly wanted to be in a position, where I could give the lovely lady something nice in appreciation of her kindness and commitment.

Unfortunately it wasn't to be, because I didn't receive a penny before the 25th December, however that in itself taught me yet another lesson in my life, which was the true spirit and meaning of Christmas and the real value of Love.

In desperation, an honest feeling of responsibility and more importantly my love of Jeannette, for the past three months against my specialist advice and all medical logic, I'd physically helped, driving and posting on Jeannette's leaflet team, whilst she worked extra hours at her other job for Trumann's Steel. It didn't earn me any cash, but it did mean that extra graft was carried out in the afternoons, work that wouldn't normally have been done. My van hadn't moved since I'd become ill and hadn't been paid for, it was an extra "set of wheels "and so as it wasn't being used for anything else, we thought that at least we could still benefit from it's presence, instead of it being stuck outside, doing nothing.

We also used it to deliver those "cheap labour" free papers, which for so long had been robbing Jeannette of the income she should have gained through leaflet distribution. Basically it was a hard, slogging, slave labour, but as I've said before "Beggars can't be choosers" and so for a mere thirty pounds, I spent hours with Jeannette, sorting and delivering heavy bundles of newspapers to children's homes, throughout the area ready for posting.

It was heartbreaking work, but it had to be done, for although it was only thirty pounds a week, it made a hell of a difference to the situation we found ourselves in, especially when considering the "all hands to the wheel" approach, needed to get us out of the shit.

Most evenings would be spent with bundles of newspapers at one side, three or four various stacks of different leaflets on the other and us in the middle of a giant mound, placing one in the other.

Because of that work, the fact that I came into contact with young mums and the financial position I was in, I managed to borrow, by the skin of my teeth, a Christmas present for Jeannette. It was a gift totally unlike anything else I'd ever bought her before, and certainly one that I hope I'll never have to buy the likes of again. Previously I'd had the delight of giving her a television set, videos, clothes, you name it, I'd bought it, but not this year, for on this occasion, my gifts amounted to three bottles of bubble bath and the cheapest pair of earrings imaginable. I had no money whatsoever and only one possibility, apart from shop-lifting, of getting her anything at all, so doing it the (honest) AA way, I had no choice but to borrow my Christmas gifts of love and thanks from one of the children's mothers, who was an Avon representative.

I even took time to wrap them up in Xmas paper, crying as I did, for I felt more inadequate than I'd ever done before, thinking to myself, "God, is this all I can give that poor girl, after all she's done for me?".

On the morning of the 25th, for the very first time in my life, I truly came to realise the real meaning of the exercise, the genuine spirit of Christmas and the real depth carried in the message, "that it is better to give of thyself".

As Alcoholics Anonymous had given freely of itself, wanting absolutely nothing in return, so had that beautiful lady, she'd done it for genuine, unselfish, caring love !!, opening my eyes in the process, by telling me that, "I wasn't that badly off!!".

It was a beautiful rewarding way to end what had unquestionably, been a very traumatic, painful, educating year, but it did more than that, for it gave me the best possible springboard to enter 1988, which was without doubt a year of change, a year where a dream was manufactured and came to reality.

I started the year off with only one goal in mind, which was to pursue Marks and Spencer for some sort of help in relation to the financial debt mountain, I now found myself landed with. Retaining belief in all the things my mother had taught me and even despite their past uncaring track record, I felt that they did at least, owe me some sort of assistance and compensation, so I set about sending correspondence to the head office in Baker Street, in an effort to get some response.

I had been trying since August of the year before, but as yet without success, so I was quite pleased to say the least, when I received an invite from the company to go down to London to discuss the situation in detail, still in the hope that I may at last find a solution to my problems.

In the last week of January, my wish was finally granted and so still very poorly, financially broke and helped along by a pair of National Health crutches, I drove down to London in Jeannette's car. The task was as clear in my mind as the sky was on the day, I had to convince the man, a Mr. Smith, that his company owed me some loyalty in return for my total commitment and that I had to make it quite clear Jeannette, who was a total outsider, had innocently and inadvertently become a victim of their policies.

Because of my poor physical state of health, it did prove to be somewhat of a long, difficult and painful day, where I found the meeting itself, just that little too much for me, especially as I had to relive the whole nightmare. When I started to talk of Jeannette, what she meant to me and how she'd been left financially insecure for the first time in her life, I genuinely broke down in tears as I couldn't contain myself any longer.

I spent nearly two hours with the man going through the whole ordeal and the sadness it had brought to others around me who'd cared, not just Jeannette, but others at companies who I'd let down, people that had trusted me, only to become victims themselves.

After two and a half hours I left the man, near enough begging him for help, pleading for some assistance to save passing on the pain they'd already caused me, only to be told, "Well I must be honest, I cannot at this moment in time see the company being in any sort of a position to help you, besides I do feel from what you've said you are strong enough to help yourself". I was gutted, so I set off in a more than angry state, with the drive home, twice as long and lonely as it was going, to arrive back in Manchester, much the worse for my thankless day's excursion down to "the smoke".

I'd originally set off full of high hopes, open mindedness and promise only to return angry, bitter, very resentful and hurt, I was both physically and mentally drained, apart from having my pride very badly damaged, but I did remember a typical piece of AA wisdom that Colin, my sponsor came out with before I'd set off, "Listen, don't be surprised if you come back with something totally different to what you expect, you might think you've come back with nothing, but you won't have, because something will come out of the trip, I promise you!".

Well!, having dragged me all the way down to London, Mr. Smith and his company wasted no time at all in coming to a decision, for on the 1st February, I received a very pathetic letter, totally admonishing themselves from any responsibility whatsoever, whilst at the same time, telling me that I had good friends, advisers and a personal resolve to sort things out, oh and of course, they wished me Good Luck!.

I reacted to such an empty, pitiful letter in the only way I knew, it was a natural instinctive response, with no holes barred in the shape of a three page reply to the chairman of the company, Lord Rayner. I held nothing back, got straight to the point and finished off with one of their own quotes which simply said, "Three generations have in one hundred years created a national institution, The business has grown, prospered and changed beyond recognition, It's principles however, do not".

I then sarcastically added four questions marks after such a profound line and decided to close the file on the case, get on with my life and put it all down to a sorry, sad experience, where I would never commit myself to any company ever again.

Chapter Twelve

A Dream Becomes Reality

My eventual acceptance of the fact that Marks and Spencer were not interested in my problems, immediately triggered off a new train of thought, one of which made me look very much towards my future and more importantly, work!.

I'd always been a grafter and so it was a natural instinctive thing to do, the only problem, however, was that I'd spent literally years working for myself, which had given me not only responsibility but also a freedom, a freedom to come and go as I chose or do more or less as I liked.

I contemplated various options, such as postman, milkman, even a window cleaner knowing full well that I couldn't possibly be tied down to either a factory or office. I even thought about gardening or greenkeeping, but with each consideration came the realisation that no matter who I was employed by or where I worked, I would have to accept discipline and take orders, all of which sent a cold shiver through my whole body.

I quickly gathered that I would once again have to work for myself, a conclusion which only served to leave me with an even bigger headache, doing what?, what could I do that I hadn't done before?, especially as "physical graft" was now a definite no go area.

Well the answer to my questionable problem came in rather a miraculous way, one which only God could have planned or thought up and one that I'd previously and wisely been forewarned might just occur as an eventuality, which did just by coincidence.

Following my seemingly disastrous trip to and from London, my friends in AA advised me to take stock of the whole experience as it wouldn't have been a total waste of time, needless to say once again, they and the wisdom they'd gained through the practising of the programme, were right, for I recalled the trip and the one significant thought that struck me on the day, "God how on earth do business men cope with trips like this, pressure from meetings, driving, even parking!".

That was it!, I'd got it!, I immediately knew there and then, what I wanted to do . . . "A Chauffeur", I could be a chauffeur.

Within seconds, care of my most powerful of minds and the imagination that lived there, I found myself driving the richest, most famous film and television personalities all over the place and in my own limo at that!!.

I had instant visions of them ringing me, "Paul!", up at home for my services, people I'd admired, adored, even respected, all requiring my company, "God, me rubbing shoulders with the rich and famous, tending to their every need, in the papers or even on the telly!! . . .

"YES!! . . . What a dream".

Rather coincidentally at around the same period of time, I finally received my large back – dated cheque from the Social Security. It was as if God had given me the "green light" to go ahead with my plans, for at last I now had well needed money, cash that automatically released the already accustomed pressure we'd both learned to live with, which in turn left me with a lighter head, plus a clearer idea of where I wanted to go, in order to repay Jeannette for her love and total commitment.

I didn't receive all the monies due to me because the state still refused to pay for the first four weeks of my sickness, but because my full attention was now focused on the new project facing me, I just dismissed it as yet another sad example of life, one not worth bothering about, leaving me a clear head to go forward.

The task facing me was daunting to say the least, I had no money to buy a car, no collateral to back the venture and no experience or contacts either, so the million dollar question was, "Where do I begin?, and how the bloody ell do I get started?".

I wasn't stupid, I knew full well that it wasn't going to be a simple case of just getting a nice limousine, then waiting for the stars to ring, so I had to sit down, think, then work out some realistic business plans that would eventually lead me to the right people.

A month later I'd drawn up my "battle plan", it was a format based on success, which ironically revolved around certain qualities that I had in the past, picked up on, policies of Marks and Spencer, for example, beliefs of Joyce Davies and finally my own, obviously gained through my experiences, all of which I believed were a recipe for a good quality service, that nobody else could possibly compete with.

I decided to set up an executive type, taxi company, that would specialise solely in running passengers to and from Manchester Airport, whereby normal members of the public would be treated to the very same standard of service as those expected by the highest paid, company executives.

Because of the numerous different companies and problems I'd personally encountered on my trips, I knew there was a definite need for such a service, as dirty cars and drivers, unreliability, plus rudeness, were all common, run of the mill practices, on offer at that time.

I believed that if I worked on the principle of referral, then I would eventually end up dealing with the people I'd originally intended, but in order to do so, I would need to establish the airport service to the public first.

With my ideas and plans firmly in mind, I then decided to start contacting various sources, such as companies, banks and of course, the airport executives, in the hope of guidance, help and assistance, or at least some positive response.

Looking back, I was once again both naive and stupid, to even think such a thing, as I found myself totally rebuffed from every corner, with the response from the Airport Commercial Director offering a pathetic, "Good luck", and a bunch of "passenger growth" figures.

Most companies never even had the decency to reply to my letters, although, when they did, it was usually a "Thank you very much, but no thanks" , type of letter.

The banks, however, were without doubt, the worst, for having sat there on most occasions, meticulously and honestly explaining my illness, loss of home and general circumstances, then giving a detailed account of the plans and ideas in mind, I would be asked, as to whether I had security or collateral, which would enable me to borrow.

Each boring manager that I saw gave me the same repetitive answer, "Well Mr. Davies, it sounds like a good proposition and I certainly admire your guts, determination and honesty, but I don't think the bank can help you at the present, without having any security, however if you can return with proof that your idea will work, then I'm sure we may be in a better position to help!".

By the time I'd been to the four main banks in Walkden, I was angry and frustrated, whilst at the same time sick and tired of hearing the same sort of robot like response. There I was trying to raise a loan for a car that would enable me to pay them back, only to have these jokers tell me they liked the idea, but needed proof, I got so annoyed with one pompous oaf, that I suggested perhaps a bike would be a good alternative, then I could peddle customers to the airport.

I'd never liked Bankers, as I'd always considered them wankers and none more so than at this present moment in time, for there I was, a hard working bloke who'd lost everything through no fault of my own, desperately trying to pick myself up again.

I didn't want sympathy for my situation, or admiration for my courage, guts and determination, I just wanted a little, small financial assistance in support of my own undaunted keenness, to make a dream come true.

It wasn't to be, for despite their beliefs, not one of those highly paid managers was prepared to accept the responsibility, or back his own intuition, so I left and returned back to the "drawing board".

Having taken stock of the situation and given many hours of serious thought to the outcome, Jeannette and I discussed the possibilities of me borrowing her nice "new" car to start up "taxi-ing" illegally.

We realised that there was no way on this earth, that I was going to succeed the "honest" way, so the only option was, the other "route", the illegal way, I realised that if the Banks wouldn't help me, then for the love of Jeannette, I'd have to help myself and so that is the exact avenue I pursued.

Jeannette and I had discussed everything in great detail, she trusted in me and my plans, but despite my own self belief, since visiting the banks a week earlier, I'd taken no future action, so in rather a "Joyce Davies" like fashion, she did.

It was a Friday evening and as normal I was at her house whilst she was at Bingo, when at approximately a quarter to ten in the evening she returned home, spot on time as usual, only on this occasion, full of excitement, "Quick love!, hurry up, I've got you your first fare!!",

I just looked at her in somewhat of a confused state, "Ya what?".

She then proceeded to tell me, how all the "regular" old girls were left stood outside the Bingo hall, as there were no taxis available, they'd been told that it would take at least a half hour for the first one to arrive, leaving each and everyone of them cold, wet and very angry.

Without having a second thought, I jumped up, set off in the car, made straight for the Bingo and dropped off four ladies, all at different addresses, all of which brought me my first one pound fare. An hour later I'd returned home having made four pounds clear profit, I was over the moon and wanting more, so Jeannette had a Bicardi, I, a cup of tea, with us both knowing full well that we were about to start off on yet another, brand new adventure in our lives.

By the end of that first weekend, I'd called into the reception of the local, newly built "Novotel", paid a visit around the corner to the Ellesmere Golf Club, typed out an advert for the Post Offices and Newsagents in the area and even sat in the car, parked outside the city centre night clubs, punting for business.

I knew from my previous experience setting up in the paper game, that I would have to go out and find the work, I also realised that I would certainly have to start by working illegally, without a license, insurance and all the other "bits and bobs", but I had no choice for nobody would help me, so I had to help myself.

That following Monday, I had a very busy day ahead of me because Jeannette was doing near enough full time at Trumanns, so I had the responsibility of looking after the leaflet team, which was obviously priority over everything else. We also had the local "free" journal to sort out, apart from me now having to tout for new "taxi" business when and wherever I could, needless to say by the end of the day I was shattered. However by now I'd recovered my appetite and enthusiasm for work and life, so despite being tired, I scoured the Manchester Evening News that night looking for possible outlets that I could utilise, which would bring in a fare or two.

I didn't have a clue what I was looking for, it just seemed the correct thing to do at the time and it was, for I came across the personal column and an abundance of "ads" for kissogram companies.

Still to this day, I don't know why I latched onto the idea in the first place, but I did and I was glad because having called maybe six or seven different companies all of whom were not interested, I finally hit the jackpot with my last attempt.

It wasn't anything like definite, but they were positive in their response, taking my name, address and other details, saying they'd contact me if my services were required, meantime for the remainder of that evening, I carried on parking up at pubs, clubs and various hotels illegally plying for trade, in order to make some money.

Because of my determination to succeed, I was prepared to take on near enough anything, no matter how short or far the journey involved was, or for how much, it was all down to getting cash in, which would then subsidise the initial outlay for printing costs, telephone bills, insurance, advertising and all the other essentials incurred when starting up a new business.

However the day after, whilst loading Jeannette's car up for the "normal" days work ahead, I got talking to one of her next door neighbours, who'd genuinely inquired about my health, as over the past months I'd got to know her and most of the others quite well. I told her how I was setting up a taxi company and of my plans for the future, which automatically brought a very interested response, "That's great Paul, you'll get loads of business in this road alone, especially as there are lots of teenagers like my girl, who use taxis all the time".

She was right, so after quite a lengthy discussion, where she told me how parents worried about "shady" taxi drivers and the general safety of their children, I wasted no time in letting the whole neighbourhood know of my new venture.

The woman also asked me if I needed any business cards producing, as she worked for the local education's printing department and could do them "free of charge". It was a question which obviously brought a very enthusiastic, "Yes please!", followed by an arrangement for coffee the following day, where she'd call around to discuss my choice of lettraset and the design I wanted.

She did call and having had a good couple of hours with me, left with me feeling "chuffed to bits", knowing that I'd probably got my printing done for near enough nothing. It was the first bit of help I'd been offered, never mind received and so I paused for thought just for a minute thinking, "Perhaps Joyce was right after all, maybe you do get out of life what you put in".

My thoughts and recollections with regards to my mother's teachings, came about because during my time on the waste paper and the earlier part of my relationship with Jeannette, we used to distribute as much food as we could to her neighbours, so I believed God was kind of paying me back for passed good deeds. Also, as the woman concerned and another opposite had, in the past been ill, I'd visited both of them with flowers, offering sincere warmth, support and friendship, even a cuddle, so I naturally assumed her generosity was a returned compliment for my past caring.

Joyce, my mother was right, "You do reap, what you sow", because a couple of weeks later, having kept me in suspense, her dear neighbour returned looking "as pleased as punch", with my business cards, an experience which reminded me of our "new football boots" saga, many years previous.

The woman placed them on the table all wrapped up in elastic bands, with such an air of confidence, I was pleased before I even set eyes on them, "There you are Paul, if you want any more, just give me a shout".

I'd originally stated to the lady that I didn't want anything too elaborate or fancy, just basic but neat, a request which definitely did prove to have been a big mistake, for they were bloody awful, they were so basic that I could have produced better at home, with a typewriter and a cornflakes packet. That wasn't all, despite the fact that she'd originally offered to produce them without cost, the woman even charged me fifteen pounds and "tax free" at that.

It was the first occasion I'd asked anybody else to do something for me, an experience which taught me a very swift lesson, "If you want a job doing properly, then do it yourself!", and so it was back to square one, with my main goal being that of raising enough cash to pay for my first real batch of printing, which would then help me launch the company in some proper fashion.

I realised that it was going to be yet another case of "make do and mend", that "Yes!", at that moment, I was similar to a beggar and that I couldn't afford to "choose", so I once again got down to the task facing me and set off in the evening, punting for work.

Within a week, neighbours, their teenage kids and friends alike, were all using my service, all of whom were close to home, people who knew us both really well, however my first big breakthrough came shortly afterwards, when we received a telephone call from the kissogram company I'd previously contacted, a call which was subsequently followed by a very forthcoming and positive meeting.

As a result I had the great pleasure of running around one of their nicest "stocking and suspender" clad girls, a lass called Jane, who by sheer coincidence I'd met some six or seven years earlier, as she performed at my ex wife's place of work. We recognized each other immediately, I mean how could I forget her, after all, she did give me the "eye – eye", at the time, but unfortunately it was yet another one of those, "missed, because I was pissed" opportunities, so we had more than a laugh on that first night, which did automatically break down any "possible barriers".

Jane and I worked for at least a month and it was good fun, but due to the fact that I was constantly getting busier by the day, our working relationship had to end .

By the time the end of March had arrived, the taxi company, without a name, was run off it's feet and "Springclough", which is what I always called Jeannette's home, was like a mad house. The poor girl, God luv her, would be taking bookings, then I would find her standing outside in the garden, awaiting my arrival home, from my last pick up or drop off, only to send me on my way again, to earn more pennies.

We had neither, a phone or radio in the car and it was mayhem, for if I dropped somebody off in Manchester City centre, I would then have to dive into the nearest available phone box to "ring in", it was crazy!. More often than not, she would answer the phone in such an eloquent manner, "Good evening, may I help you, please?", then panting away having sprinted to the phone box, I would say, "Oz cabs one, where to next?" and that's how it carried on all night.

By say, one thirty in the morning, her typical response would be something like, "Oh it's you, quick, go to such and such a place, it's absolutely mad here!!, we must be bloody barmy", it was and we were, but with the poor girl getting to bed at about two in the morning, there was one thing we both knew for sure, "We were definitely onto a winner!!".

Sometimes to make extra money, I would drive off down to the airport, then hang around and just wait for someone to utter those magic words, "Excuse me, are you a taxi?, only we're stuck here, ours hasn't turned up", which more or less meant that by the time Jeannette was getting up on a Sunday morning, I'd be returning from somewhere like Scotland say or London.

After three or four weekends of the same and then accumulating a large volume of hotel and Golf Club work for mid – week, I was now confident enough in my own mind, to know that I was now ready to place my typewritten "ads" in the shops, also I had enough cash to fund the exercise and so I went for it !, in an effort to bring "a dream to reality".

On the 28th April I spent the whole day driving around to every sub post office and newsagents in the area, asking each and everyone of the owners to display my simple, "ad" in their windows,a request to which, most of them agreed, so with the footwork complete, all I could do was sit tight, wait, hope and pray.

I was still sore and smarting from my earlier efforts to find "free" help from a bank, even worse the, "Come back with proof", statement they'd all repeated, so I wanted to return in the not too distant future saying, "I told you so!" and "Well, here I am".

However I didn't have to wait long, before I once again spoke to my own manager, for by some strange quirk of fate that very evening, The Manchester Evening News carried an article, which told the story of despairing to – be married couples, who'd been let down by the company supplying their wedding limo's.

I picked up on the story immediately and wasted no time in contacting the reporter who'd written the item, I initially thought, that perhaps the bank could use the exercise to their own benefit, by starting me up with a car, thus enabling me to supply a free service to the couples involved, then using the whole saga for the best P.R. stunt imaginable and without cost. So fired with enthusiasm and a keenness on the reporter's side, I contacted the bank with what any normal, intelligent, entrepreneurial thinking person would have considered quite a realistic, beneficial proposal. That of course is, unless you're a Banker!.

Their response was different, you see they are a totally unique species, a breed unto themselves, who live by a strong guide line, which is summed up in one word, no, not law, order, or even religion, not even faith or belief but "procedure", for they cannot even wipe their own arse without instruction.

The bank we were told, couldn't accept the responsibility if something went wrong, they couldn't trust the press, especially as they didn't like dealing with such people, Oh and of course, collateral and projections, I needed those two commodities also, which meant that it was back to the basics again and the "goal" of proving that I had indeed got a viable venture, something which could eventually entice assistance out of them.

Although dejected, I wasn't down, so the next day I once again set about "doing it for myself", the hard way, by doing Jeannette's job, taxi-ing in between and that most frustrating thing of all, waiting for the phone to ring in response to my adverts.

Well I didn't have to wait long, because the very next day the calls started to come in from all over the place, with airport bookings being made for all sorts of times of the day. All at once it seemed to go absolutely stupid, as everybody seemed to ring in at the same time, the Golf Club I'd done work for, then another at Swinton, who'd been referred to me, then holidaymakers going away to the airport and local businessmen also, all sick and tired of the poor services of the past. I was run off my feet, then on top of all the existing commotion came the one call I'd been waiting for . . . the Novotel Manager.

For weeks I'd picked up the odd guest, even a few of his staff, but never the man himself, or any of his management, yet funnily enough after waiting for so long for his first call, it couldn't have come at a worse moment, as Jeannette and I had only just finished loading up the car ready for her to go to work, posting leaflets.

Needless to say I was panic stricken, I ran out to her just as she was placing the last boxes into the boot of the car, "Oh bloody ell, you'll never guess what, that was the Novotel, they want a car for the manager in an hour's time, what are we going to do luv?".

We were both well aware it was a chance of a lifetime, one not to be missed, but we also knew how busy Jeannette's leaflet job was and how important it was to keep it ticking over, so we found ourselves in a bit of a dilemma.

Following a brief discussion, it was agreed that I should do the job for the hotel and that Jeannette's team would have the morning off, after all there was more of a future at stake in the taxi-ing side, so once again it was "all hands to the wheel" as we had just under an hour to clean both the outside and inside of the car. It was a perfect example of the perfectionism, we as a couple possessed, for in spite of the fact that it was a new vehicle, less than a year old, we wanted it looking in best showroom condition and so by the time we'd finished, it did!.

With only fifteen minutes spare, I started to get really nervous as my next problem was clothes, you see I'd never previously paid much attention to dress or fashion, because apart from "working tackle", jeans and T shirts were always the main accent of my style.

I wasn't totally void or bankrupt of decent, tidy looking clothes, it was just that they were never in a great abundance, so it came down to whether the one pair of black pants and the sole white shirt I possessed would fit, plus the other final important item for any chauffeur, a tie?, did I have a tie?. The answer was yes, which meant that although I did sort of resemble somebody attending a funeral, I did look clean, bright and very tidy.

With the car absolutely gleaming and myself looking just as presentable, Jeannette wished me, "Good Luck" and so I went, on what was really the very start of making a dream come true, the birth of "Exclusia Travel".

Wearing black trousers that were a little on the "tight side", a white shirt that was very much on the "choking" side and a plain black tie fit for a funeral, I entered the main reception hall, remembering passed advice from my good friends in AA, when they said, "Be yourself Paul!, be yourself!". Well, I couldn't have asked for a more seemingly difficult man to deal with for my first real account customer, as he came over in somewhat of a pompous, arrogant, "I love myself manner", a man who was nothing less than condescending in his attitude. However because of my very committed, strenuous effort, he still parted in a very gratifying sort of way saying, "Thank you very much, it's a nice service, what's you're name again?", so I told him and left in somewhat of a half confident, unsure frame of mind, more believing I'd succeeded than failed.

We never heard from them again for over a week, so you can imagine it was a seven day period, where despite still being constantly busy, I experienced those horrible "failure" feelings, but like I say, with a week gone they once again contacted us, requesting only one person, "Paul", no one else, just "Paul", as "Mr. Wright was very pleased with him and doesn't want any other driver".

Little did they know, I was the only driver, but that was the idea in the first place, they were all supposed to imagine us as a giant company and it had worked, which meant that Jeannette and I now only had one other hurdle, which was the Bank, with the task of proving our case, now the firm goal, plus constant growth with what means we had at our disposal, the priority.

By the day the volume of work I was carrying out increased four-fold, which meant that I was now, more sure than I'd ever been before that I was sitting on a potential "goldmine", a notion which was confirmed by two separate incidents within the space of a week, both of which came by way of intimidation.

The first incident occurred at the airport, which came by way of the Black Cab drivers who worked from the rank there, they resented the fact that I'd placed my very basic business cards in the telephone kiosks and on the notice board, whilst at the same time touted for business, saying it was illegal and that I'd get my legs broken if I pursued along the same lines.

Although there were four of them and they were all big blokes at that, I was definitely the last person in the world to be frightened off by threats, so I responded in typical "Davies" fashion, "Do you really think that you lot frighten me?, do ya?", I looked at them and I actually think that they were shocked by my response, so while I had their full attention I thought I may as well give it to 'em straight, "Listen, you lot want this place all to yourselves, you're greedy, rude and most un-obliging to the public, you even 'rip 'em off' at that, apart from the fact that you're cabs are crummy, dirty and smelly, so don't try and stop me doing a hard day's graft, just because you're not prepared to do the same".

They looked dumb struck, so I thought I'd part leaving them nothing short, which was just typical of me, as once again I had to have the final say, "You might frighten most other people off with your 'bully boy' tactics, but not me and I'll tell you this now!, if you really fancy ya chances, carry on at your own peril!".

Well I returned home with the satisfaction of knowing full well, that I'd probably got over what was without doubt going to be the biggest threat possible at the airport, although at the same time I knew that it certainly wouldn't be the last I'd heard from them, as it was quite apparent that there was a lot at stake, "earning wise".

As if to rubber stamp that thought and belief the second incident quickly followed only this time care of an arrogant, self righteous gentleman, who was the local licensing officer from the council.

I had no respect for the man from the first minute I'd clapped eyes on him because his mere appearance and presence told me what he was all about, as he looked a real two faced, lying little creep who'd stab his own Mother in the back, he was a worm and I knew it, so there was no love lost from the outset.

He'd called around to "Springclough" carrying a folder tucked underneath his arm, an arrogant, cocky "I'm in charge" approach and even worse an "I'll show you" attitude, all of which achieved nothing other than set us off on a poor start to what eventually ended up being a very torrid, hot and cold relationship, based mainly on hate and revolving around turmoil.

He was totally the wrong man for the job and certainly the wrong type to be dealing with me, especially as he was only confirming my initial beliefs before setting off on the adventure, you see I was quickly "getting the picture", with the realisation that there did seem to be a sort of clique, or mafia type system operated in the "taxi business" world, one which only survived with the help and assistance of people like himself, ie people who took "back-handers", a system which I desperately wanted to beat.

I didn't like what he had to say, or the stipulations he was making at the time, but there was nothing I could do other than just for once in my life conform to regulations and the system, so I obliged doing everything I was requested to and so in the first week of June it was official, Exclusia Travel was born!!

I was registered, the car was plated and tested, Jeannette's car and the company were fully insured and the bookings were flying in, my earnings had risen from a mere thirty six pounds to a colossal three hundred and thirty six a week and so it was now time to go back to the bank.

On the 23rd June I once again called the assistant manager, where upon I was told to take my figures in that day, the man briefly discussed the venture, asking me how things were doing, after which I left, with him telling me they'd take a look at what info I'd given them and give me a ring within a couple of days.

Because of tiredness brought on by the work I was getting through, added to my still "unwell" condition, I'd returned home to Jeannettes' and gone to bed for an afternoon nap. I didn't have any immediate work on and I was drained having been to the bank, so it was an ideal opportunity to catch up on some sleep, however it didn't happen and I'm glad, for at a quarter past three that afternoon the phone rang with Peter the assistant manager on at the other end, "Hello Paul, it's Peter Williams at the bank, look we've had a look at your figures and we like what we see, if you can get on the Enterprise Allowance Scheme we can do something to get that car you want, can you pop in tomorrow?".

I couldn't belive it, we'd finally got through to them and proved our case, so with my original desires for sleep miraculously vanished, I wasted no time in calling Jeannette at work, where I apprehensively waited to be put through to her, however when she picked up the phone I couldn't restrain myself, "We've done it luv, we've done it, the bank 'll back us, after all our effort, they want to back us!".

Needless to say we were both really excited and so the next day I returned back to the bank where the wheels were immediately set in motion, following which Jeannette and I wasted no time in heading to our nearest Ford dealers with a view to buying our first company car.

The financing of the vehicle was obviously the most important factor, but even more so in my case because my brother Eddie worked for the car making company, which was in itself a great help, as all staff had the opportunity to buy whilst enjoying the benefit of large discounts.

They were given transferable tokens which at the time allowed twenty per cent off any purchase, a discount which automatically gave us more options than anyone else would have in the same circumstances.

Sitting in the rear of the Granada for the first time was an experience which I shall never forget, for having looked at every other model in the showroom, Jeannette and I eventually sampled the delight of the one they had on display. She truly looked the part, as I stood watching her behind the wheel, where upon I immediately decided, "That's the one luv!, it's perfect". It certainly wasn't chosen in a hasty fashion, more carefully picked out after an enormous amount of thought and consideration, with leg-room, boot space and general comfort, all important items when thinking of our future passengers.

The price we were getting the car for, in view of the substantial reduction care of my brother, was no different than that of a much lesser model, so with our minds firmly made up there and then, we left having ordered our first Granada Ghia.

With the banks full backing, the order by way of a deposit was completed, which meant that Jeannette and myself had nine weeks before taking delivery of the car on the 1st August, which also meant that it was once again decision time, whereby we had to make our minds up as to whether it was worth carrying on with her leaflet distribution team or to finish the job altogether.

In the end we had no choice, for as I said earlier, the job had changed so much for the worse over the past year or so and her staff themselves had in that time messed her about somewhat, so we immediately cancelled any outstanding contracts she had, which automatically gave us less to worry about.

By this time my lovely Jeannette was tired, she was working full time at Trumanns Steel, whilst at the same time supporting me in my new venture, as well as running a home, so with the ending of the leaflet team, which technically was the closing of a large chunk or chapter in her life came the opportunity of a holiday and a chance to return to Portugal.

This time it all went without a hitch, I wasn't ill, they knew where they were staying and they'd done it all before, the weather was fantastic and so without having to worry about anything back home, she'd returned after a week away looking much the better for the break and me signing on the unemployed register for the first time in over fifteen years.

It was a necessary action which due to procedure had to be carried out because to qualify for the Enterprise Allowance Scheme, all applicants needed to be registered unemployed for at least eight weeks. Luckily it didn't affect my benefit, but as it was a regulation, it had to be done and so once again I had to conform to the system, having said that it was worth it, as not for the first time in my life, history seemed to be repeating itself.

Due to the conditions of acceptance, all applicants had to attend a two day seminar at the Y.M.C.A in Manchester, it was actually the first such gathering of its sort that I'd attended since my experience at the large construction company as a teenager, although despite the years that had passed and all that had gone before in them, nothing much had changed.

I found myself amongst a crowd of between fifteen to twenty people and me once again looking around with a critical eye thinking, "What chance do these lot stand of succeeding in business out there?".

They were all in a "similar boat", either unemployed, couldn't find suitable work, or like myself couldn't bare the thought of working for somebody else, some foolishly just fancied having a go, doing a bit for themselves, either way, there was a hell of an assortment.

It was the biggest waste of tax and rate-payers money I'd ever had the misfortune to witness, as a couple of blokes who obviously had contacts within the civil service, waffled non-stop about self-employment, franchises and God knows what, they spoke about tax, tax years, sickness pay, insurance stamps, then about books, book-keeping and of course my favourite subject banks.

Most of the poor helpless buggers who were supposed to be there for help, were either frightened to death, absolutely bam boozled, or had just plain fallen asleep with the boredom, so by the end of the two day period a mere handful were still interested in the prospect of working for themselves.

Having completed that exercise all I had to do was complete my last six weeks on the dole which would take me through to the end of July.

It was a hectic time and an exciting period, one which saw me running all over the place, because we had a phenomenal response to the cards we'd posted care of Jeannette's leaflet team, the neighbours' kids kept me running about all through the night, picking them up from night clubs etc and the Novotel work had increased ten fold.

It had got that busy by the mid July, that the small calender we'd started using, had to be abandoned for sheets of A4 plain white paper, in order to accept the numbers of bookings and so yet another decision had to be made, a decision on whether Jeannette should leave Trumanns Steel to come and work full time in the business.

Jeannette had been unhappy for quite some time, feeling that she wasn't getting a fair deal within the office framework, long standing family ties and loyalties had been severed with a change of management and an influx of new, not so nice employees meant a very uneasy atmosphere in work, was common place, which were obviously not suiting to anyone of a genuine, honest and sincere nature.

I'd personally been upset for quite a while, as seeing her go to and return from the place, in such an unhappy frame of mind was nothing short of painful, I'd had many a "close shave" with regards to running late because of double bookings and delayed flights, even though a few of the neighbours were earning cash in their own cars working for me and so in my mind it was more advantageous to have her working alongside me than to be losing money, through giving work to others.

With one week to go before the official start up date, I'd finally persuaded Jeannette to leave, so we cleaned and polished up her car, which was only a year old, drove it round to the local showrooms where she'd originally bought it from, worked out a decent "trade in" deal with the salesman and arranged to pick up our second brand new company car, a week later.

The date of August 1st 1988, was one of those days in my life that I could never possibly forget, for it was a day which comprised of so many different, mixed emotions, where two hard-working people, who had been over so many hurdles, in each of their own, previous, separate lives, embarked on what was to become one hell of an amazing experience, where so many dreams were to become reality and an already deep affection for each other, eventually grew into an unbreakable, un-destructible bond of love.

I'd always called Jeannette "My Inspiration", for that's exactly what she was and what she did for me, as her mere friendship and presence, genuinely inspired me to pick myself up, dust myself off and not just start again, but "bounce back" and succeed, which is probably why, whilst stood in the showroom awaiting service, all manner of thoughts and recollections raced through my mind. I recalled how when the bank originally asked me for my plans, projections, where I wanted to go and how far I was prepared to go, I told them, "I intend to go as far as you'll let me!!". "I want to cover every level possible, taxis, middle market, top, I'm going to deal with Private, Business, Hotels, Commerce, General Travel, you name it, I want it!!".

I then went one step further by highlighting the work available in the holiday sector, "I'll carry anything I can, baggage, airline tickets, holiday passengers, with my main 'dream goal' the air-crew transfer market!".

Once I'd explained that side, I then went onto a few more of my "dream aims", Weddings, Film and Television, the real, creme de la creme of chauffeur work, all of which were "pipe dreams" to the man sat opposite me. These and many other memories of past struggles came flooding back, my numerous battles with Banks, the Social Security, Marks and Spencer and of course my creditors, all bad memories, now once and for all, problems of the past.

As we drove away from the showroom having picked up our first car I looked at her thinking "God luv it's finished, the nightmare is all over and behind us, we're on a good run at last!".

We were so proud as we pulled up at "Springclough", checking each and every dial and button, enjoying the smell from the newness of the interior, then the excitement of the car phone and the making of that first call to see if it worked, even though we were parked outside at the front of our home.

We'd already decided that I would drive the Citreon as much as possible, it was the cheaper of the two models, a diesel engine and so, as I was going to be doing much more mileage than Jeannette, it was much more sensible for that car to be the "work-horse" of the fleet.

So with our inspection and the first excitement of our day over it was time for a brew, something to eat, then off to pick up our second vehicle from Fords.

Watching "my inspiration" drive off proved to be one of the proudest moments of my life, for in the time we'd known each other she'd "freely" tolerated me, supported me, cared for me, but most of all loved me.

The lady had taught me so much in my sobriety by just the power of her example and now she was totally trusting in me, so I was both proud and pleased that at last, without "wanting" she had something in return, something to show for her general loyalty and commitment.

It was crazy and probably the most unromantic scene that one could possibly imagine, for unlike most couples who go off to pick up a "brand new" expensive vehicle, we were in a rush to get away. In fact I don't think the salesman had ever experienced anything like it before, we didn't want coffee or a chat, weren't interested in sitting listening to his explanation of this or that, we just wanted to get away.

Because we were busy, she drove off one way whilst I went the other, as I had a flight landing and she had passengers to take, so the only way I could ask about the car or tell her that I loved her was from car to car by phone.

It was an experience which although rewarding was a bit of a "mad rush job", yet sadly that unpredictable sort of a frenzied running about style did immediately become the "norm", as our lives mainly due to our success became "one hell of a whirlwind, or tide of chaos!".

A week later in our "by now" positive fashion, we decided to spend some of our profits and chance placing a couple of "ads" in those same local "free" papers that had been the scourge of our lives for the past twelve months.

It was a gamble that paid off, for within a few days the already hectic schedule we'd become accustomed to had got totally out of control, bringing with it an avalanche of airport bookings. We were taking over ten bookings a day and even though a couple who lived over the road, were helping out in their own vehicles, it wasn't enough, I'd even employed one or two of our "new" customers, who themselves had asked for work whilst going on their own holidays, but it was still a struggle, as it was a case of them all wanting to earn the "nice cash" when it suited them, needless to say we had to seriously, although reluctantly, think of employing someone "full-time".

In the same week, we'd received telephone calls from two large companies, one through referral and the other by way of the advertising we'd done, so my mind was immediately made up for me, even though I'd constantly had reservations about such ideas.

The first company who'd contacted us, wanted our services on a twice daily basis, five days a week, it was to pick up three ladies in the morning, take them to work, then they were to be picked up later in the day and returned home.

Funnily enough the second company who'd contacted us through the paper, were a local travel agents who I'd called on when I originally started up, the girl at the time was rude and un-interested in my proposals, so on this occasion, especially in view of the fact that I was dealing with the manager, I in typical "Davies" fashion, got my own back by explaining to the owner that he could have had my services some two months earlier and cheaper, had it not been for her abrupt arrogance.

With those two new contracts safely under our belt and a holiday client bank that was growing by the day, I believed more than I ever had done before, that God was truly on our side. It seemed that there could be no stopping us, as everything we "touched" turned to gold, however once again I was guilty of "counting my chickens before they'd hatched", for in the first week of September, whilst taking the three ladies to work on our regular contract "run", I was involved in an accident which severely damaged both the car and my pride.

Nobody got injured, but looking back it was God's way of telling me that I was doing far too much work and so we employed our first full-time driver, which was something of a shock to say the least, as I would never of planned, less anticipated, doing that in a million years when I originally dreamt the whole thing up.

Keith was a great lad, he was young, enthusiastic and desperately keen to work, he'd longed for a driving job and really fancied being a chauffeur, so we decided to give him a chance, especially as he'd contacted us through our advert, and his own initiative.

Two months later he'd well and truly become part of the company, he was welcomed into our home and although he was staff, accepted as a friend, which meant that now, I at least got the opportunity to catch some sleep in-between my "twenty hour" working days.

The service we provided to the public meant that any driver, whoever it maybe would automatically take time and make the effort to find the clients a baggage trolley, then escort them to the correct check-in desk. It was one of the many extra specific details that made the general service stand out from any other available, consequently because I personally ended up handling the larger majority of work, my face, tidy appearance, plus the general manner in which I dealt with passengers inside the airport building, soon drew the attention of airline check-in staff.

That fact, plus my inquisitiveness and a search for cheap airline tickets, brought about yet another encounter in my life, a meeting which had everything to do with destiny, fate and more importantly God's plan, where once again, I went off my instincts, feelings and the other person's "body chemistry".

For years I'd heard about the cheap "last minute" seats that were supposedly available at the airport, how you could roll up and wait to see if there was any room on flights, then board for a minimal fee, so as I had some spare time I'd promised

Jeannette that I would have a "mooch" round and make a few enquiries.

I'd been downstairs with no joy whatsoever, so on the advice of staff I'd already asked, I made my way upstairs to the main departure floor to see if I could do any better up there. Having been to several desks, all of which were of no help whatsoever I decided to quit, as it was obviously all hearsay, however, just as I made my way to the exit doors I passed one last desk, which I hadn't already approached, so I decided to give it "one last shot", in the hope that something might turn up.

By this time I'd become accustomed to a very rude "Don't be stupid!", type of response from staff, who for one reason or other believed they were all important or something, so I was more than surprised when the "rep" concerned, actually "came over" as pleasant.

The woman, Kath, was a well built, attractive lady of maybe forty five, possibly forty six years old, who reeked of warmth and caring, yet had an enormous amount of sensuality about her, with those ever common, sexy, brown eyes which always suckered me, to compliment her voluptuousness.

Unfortunately she was unable to help, but we did "hit it off" immediately, so after quite a long, lengthy and enlightening chat, I once again decided to give up my search for cheap, last minute flight seats and left the airport to make my way home, knowing full well that I'd not only made a new friend whom I liked a lot, but that I'd also inadvertently found a contact who had knowledge of the airport and more importantly how it operated.

It was a stepping stone which I immediately realised could eventually lead me to much greater things, an opening that I'd long since dreamt of, without having the slightest, remotest anticipation of it happening so soon after starting up, needless to say I wasted no time whatsoever in drawing on that most essential of my resources, "manipulation". With each lot of passengers I checked in, came a regular wave, wink or if I wasn't rushing a chat, which meant that within a week not only did she know all about me, but most of the other airport staff did also.

I knew in my own mind that it would only be a matter of time before they started to think about using my services, so I decided to "hurry" things along a little, by purchasing Kath some flowers in return for her rather sensual "flirting" manner, thus attracting not only theirs, but other companies attention, who operated travel desks in the departure lounge.

I'd told Jeannette all about the woman, how nice she was and what "potential" there was in our friendship, especially when considering how much work could be got as a result of such a relationship, which obviously meant that she was more than keen to meet the woman, having heard so much about her.

Well typical of me, she didn't have to wait long because by now we were both shattered and desperately in need of a well earned break, Keith and his devoted wife were more than capable of looking after the job in our absence and so with the bank manager's blessing we decided it was time for a holiday and a return to the Algarve, so for once instead of our passengers flying off to the sun, it was our turn.

There we were, already the talk of the area, the proud management team of probably the most successful new business venture in years, the owners of the most reputable chauffeur/taxi company in the area, being taken to the airport by our one and only driver in his wife's little battered, old Escort.

Having already looked after well over a thousand couples, treating them to the best service available, by means of brand new "limo's", door to door service, the most courteous manner possible and the smartest looking uniformed drivers you could get, we found ourselves in a car that had a boot full of junk, which left us with cases on our knees, a front passenger side window covered with polythene, as it had been broken into during the night and a driver looking as if he'd just fallen out of bed, with not one item of uniform in sight.

He dropped us off at departures, where upon we rapidly snook into the main building in the hope that none of the drivers from the other companies who knew us, would witness the pantomime, which is where Jeannette and Kath met each other for the first time.

As promised she'd arranged our seating on the plane and the processing of our tickets, so after a bit of a chat, Jeannette, Nick and I set off for a well earned break, with Jeannette understanding full well what I saw in both Kath and the friendship, whilst as the same time wondering what the hell we'd be returning to . . . "I wonder if we'll have a business left?".

We had a good relaxing holiday, with the Portuguese climate doing us proud, so we returned fully refreshed, clear headed and ready to put our whole new array of ideas and plans into action.

In our absence Keith had done extremely well, so we wasted no time whatsoever in setting about the task of building up our little empire, especially as we knew we could now rely on the lad.

Our first move was to re-advertise, only on this occasion with our already rapidly growing reputation behind us, it was a far more wide ranging campaign, both area wise and in content. We'd had our very first "Wedding booking", which yet again was one of my more distant dreams when pre-planning the whole adventure, so in order to capitalise on the exercise we took photo's of the cars whilst they were ribboned up and ready to go, which meant that within three months of our first official start up date, we found ourselves actually fulfilling one of our more futuristic aims and promises.

Despite my nervousness, that first wedding went as well as anything else we'd tackled, so the second advertisement was purposely and more tactfully aimed at a much wider market, as our confidence by way of experience was now "sky high".

It worked a treat, for the response we got from companies and the self-employed alike was phenomenal and so by the time we'd reached mid December it was absolutely chaos, no mayhem!

We'd been contacted by a local self-employed woman who held consumer product parties at home, with regard to picking up the very important researcher, from either train station or airport, then returning for them afterwards, M.E.L one of the two "major" local companies, gave us a verbal and written contract immediately, with the second, Chloride, asking us to call in with one of our cars, so that the office manager could check that we were what we claimed to be, "immaculate", then as if to really put the "cat amongst the pigeons", Kath and the company she worked for at the airport also required our services.

As if all that wasn't enough, we received a call from a local lad who faced losing his "night job" if he didn't obtain transport to and from work. The poor lad was a cripple, so because of our soft, genuine and sincere nature we couldn't refuse, which just about finished us off altogether, because the whole chaotic situation basically brought a totally different Christmas to the year previous, one where this time I could afford to buy Jeannette something really nice, but unfortunately I couldn't afford the time to see her.

We both worked incessantly throughout that first Christmas and New Year period, so with our first six months successfully behind us, we entered 1989 full of hope, enthusiasm and promise.

Rather predictably, despite the very positive outlook we'd adopted, our personal aspirations and the great expectations as a result, things didn't quite go according to our plans, for it was a year, in which I personally, care of a good few hard painful lessons, learnt more about life and people generally, than I'd ever done before.

It kicked off with an enormous bang, by way of the sudden departure of Peter, the assistant manager at the bank, he'd been promoted and moved to another branch, which for me was not to dis-similar, to losing my right arm.

He'd been with me since the conception of the whole idea and supported me all the way through, so I was devastated to suddenly learn that he was leaving, even worse I couldn't follow, but the bad news didn't stop there, for he then informed me that a young woman had taken over his position and that she was out to impress!!.

The next thing I knew, he'd gone and I like a few other account holders was summoned to the bank to, as she put it, "Discuss the state of the account".

Well, the minute our eyes met it was a "no go" area, for she was young, inexperienced in life and it's problems, arrogant, cold and even worse, ugly, rather like a sort of effeminate, lesbian type. It was a case of "I'm in charge" and "This is what you're going to do, Mr Davies", as the woman explained to me how unhappy she was, with regard to my enormous unsecured overdraft, which amounted to all of a mere one thousand, five hundred pounds.

Then already having made a mess of things with her condescending attitude, she totally "cocked up" her representation on behalf of the bank, by "telling me" that I will oblige her demands and immediately.

Sadly, even in spite of my four years sobriety, that without doubt, was her biggest mistake, for still to this day, I'm as defiant and rebellious as I ever was, forever reluctant to do as I am ordered, even worse, told or threatened.

With some sort of thick, stupid, ignorant persistence, the young woman opposite continued to pursue along the same direction, "Well, Mr. Davies, how soon can we expect this overdraft to be cleared?".

By this time I'd had enough, so I jumped up to give her a piece of my mind and some honest advice, "Listen luv, your approach will get you absolutely nowhere with me, I really think you want to learn how to communicate with real people, before you pursue your career, sadly you lack things like Christianity, caring, understanding and trust, you have no respect for anyone else and with your outlook, plus the chip you're carrying on your shoulder, you young lady are going nowhere in life!!" then as I left her office, I let her know my full intentions with regard to the position of the overdraft, "Oh and by the way, because of your arrogant attitude you can shove the account, as it stands, right up your selfish arse, I'm sure it will fit!!".

Like all "Finance" minded people, she and the bank, in their own cocky manner, naively believed that I needed them, not on your life!, because my next immediate action was to place all the cash we received into Jeannette's personal account, consequently a flood of crappy letters soon followed all "requesting" my attention to the matter, which of course I ignored.

Up untill this moment in time, we hadn't really experienced any bad "cock ups", nearly all our customers had been punctually met or picked up, so the client bank was in a constant state of growth. Chloride the other large, local company had also joined our account list, so with the work I was getting from the airport growing by the day, I instinctively became wary, because whenever times were like these, something usually went wrong.

Well once again, God didn't disappoint me, for as I fully expected, a mini-disaster lay just around the corner because Keith, who as yet hadn't let us down, started to go wayward, by oversleeping in the mornings.

That first time it occurred was a nightmare, one which I didn't want repeating because the phone rang at four o'clock in the morning, with one very irate customer on the other end, wanting to know where his taxi was.

The driver's failure to turn up was bad enough, but it was an occurrence made ten times worse by the fact that our passengers always got a regulatory courtesy telephone call the evening before and as the couple concerned had only received theirs some seven hours earlier the whole matter was embarrassing to say the least.

It was the first of quite a few similar mishaps, which always ended up with us forgiving, whilst he was ever apologetic, however by the end of January he'd left us to go working for his brother-in-law, as his wife wasn't too happy with the odd, unpredictable working hours that he had to keep.

Keith's departure left us disappointed, we knew he liked the work, and we all got on well together, but we understood his wife's misgivings and so we had to let him go, which unfortunately put us in yet another predicament, for now more than ever before we were short of a much needed driver.

"When one door shuts another opens", well that's how the saying goes, but in our case it was "as one driver leaves another starts", because by sheer coincidence we received an approach from another young man, who on this occasion already knew all about our company, as at the time he was working for one of the more well established firms, who offered the most basic of taxi services.

We already knew we were the talk of the North West area of Manchester, but until we'd met Gary we'd no real idea of the impact we'd actually made on the other firms who'd operated and manipulated the market for the previous five or six years.

Having initially inquired over the phone, he came around to meet us both at "Springclough", where he was very honest, open and direct, he had a lovely attitude and manner, plus a nice clean car to compliment himself, all of which impressed us both immediately.

He took time to explain how he admired us both for what we'd set up and achieved, then how he'd always wanted to do the same, he finished by shocking us both with stories relating to the anger and bitterness running throughout the other firms because of our success. He was unhappy picking drunks up, despondent with working permanent nights and totally weary of listening to colleagues constantly moaning about Exclusia Travel who we were taking the "better" airport jobs off themselves, so he'd come to us for employment in the hope of a fresh start and a higher standard of work.

After a good, long, open chat where salary, hours, standards, everything barring a starting date were discussed, he left with an agreement that he had time to think over everything we'd said and that he'd keep in touch, leaving us both absolutely amazed.

We already knew that we'd "ruffled a few feathers" because so far we'd experienced more than enough harassment from the licensing office, but never in our wildest dreams could we ever have anticipated the resentments and nasty actions that Gary told us had grown, or the lengths that our opposition were prepared to go to, in order to stop us working.

It only took him twenty four hours to make up his mind and so he handed his week's notice in, without letting slip, that he was in fact going to work for us, the opposition, the scourge of "mafia run" taxi market.

It was a good job as well because it gave us the opportunity to find out for ourselves what depths the pathetic lot were prepared to sink to.

Because he was working on their radio wave band, he witnessed the constant "tracking" and harassment which they carried out, the threatening phone calls that were made and the false bookings they attempted to make.

By far the worst of their actions was the night that they actually followed Jeannette and her sister to the Bingo, yet in spite of the many numerous complaints to the local enforcement officer, not one was followed up.

By the time Gary had joined us, our ever growing popularity was hurting everyone of them, with constant advertising and even independent appraisal in the media generally proving too much, they'd near enough lost all of their decent company contracts to us, so things were beginning to hot up.

Heading towards the last week in January we hit yet another saga, which in hindsight most people setting up a new business would have loved to have had, it was a simple "poser" of a question on the face of it, but sadly in our innocence, one we didn't know how to solve, with the problem being, "Where can we put all these cheques?".

Because of the unsettled dispute with Barclays bank, plus the vast number of large cheques I had collected from the numerous company account paying customers, I needed new facilities so that I could capitalise on what was in fact "dead money", I didn't want to settle up with the first outfit so, "What should I do?". At the time, due to inexperience, I believed that I had no other option, so as a result of a regular business client referral, I ended up approaching another one of the main high street banks, which unfortunately meant that my original debt would actually have to be settled, before the account could be closed.

Once again, when discussing the possibilities, the manger in question was impressed with the figures, he could see the potential and wasted no time in opening the account, even in view of my past problems with the last organisation, and so come February 1st we had another account, only this time, with the benefit of lots of funds in it, care of the Nat West Bank.

The manager Mr Ged Kurns couldn't have been more enthusiastic, in fact he was so keen that within a week of banking with him, he'd paid us a visit at "Springclough", which was obviously a "recce" to see what sort of background we had.

The man absolutely overwhelmed us with his instant belief and confidence in us both, following which he went on to discuss all manner of subjects in relation to the running of a successful business, he told us how we needed to start employing office staff, so that Jeannette could do more driving, advice which then led him onto extra drivers as back-up, "You need lots of back-up!", he stressed, before going onto something else. Then halfway through his visit the phone rang, meaning Jeannette had to leave us to take the call, which left me alone with Ged and the problem of trying to listen intently to him, whilst at the same time "earwig" in on her conversation.

You see I could tell by her body and eye movements and the way she was answering, that the call was obviously very important, her telephone manner, although usually brilliant, was at it's very best, impeccable in fact, all of which left me puzzled thinking, "I wonder who the hell it is?".

She must have been on the phone at least twenty minutes explaining every important detail imaginable about our company, during which time Ged had near enough restructured our whole life, so by coincidence he got up to leave as she put the phone down, bidding us both a farewell with these parting words, "Well I'd better get a move on because I can see you're both very busy", then just as he got to the front door he stopped, "Oh by the way Jeannette, I think it would be of great assistance to you, if you thought about getting a cleaner, this place is spotless but it must be very time consuming, time you cannot afford to waste, especially if you're going to be as busy as I think you are, anyway cheerio!".

Once that front door had closed and he'd driven off, we stood there with our hands to our mouths in total silence, then simultaneously burst our laughing, "Great stuff, what d'ya think luv?", Jeannette just looked at first, obviously still in shock and disbelief, then eventually she agreed, "We can't go wrong with a man as enthusiastic as that behind us, can we luv?". We were absolutely elated, for at last we'd found someone who was prepared to back us all the way, without fear of putting his own head on the block, so after a good, lengthy chat about the many various points he'd made and the advice he'd given us, I finally asked Jeannette who it was on the phone as it sounded really important.

She looked at me with a really pleased look on her lovely face, then said "I didn't want to say anything while he was here, but you'll never in a million years guess who that was?".

She was right because never in my wildest dreams could I have envisaged receiving a call from Loganair, one of the national airlines, enquiring about the services I offered and with a realistic, genuine view to contracting us.

The company wanted to know whether we had a vehicle that could accommodate between five and seven crew members, which had to be spacious in order to carry their vast amounts of luggage.

They also wanted to know what size of fleet we had, whether or not we had back up and how many vehicles could be supplied at any one time.

Of course we had the lot, or least that's what Jeannette said, she had no choice, after all it was the chance of a lifetime and a "God given" opportunity to fulfil yet another one of my initial dreams.

I think that within an hour of that discussion, we were both off looking around the various car showrooms of Greater Manchester, trying to find a suitable mode of transport which would help us seal the contract, we had to, because Jeannette had already made an appointment with someone from the airline to view and inspect the vehicle to be used a week later, but of course we didn't have such a thing.

It was a massive gamble which had to be taken, one that cost us seventeen thousand pounds but more importantly and as a direct result of listening to the finance agent who represented Lloyds Bowmaker at the time, Jeannette as a consequence of being forced to buy the car in her name, eventually lost her good reputation.

The man concerned didn't wish to do the deal in the name of the company, he said that because it was a new venture and that so far it had neither a good or bad name, the agreement could only be finalised if it were in Jeannette's title only and so because we needed the car she signed up for it, then a week later I won the contract meaning that the gamble "for now" had paid off.

As each day passed the work constantly grew at an unbelievable pace, with both the general public and the local companies all demanding our services, which meant that we entered the month of March running round like headless chickens. One minute I'd be here, then the next I'd be there, as one company would want a car, then another would require four maybe five, with the neighbours in Springclough keenly sitting in their homes, awaiting our call, as well as customers, who themselves had only just used us, all dying to earn extra cash.

It was like a merry-go-round of success, with everyone involved reeping the benefits because as more people joined the band waggon, the faster it went, picking up more work as it did.

The whole experience for me personally was nothing short of educational, with the general public, without doubt proving to be the most enlightening of all. My friends in Alcoholics Anonymous had spent years teaching me not to pre judge, as people are always full of surprises, well my next story pays full testament to that fact, for it was an experience which also taught me that there are more ways than one of showing gratitude.

The customer concerned was a Mr.Dee, a man who rather typified a majority of our clients from "The Green" area of Worsley, as both he and his wife really thought they were something and so did their kids. The "Green" as it is known, is a piece of grass, which is no different to any public park, it has an enormous, grotesque looking "bandstand" type of construction on it, which is more likened to a public toilets, it's a meeting place for the local druggies, drunks and as one resident put it "queers", but for some reason or other, the locals seem quite proud to say they live on the "Green".

That in itself should give you some idea of the type who live there, because they seem incapable of sounding their "R's", you see green is gween, raining is waining and drive is dwive, all of which pisses you off, especially when you hear it in the very early hours of the morning.

It proved to be very hard work dealing with the Dee family, their kids were obnoxious, they were both arrogant and snotty, added to the fact that they hardly said a word, on either their outward or return trips, so I was more than surprised when I returned them home safely and received a very complementary "Thank you", there was no tip, although I never expected one, but in his case the "Thanks" was enough.

By this time I'd started putting comments down about clients, which would automatically help the next time we picked them up, so in order to give us warning for that next occasion I put, "He's decently obnoxious! and they love themselves".

I really didn't expect to hear from them again for another twelve months at least, so you can imagine my surprise when I received a call from his secretary at work, a couple of days later, with a request to pick up a young lady from the airport, then take her to a building site on the other side of Manchester.

As far as I was concerned not only was it a nice way of paying my company a compliment but it was also a lovely way to say "Thank you", so without hesitation I took the job on and enjoyed every minute of it.

The young lady concerned was pleasant, attractive and a pleasure to deal with, she worked for a public relations company, who were organising the opening of the building which Mr. Dee was the site manager in charge of and so she'd come up from London to pre organise the event.

It proved to be a lovely day, one where yet again I did us proud, so Francis left with the promise that whenever she was returning to Manchester, she'd be in touch.

I really didn't envisage seeing her again, but it was always rewarding to look after someone, no matter who they were, or what walk of life they came from, then see them leave happy, so with her departure it was back to the regular work believing that there was always a chance of her "referring "us to someone else down South.

That very same week and as a result of more recommendations, we picked up three more regular contracts, which once again all boiled down to hard work, determined effort, with the taking of extra time and care proving the most outstanding feature.

The first contract was another daily run for one of the large local companies, whilst the second was for the AA travel agents in Aberdeen, which at the time proved to us both, "that the power of example" was really far greater and wider ranging than any possible advertising could be, especially as they knew all about us in the far reaches of Scotland.

The third approach came from Ferranti's of Wythenshaw, they only had a couple of lady chauffeurs who constantly ran themselves ragged, consquently, we continuously bumped into each other at the airport and so having given her one of our business cards, she in turn had passed it on to their transport department.

They urgently required a number of cars to ferry quite a few important visitors over to Blackpool for a weekend seminar and that's where their problem arose, because their own staff weren't available, they didn't work weekends!!.

Once again we completed the job without a hitch, which meant that although hectic and chaotic it was a very successful two week period, where the already gathering snowball was growing bigger and faster with it's own momentum.

It was during the same month that we realised there was no way we could continue without either, reluctantly taking on more full time staff, or even worse releasing some of the "normal taxi" work we'd done since originally starting up.

Gary was getting ear-ache off his wife, as once again, whilst the lad we'd employed was prepared to work "odd" hours, the woman behind him thought more of a social life. She wasn't prepared to sacrifice anything for the luxuries, so we suspected that his departure was looking rather imminent, which meant that as a result we could end up letting our own customers down, by being short staffed.

By now Jeannette and I were beginning to see that being successful did have more than it's fair share of problems, that the public generally, were somewhat difficult to deal with and that employing staff was an even more difficult task or burden to bear.

We were now experienced enough to know, through body language, chemistry and actions, what the people we were dealing with, were actually thinking, or "up to", we also knew that we had to try looking after ourselves first and so in an effort to safe guard our own interest and even though it was one of the many painful lessons I'd learnt some years earlier with Marks and Spencer, there wasn't much we could do, so the "bread and butter" work had to be sacrificed in order to keep the larger, company contract work.

I immediately stopped picking up the neighbours, their kids, long standing customers and any other normal taxi "pick ups", work that only earnt the odd pound or two, which automatically released some pressure, by giving me more sleeping time.

As if by coincidence the release of that old, original work coincided with the promised confirmation of my very first trip for Loganair, they originally told me that my services would be needed from the end of the month, but it had been brought forward somewhat, obviously to the delight of myself, which once again was the start of yet another experience, one that brought lots of pleasure, much laughter and an abundance of friendships with a bunch of the nicest, young people I've ever had the pleasure to meet.

My first trip was nothing short of a personal disaster, brought about by my own nervousness and a constant yearning to do well, I needed that work for a variety of reasons, all of which revolved around "the unattainable", "the impossible dream", oh and of course, "pride". I'd already experienced the "closed shop", "mafia" style running of the airport which was supposed to be a publicly owned concern and so rather like my "run in" with the local, licensing office, who with a chosen few taxi companies had a "grip" over the innocent public, I wanted to once again, prove that it was possible to break the strangle hold, held over this sector, which seemed to be in the hands of "Selwyns Transport" and the airport authority itself.

I despised monopolies or cartels and in both instances had it proved to me that they existed, so the mere fact that I found myself actually taking a full aircrew up to Glasgow, was a dream turned reality and one hell of an achievement.

The car looked absolutely immaculate as I pulled up to the crew room entrance, it was a part of the airport where only airline or airport transport was allowed to park and so it wasn't long before one of the traffic wardens rolled up to tell me I had to move.

I knew the warden quite well, so I obviously felt very proud as I explained that I was indeed picking up a crew, then taking them up to Glasgow Airport, where by he looked stunned before questioning me further on how I'd managed to break into the market, knowing full well as I did about the "closed doors" cartel it was operated under.

The original arrangements made, were that I should be at the gate for ten o'clock on the Sunday morning to await the arrival of my crew, their operations staff had my car phone number and so when the thing actually rang whilst I stood talking to the warden they couldn't have timed their appearance any better, as the head of "ops" desperately wanted to speak to the Captain.

They were all so nice, friendly and complimentary about the car and myself that I felt on top of the world, especially as I knew full well that Steve the traffic warden would be going off to tell most of the airport about what he'd witnessed, so feeling ten feet tall, I set off fully loaded for Glasgow Airport on my very first trip.

The Captain who chose to sit in the front passenger seat talked non stop, with the other four crew members much the same, they told me how they'd spent all winter going to and from Glasgow in one of Selwyn's old tatty, mini buses, which had no heater, no radio, and where the driver was a real, old, miserable sod. They then told me of the hours they'd spent hanging around waiting and how unsafe they felt whilst being blown from side to side on the motorway, even worse, the time the journeys took. Because of my interest in what they were saying, the other distractions from within the car and my nervousness and keenness to do well, I'd stupidly ended up taking them onto the M62 motorway to Leeds and Yorkshire instead of the M61 for Scotland.

I couldn't believe that after all my travelling I could do such a stupid thing, in fact I don't think I'd previously felt so embarrassed in my life, I was heartbroken inside, with my stomach turning over and over again, however luckily none of the others had noticed, so I turned the car around and headed back for the direction of Manchester. In typical waffling "Davies" style I managed to make light of the situation by claiming that I'd already heard of a bump on the correct route and that I'd tried to take an alternative detour around the problem area, an idea which unfortunately hadn't worked. It was a debut trip that I could well have done without, but after stopping for breakfast at a service station, then buying the girls a few chocolates and a drink each, I'd safely, "won them all over", by the time we'd reach Glasgow, with "Thanks Paul", "That was great!", "Will we see you next week?", being a few of their parting words.

My return journey back to Manchester with a second crew was fifty times easier and consequently more enjoyable, the other crew had told them all about me and the service, as they changed over on board the plane, leaving me confidently knowing that it was the first of many trips I'd be doing.

At that point in my life it seemed changes were constantly taking place all around me, nobody wanted to commit themselves, yet everybody wanted the "cash", even demanded it for doing very little, whilst at the same time, on their own terms. The four or five people who'd all previously earnt vast amounts of cash seemed to change their attitude to my success, by either wanting more money or working only when they wanted, usually in the daytime, between nine and four o'clock.

One bloke only wanted to pick up from the Novotel, while another and his wife could only do mornings, there was one chap who made no bones about the fact that he only intended doing jobs for one company, then there was the fella who was only available between taking his wife to work and picking her up. Even Kath at the airport had finished, yet despite the ever present, good reliable service, I'd always given, I was dropped because my face didn't fit with the manageress and so for the first time since I'd started, I was beginning to feel and see resentments, as they crept into people's lives, all in envy of our success.

Predictably one by one the neighbours gradually dropped off, eventually leaving Jeannette, myself and Gary, to cover the enormous amount of work we had booked in, which looking back was an ideal opportunity for the young man to see just how much commitment is needed to succeed, something which I honestly thought he would benefit from. Instead he was mesmerised by the driving I was capable of doing, plus the hours I was prepared to put in, which left him saying "Well I couldn't do that much, anyway Mary wouldn't let me, not even if I was earning a thousand pounds a week!!".

His view and attitude saddened me because he'd previously told me how much he'd wanted to do what I was being so successful at, yet there I was showing him how, but he still couldn't see and didn't understand that I was trying to lead by my own example. Jeannette and I even took him, his wife and his child down to the airport, as we took photo shots for a glossy brochure we were having produced, all of which they seemed to enjoy, but no matter how hard we tried to get him involved, he or should I say, his wife, refrained, wanting only set hours and an average wage per week.

Towards the end of March we'd received a very surprising call from Francis the PR girl in London, she wanted me to meet her off her flight, then chauffeur her around for a full day to various destinations, all over the North West, a job which I was more than happy to accept and looking forward to doing.

However on the day in question I got the shock of my life as she explained how in a couple of weeks, not only would I be picking her up, but also others, all very important film people, news which left me absolutely breathless, with nerves and excitement, thinking, "How the bloody ell has all this happened to me? and in such a short space of time, here I am, I've been doing this for a mere twelve months and I'm achieving my wildest dream and ambition, driving VIPs around from the film industry". That news meant that we once again had to think about the nightmare of employing staff, only this time seriously, because even a blind man could see we were going to get swamped in work as a result of our own success, so having discussed the situation with Gary, he came out with a suggestion of talking to a couple of drivers who he used to work with.

They were a brother and sister pair, who's mother, unknown to us, ran her own small, one car outfit, in one of the more un-salubrious parts of Salford, a place called Little Hulton. It's a rough area and that's putting it mildly, so we certainly weren't surprise to find, that they were both a bit on the "shady side", with what we suspected as having rather deceitful intentions in their approach to work.

We met Stuart, the brother first, who came around to Springclough, alone one afternoon, he looked presentable enough, wearing a clean shirt and tidy trousers, but his eyes were "shifty" and he asked far too many "nosey" questions relating to the business, which were really none of his concern. His sister, Lisa, well she left us both gob smacked with just her appearance, as she looked more like a tart, than someone trying to get a job as a lady chauffeur. The girl wore the shortest mini skirt possible, thick black fish net tights and a grubby looking off white, see through blouse, under which was a black bra, she did have nice dark, brown eyes and unlike her brother, did her best at least show some enthusiasm, but that was the best she had to offer.

As soon as we'd met them both we were very suspicious, we had the niggling thought at the back of our minds, that it may all be a very crafty ploy on the part of the ruthless taxi company they worked for, to very cleverly destroy our reputation, even stop us trading from within our own company, after all they'd tried near enough everything else, to put us out of business.

After a considerable amount of thought and a lot of deliberation we decided, against our better judgement and instincts, to give them a chance, but in order to cover our own backs, we made a stipulation that they had to show some sort of commitment, by each purchasing a "brand new car". Their vehicles just weren't suitable enough for our standard of clientele, so in buying a new car they would at least show us how serious they actually were about the idea, we also had a sneaking suspicion that they really wanted to see how we operated, so that they could eventually work along the same lines with their mother. We thought that they had long term plans of setting up in competition, but that didn't worry us in the slightest because we already knew just what was required to survive in the "game" and they certainly didn't have it!, so with scepticism we agreed to them joining us on a self employed basis, as soon as they'd bought their cars.

Meanwhile my most rewarding moment had nearly arrived, I'd spent the previous day with Francis and Carolyn her partner, chauffeuring them both here, there and everywhere, even managing to find them a suitable hotel nearer to the venue, but this really was it, the morning of my "biggest day", when my "dream of dreams" actually occurred. It was my very first experience of working with what I now call the "arty, farty" people of the television and film world, a world where, chaos, madness and illogical thinking all rule.

At the time, I thought that the way they acted was down to their own stupidity, selfishness and plain inability, but a couple of years later and with much more experience behind me, I realised that the two girls were just par for the course, in that industry.

As they had a busy, hectic day ahead, they were up bright and early with my schedule for the day, which until now had been kept top secret, probably the most important thing left to discuss. "Ha!, well that's what anyone normal would think!!". Not Francis or Carolyn, in their mind, they had far more important things to worry about, buffets, champagne, a red carpet, oh and of course a "Gold Spade", for that first dig, which Miss George herself, was to perform.

At the time I thought I was hearing things, "Did you say Miss George?", at which point I started to get a little inquisitive, you see, I was under the impression that it was just a small ceremony, with no mention of a famous actress being present. Then right out of the blue and in a real "matter of fact" manner, Francis came out with a "pearler", "Paul could you arrange to have a car at Manchester Airport for eleven o'clock this morning, to pick up Susan George?". My face must have said what I was thinking for me, because the two girls looked with a questionable expression on their faces, then said, "Is there a problem?", "No, no is there hell, it's just that you've left it a little late in the day to tell me about it!!".

Indeed there was something terribly wrong, but there were so many "dramatics" about the way they handled everything, that I didn't want to get involved, so I left them to finish their coffee, whilst I, in panics-ville state, rang Jeannette up, to try and sort something out.

You see, as with my first trip for the airline, it was just the start to what I hoped would be a long career, that I didn't really want, because to make matters ten times worse, the two girls insisted that I stayed with them until the ceremony had started, which unknown to both of them caused me problems, ten fold.

One, I only had one Granada, or limo as they preferred to call it, two, Jeannette had no idea of how to get to the site in the first place and three, even if she could, it was an impossibility because she was too busy on another job.

To make things even more difficult, God had decided that it would be a good time for my car phone to break down, so needless to say I'd got myself into one hell of a state. The two girls meanwhile were totally oblivious to my problems or the predicament I found myself in because they were wrapped up in their own and hopefully I'd hidden my despair and worry so well that everything was as they say, "Hunky Dory". Having spent twenty minutes or so phoning around my list of part time drivers, all of whom were unavailable, I began to sweat, I could feel my heart thumping, the blood pumping and my head feeling like it was ready to explode, then all of a sudden as I fumbled through my address book, I came across the number of a lady who'd worked with Kath at the airport.

The woman, Marion, was forever asking me if I ever needed any drivers, she was tidy, very presentable and was the proud owner of a nice big Volvo estate, a large car, ideal for the job in hand, she knew the airport well, and so in desperation I once again picked up the receiver, whilst at the same time shooting more prayers up to God than I'd ever previously done before.

Thankfully my prayers were answered, for not only was Marion available and willing, but her car had just been cleaned as well, better still, she even knew the area where the site was, which immediately took a ton weight off my shoulders. In the end everything worked out OK, with the opening ceremony kicking off spot on time, after which both Marion and myself were invited into the same private function as all the other dignitaries.

Marion had done me proud and so I paid her well, with the promise that if she ever wanted to do any more work, then I was more than happy to have her along, so with only one car now needed, she left with my most grateful thanks and the realistic hope that we'd do it again.

Meantime, I still had a fair bit of work to do, work which in the end proved somewhat dramatic and very, very fulfilling.

Quite suddenly without an ounce of warning, Frances came over to ask me if the car was ready, "Yes of course it is, it's at the main doors now". Then with a nod of her head and an acknowledgement from Miss George's manager, Susan was escorted to the car and we were off, in a mad frenzied panic, with a seven minute deadline to get her back to the site where the ceremony had taken place. I was amazed because the eyes and attention of all those who'd arranged the opening were firmly focused on me, as they totally relied on the knowledge I had of the area and my ability to get there on time. The whole experience was incredible, because for once in my life I felt really important, I knew that there were all those VIPs wondering if we'd make it, then at the site, there would be the public all waiting to wave her off, you see, Miss George was being taken back by helicopter which was landing at the site, but if we didn't make it in time, he'd have to leave without her. There we were doing at least seventy miles an hour pulling into the landing area, greeted by the jeers and cheers of the public and the building site workers alike, all frantically waving, trying to get a glimpse of Susan before she left.

As I opened the door for her, she kissed me on the cheek, "Thanks for all your help Paul", before making her way to the "chopper", which within seconds was ready to take off, then to my amazement and embarrassment, she winked and waved to me as the thing whirled away, all of which brought even more cheers from the builders and an avalanche of questions from the public such as, "What's she like?" and "Was she as nice as she seemed?". A few minutes later the excitement was all over, the crowd had dispersed through the settling dust caused by the helicopter, whilst I was left stood alone, more than pleased with myself for without having the advantage of an advanced warning, I'd successfully carried out my first ever contract. However my mission wasn't finished just yet because I still had one task left to complete, that of taking Francis and Carolyn back to the airport, so having put my own "mental" celebration on ice until I'd got home, I carried on with the job in hand.

The two girls left me at the airport full of gratitude, appreciation and the promise that they would be seeing me again in the not too distant future, all of which meant that I could at last return home to my inspiration and finally take stock of our joint achievement.

Not surprisingly, by the time I did eventually sit down, I was shattered, the worry, the excitement, the nervousness, all contributory factors to my mental and physical state, I'd even made my first television appearance, on the news without knowing it, which Jeannette had taped, but I was too tired to take it all in, so with one of her lovingly cooked meals inside me, I retired to my well needed bed, for some more than deserved sleep.

The next day it was a case of watching the video showing my first appearance on TV, which was all of ten seconds, then patting each other on the back with a "Well done", having a cup of tea, accompanied by the briefest of chats then off to my work. That's all we could do, because unknown to us at that period, our lives were already running at such a fast uncontrolable pace that we had no time to sit and wallow over anything, whether it be good or bad, with each day providing something new, different, or totally unexpected.

The day after the event proved to be no exception because the bother and sister pair turned up displaying the brand new cars they'd bought, with him looking as tidy as the last time we'd seen him, whilst she still needed to be reminded that the "fish nets" she'd donned just weren't suitable, anyway they started, although Jeannette and I still had reservations.

It wasn't long however before they started moaning, in fact I think it was all of a week, their major complaint was that they weren't busy enough and that working all hours wasn't exactly what they'd been used to, but both areas had been clearly and openly discussed at that first meeting, something which I quickly reminded them both of.

Towards the end of April Jeannette and I were exhausted, we'd worked incessantly since our last holiday and so having a fair bit of back up we decided that now was a good time to get away and unwind. We knew we could rely on Gary to keep a check on the other two and that the work, whilst busy wasn't chaotic, so we thought very carefully about the idea before definitely deciding to go.

With only three days to go before our departure, Gary himself decided to "rock the boat" by informing us that he was leaving, he said it was nothing personal, that it wasn't even the money, it was the irregular hours and the fact that his wife wasn't happy. However looking back it was an odd thing because it was actually him who told us about Lisa, a girl, who as Jeannette said at the time, he obviously had the "hots" for, which was something even apparent to me. On reflection, I now wonder whether or not it was his wife's jealousy which made him hand his notice in, anyway with only a few days to go before we left for our well earned rest, Gary had gone leaving the two we didn't really trust as our only staff. Once again we found ourselves in a bit of a predicament, because whilst we needed the break to recover from our exhaustion, we couldn't really afford to leave everything we'd built up, in the hands of "Bonny and Clyde", as we'd christened them, so we needed God to perform one of his miracles, because other than that I would have to stay at home, leaving Jeannette and Nick to go alone.

Well, my prayers were well and truly answered because right out of the blue, we got the craziest of phone calls from Kath, my friend who used to work at the airport, we hadn't seen her since Christmas, when Jeannette and I had taken her out for dinner and originally offered her a job, so it was a totally unexpected shock to hear from her. She had intended to try and surprise us by making her own way to our house, but had got lost on the way, so having found out exactly where she was calling from, I went to pick her up.

Kath was a qualified supply teacher and had returned to doing the job since leaving the airport, although she wasn't totally happy as she'd missed the whole atmosphere of the travel world generally, so she really wanted to return to working in that field. Unlike the last time we'd discussed work, she now saw our adventure as a whole new challenge in life which she wanted to be part of because over the past months since we'd first met, the woman had seen all that I'd achieved before her very own eyes, something that she'd constantly remarked about. Apart from seeing that I was going places, I was a sort of an answer to some of her problems because working with us would mean she was back in the environment of the airport, which I knew would once again throw up other job opportunities, so after a long, lengthy discussion it was agreed and she joined our little company.

It meant that I could at last enjoy the holiday which up until that point in time, had looked very distant and so we prepared to depart with Kath in charge, totally confident that all was safe in her hands. Before leaving we gave her our contact address and telephone number, numbers of back up drivers, mechanics, electricians, you name it, she had it, she even had cash, authorisation to sign on any accounts, everything!!, but more importantly because of my suspicions about Bonny and Clyde, a warning !!, "Listen Kath, watch them two, they're up to no good, I don't trust them but I have to try, just be careful they're quite likely to let you down!!". I also told her that she wasn't to take too much work on and that if she felt it was necessary, she was to enrol the extra help and assistance of Janet, a girl we both knew from her days at the airport, who had been unhappy since leaving and consequently like Kath, looking for a return to the travel industry.

We eventually left shattered, but fully confident that all would be OK in our absence, especially with Kath, one of very few people I'd ever trusted, liked or respected in charge, however within a few hours of our arrival I'd received a phone call from her, telling me that Bonny and Clyde had let her down on the very first two early morning pick ups.

Despite my ever present suspicions, I couldn't believe it !, I mean the very first jobs, after all their previous moaning about not having enough to do and they couldn't even do them, I was so annoyed with myself because although desperately needing a break, I realised there and then, that I shouldn't have even gone on the trip, feelings made ten times worse by the fact that Kath, the woman who I'd confidently entrusted, couldn't even handle a simple problem like that, without ringing me up asking for help.

The question she posed of, "What shall I do Paul?", was answered quite eloquently by myself, in my usual, most basic of manners, "I told you before I left Kath, the minute they mess you about, then get Janet to give you a lift!!", which then brought a second question from her, "But what about Stuart and Lisa, what should I do about them?". Once again at most inimitable best, I summed it up quite simply, "Fuck em, Kath !!, Fuck em!!, they're not pissing me about, I'll sort those two out when I get home !, you're in charge and I trust your judgement".

Thankfully we never heard from her again during the holiday, which meant that both Jeannette and myself enjoyed the rest of our break to return refreshed, charged up and ready to resume our hundred miles an hour lifestyle.

When we appeared at Manchester Airport, we got somewhat of a shock because instead of Kath meeting us, it was Janet, Kath was ill in bed as a result of exhaustion, she'd worked hard, non stop in fact, but contrary to my advice, the woman had endeavoured to do as much as she possibly could, consequently she'd knackered herself up.

Instead of going straight home, we immediately called round to Kaths', where we found her in bed, looking bloody awful, we told her to take a week's rest, give us a call when she was fit enough to resume work and that we'd see her when she was ready. With that we then took Janet home, discussing her new wage structure as we did, after all she'd helped Kath look after the business in our absence, so it was only fair that we showed our loyalty, by giving her permanent employment in return.

As per usual it was "back to the grindstone" immediately, so by the time we'd got home, we felt as though we'd already done a days work, knowing full well that I still had Bonny and Clyde to sort out, apart from any other "as yet" unknown problems.

Sure enough they came round complaining that they'd had no work off Kath, that they felt as though we'd used them, Oh and of course the root of all evil, "MONEY!!", the pair even had the cheek to tell me that I owed them money!.

Well Jeannette and I were in no mood for those two, so we let them have their say, before giving them a few "home truths" on just how much commitment, loyalty and hard work was needed to survive, never mind succeed in such a business, all of which was too much for them to swallow, so they stormed off, thankfully saving me doing the honours.

With over a week passed since our return, we'd neither seen sight nor sound of Janet, she herself wasn't feeling too good, but her boyfriend had been to collect her wages, whilst Kath had at least spoken on the phone on a couple of occasions, so needless to say Jeannette and I were once again beginning to get suspicious.

Sadly we didn't have to wait long before those thoughts, doubts and suspicions were confirmed, for on the Sunday morning, whilst I was in bed catching some sleep, I was awakened by the noise of slightly raised voices. Although I'd previously been in a deep comatosed type of state, I hurriedly put my shorts and sweat shirt on, then raced downstairs to find what I can only describe as some sort of deputation, or Spanish inquisition, for there in our own living room were Janet, Bonny and Clyde, Bonnie's boyfriend and Ma Baker herself, Kath.

Despite the fact that Jeannette could have easily have handled all four of them alone, I was immediately incensed to think that they were all coward enough to air their grievances in a "bullying" fashion with her, misguidedly believing that Jeannette wouldn't cope and that I was out of the way in bed. I was also angry because they had no regard whatsoever for young Nicholas, Jeannette's son, who at the time was only fourteen years old and still asleep, but on top of all that, the things that they said, plus the accusations made, just about put the icing on the cake for me.

It appeared that Kath for some "still unknown" reason, had basically decided to "shit stir", with the destructive, vindictive sort of manner that a scorned woman would usually apply. She'd discussed all of our business with everyone imaginable, whilst at the same time, inspite of all I'd previously done for her, totally "turned round" and changed her view of me.

It seems looking back, that she generally orchestrated a hate campaign of all those people who I'd either given a chance to, or even come into contact with in the past, intent on destroying my relationship with Jeannette and the business we'd built up.

There were even accusations on Bonnie's part that I'd slid my hands up her skirt, all of which just about summed up the depravity and pathetic state of their attack, especially as I'd always considered her a slag or a tart!!.

Further accusations that both Jeannette and myself had used each and every-one of them, were followed by yet another insinuation that I'd previously made a pass at sixty year old Marion, the woman who'd helped us on the film contract, all of which led me to think, "God at this rate there must have been a North West area seminar on Jeannette and Paul of Exclusia Travel".

The pathetic sadness of their worthless accusations was well and truly summed up by myself when I turned to Kath in front of Jeannette and stated quite categorically, "Kath of all the people I'd even think of making a pass at you'd be the one, so answer me, have I ever touched you?". There was no other way she could possible respond, for even as bitter as she was, the woman knew deep down that I'd even sat with my arms around her comforting her, as she sat weeping alone at home, dressed only in the skimpiest of satin underslips, following a trip abroad chasing after her estranged husband.

At the end of a lengthy, heated argument, my case with her was secretly proved and that same woman, who I'd given my all, in terms of friendship, left our house, well and truly suckered by the two cronies I'd initially warned her about, so yet again it was back to the successful winning formula of just my inspiration and I, proving once again that our love was much stronger than others gave us credit for.

That experience did enlighten us both to one fact, a lesson which thankfully looking back we did well to learn from because we were now more sure than we ever were before, that the more successful we were becoming, the more resentments other people were growing, which meant that we had to start being on our guard more and "toughen up".

Our new "get tough" policy was immediately enforced on the 4th May, with Jeannette and myself deciding that for far too long we'd been too polite, too nice and too much like doormats, with our first victim being the local "lady" who held research parties at her home.

Anne was a big, fat woman, with a gob to match her physique, she was cocky, full of herself and one of those types who was never wrong. During the time Anne had used our services, she'd never had cause to complain, despite the fact that more often than not, either the woman herself or her clients had kept us waiting, so it was rather fitting that she was our first "rejection".

Unknown to her, I had waited as pre arranged outside a house for one of her clients, however after fifteen minutes nobody had shown, so I left to return home. Sometime afterwards in the belief that it was another driver who'd been, the woman got on the phone in her typical, "I'm right " attitude, "gobbing off" to Jeannette, that the car she'd ordered had not arrived and so with the presence of the lady she is, my inspiration refused point blank to have anything more to do with the rude, "mannish" type of woman, saying, "I think it would be better for all concerned, if you book your cars elsewhere as we don't particularly wish to deal with you again!".

Because we were getting pissed off with that sort of attitude and as a result of feeling better for our actions, we immediately adopted the very same stance with the public, whereby if they were extremely rude to us, then we returned the compliment.

However not for the first time in our lives as we said goodbye to one face, it was "Hello" to another, only this time one from the past for the month of May brought the return of Keith, the young lad who was our first ever full time driver.

His return brought immediate relief to both Jeannette and myself because only a couple of days earlier I'd started employing a good, long time friend of mine, on a part time basis, which meant that at least this second time around, Keith would have regular working hours and I'd increased my staff.

However by the mid May, even though we had two other drivers, apart from us, things were still hectic, so by sheer chance or should I say through a conversation with a painter working at Springclough, I made one of my biggest ever mistakes, by offering the chap concerned a job.

The man in question was a local bloke, who only lived around the corner from Jeannette, he was pleasant, well mannered, with only one real problem, which was that he smoked, but with that being his only downfall, I took him on.

It meant that for the first time ever, we were well staffed, and more than capable of taking on more work, which through God's will, is exactly what we did!! because the work kept flowing in, meaning that all the drivers employed were kept busy, whether it was day or night.

By now we were covering all sorts of work, group bookings of up to fifty or so people transported by coach, one, two, even three loads of people at a time and then our company contract work on top, plus my airline work.

We were doing well and we knew it, but unfortunately for us, so did the rest of the residents in Springclough Drive, all of which meant jealousy, envy and anger were emotions festering within the natives, meaning that bitter resentments and "trouble" were once again brewing just around the corner.

It always seemed that whenever somebody had it in for us, we would find ourselves picking up more new work, without even trying, all of which just rubbed salt into the already stinging wounds of our enemies, with this last episode being no different.

Because on the very last day in that month of May, we received a call from the only company I'd ever made any sort of personal advance towards, in a search for work or to achieve any of my initial ambitions. It was a large TV company and as a result of the rudeness shown to me by the woman I'd originally met, a call which I certainly didn't expect would ever follow.

A month earlier I'd been down to Granada Television, to keep an appointment with a lady called Barbara Jervis who was in charge of the travel department. She wasn't very forthcoming, positive or even particularly keen to meet me when we'd first spoken on the phone but through my own perseverance, eventually conceded to my requests to, at least, have a brief chat.

Apart from being off hand and very self righteously arrogant, the woman was dammed rude, as she basically tried to "fob me off" claiming that they already used a company and that there really wasn't enough work or room for another.

I could tell from the way she was dealing with my interest and enquiries, that the woman was obviously on a good "back-hander", that there was absolutely no way on this earth, anyone else was muscling in on the act and that she didn't like me, "one bit" for asking.

Needless to say I'd left all immediate hopes of breaking into TV work aside for the time being, concentrating on more realistic possibilities for the near future, that was until now, when we'd received their call and an urgent request for a "limo".

Since originally starting up, I'd always believed in myself and my own ability, but I knew that out there in the real world I would, at more than one point depend on someone, somewhere else and this was one such time.

I wasn't stupid or anything like that, I knew full well that the horrible woman I'd met at Granada had rung us out of desperation not choice but I also realised that having done so, it was now down to me to "win over", whoever this VIP was, so that I would at least get one foot in the door, in spite of her and the deceitful way she operated.

It was all rather like a repeat performance of my very first job for the Novotel, only this time I was fittingly tailored out for the occasion, as well as having the ideal mode of transport for the job, it was also a last minute rush job, as we once again frantically cleaned the car but we did it and I arrived outside the man's home, spot on time.

Inwardly I was obviously very nervous, as not for the first or last time in my life, I desperately wanted to impress but those apprehensions were soon dispelled as the man, a Mr Doherty although important was both friendly and pleasant.

I chauffeured him down to Leicestershire, waited for four hours, then returned him home, knowing that it was another job well done, without a single hiccup, all beliefs rubber stamped with his parting words, "That was an excellent service Paul, thank you very much indeed", so I made my way home, confident that Jeannette and myself would at some point in time, be hearing from the television company again. As usual the following day Jeannette and I would "catch up" on what had gone on in my absence, work, drivers, the home, all manner of things, however this time our major celebrations were slightly soured by the news that her next door neighbour had actually been out to have a few words with Neil, my long time friend who now worked part time for us.

It was the very same woman who had previously made the pathetic, disastrous attempt to produce some business cards, the same person who I'd been kind to when she was ill, by being caring and friendly and the same person, who'd gladly accepted all our waste food when her husband had lost his job but she'd kindly forgotten those things, as they obviously were not important. She objected to Neil parking his black van in the road whilst he was working for us driving one of our cars and it was the first real aggressive action shown by anyone of the neighbours in the drive, so typical of Jeannette, she tried "in a nice way" to find out what all the fuss was about, only to be met with the most volatile, sick response imaginable.

It was a sad case of jealousy and nothing more but at that exact moment in time, something we had to totally dismiss, misguidedly believing it would go away but unfortunately it didn't, unbeknown to us, it grew, spreading within the road, as the very same people who'd all used and in some cases worked for us providing the service, resented our rapidly growing success.

Meanwhile unaware of the depth to the underlying problem, we carried on with our own lives and in our own way, we had no choice because the work just kept coming and coming, so we battled on "grafting away", naively thinking that it was all a temporary thing and that they'd pick on someone else, when they'd got fed up of us.

God being the script writer, was as ever watching and so in his wisdom, he once again decided to act, making matters ten times worse and sort of showing a "red rag to a bull", by giving us yet another totally unexpected telephone call, one which actually brought my wildest, most imaginable dream, come to true, factual reality, an experience never ever to be forgotten, memories of which, will live with Jeannette, Nick her son and myself, . . . forever!!.

It was a call from Francis in London, the "PR" girl who I'd already worked with, I didn't really expect to be hearing from her again for quite some time, but there again, due to the pressure I was under on their last visit, I hadn't listened to much that was being said. She informed me that the actual opening of the Mutiplex Cinema being built was taking place in a couple of weeks and my services would be required for a period of not less than seven days, she was coming up the next day and would be grateful if I could meet her at the airport.

Once again I was there and of course I looked after her, however as with their previous visits, it was all rather "cloak and dagger" type stuff, where the discussions she had with people, whilst I was present seemed coded. In hindsight it was all unnecessary secrecy, which only served to cause even more chaos and uncertainty for the more important tasks such as ours of providing transport because without any warning she asked me if I could provide a couple of "limos" the next day to pick up several "film celebrities" from the airport. They were only the stars of the "Police Academy" movies, who were arriving to promote the "premier" of their latest of six films, which was going to be used at the opening ceremony, needless to say the realisation that we were going to be responsible for picking them up, only served to make us nervous with excitement and that's putting it mildly!!.

Still pursuing the same crazy avenue of mystery, we weren't told until the very last minute of their arrival or even what flight we were meeting but as usual we were there with Jeannette, myself and Keith all immaculately dressed with cars to match.

As arranged we'd arrived spot on time with us knowing far more about flights and the airport generally than Francis, Carolyn and the others ever could, all of which meant we spent the next half hour hanging around, listening to all the fuss and palaver being made by them.

It had always been our policy that no matter who we were dealing with, we'd treat everybody the same, with no extra fuss made to anyone in particular but not in their case, they acted as though they were dealing with Royalty, Gods even and so we waited like all of the onlookers, in anticipation, believing that they were going to be arrogant, selfish, pompous and very hard to deal with.

The minute their shuttle touched down there was an air of expectancy about the place, with the press and media gathering outside, whilst we stood in the back ground awaiting their appearance.

By now the small crowd that had gathered inside the building buzzed with excitement, as even the "black cab" drivers who despised us, muscled their way into the arrivals hall to see what was going on. Then suddenly they were escorted through by one of the airline staff, to be greeted with cheers, a round of applause,

Carolyn on behalf of Warner Brothers, Oh and of course us, their drivers!!.

What a surprise we got!!, for contrary to what we'd been led to believe, they were all very nice people and so from the very first minute we met, both Jeannette and myself knew that everything was going to be alright and that inspite of the pressure, we were going to enjoy every minute of our time with them.

For four days, I near enough lived with those people, because everywhere they went, I went, if they wanted to go somewhere special, I took them and whatever work they were carrying out, whether it be a photo session for the press or a radio/TV interview, I was invited in alongside them, in fact we became so close, that within such a short space of time a true friendship had been formed.

It was a period of time I hardly saw Jeannette or anyone else for that matter because I spent day and night with them, however I did get the fifth morning off, which ironically came as a result of Granada, the very same television company I'd previously done one job for, which not just by coincidence, was the first and only "cock up" or complaint that occurred during the whole of their stay!. They were appearing on a live morning programme for the company at Liverpool and so my services weren't required, as they were supplying "limos" of their own.

It was a fact which by it's very nature annoyed me because I already knew that the company with their contract monopolised the market, so I immediately panicked, fearful that they may "muscle in" on this one. Well I needn't have bothered, for in the afternoon I discovered that they'd had a disastrous day of it already, as the limos supplied were in fact normal "tatty", dirty, smelly taxis, that were falling to bits, they said that all the drivers had got lost and that they'd actually missed having me take them all together in one giant "limo". Whilst over the moon at such news, we were left somewhat confused as to why, why had the woman in charge of travel, previously told me they were happy with what services they were already using. It was a puzzle, which because we were so busy, couldn't be dealt with just yet, so we carried on with the task in hand, believing more in ourselves, than we'd ever done before.

Two days later on the fifteenth of June 1989, we had our biggest ever day since starting Exclusia Travel, the Gala opening of Warner Brother's Multiplex Cinema in Bury. It was a day where yet again Jeannette and I were put on the spot, to be left running around at the very last minute, like two headless chickens, a day where Jeannette, God bless her, worked more than two or three miracles and where without her, everything would certainly have been a total disaster!.

We'd constantly worked as a team, even when she was working at Trumanns, which is probably why we were so successful, but I've always maintained in my new life, that she is actually the success behind me.

Well this day was no different because still, as I write this now, I don't know how she managed to arrange it all and make the whole thing happen. I was already more than drained, when I returned home at mid day for a bite to eat, to be greeted to a vision of no less than six "brand new" expensive cars, parked up in "Springclough".

I can see us both now, stood looking out of Jeannette's front window, laughing and giggling with, I don't know what, nerves, excitement, call it want you want!!.

Then there was the anger, bitterness and resentment, on the faces of those lovely neighbours, as they watched the commotion, all of whom had taken so much from us in the past, waste food, free samples, flowers when they were ill and of course the trips I'd given them and their families, all without charge!!. Two or three of them had already been out into the street, obviously gossiping, wondering what was going on but unknown to them, there were more to come in the afternoon. By now though we were past caring, after all we owed them nothing, so we treated the whole thing as a huge joke, thinking how sad their pettiness really was.

Being told less than twenty four hours before the event, that we were going to be picking up numerous, famous people and of course having to arrange the extra cars enabling us to do the work was bad enough but to be told on the very last minute that I was to go to the airport to meet the great Liza Minelli no less, was a joke. I actually thought that Francis was "piss taking" but she wasn't and so off I went in one of the "brand new" Daimler Jags we'd rented, to carry out the job in hand.

By this time, Jeannette and myself were getting a little fed up, as we realised that Francis and her friends from down south, seemed to be living in another world to us, they obviously thought that with a click of the fingers anything was possible and that we could just as easily quickly provide. I say that because as we stood in the airport building, one of the girls suddenly came out with another one of their magical statements, which went something like, "Paul, I thought you were providing a 'limo' for Miss Minelli?". I could have smashed her in the face there and then !!, I couldn't believe my own ears, all week and ever since I'd started looking after them, my "brand new" Granada was a "limo" in their "OK yah" world. Now, when I'm stood in the middle of the airport, having only been told half an hour earlier that I was even going to be there at all, the fifty, thousand pound Daimler parked outside is not a "limo" because a "stupid limo" has suddenly become a Rolls Royce!!, of all things.

Still totally disbelieving what I'd just heard, I went straight over to Jeannette, "Those two are totally off their trolleys", D'ya know what they've just said?", where upon I started to relate my story and their change of plans and ideals.

Well, I don't know how she did, or where it came from but Jeannette somehow managed to half arrange one whilst we were still awaiting the stars arrival in the airport, although it wasn't definite, so after a dramatic appearance through customs, I made a swift departure with Lisa Minelli in the back, secretly heading straight for the Midland Hotel in the centre of Manchester. It was as dramatic an exit as one could have asked for but not half as dramatic as the sight that greeted me when I eventually got home because not for the first time that day, Jeannette had near enough performed a miracle, for as I turned into Springclough, I just burst out laughing, "Why ?", because there amongst eleven other very, large expensive cars, stood a white, Rolls Royce!!. "She's done it !, thank God !!".

Due to the fact that I was never actually involved on that, the more important side of the business, "The organisation", I'm unable to describe the feelings brought about by the pressure and the responsibility. All I can say, is that on the many occasions such as the evening I'm describing, I was always proud of "My Inspiration", forever grateful that she was there!!. Having said that, on this particular occasion she did us more than proud, because as I slowly rolled up the cul de sac, I could see the faces of all those jealous neighbours, green with envy, as they peered through their living room windows. Having joined the queue of cars, I then had a cup of tea in the garden with all the drivers I'd employed and I was proud because parked the full length if the road were brand new Daimlers, Jaguars, BMWs, Mercedes Benzs, the Rolls Royce and of course my own vehicles, with each driver identically matching the other, as they all donned the same uniform.

I desperately wanted to stand in the middle of the road and shout, "Fuck you all, you evil, jealous bastards!!", to each and everyone of them, for had they not acted in such a despicable manner, some of them I'm sure, would have been driving instead. Never the less, instead of succumbing to their more evil, naturally common ways, I opted for more of a sober "fingers up" attitude and so we all left together in a giant convoy, destined for our own individual hotels and pick ups, led by myself in the white Rolls Royce.

The next hour or so for me personally, proved to be somewhat of a nightmare, as my only job, which was to pick up Lisa Minelli from the Midland Hotel, left me with more than enough thinking time. Consequently worrying and projecting doom 'n' gloom took over the main stage of my head, with thoughts like, "I hope Jeannettes' alright!!", or, "God what if someone breaks down!!", then there was Mike, our totally thick, stupid driver, the one who wasn't all there, "I wonder how he's doing?".

In the month or so that Mike had been with us, he'd had some terrible "cock ups", many of which I'll write about in the next chapter, cock ups that mainly came about as a result of his total ineptness to do near enough anything right, so although I only had the one pick up to make, albeit the most important one, I did have more than my fair share to panic about.

On the night, we were all tied to a very tight, careful planned time schedule, cleverly worked out by Jeannette, with me arriving first, then the rest following at twenty second intervals. It was done purposely, so that each car load of celebrities could roll up to receive their own individual acknowledgments and picture shots but first and foremost, I had to get there.

Reliving moments such as these, is rather like having a recurring nightmare, for that's exactly what a job such as this was, Oh yes!, it's glamorous alright and at the time you are the envy of most people around you but it is never the less, a nerve wrecker!. Constant worries run through the mind, such as, "What if the car won't start?" or "God, say the door jams!", then there are the other multitude of problems, things that at the time you know full well you have no control over, whatsoever, such as major traffic problems, caused by some unimaginable or unforeseeable disaster, then there's the stars themselves, who often run late with an, "Oh well I'm alright" attitude all things that run through the already drained mind.

Despite my many projections of impending disaster, we did make it spot on time without a hitch but nothing could possibly have prepared either myself or the others for what lay ahead, as it proved to be one hell of a magnificent experience, "a one off" and a chance of a lifetime!!.

For over a week I'd driven up the very same entrance, time and time again but never before had it appeared as it did now.

I was absolutely shocked to find that even the streets approaching the cinema were lined with local people all waving flags and cheering as we approached the entrance to the car park, escorted by a police bike rider. Then as we actually drove in I couldn't believe my own eyes, I remember thinking, "Please God don't let me break down now, not in front of all these folk, let me make it all the way".

There were literally thousands of them, young and old, all facing me from different directions, as I slowly weaved my way through the specially marked out route giving everyone the chance to see the stars. The adults clapped and jeered, whilst their children waved flags, all with their eyes firmly fixed on the car as we gently toured the car park, then I suddenly found myself opening the car door for Lisa at the main entrance to the cinema and for the first time since originally picking up Francis, I truly realised what I was actually involved in.

Numerous television cameras rolled, boom microphones wearing fluffy hats were held out or raised, then literally hundreds of camera flashes simultaneously exploded, it was here and I was a major part of it, Hollywood had come to Manchester!!.

With the main star's grand entrance over, I stood nervously awaiting Jeannette's arrival, then spot on time she pulled up with her two own personal favourites from that week, at which point the cameras once again rolled with the accompaniment of yet another million and one flashes. She looked absolutely beautiful, she was mine and I loved her more than I'd ever done before, but more importantly I was so, so proud of her, because our performance was all down to her, nobody else, her and seeing her stood there amongst all this attention was both fitting and right, she deserved it!.

At that point both Lance and GW, the actors she'd brought were supposed to face and acknowledge the watching crowd, have their pictures taken, then enter the cinema building, clearing the way for the next approaching car. Not on your life!, not these two characters because unbeknown to me, on their way to the Gala they'd asked Jeannette where Nick, her son was, the whole bunch of them had been dying to meet him all week, only to be constantly told by me that he'd be at the event, so as soon as they'd got out of the car, they only had one question, "Paul, where's Nick?".

It was absolutely chaos!, there we were for all the press, media and the public alike to see, stood chatting on the red carpet with not a care in the world, while the ushers and other officials who were all full of their own importance, having kittens, looking on in amazement. Thirty seconds later, the next car rolled up with exactly the same thing happening, by which time Jeannette's son had himself become somewhat of a celebrity. The viewing public must have wondered who he actually was to be receiving so much attention, they'd said all week that they couldn't wait to meet him and they meant it, which for me, was probably the biggest lesson I learnt from the whole experience.

With the arrival of the third car, they finally entered the building leaving us to stand, pray and wait, that all the cars would turn up on time, in order and without any problems along the way, which they eventually did and so with only one major, "not too difficult" task left to complete that of returning Miss Minelli to the airport, the pressure was at long last off, or so we thought!.

Whilst the premier of the movie was being shown, Miss Minelli was to leave, via the side door, it was only ever planned as the briefest of appearances, which is exactly what it was.

As a result the rest of our fleet were parked at the rear of the building, whilst I stayed on call ready to return her to the airport, it was an easy exercise, which shouldn't have proved a difficult task but unfortunately as with everything else I seemed to do in life, nothing is that simple!.

Jim, Jeannette's brother in law, who'd always professed to know something about cars had noticed water leaking from under the Rolls, consequently I'd switched off the engine, something I never liked doing especially if the vehicle was suddenly going to be required, enabling him to investigate the possible cause. Having had a good look at it, he told me that it was probably the water pump, saying it was driveable, as long as it was topped up with water, which he duely did, leaving me looking up at the sky breathing a large sigh of relief, "Thank God".

With that panic over we once again waited patiently for the ensuing sudden departure of the star herself, although we didn't have to wait long because just a few minutes later the nod was given to prepare the car. With my fingers crossed, I turned the key in the ignition and there it was . . . nothing!, yes you heard me, nothing, not even a click of the ignition because that stupid car was as dead as the animals we'd buried in the back garden some twenty or so years earlier. Jeannette, bless her, thought I was joking when I turned to her saying, "It won't start, the car won't fuckin start!!". It was our worst nightmare come true, there in front of thousands of people a white Rolls Royce for all to see and it wouldn't fucking go, with Lisa Minelli herself no less, coming out at any moment expecting to get into the heap. I personally wasn't prepared to fanny about, especially in the sort of mood I was now in, so I ordered one of my drivers to bring a Daimler round, without trying to cause too much attention which he duely did, meaning we'd only just escaped serious embarrassment by the skin of our teeth.

It was a saga which still brings a tear to our eyes when we recall it because the pompous oaf from Warner Brothers who continuously repeated "The car, the car, for Miss Minelli!", sounded more like the midget on Fantasy Island with his exclamation, "The Plane, the plane!!".

Even more laughable was the fact that Lisa couldn't even tell the bloody difference between the two vehicles, as all she seemed interested in was having some popcorn and English chocolates!!.

Anyway I got her to the airport, then happily made my way back to the cinema complex, knowing that we'd got over the worst and that we'd more than done ourselves proud, however at that point I personally had no idea of the surprise facing me on my return.

By the time I'd got back, the movie had finished and the Gala had only just begun, I could find neither Jeannette, Nick or any of the drivers for that matter, so I made my way to the marquee entrance where the as yet surprise to me, quickly unfolded!.

My appearance at the entrance was greeted with various shouts from all directions, "Paul", "Paul", there were acknowledgements from the dance floor, the buffet, this table and that table, then I heard the only voice that I really wanted to hear, "Here love, over here!", which of course was my inspiration calling from the table right in the corner of the marquee, which had secretly and specially been reserved for us . . . "Exclusia Travel!!".

It was as if we were in a movie ourselves or should I say more of a fairytale, for there we were surrounded by a sea of very important people and dignitaries, all wearing tuxedos, evening dresses, even diamond tiaras as the ball really got under way.

Each guest was met at the reception area with a large glass of buck's fizz, which was topped up every time they took a sip by their own attentive waiter, they were then escorted to the main function room, where God knows how many large, round tables invitingly stood, each one capable of seating twelve guests, all were littered with expensive chocolates, cigars and cigarettes, then just to add that party atmosphere, delicately coloured fancy balloons and streamers hovered above each setting.

As the night wore on the party really exploded into full swing as waiters, constantly paraded around replacing the empty bottles of wine with more of the same. The privileged people who were present began to let themselves go as the alcohol began to take effect, with our sober drivers making the best of the entertainment provided but for Jeannette and myself it was a time to take stock, to reflect and to realise our joint achievement.

We still had lots of work to do because we had to get the drunken lot back to their hotels and then the following morning take them to the airport but that was easy compared to what we'd already been through, for now the pressure was well and truly off.

Midway through the evening it was "nose bag" time, a point where all of these pissed up, well to do people, lined up in a queue, then paraded along an enormously well presented hot and cold buffet. There were smoked salmon, shrimps, prawns, lobster, even caviar, then on another table, chicken, duck, turkey and above all else a pheasant. The display of deserts was incredible too, but by far the most impressive of all was the carefully constructed mountain of chilled bottles of champagne, accompanied by the even larger well stacked, display of champagne glasses, all to be consumed on the night.

After the mammoth feast, where these highly respected folk had turned savage like, it was back to business with more drinking, dancing and the customary kissing and cuddling that becomes the norm, when people get into such a state.

Whilst all this was going on, the numerous photographers present continued to mingle amongst the crowd, snapping countless shots, whilst the reporters accompanying them, interviewed those very same VIPs, which is exactly where the photo on the front cover of this book comes from, only in our case, this picture tells a completely different story.

Unlike nearly everyone else present, we were shattered, still working and sober, we were madly and passionately in love, whilst at the same time proud of our enormous achievement, realising that we'd even surpassed our own high standards and expectations.

One or two of the reporters had already been over to our table during the course of the evening, out of fascination, wanting to know who we were and why so many of the stars present had been over to our setting spending so much time with us. In fact it was actually one of those reporters who quite eloquently summed it all up for us, when he said, "They all have so much respect for you both!!". They did!, for as the orchestra continued to play and the night rolled on, their presence in our company became even more apparent for all to see, which was more than a pat on the back for Jeannette and I, it was the nicest possible way of saying, "Thank you" and it meant something very special to us both!.

By approximately three o'clock in the early hours and after a great deal of effort, the last guests were finally dropped off at their hotel, they were two of the stars from the TV series "The Bill" and they were well out of it!. Even the full orchestra had given up on them both, having serenaded the pair with the last waltz for over an hour, which wouldn't have been half so bad if they'd been of the opposite sex, but seeing two men dancing whist holding a half empty bottle of champagne each, was truly a sight to behold.

Jeannette had dealt with the lads since their arrival at the airport a day earlier, they'd been nothing but charming to her and so she was the poor unfortunate, who had to wait for them both.

She didn't mind for as she put it, "They're a lovely couple of lads!", so whilst Jeannette saw to them, I took the Rolls back, meaning we all eventually got home together at about four o'clock in the morning.

Going to bed was a pointless exercise because we were all back at the various hotels in Manchester for six o'clock, so we had a cup of tea, a piece of toast and a form of chat, which resembled some sort of mumbling noise or use of a foreign language.

By now we were dead from the ankles up, meaning that even holding a conversation was hard work, so very little was actually said knowing full well that we'd soon have to put that "other head" on, don the "alternative face", the one with the smile and finish the job in hand, by pretending to be fresh as if we'd had ten hours sleep.

During the course of just over a week, Jeannette and I had dealt with over thirty famous Film and Television celebrities, we'd also looked after more than twenty, very important and powerful film directors, producers and executives in general, so it was rather ironic that the first people to leave that morning, were in fact the cast of the film itself.

They couldn't have been nicer to us both if they'd tried and so instead of me picking them up in the seven seater limousine that I'd always previously used, Jeannette came along with a second Daimler, enabling us both to say "Thank you" and "Goodbye" together. We knew that it wasn't going to be the happiest of occasions but typical of them, they had us laughing right to the end, for looking very delicate and much the worst from the night before, they all appeared wearing dark sun-glasses in typical "Hollywood" style. In saying our farewells, we felt as though we were losing good friends but I distinctly remember saying to Jeannette, "I don't know why but I have the feeling deep down, that we'll meet them again!" and so with a hectic morning schedule ahead of us, we made our way back to the city centre hotels, for one of the many trips left to complete.

Once again everything went totally according to plan, with each and every guest punctually picked up then returned to the airport, trips which saw me personally work right through until mid-day, however none were more important than that last couple of people, for it was none other than the President of Warner Brothers himself, Mr Salah Hassanein!.

He was a lovely man, who inspite of his power and influence, came over as just a normal, likable chap, however as a result of my commitment to looking after the cast, I wasn't able to tend to his every need, therefore another driver had to be seconded to him full time for the duration of the event. We both got on extremely well from the minute we'd first met, but not half as well as the introduction I'd experienced with his wife, who from all previous accounts was less than awkward. Well if there's one thing that I do not get involved in, it's hearsay, it plays no part in my sober life, never has and never will, something which on this occasion I was more than glad of because on the day in question, she was due to arrive at Manchester Airport, alone and so at the special request of Francis, I went to pick her up.

They'd told me Mrs Hassanein was allergic to this and allergic to that, warning me that she could only drink fresh water, whilst at the same time telling me, that the woman was agoraphobic, schizophrenic, even a manic depressive, in fact you name it she had it!, all which left me thinking, "She sounds a bit like me, I'll bet we get on a treat!". Well the lady walked through the arrivals hall and we, not surprisingly, "hit it off" straight away, she was charming, friendly, quite attractive and we talked non-stop all the way to her hotel, getting on like a house on fire!.

It was probably the most educating example of the whole experience, one which more than served Jeannette and myself well for the future because as I'd been taught in AA, we are all people with only one day to live, that's all, one day, with even that being a gift from God!.

Consequently that last journey back to the airport was more than a pleasure, one where I actually learnt a hell of a lot in just twenty minutes from two people I had nothing but respect for.

Salah wanted to know what I thought about the show and the two PR girls Francis and Carolyn, who arranged it all, then he criticized the renting of the Rolls Royce, "Was it really necessary?", with most of his comments things I'd already remarked about to Jeannette in private. Elyse his lovely wife paid me the biggest compliment of all, when she asked me if I'd like to go and work for them over in the States, all of which made me shrug my shoulders, smile, then jokingly reply, "Well even if you were being serious, I couldn't go until I've accomplished everything I want to here!". I actually thought that Elyse meant as a chauffeur, that was until she'd corrected me by saying, "No Paul, I didn't mean driving, I mean in PR work, I think you'd make a great Public Relations guy!".

I was overwhelmed by her comments and her kindness but dismissed them by saying, "Perhaps one day when the time is right!", well if you do ever read this Elyse or Salah, "I'm ready when you are!".

Once we'd arrived at the airport I escorted them both to the correct check in desk, then presented the lovely lady with a bouquet of flowers, I thanked them for being so nice and wished them both a safe journey, in the sincere hope that we'd meet again, then left knowing that it was the end of what was truly a "fairytale" experience.

Chapter Thirteen

A Nightmare Begins

Due to the fact that we were so busy, we very sadly had no time to either enjoy or celebrate our success, our own very regular work was as hectic as ever, with more companies requiring our services by the day.

We were constantly being contacted by the press for either interviews or local advertising, apart from an enormous increase in the main holiday airport bookings, so a decision was immediately taken to retain a couple of the lads who'd helped out and start thinking about purchasing a second Granada Ghia.

The month of June had been as busy and as successful as anyone could possibly have prayed for but unknown to us at the time, it was to become even busier, for in the very last week we received a call from Loganair, asking me to pick up a Danish, two man aircrew at the airport, then just by coincidence take them to the Novotel at Worsley, where we lived.

It was the start of a contract which lasted for three months, a job that certainly opened my eyes from that first pick up because as I stood awaiting the appearance of those first two, baggage laden, pilots I got the shock of my life. Oh yes they came through alright, carrying their briefcase and document holders but that was it, no suitcase, no clothes, not even a razor blade or toothbrush between them, they didn't even have enough money to buy the essentials, never mind trousers, shirts or a jacket, so I had to chip in out of my own money, "Thus starts a new chapter in my life and once again a very entertaining relationship!". The month of July and the following six months brought with it a whole host of unwanted problems, that really we could well have done without, most of which arose once again out of other people's jealously.

You see the delivery of two brand new, matching Granada Ghias had just about creamed off all the lovely neighbours, who'd already had a belly full of seeing us in the papers and on the telly, so this next instalment was just that little too much for them to take.

We'd received notice that we had to appear at a council hearing as a result of residential complaints, arguing that we should not be working from home. It was an incident which coincided with yet more harassment from both the council enforcement office and the other ordinary taxi companies, all once again brought about by us mass advertising, so not for the first time since starting off, I took legal advice from my solicitor and turned up on the day with him representing me.

It was a hearing that lasted a good twenty five to thirty minutes, which left me with no doubts whatsoever that, as I first suspected, the whole thing was a fix and had been orchestrated by the local authority with the help of Jeannette's caring next door neighbour who had council contacts.

We were told that we had to find premises to work from and that we had six weeks to do so, if not we would be stopped from working altogether, which would then mean the crooked bunch sat opposite us, would have won!.

There was no way on this earth that Jeannette or myself were going to give them that satisfaction, so despite the abundance of work, the resulting chaos and the pressure it caused, we immediately set off looking for a small office that would be suitable to our needs.

Meanwhile the job carried on with the endless rushing from here to there and the brief periodic chats at home becoming a regular feature.

The atmosphere within the road generally was beginning to get nastier, as faces were pulled when either us or our drivers left or entered the street, which all brought about a little unwanted discomfort. We were beginning to see more problems appear by the day as the pressure on us began to tell, all made worse by outside distractions that we could ill afford, so it was only a matter of time before somebody "copped it".

Having dealt with so many nice people from the states some six weeks earlier had made us realise that our approach to life was right but it had also made us wake up to the fact that we were not only good at what we did but that we were also very specially gifted people too.

Consequently it was as a result of the "snotty", "pigheaded", male chauvinistic attitude of a Managing Director from DAF trucks that we decided to give their company the push and change our ways.

It was a perfect example of the outlook held by most companies when dealing with the "providers of services" such as ours, a view or opinion that we were in fact second class citizens. It was also an outlook that we were soon to see was the "norm", which in turn forced change in both Jeannette and myself, which sadly we'd have done well to adapt to long before.

We'd looked after the man concerned all day, as he'd been over with a delegation of staff from Europe to open their new headquarters in Salford. Once again it was a day of frantic running about, pampering and "moly coddling", in fact we'd been here, there and everywhere with them, making sure that everything, despite their own staff's inefficiency went strictly according to plan, making it the perfect day for everyone.

Well that's what we'd originally thought, however following a booking made by the usual girl in charge of travel, I enquired as to whether they were pleased or not with our service on the big day, obviously expecting an emphatic "Yes". The young lady concerned replied by telling me that everything baring one incident was perfect, which did leave me somewhat puzzled, so I asked her exactly what the problem was, only to be told that the Managing Director objected to me kissing his wife on the cheek, as I said goodbye. Jeannette was as annoyed as I, so after a very brief conversation we decided to end our contract over the phone there and then, informing them that we no longer wished to deal with their company, if that was the sort of childish attitude their higher management adopted. Later on that day we received yet another call from DAF, only on this occasion it was the office manager in a somewhat apologetic manner, desperately wishing to sort out the situation, mainly because they'd previously looked long and hard for a service like ours.

Never the less we stuck to our principles, refusing all further requests, fully believing in our own attitude and standards, thinking how sad it was, that one could shake the man's hand but not kiss the lady.

During the next few months we did continually see their staff being picked up at the airport, although I have to say, that the tatty transport and scruffy drivers doing the job were slightly less presentable than us, having said that it was the type of service they deserved!.

To just about put the icing on the cake for Jeannette and myself, Jim our positive thinking bank manager, who'd suggested this and that when he was last at our home, decided as all men and women in the same position do, that he'd have a sudden charge of heart and as did the other bank, start returning cheques that we'd issued, which would take us all of a few pounds overdrawn. It was the start of yet another bust up but for the time being not so important, as we had far more important issues to worry about, things such as neighbours, council officials and the ownership of two band new Granadas that we hadn't even signed for.

At the time I initially thought that God for once had actually gone out of his way to give me something, without me having to struggle for it because some six weeks after taking possession of the cars, we received numerous visits from a very polite, distressed but very apologetic man from the garage where we'd bought them.

My suspicions that something was radically wrong were initially aroused by his niceness, after all, whenever you buy a car from any garage, it's very difficult, near impossible for them to show you any time or interest after the sale. Then there was the fact that he'd left me two new documents to fill in, so in order to get a better and fuller understanding of the situation, I immediately raced round to my solicitors for advice.

Now by this time I'd seen quite a lot of my solicitor, what with council hearings, taxi laws, setting up the business and a multitude of other problems, it seemed we'd been through hell and high water together. He was a decent bloke, who'd always made extra effort to fully explain every detail to me and he was honest but each time I left him, it appeared to me that I was either in the wrong, or that I had no case against whoever I had a disagreement with.

Well having gone in fully expecting him to say that I could legally keep the cars, I left totally disappointed, with the knowledge that some day in the not too distant future, I would eventually have to sign up the new documents, meaning that my illusions of owning two new Granadas, which didn't need to be paid for, were quickly shattered. In the end I did concede by officially completing the deal but before doing so, I made a point of having the "cock up" and my honest generosity which made life a lot easier for quite a few people involved, noted at the credit company for reference, so with that unrewarding excitement behind us, what spare energies were left, then had to be placed on the council enforcement problem.

Our second hearing was on the 15th August, it was held in the very same chambers with the identical committee present that were there the first time. During the hearing a petition containing names of local residents was produced, that had been put together by the Westons' next door. It was something that neither of us knew anything about, which in itself was a sad indictment of the people who lived there, I say that because Jeannette had lived in Springclough since the houses were originally built, in fact she was the very first resident to actually move in, she'd been nothing short of a good neighbour to everyone, which was in her genuine nature anyway and the mere fact that although only a few, not one of those who hadn't signed didn't even think to bring what was actually going on to her attention!!.

During our own relationship, Jeannette often spoke about the various goings on that she herself had witnessed over the nineteen years she'd lived there, the affairs, the wife swapping at parties, all things she wanted no part of, then there was the gossiping, nosiness and scandal mongering all of which caused endless wrangling and arguing within the drive, which I believe on more than one occasion caused marriage break ups, sometimes even forcing a few poor souls to move, altogether.

She'd always told me that it was a case of a certain few, like Sue, the nosey blonde who lived opposite wanting to live in each other's homes, wanting to know anything and everything that was going on in the cul de sac but as Jeannette wasn't made like that, they were never invited in, thus she kept herself to herself and her own life private, even though she could well have written her own book about "The goings on in Springclough Drive".

Upon reading the list of names presented before us, we were shocked, disgusted and very annoyed, for the petition had been signed by people who themselves had in the past worked for us, earning cash, people such as the Johnsons' from number fifteen.

Then there were the Kays' at number six who'd also joined on the bandwagon, even though they made far more noise than us and at earlier hours of the morning as they ran a cake and biscuit delivery business from their garage, a man whose wife loved to sit on the garden wall, displaying her bikini clad body for all to see.

Without thinking, the Shears' from number eighteen must have signed, even though he was running his own alarm fitting business, whilst working for British Telecom at the same time but having given it a second thought, they crossed their support off. It didn't alter the fact though that they'd originally gone along with the scam, seemingly forgetting the care and effort I'd always previously taken to look after their daughter, who like a lot of other kids in the road had found themselves stranded at the most God unearthly hours of the morning!.

Then there were the Carrs' at number eight, he was an ambulance driver, who frequently popped home to have a brew, whilst some poor bugger was dying somewhere. It was a regular feature in the road regardless of what shift he was on, mornings, afternoons, nights it didn't matter, but you could always tell because he'd leave the radio on full blast, just in case there was an emergency call obviously so that he could hear it.

But by far the most hypocritical of all those people that signed, was Evelyn herself, for she was the very same person who was prepared to accept non taxable cash in return for the horrible, cheap tatty business cards she'd supplied, albeit in rate and tax payers time as she worked for the local authority.

Whilst at the same time, like everyone else involved, she was guilty of forgetting the kindness both Jeannette and I had in the past shown, being good caring friendly people. Their daughter's had benefited from our service too but having said that, I could go on for another three, maybe four pages about the whole horrible, worthless bunch of them, so instead I've devoted the next two pages to them all, in an effort to share with them my success from writing this book, by placing the exact petition in, as a "Thank You!".

WE, THE UNDERSIGNED, BEING RESIDENTS OF SPRING CLOUGH DRIVE AND SPRING CLOUGH AVENUE WISH TO DRAW YOUR ATTENTION THE APPARENT USE OF 12 SPRING CLOUGH DRIVE FOR A COMMERCIAL TAXI PRIVATE HIRE BUSINESS, WHICH WE BELIEVE TO BE IN CONTRAVENTION OF THE APPROPRIATE LICENSING AND PLANNING LEGISLATION, AND WHICH IS CAUSING US DISTRESS BY VIRTUE OF:-

EXCESS NOISE AND SLEEPLESS NIGHT - REVVING OF ENGINES, SLAMMING DOORS ETC.

INCREASED TRAFFIC AND DANGER TO CHILDREN WHO PLAY IN THE VICINITY.

OBSTRUCTION OF DRIVE WAYS - INCONSIDERATE PARKING MAKING IT IMPOSSIBLE FOR VEHICLES TO GAIN ACCESS IN OR OUT OF THE DRIVE.

WE WOULD WELCOME YOUR INVESTIGATION OF THIS MATTER AND A SATISFACTORY OUTCOME AT THE EARLIEST OPPORTUNITY.

Mrs E Weston 10 Springclough drive worsley
Mr J Weston DITTO.
Mrs. S. Hargreaves. 9. SpringClough Drive "
A. Hargreaves. " " "
F. Allington 5. Spring Clough Ave
[illegible] Moss 13 SPRING CLOUGH AVE
[illegible] Moss 13 SPRING clough ave
H. Moss " " " "
M Darlington 15. Spring Clough Avenue.
R. McLaren. 4 " " Drive
J. McLaren. 4. Spring clough Dr.
C Fairclough. 2. " "
K Fairclough. 2. " " " "
S Parry 11 spring clough Ave.
N. Alcock 5 Spring Clough Drive
Mrs. S. Bleakley 1 Springclough Drive
S. Bleakley 1 Springclough Drive
[illegible] Sharples 11 Springclough Drive
M. Sharples 11, Springclough Drive
[illegible] 19. Springclough Avenue
[illegible]

Mrs. [illegible]
Mr. W. Pinch Esq } 21 SPRINGCLOUGH Drive.

[illegible] 27 Springclough Drive, [illegible]

L. Bell 20 Springclough Drive
S Bell. " " "

[illegible] [illegible] " "

[illegible] [illegible] " "

[illegible] C 27 " " Gillis

E. Wilson 35 " " Conner.

[illegible] 22, SPRINGCLOUGH DR. — NW.

G. Dyson 22 " "

Laura A. Johnson 15 Springclough Drive

G. M. Johnson 15 Springclough Dr.

A DiCocco 2 Crosby Ave.

D. Carr. 8, Springclough Drive.

L. Carr 8 Springclough Dr

R Kay 6 Springclough Dr.

Mrs McKay 6 Springclough Drive Worsley.

As we'd only just had the petition put in front of us, there was no time to reveal these details, so we left that hearing with another three month period, in which we had to find premises to work from, which we now knew we had to for our own sakes.

However once we'd left the civic centre Jeannette and I took time to calm down, then once again read the list of names and their complaints, after which I was more convinced than ever before, that there was in fact, a vendetta or hate campaign being waged against us, from within the council itself.

It was an opinion not shared by our solicitor, as he thought that it may well have been a figment of our own imaginations, all of which annoyed me even more, especially as he was supposed to be on our side, so undeterred we made our way home, knowing we had a lot of work to do, whilst at the same time, we had a hell of a battle on our hands!.

By the time we'd reached the month of September, bad relationships, bad luck, legal wrangles and a whole range of other problems seemed to be drowning us both, as one after the other, people from various quarters "had a go".

What with drivers we were employing, abusing our kindness and trust, the neighbours and the authority doing their bit, then the bank sticking their ten penny's worth in, the past glamour was fast turning to gloom.

On top of all that we'd received our first ever county court summons, relating to a Jewish paper who demanded payment from us, despite the fact that, they'd made a total "balls up" of the article they'd produced, needless to say, we weren't very happy.

Good news at that moment, was in very short supply but even though we appeared, despite our efforts, to be submerged in a sea of shite, we persevered, believing that something positive would shortly happen and sure enough it did, for in the second week of September we received a long awaited call from Granada Television, the company we'd previously done that one job for some, four months earlier.

It was the new man in charge of booking cars, who'd been referred to us by Mr.Doherty, the executive producer of sport programmes, who I'd taken to Leicester. He'd demanded that his department used only my services for the forth coming season and so I'd finally achieved another one of my main ambitions, for at long last I'd broken into the, so far, closed world of TV chauffeur work.

By way of referral from within their company, word soon spread, about this new, caring, reliable and very immaculate service, consequently within a matter of weeks, we found ourselves dealing with near enough all the higher management of the company.

It was just the tonic Jeannette and I needed, after all we'd put up with so much rubbish from other folk that it was no more than we deserved and so with what seemed like the blink of an eye, the weeks had flown past and we were in the middle of October.

It was the twelfth actually, we were very busy and I was on my way home, having been up all day since the early hours of four o'clock that morning. I wasn't in a rush, I just wanted to get home, have some tea, then relax, the traffic over Barton Bridge looked as bad as ever and so that little bit of extra patience was needed, as I could see the queue mounting up ahead of me.

Suddenly the traffic came to a stand still meaning I too had to stop, however the bloke following me and the two behind him, all failed to see the danger, which as a result, meant that I was hit in the rear, by a car doing no less than fifty miles an hour, then concertinaed twice by the other two.

Having had a lot of experience I was calm, I didn't think I was hurt or badly shook up, so I got out to check that everybody else was ok, then immediately phoned Jeannette from the car, asking her to contact both the Automobile Association and the Police.

It was a long, late night and an accident I could well have done without, especially as the car and more importantly the phone in it, would be off the road for quite some time to come but thanks once again to Norman, my friend at Garners' Insurance, plus the high premiums I'd always paid, another vehicle was supplied the following day, leaving me with unwanted time off and the immediate task of finding another driver to take my place.

Thankfully the search for an extra full time driver, was easily and very quickly resolved because Neil, my long time friend who'd been working part time for us since the early part of the year, decided that he'd love to join the team, so within twenty four hours a major headache was unexpectedly cured, leaving me one less hurdle to clear.

It seems looking back, that my life was just one problem after another, with no rest in between solving them because two days later on the 16th October, the aggro with the licensing authority and the neighbours reared it's ugly head once again, with our three month stay of execution up, bringing with it our third appearance before the "kangaroo court" of Salford Council.

Since our last hearing things had predictably got worse in Springclough, with neighbours awkwardly, even stupidly parking in the most ridiculous manner possible in an effort to inflame the already bad situation, where any of the drivers calling round to our house to pick up a car were either snarled or sniped at. It became apparent that for some strange reason, their grudge was solely directed towards myself, whilst at the same time, they couldn't see how much they were affecting Jeannette.

Silent telephone calls throughout the night were accompanied by sarcastically made daytime ones, along the lines of, "I believe you've got a taxi business to sell!!", or "Social Security benefit is good these days!", incidentals which made us all the more determined to win!.

We'd already arranged to meet our solicitor before entering the town hall, so as to erase any chance of a conflict outside the meeting room, which was the first of many a smart move we'd pre planned and I'm glad we did, for as we appeared in the waiting room there they were, all as bold as brass, smirking confidently as if they already knew they'd won. This time however, having had three months to prepare, we were more than ready for them and so we entered knowing full well that we ourselves had a few tricks up our sleeves and I was more than ready to use them.

By choice we let them have their say and air their grievances first, I wanted to let the committee see exactly what sort of people they were dealing with, knowing full well that their anger would seep through and that their inability to express themselves would let them down badly. Well, the evil bunch didn't disappoint me, as they shouted, screamed and even got the old man from over the road, to turn up and do his "dying swan" bit, all of which looked very impressive I must say. But then it was my turn and so through our solicitor, the announcement of our long kept secret was made. After listening to them cattle on like a load of old fish wives for half an hour, he informed the committee that we'd found alternative premises since our last appearance and that with the assistance of the planning department we were in fact there to apply for permission to use the offices immediately.

Well dare I say it, their faces were a picture, as they sat there, stunned and utterly gobsmacked, they couldn't believe that after all their effort, their ranting and raving and the pathetic Oscar winning performance of the old man, that we'd silenced them with our very first defence, one statement and more importantly one piece if action.

They were disappointed, disillusioned and at long last we'd shut them up and so following a short break where our application was discussed, then granted, we left the room, them with their tails, well and truly between their legs and us more than pleased with ourselves, even though our licence would once again be reviewed in another three months.

As we actually left the building, Jeannette and I overhead something which was said, a comment that at the time made me smile, it was a statement that also saddened me somewhat, even though it did confirm my initial thoughts and beliefs, for as we passed Evelyn and Mr Ashburton, the licensing officer who'd constantly harassed us in the past, we overhead their discussion, a discussion which prompted him to answer her question of, "Well what do we do now?" by saying, "You'll just have to keep an eye on him and let me know if you see anything". It was proof that I really didn't need, as my instincts had been telling me as much for quite some time, however further confirmation did come from a direction that I would never have previously anticipated, news which saddened me wondering, "How many others had been through the same sort of ordeal but not been strong enough to make it?".

Because two days later, having just decorated our new office, we received a visit at home from Danny, the lad from the planning department who'd helped us so much in our search for suitable premises. He was pleased that we'd made it and that we'd not been put out of business, well not for another three months anyway, all of which surprised us, as he was the first person from the council that we'd dealt with, who was enthusiastic to our cause.

It was then, in answer to our question of "Why?", that he told us of the strange "goings on" within the town hall, especially the licensing department, of how inexplicable pressure was forced upon him and the department he worked for, to obstruct any of our plans or efforts.

He then told us of how he'd approached his superiors, perturbed and worried, wanting to know why so much unneeded attention was being paid to Exclusia Travel, complaining about the strangeness of the situation as a whole, only for his questions to be dismissed outright. Mine was a frustrated, angry response, wanting to know why he hadn't said anything earlier, so that I could have taken the matter further, to which he replied, "It's not that simple Paul, I have a wife, children, a home and mortgage, I'd probably lose my job, pension and any pay-out that goes with it, I'm sorry!".

My initial emotions soon evaporated with his response, for I understood how he felt and so did Jeannette, all of which immediately made our minds up for us, on the question we'd long been asking ourselves of, "Should we move and get away from this bunch of 'riff raff'?".

As a direct result of what he'd told us, we knew that we were always going to have problems as long as we lived there !, that the desperate attempts the licensing officer and the neighbours were prepared to go to, although nothing short of disgraceful, were still never the less unprovable without Danny's assistance and so we decided that it was time for a fresh start!.

The very next day, Jeannette came in having been shopping with her sister, where upon we had the usual cup of tea, a sandwich and a chat, talk which ranged from the drivers who were out working to the sour faced crowd living in the same road. Then we went on to our existing problems with the bank and the task of looking for a new house, a subject which to my surprise brought that, "It's funny you should say that", statement from "my inspiration". Now in our house that remark usually meant that there was something quite profound coming and sure enough this occasion was no different, for less than twenty four hours after deciding to move she came out with these words, "Listen love, sit down and listen to what I've got to say". She then proceeded to tell me about a house she'd just seen and immediately fell in love with, asking me to go with her, to take a second look at it, whilst at the same time keep an open mind, after which we could as always discuss the situation with each other.

I had no objections and so after dinner we went off in search of this "new ideal home", although I have to say, I was at that point rather sceptical, thinking that Jeannette was so desperate to get away from Springclough, that she'd take anything. In the end they were fears, doubts and apprehensions that were soon dispelled, for I suddenly pointed out to a very prominent, large, new property, saying, "That's what we want, look! that house there, now I'd love to live in a place like that, it's enormous, no neighbours, no kids and loads of space!!". Jeannette agreed, in fact it was the very same house that she'd seen, so we pulled up to the show house opposite to make enquiries with the representative who worked for the company building on the site. She was so helpful that she even took us round the place and boy was it some house, four bedrooms, a large living room, a dining room and two bathrooms, there were three toilets in the place and even a study.

The young lady told us that although new and un-lived in, it was being sold privately by a Pakistani gentleman, hence the reason for the basic, bright yellow and orange "for sale" signs, displayed in the windows and that she had the keys in her possession because she was actually on commission to off load it.

The fact that it was a Pakistani selling the place probably put most other potential buyers off but not me, for it gave me the chance to carry out one of my "by now", long standing threats to Jeannette of "I'll tell you luv, when we move from here, I swear I'll sell this place to a Paki or an Indian!". So having been inside the place, then immediately falling in love with it and following two or three return visits, we contacted the gentleman concerned for an initial meeting.

It was following that first introduction, that both Jeannette and I realised, God had more than a helping hand in all this, for in the space of an hour, we'd agreed not only a price for Mr Ali's house but also a figure for him to buy "Springclough".

There was no chain involved, his place was obviously empty and of course I in my most revengeful way, was getting my own back on the "swines of Springclough", it was perfect!.

Unfortunately as with anything else I did, nothing was ever that simple because obtaining the mortgage brought yet another encounter with one of a few shylocks I've come into contact with over the years, a bloke who worked for my good friend, Norman Hill of Garner's Insurance. Norman had always done me well, he'd always looked after me and was a good friend, a man who I'd always respected, so leaving my affairs in the capable hands of Fincher and Co, didn't worry me too much, forever saying to Jeannette, "Oh don't worry luv, they must be alright if they work for Norman!".

As with all home purchases the odd call was often made, just to check that everything was going through ok, that my new, "first time buyer" mortgage was alright and there were no "hiccups", all calls that were met with the same answer, "Everything's running smoothly, you can carry on as normal and I'll let you know when you need to sign".

So I did, I got on with my own "normally, abnormal" life, of running here, there and everywhere at a hundred miles an hour, employing and sacking drivers, whilst at the same time trying to keep track of what they were up to, when they were supposed to be working.

The constant battles with the neighbours in the Drive about parking raged on, and so did my other disputes with the bank, all of which meant that I was more than preoccupied with my time.

In the end I had no choice, I had to vent my "built up" anger onto somebody, so I decided to put am immediate stop to the pressure that the bank, had in the past five months been increasingly placing on me, by threatening the area manager that I'd release tapes in my possession to the press and media, tapes confirming my accusations of Mr Kerns's rapid turn around, change of thought and eventual mal-practise. They had no choice, they had to concede, which they did and so having cleared the air, the search for yet another high street bank got under way.

Meanwhile, the day our mortgage application was due to be processed had arrived, it was a day where all else was secondary, where drivers, customers, neighbours, could all please themselves as nothing else mattered, except one thing, a decision, a decision made by somebody else that was so important to both of us.

I'll never forget it, it was a Friday and it was one hell of a long day, a day that both Jeannette and myself spent living on our nerves, unable to do anything else but wait, in the hope that the phone would ring, bringing us the good news. It was awful, no painful would be a better description, for we waited and waited and waited, seemingly forever, in fact, by about five o'clock that evening, I could wait no longer, so I rang Mr Fincher myself, only to be told that there was problem!. He informed me that our application had not been accepted because of a county court judgement against my name, even worse he'd found out about it over a week earlier but failed to contact me, so that I could do something to sort out the problem.

The judgement was actually a legacy from my illness, the one that resulted in me losing my business, which also ended my days with Marks and Spencer, in fact it was the thousand pounds I owed off the van to the HP company, one of the debts I rightly or wrongly held them responsible for at the time. Anyway who I owed the money to, or how much it was for, was immaterial at that stage because I was angry, I couldn't understand how "so called" professional people were capable of doing such a thing, which left me with no alternative other than to ring Norman up and tell him what had happened.

It was something that I had to do, not just for my sake but for his and other potential customers, after all he was a good friend and a well respected servant of the industry, a reputation that could well get tarnished by this sort of character, so I did and yet once again he was brilliant which was just typical of the man, for he was magnificent!, "Paul mate!, don't worry, by first thing Monday morning, you'll have your mortgage, I promise!!".

Well true to his word, we did!, which meant that heading into the month of December we had to once again make an appointment with Jack our solicitor, only on this occasion, for a much better reason, than the last time we'd seen him.

"There's no rest for the wicked", well that's according to the saying, all I can say in answer to such a statement, is that I must have been an evil bugger, for amongst all of this chaos, we found ourselves keeping another appointment with yet another one of the high streets banks, which once again came as a result of a referral from one of our customers, a man who actually worked for the same outfit . . . The Midland Bank.

The surroundings for our meeting were unlike anything else we'd seen in our dealings with banks, the offices were plush, newly fitted and generally gave a welcoming environment.

The manager a Mr Phil Fairhouse had already seen our figures and obviously knew all about the business from his colleague, so the appointment was a formal opening of the account as well as an official welcome to the bank. He was, as were the other managers when we first met, keen for our business, anxious for us to expand and enthusiastic to our cause, with similar questions such as, "How many people would you like to employ?" and "How far will you go?". However leaving Phil's office that first time did, inspite of our past experiences, lead both Jeannette and myself to say, "This is different this time luv, I really think we can go places with him!", a statement with which she agreed and so we made our way home confidently looking forward to our impending move, knowing full well that we had our new bank's full blessing.

Sadly on the 8th December, Jeannette fell foul to a very bad virus, a flu virus which had already near enough disseminated the working public generally. It was of epidemic proportions and really couldn't have struck our home at a worse time, for four days later whilst already struggling looking after her, Nick and the business, I got a shock telephone call from Loganair, the airline I was sub-contracted to.

Unknown to me because I was so busy, the airport had suddenly been closed due to a union dispute, consequently all flights were being diverted to Liverpool Airport, some thirty miles away.

Martin the lad in charge of the airline's operations told me that Manchester would be closed for at least five maybe six days, that he needed my services and that he would shortly be sending a fax to the office, which I duly picked up, remembering his last words of, "Give us a ring Paul when you've got it", as I did. Ten minutes later I'd returned home, sat down and proceeded to enjoy a nice cup of tea, whilst at the same time read the fax he'd sent, which read, "Paul can you pick up the crews off flights enclosed?". "Please call back to confirm". Upon studying the details on the second page, I coughed, spluttered, then spilt tea all over the place for I couldn't believe my eyes, there before me was an A4 sheet of paper, literally covered in squares, all containing flight numbers. I felt that it was either a joke, I was confused, or that a genuine mistake had been made on the part of Martin, so I immediately rang him back to find out.

I sat there in shock and disbelief as he confirmed my worst fears, no it wasn't a joke, neither was it a mistake nor was I confused, I had understood it perfectly, I had read it correctly and worst of all I desperately needed HELP!.

Usually in this sort of situation I would have "my inspiration" alongside of me, I'd be out there in the middle of the chaos and she'd be at home, bringing some semblance of normality to the situation but not this time, this time I was alone, alone, vulnerable, feeling inadequate and right in the middle of it but the job had to be done and so I got right down to it.

I delegated Nick the task of looking after his mum knowing full well that I'd hardly be at home, then I called all the drivers in who worked for us, warning them, that they too would hardly be seeing their beds. Having done that I worked out a roster, making sure that cover was available at all times, after which I made sure that each and every one of them knew their way to Liverpool Airport and exactly where to pick up our crews from.

It was a week of utter mayhem, chaos the likes of which I'd never seen before, where everyone willingly worked from four in the morning till four the next day, shuttling countless air crews from Manchester to Liverpool then back again. By the end of that week, everyone was shattered, pilots, drivers, hostesses and engineers, all knackered but it was a week of endless confusion which produced so much laughter, where new friends were made, producing even more tall tales that could be told in the future. It was a week that I personally never thought we'd get through but we did and so yet again Exclusia Travel had turned up with "the goods" and in the most professional way possible!.

As a "thank you" to our staff for their help, I decided to take them to the airlines Christmas party, we were invited as a result of that chaotic week, so I paid for the tickets and drove our seven seater limo to make sure that just for once, everyone else could have a drink.

In a crazy sort of way I was proud because when I originally started off on this adventure, it was one of my more imaginative, wilder dreams to think I'd end up working in the airline industry at all, but to actually be sat there at a specially booked table for my staff, at an airline function, was something else!.

It was a good night, where lots of fun was had by all, a night that left Jeannette and myself driving home alone to Springclough together, for probably the last time, you see none of the others knew about our forthcoming move, we didn't want them to, until the time was right, so it was a brief time for thought, reflection and a pat on the back for each other.

We'd had one hell of a year, which seemed to be ending in the most unexpected way imaginable, for despite the comings and goings of countless drivers we'd finally got what we thought was a settled, loyal team together. Then after all the problems in the drive, we were actually leaving without them having the slightest notion of us doing so, or that we were going to be replaced by "Pakistani neighbours", so with just one thing left to do, which was move, we said goodbye and good riddance to 1989, to enter '90 with a new home and a fresh start!

We'd actually been preparing everything at Springclough for a good few days, knowing full well that our new home was ready and waiting for us to move into it, with large furniture such as wardrobes, beds and display units already dismantled and ready to go, the place was already fitted out with brand new carpets and so there really wasn't all that much to do.

It was amazing for I swear it must have been the quickest "moonlight" anybody, anywhere, has ever done because four van loads later we'd gone, even taking half of the garden plants and shrubs with us.

The next three and a half years of our lives saw more changes than ever before but it would be near enough impossible for me to catalogue each and every event, therefore I've decided to write about just some of the horrendous experiences encountered through employing staff and of course the drivers themselves.

Then having done that I've devoted a few pages to the world of Television and finally a few lines to outline the many other problems experienced during those last years to present day but for now it's back to the January of 1990.

Not for the first time we'd entered a new year full of hope, promise and a very positive outlook, however our aspirations and efforts were dented in the first week of that year, for having shared our plans, secrets, cars, even our home with Neil, my longtime friend, he suddenly decided to leave. Without even a murmur or a previous warning, he suddenly turned up at our new home and like a bolt out of the blue, told us that he actually wanted to have a go at the very same game, working for himself. We couldn't believe it because I'd near enough treated the bloke like my own flesh and blood, a brother in fact, I'd given him a good wage, basically put him in charge, even let him have the seven seater "limo" for his families use, so I was angry, any how he left immediately which meant that Jeannette and myself had once again given our all, only to be let down badly.

His sudden departure immediately left us wondering "God what next?, it's going to be another one of those years!", well we were right, although we had no idea at the time, for only a matter of days later Mike, our doziest of dozy drivers, really just about crowned his long catalogue of disasters and mishaps with one of his best efforts to date.

On the day in question it was a cold, frosty morning at about seven thirty and it had been snowing, I'd been up early and so I was already working, when I received a call from my Jeannette, who sounded in somewhat of a semi-distressed, semi-angry state.

The mere fact that she was even up at that hour, never mind called, alerted me to realise that something was wrong but by this time, having employed the man for so long nothing came as too much of a surprise, especially when she came out with those awesomely worrying words, "Paul love, listen I think you better ring Mike in the car!". Whenever she said that my mind would automatically take me into another world, another dimension even, for Mike was a real "one off", a character of his own, the likes of which I'd never seen before or never want to see again.

In the eight months that he'd been with us, he'd put years on us both, for more often than not the man would be running late or getting lost, both nerve wrecking experiences for those sat in the office or working elsewhere unable to do anything at the time and so with her call came my usual response "God what's he done now?".

Having reluctantly asked the million dollar question I was told that he'd only gone and reversed the car over our snow covered rockery, getting stuck on the top in the process. Then instead of getting out to take stock of the situation or even ask for help, he decided that in some sort of rally-cross manner, he would somehow go forward have a second attempt believing for some strange reason that it would be better a second time around !. In the end having totally decimated the rockery left countless tyre tread marks on the snow covered lawn and woken everyone up with his antics, he'd set off for his first pick-up some two miles away, even though the car was making one hell of a noise.

With this information on board I immediately rang the vehicle he was driving to find out what the hell he was playing at, a question which was met with the answer "What d'ya mean Paul?, I don't know what your talking about". How the bloody ell he was capable of doing such a thing was beyond me, especially as I could hear the noise that the car was making from down the phone, so I told him to leave the passengers who were waiting for him, saying that I'd pick them up and that he was to return the car to our house, then go home himself.

Some two hours later I returned home to Eden Vale, which is where we now lived, only to discover the true extent of the damage he'd caused, even worse the stupidity of the man for driving the car, in the first place.

There for all to see was a front lawn covered in tyre marks, that resembled a stock car track, a rockery which comprised of broken and crushed rocks, and a car that had miraculously lost it's exhaust!.

Yes!, that was Mike alright, never mind the mark of Zoro, that was the mark of Mike, a trail of disaster!!. I was angry!, no I was worse, I was fuming but we didn't sack him after all he'd done far worse on his travels, so having sent him home, Jeannette and I at least had time to calm down, before speaking to the man again later that day.

When we did, we got the shock of our lives as the first words out of his mouth were "Well I'm not bothered I'm packing it in anyway, so if you'll pay me what you owe me we'll be straight". The dam cheek of the man stumped us more than anything else, for having destroyed our garden, our car and left our passengers late, the man didn't even have the decency to accept responsibility, never mind apologise, completely dismissing the whole incident as a figment of our imagination, so we left in a very angry state, with me telling him that he could whistle for his money.

Looking back it would have been easier to have paid the man his wages then said goodbye, thus shutting the door on another chapter of my life, that being the sad experience of ever coming into contact with him, for just to be rid of the man, should in hindsight have been recompense enough, especially in view of the damage he'd caused to the company and the heartache to Jeannette and I personally.

Just remembering those countless calls from passengers who were either waiting at home to be taken or those actually in the airport, who'd landed some time earlier, desperately tired and longing to get home for that first "cuppa", is painful enough. But thinking of other incidents is twice as painful, incidents that should never have occurred, like the time he took passengers to Birmingham Airport, where yet again he was running late, only not just, on this occasion, he was over two hours late!.

It was an occurrence that even to this day I blame myself for because it was I who succumbed to his pleas of "I'll do that job boss", that initially prompted me to allow him to go in the first place, where his parting words of "Don't worry, everything will be alright, I'll look after them" for once left me confident believing that it would.

It wasn't, in fact it was far from alright because some two weeks later I discovered that the plane the couple were catching, was four hours late taking off, which of course is the only reason they made it at all, for they arrived at the check in desk at around the same time they should have originally been landing at their destination airport!.

It got worse!, for not only were they some two hours late but the idiot had taken them to the wrong airport altogether!, as instead of being at East Midlands they found themselves stood in the centre of Birmingham.

Knowing how slow he drove and how incompetent the man was generally, still leaves me cold and somewhat mystified, as to how he then got to East Midlands on time, never the less he did, even though it was nothing short of a miracle.

Another one of his great achievements was the time that he'd decided to place our customer's luggage on the roof rack, an unnecessary procedure when considering that there were only four passengers in a seven seater car, with plenty of room in the giant boot.

"What's wrong with that?", you may well ask, it's simple, the prat never tied them down and so as a consequence they fell off, luckily for him and us, landing on the hard shoulder of the motorway. In his wisdom he decided not to tell us, all of which only made matters ten times worse, when I eventually received a caring call from the "regular" customers concerned the day after, telling me what an idiot the driver was whilst at the same time, advising me to get rid of him!.

When I eventually approached him on the subject, he replied saying, "They weren't damaged, so I didn't think it was worth bothering about". Sadly that was his attitude but the man was so nice in one way, yet sad in another, that there wasn't much more could be said, other than, "Don't let it happen again! ", so once again I dismissed the incident putting it down to his stupidity, whilst at the same time trying to think of his nicer points!.

Well!, stupidity is one thing but ignorance, thoughtlessness and stupidity are another and I say that because less than twenty four hours after the first incident, another occurred, only this time I witnessed it for myself and it was ten times worse!.

There on the carriageway below was our seven seater limo, which sadly since Mike had been driving it, had become a regular sight. It was a lovely vehicle, one which always turned the heads of passers-by, sadly however I'd become accustomed to regularly seeing it parked up on lay-bys somewhere, usually on the motorway. As I looked down whilst passing on the carriageway above, I couldn't believe my own eyes, for there in a line were our passengers, all carrying their luggage above their heads!, in a sort of "Arab fashion", rather like a caravan crossing the dessert or a line of African tribes people on a trek. I couldn't understand it, "Why the bloody ell are they carrying their luggage, in a line and towards the car instead of away from it?", so I quickly made my way home to be in the company of "my inspiration", before daring to make, "the call", which would explain all!.

Yes!, unbelievable as it may seem, by this time I'd got to the point where I was ready to tear my hair out and I was too frightened to ring myself for fear of what I'd either say or do!, having said that in the event I was glad because the news that greeted Jeannette was nothing short of incredible!, no unbelievable! even unreal, for Mike had only gone and done it again!, he'd put the luggage on the roof without securely fastening it on!, only this time the consequences were far more damaging.

Jeannette and I sat there in disbelief, unable to understand what the hell was running through his mind, did he have a mind!, how could he possibly do the same thing again, especially after the previous day's occurrence?. His response when later questioned was even more of a shock, as he stood there, in the most "matter of fact", casual way possible saying! "Oh there was no damage done!", even laughing as he explained about the Policeman, who had sat in the Range Rover holding one of the cases on his knee, with the question to Mike of "Are you looking for something by any chance?".

By now we had become well used to Mike's habitual lying, so his claim that "No damage had been done", meant nothing whatsoever, therefore Jeannette and I later went around to our client's house to check for ourselves, where upon we once again got the shock of our lives!. For there lying in the centre of the living room, was the remains of what was once a suitcase, full of dirty, shredded, oil stained clothes, all worthless as a result of the forty ton lorry which had steamed rollered over them all, the very same lorry which Mike had kindly forgotten to tell us about, when telling us that "Everything's alright, no damage was done and the clients were great about it!".

As with most "cock ups" they always happened to the nicest of people, people who for some strange reason or other, often experienced a bad holiday generally, where either somebody was ill, the hotel or resort were poor, or the company they were in was bad. So it didn't surprise us one bit, to learn that the young couple and the others they had gone with, had already experienced enough of a nightmare, before Mike had got to them, never the less they were nice about the whole episode, gratefully accepting our quick settlement of cash, flowers from Jeannette and myself and the promise that in future we wouldn't send the idiot, we'd go ourselves!.

His adventures however, weren't restricted to just holiday-makers, for it seemed that he could quite easily cock up any task or job, given to him, in fact looking back if there were any heart stopping moments you could always bet Mike would be there or there abouts!.

For instance, the chaotic week we looked after the air crews from Loganair immediately springs to mind, a week where only three mishaps occurred, all on account of his stupidity.

The first being a trip from Liverpool to Manchester, a journey that had already been completed at least five or six times by the man, where speed was of the essence and a quick turn round at Manchester was all important. Originally three vehicles had set off together but unfortunately only two had arrived, guess who was missing, the brainless nerd had taken the wrong turn, which ended up with him taking his crew off to Chester, seemingly to go shopping or something.

The other was the morning he disappeared out of sight completely, something which he was very good at, however on the morning in question, he was suddenly needed elsewhere, for as previously instructed by myself, "Anything could happen this week, keep in touch!", of course Mike didn't and so I plus a few of the other lads, near enough had a heart attack, chasing around looking for him, only for him to turn up an hour later, telling us all what a lovely time he'd had on the plane with the crew he'd dropped off.

I could have killed him there and then, especially as I was near enough at my wits end but it didn't make any odds, nothing ever sank in with him, all he was bothered about was the fact that he'd been invited to have his breakfast, "breckers" as he put it, on the plane, especially as he'd never ever flown or been on one!.

Which aptly brings me to what was without doubt his greatest of all great achievements, the day Mike ended up lost in the pitch black of night, stuck in the middle of an airfield with a car full of airline crew, as jets and other aircraft of all descriptions taxied past on both the left and the right, with him stuck slap bang in the middle. Although one shouldn't laugh as it could have been catastrophic, I can't help but smile as I picture the faces of those either in the car or the crews on board the planes, for just the mere sight of seeing Mike dodging and weaving between any number of 757s, or 737s, must surely have been a sight to behold.

You see that was Mike, he was so stupid and irresponsible, he didn't think but looking back I can't make out whether he did it on purpose or he was just plain bloody gormless!.

There was one occasion when he got out of one of our cars, opened the doors for the clients then locked himself and them out, leaving all the luggage they were taking away on their holidays with them in the boot of the car. Now anyone normal would ring the office in a panic, worrying about the predicament they'd put the customers in, not Mike!, Oh yes, he did ring but not to tell Jeannette that he'd dropped a right cobbler, or that he'd made a terrible mistake of mega proportions, Oh no! because he had other things on his mind, "Bloody ell Jeannette what am I going to do?, I've locked myself out of the car and the keys are inside it but what's worse is I've left me fags in it!!".

I mean talk about getting one's priorities right!, he stood there with passengers who can't get their luggage out of the car to go on their holidays and all he can think about is a smoke!.

Before I finish talking about Mike, I have to write about the day he was given the task of chauffeuring around five, French businessmen from the Novotel, men of high importance who were here on a mission to look around for potential new sites within the Greater Manchester area, for the possible building of a second Novotel.

Once again, a day where against my better judgement, I was forced to delegate the task to none other than Super Mike!, my star driver.

The basic idea was that he'd take them wherever they wished to go, in an effort to view as much of the area as they possibly could, within the one day available but as a result of the bloke's total ineptness they saw far more than they'd ever originally expected because thanks to dear old Mike, they ended up getting stranded in the middle of a field, stuck God knows where!, needless to say thanks to Mike we never worked for the Novotel again.

Although the bloke was, by far the worst, he certainly wasn't alone because at the end of a good eighteen month period, where we constantly searched for that one perfect employee who had all the qualities we desperately required, not one was ever found.

We had nice lads who came to us for jobs, who were triers, they weren't frightened of work and they had a good manner about them but they either smoked, which meant they constantly reeked of tobacco or just stank full stop.

One lad had all the above qualities that I've mentioned but no matter how hard I tried, I couldn't get him to wash himself properly, which eventually led to me presenting him with a can of deodorant but sadly all was to no avail, so he had to go.

Then there were the others, the "cocky" type, who were far too clever for their own good, the ones who came to work for us with the sole intention of setting up for themselves at a later date, who thought they were conning us but they weren't, not for one minute!.

Sadly we encountered a few drivers who were great but like every other, there was some drawback to employing them, only these few had the very same problem as I, which was booze, yet not surprisingly each and everyone of them was a bloody good "grafter". Unfortunately though, as soon as they'd started earning quite a lot of money, the booze predictable got a hold, making them all totally unreliable!.

We had others that started for us who came with glowing references, such as the man who produced a CV as long as his arm, with recommendations from The Ministry of Defence, The Army, Navy, you name it he had it, yet on his first job, he was some seventy minutes late, when found waiting at the airport for his customers, when he should actually have been at their home, as they hadn't even gone away yet!.

In a period of time that I've mentioned Jeannette and I experienced all manner of things, as staff tried in whatever way they could to "take".

We had them pocket tips that they weren't supposed to, even steal on occasions by taking fares, then there were the car phones and the abuse of them as drivers such as Neil, Pete and Andy, all constantly rang up their secret woman behind their wives backs, even worse at our expense.

Then there was the state of the cars, that those same few would bring back, covered in mud or soil and carrying half a wood with them, as overgrowth from where they'd been shagging the night before, clung onto the axle or wheel arches!. Oh yes! we've seen and heard them all alright! even women, the young girls such as Jane, Rachael and Gaynor, who wanted so much to work, so we gave it to them, only to be told that it was too busy for them, after we'd stood by them all though the quite winter months, or that the money wasn't good enough, even though they were doing very little for it.

We had people who came to work for us, people who were at the time claiming vast amounts of money in insurance claims from other employees, as well as sickness benefit from the state. We had others who just wanted money for doing absolutely nothing, yet all the time we tried, never, not once, did anyone of them ever say sorry for being late, damaging a car or any cock up whatsoever, so in the end we decided to quit, to stop employing people and to go it alone, whereby if we needed other vehicles, we'd subcontract, "After all Jeannette, anything's got to be better than this!".

Chapter Fourteen

Learning to Survive

Employing people to do the work was bad enough but the people who we were doing the work for, now that was an entirely different matter. If it were the general public we were dealing with as they were going on their holidays, all manner of things could go wrong, for they are capable of absolutely anything. They would give us the wrong time, wrong date, even the wrong address in some cases, then having had countless reminders before getting into the car, still somehow manage to forget either their passport, tickets, money, or even them all!.

If I had a pound for every passenger that's forgotten to give me their return flight details, then swear blind that they had, I'd be a rich man!. Or maybe a tenner for every couple who have left their home at four o'clock or some other similar ridiculous hour, only to post their key through next doors, then half way to the airport remember that they too have forgotten something, I'd be even wealthier.

Lost luggage, lost days, lost souls, even lost teeth, that just about sums up most of the travellers I've dealt with over the past few years . . . hopeless!! but what about the other side, the companies!, especially Television, now there's a tale!.

Because of the set "norm" that companies over the years had been used to dealing with, secretaries and staff generally tended to speak to us as though we were some kind of illiterate, brainless moron, you know the type that usually works for a normal taxi company. Obviously at first it wasn't their fault, for as I said it was what they'd normally been used to, however the same excuse could not be made once they'd either met us or experienced our service.

And so it wasn't long before we'd started getting fed up with such a manner, a manner which we soon discovered, as I said earlier on in my story, tended to treat us as some sort of second class citizen, with most of the ignorant, pompous sods at the other end of the phone, totally unaware that we were in fact probably twice as hardworking, twice as intelligent and three times as wealthy as themselves!.

It was absolutely ridiculous, there we were listening to either a bloody kid, young enough to be our own, or some self righteous clever shit who thought she was talking to some imbecile. They were so full of their own importance, it was pitiful, yet those very same people, who thought so highly of themselves were in fact the major cause of most, if not all of the chaos endured. Having said that, most of the staff that I did work with, whether they be a producer, director, or a researcher, did think that their own immediate task was far more important than anybody else's, consequently chaos did rule, generally meaning that the not so important people such as ourselves, "the second class citizens" predictably ended up pulling our bollocks out at the very last minute to save the show, usually without even being noticed!.

In my time working within the industry, I have on more than a few dozen occasions saved both time and money and on more occasions than I care to remember saved somebody's face, even job, for the people behind the scenes are as incapable of organising, as a few of those famous faces you see on screen are of looking after themselves!.

I've witnessed all sorts of goings on in the entertainment business and I've done a lot of crazy things that I've been paid to do, things that did annoy me at the time, yet I've always been nothing less than professional throughout, by being loyal, trustworthy and above all reliable but most of all I've retained my integrity by keeping their anonymity, something which despite my present day feelings, I still intend to do!.

There have been so many "cock ups", so much bad organisation, so many last minute rescues bids that I don't know exactly where to begin. Then the stories of my experiences, the boozing, the womanising and the general antics of the stars, or production teams as a whole, are so many that once again, as with my own sex life and the boozing experiences I had, a separate book dealing with this subject alone could be written. But by far the most annoying to me personally was having to witness the wasting of vast amounts of money, even sadder how it was actually wasted, for if there is one lesson I could pick out from the many that I've learned through working in the Television World, it would be "misplaced priorities" and "double standards", for they are ever present in an abundance. No!, it's not sour grapes, it's a fact that I was paid money to run around like a monkey chasing it's tail, for certain items with no expense spared! but of course only if it was for either a celebrity or higher management!.

I've wasted hours, all told, chasing round for chip shops, burger bars, sandwich shops the lot, on one occasion I even spent an hour in search of a bucket full of ice because the "Star" concerned wanted her Beaujolais Nouvelle chilled!.

One man, who at the time was programme controller, sat in the back of the car with his wife eating Stroodles, from a delicatessen, chicken nuggets from McDonalds and a bottle of chilled champagne from glasses that had all been kept chilled in the ice box.

All pre arranged by myself in an effort to fulfil their earlier wishes, following their night at The Liverpool Concert Hall, ironically the last job I ever did for the man!, inspite of his words on the way back of, "That was great Paul, we must do this again sometime!".

Waiting charges were another questionable area of wastage because it was a period of time that we or any other company working for them, had to charge for, as both the car and driver were in effect unable to work elsewhere. It was always a good excuse for a row, all once again as a result of the double standards that I spoke about earlier, for the question of, "Why is there so much waiting time?" was always asked of us and not the "star" or "management" concerned.

Once again if the presenter of a show decided he or she was going around to his or her friends for a "leg over", then I had to wait outside, with no questions asked and it was all OK!.

As with the celebrities, if a member of higher management missed their flight then once again no questions were asked, where upon the driver which was usually Jeannette or I and obviously the car had to wait there until the next flight had arrived, which meant that we would sometimes be stood around for over three hours!.

In stark contrast to all of these "goings on", the companies financial directors and accountants would be spending time slashing budgets here and there, whilst at the same time cutting this or that, in order to make up for those losses, it was mayhem!.

Time and time again payment was more than two months behind because there would a question mark over our bill, maybe five pounds here, or a fiver there! and so in order to save paying up on time, the query would be left for as long as possible, in order to delay!. It got that bad at one point, that Steve Morrison the programme controller, who was a buggar for constantly using the car phone, once again picked it up only to find that it had been disconnected because the bill hadn't been paid!.

In my own naivety and stupidity and especially after giving him such loyalty and reliability, I expected him to be annoyed with the realisation that such a thing could happen, however having explained that Granada were nearly three months behind with their payments, he just laughed saying "Bloody Hell that's the second time today!, the same thing happened to the driver that picked me up in London!".

You see that was the measure of the man because as long as he was alright then everything was okay, even despite the fact that on countless other previous occasions, that very phone had more than "saved his bacon".

I'd done all sorts for that man and his family, I'd freely put myself out even at the expense of other work, pulled him out of the shite on more than one occasion and even delayed the take off, of one of his flights, as he regularly ran late, all apart from being nice and making them feel special but in the end it really meant nothing, for if it had he'd have been into work like a shot to sort the problem out.

I remember one occasion in particular, where as a result of the regular confusion within the company and as a bi product of the pompous attitudes that I've already spoken about, there was a major "cock up" which ended up with me once again pulling them out of the shite. In the end and after a long discussion some days later, Steve himself asked me about their transport side, he wanted to know my thoughts, plans and ideas for such a department, all of which prompted me to send a detailed letter listing costings, savings and plans to their Finance Director, a Miss Kate Stross, predictably however, in typical Granada style, it was never even acknowledged, so I carried on observing the "cock ups", watching the money being wasted and logging the ensuing chaos it all caused for some time to come!.

Sadly Steve wasn't alone in his attitude, as there were countless others, all the same, who'd constantly demanded our service, our trust and our friendship, yet once again, time was to eventually prove to both Jeannette and myself that all our effort and the above things I've mentioned really meant very little at all, for just like Steve, if they were okay, then everything was okay and it was a case of "Sod you!".

During a period of eighteen months with Granada Television, we worked on all sorts of different programmes, which varied from quiz shows to sport and from kiddie's programmes to audience participation such as debates.

There were the light entertainment shows, as well as the one offs, such as the "Specials", then there were a multitude of outside broadcast programmes such as football, rugby and bowls, yet no matter what programme we ever worked on, the most important factor, feature, call it want you want, was the "nosh up" afterwards, the buffet, the booze up, the celebration, which always said, "Didn't we do well!".

God it was pathetic!, talk about pat yourself on the back, there they were all stood, congratulating each other on what a good job they'd done and how hard they'd worked!, as they basically got fed and watered, or should I say pissed, yet in truth they didn't have a clue what a bloody, good hard day's work was!.

Earlier in my story I described the shock of working with Francis and Carolyn, the girls on contract to Warner Brothers, my amazement at their disorganisation and the last minute panicking that those weaknesses caused. Well with the benefit of hindsight and experience they were organised, when compared to the staff at Granada and other TV companies, as more often than not we'd be given notice that our services were required immediately, without even a warning!.

It seems on reflection that it was a case of "Oh give Paul a ring!", where upon I like a fool suffered the panic attacks, the anxiety and the stress all in an effort to impress, which is obviously what happened but why?, why did I carry on in such a manner?.

The answer to that question is simple, it was in an effort to gain their commitment and that elusive contract, the one that my mother had always believed in, for it would bring with it security, the very same security that others before me had in the past gained for doing far less than I, for a contract wouldn't only have made all the worry worth it, it would have been Granada's way of showing their gratitude, their loyalty, their trust, in fact it could have been their nicest possible "Thank you!".

The last major job we completed for Granada Television was actually the Coronation Street Gala, a presentation and thirtieth anniversary of the street's long running success on screen, which actually took place on the 8th of December. It was probably one of their biggest ever days, a day when as usual millions of viewers would be glued to their sets, a day when all eyes were on Granada Television!, a day of celebration and a day of success!.

Well it was but had it not been for Jeannette and myself and a few other people, it could well have been the biggest disaster imaginable, as once again self righteous, pompous "know it alls" nearly made the "cock up" of their lives.

We'd first received notification that we would be asked to work on the event some three weeks earlier, following which we both went down to Granada Television Studios. Then on the 13th November we received written confirmation of that previous discussion and a detailed account of exactly what they required us to do, it wasn't difficult three, maybe four cars at the most, so there was no problem.

That was until the 5th December, a mere three days before the event, when we suddenly received a telephone call asking us to call into the reception to pick up an envelope containing a list of the celebrities who were coming and what time they were to be picked up from the hotel.

Well two weeks later I was due to drive Cilla Black around, on her programme "Surprise Surprise" but I swear to God at that exact moment in time, we thought that either my old friend Jeremey Beadle was about, or what we were reading was all part of some elaborate hoax, for the original order of three cars travelling to and from the Ramada Hotel had suddenly changed, to no less than twelve or thirteen cars travelling as far as Rotherham, Blackpool and Southport.

Apart from those few, slight problems, thirty other guests were arriving via either the airport, the coach or train station!, needless to say not for the first time in our lives, it was "panicsville!!", where once again Jeannette and I were left to cover up the incompetence of others.

However this occasion was unlike any other, for only a month earlier we'd fired all our drivers having decided that employing staff was an impossible, fruitless task, so there was more than enough to be done and not much time to do it in!. Nevertheless through our solid determination to succeed, our defiance and refusal to be put down and our loyalty to Granada we somehow made it, for on the morning in question, various drivers and companies that I'd borrowed, on a sub-contract basis all turned up to our home.

As with the Warner Brother's Gala, Mitchell's car and van hire, had once again supplied the limos and so against the tallest odds imaginable, Jeannette and I had done it again, well the first bit at least, now all we had to do was pray that our preparation was right and that all would go well on the day!.

Well as I've previously stated in this book, there are many things entailed in travel and the transport industry generally, that one can prepare for, having said that, there are others that one cannot, with the weather being the operative in this instance, so it will come as no surprise to you, when I say that within a couple of hours, the weather had changed for the worst, bringing with it a whole array of new and unexpected problems!.

You see The Gala was being filmed all day in the studios at Granada but due to the size of the operation and the various numbers of artists, time was of a premium because even allowing for cuts, retakes and any other delays, by the time the thing had been fully recorded and the final editing had been completed, the start would actually be showing on TV to the viewers, the following Sunday evening.

It was a schedule that was bad and tight enough without the added hindrance of freak snow blizzards that paralysed the trains, planes and near enough anything else that moved, yet against all odds, thanks to the support of the drivers who helped, Jeannette's organisation and above all else, our stamina we made it!, with everybody miraculously arriving spot on time!.

Having said that, as with the Warner Brother's job I missed the start, for yet again I found myself doing my Captain Fantastic bit, as costumes desperately needed for the show were running late, arriving by plane at the airport, so once again it was Paul off to the rescue in true theatrical style, with the cause being "To save the show!".

However when I returned Jeannette, Nick and the drivers who'd help get the thing off the ground in the first place, had all been left standing in the cold, miserable security lodge, supposedly expected to wait for over four hours, whilst the show was recorded and the gala rolled on!. Ha!, not on your life!, I wasn't having any of that, especially after all the effort each and everyone of them had gone to, so we gate crashed the party immediately, to enjoy the celebrations that we'd worked so hard for, to ensure they even took place!.

As with all of these jobs, my work was never actually finished nor the task complete, until the very last guest had been safely returned home or taken to the airport, train station or bus station necessary. It was however by sheer coincidence, an honour which nearly always fell to me for some strange reason, with this occasion being no different, only this time, it was more of a pleasure, as the final guest to be collected that Sunday, was none other than the "darling of the street", Jean Alexander, yes, Hilda Ogden herself!.

She was a lovely lady, a woman who took me totally by surprise, for she was quiet, nervous and very, very shy but her real beauty lay in her unassuming attitude, which came through in her caring down to earth manner!. The lady didn't like flying, in fact she was petrified, so naturally, following a very special request that I personally took care of her, I did! and it was a pleasure to do so, though sadly it's more than I can say for Granada Television because our arrival at the check in desk and the anticipated picking up of ticket which had supposedly been left there, amounted to nothing!.

You see those efficient, caring, intelligent people at Granada had forgotten to book the dear lady on the flight. You know the very same person who'd pinched the limelight the night before, the one who'd done so much over the years to boost the ratings, yes, that very same woman who Granada loved so much, "Well that's what they said!". The poor lady was just about ready to cry when we found out, as she was a bag of nerves already without this, "Don't worry Jean I'll sort this out!".

Not for the first time in my chauffeuring career, I used my knowledge of the airport, the friendships I'd built up in the past and a lot of initiative to sort the mess out, whilst the dear lady looked on in amazement and within a few minutes I found myself in a position that I'd been in so many times before, saying "Good luck!, goodbye, I hope we meet again!".

It was one of those very gratifying moments that came with the job, where somebody we'd looked after actually appreciated our efforts with words such as "Oh thank you , I don't know what I'd have done without you!" and so I made my way home, in the sound knowledge that both Jeannette and myself as "Exclusia Travel", had once again proved by our professionalism that we were without doubt, the best!, by coming through against unbelievable odds, "unscathed!".

By the time we'd returned home it was Sunday evening and the show was being broadcast, we were obviously shattered but very proud, yet as ever there was no time to celebrate for we had other work to do and so we carried on doing the "bread and butter" work, that of our own clients, whilst once again putting our own "pat on the back" on ice!.

Ironically that last job coincided with the one and only official "thank you", we ever got in our time working for Granada, a thank you which we received on the 14th December from Jane McNaught, the producer. I say ironically because what should have been a rubber stamp, a qualification or confirmation of our professionalism, actually turned out to be our own downfall!. Because it eventually ended up with us doing no further work for their company, county court action being taken against us and me with a black eye, all due to the delayed payment policies of the Financial Directors of Granada Television.

It was a typical example of our outlook because where Jeannette and I "like mugs", were prepared to wait for our money, others weren't, it was also more proof, qualifying our own past beliefs, that they like most other large concerns, demanded the best service on offer, whilst at the same time they were reluctant to pay up, thus expecting poor souls like us, to survive on fresh air!.

You see one of the companies who'd helped us out on the job had become impatient with the delay in our payment, as a result they took it upon themseleves to contact Mr Pinson, at Granada, who then kindly took it upon himself to disclose our own private invoice and charges to the man concerned. Needless to say a meeting was arranged with Mr Pinson, a meeting where more insults were to follow, as personal questions relating to our business were asked such as "Are you experiencing financial difficulties?", all of which only succeeded to annoy us both even more.

In the end Jeannette and I stormed off having told him what a rude, ignorant, sly, supercilious worm he was!, following which we sent a letter to the board withdrawing our services.

We felt that if any of those people, in either higher management or on the board had anything whatsoever about them, then they'd stand up, be counted and for a change show us a bit of loyalty, support and friendship in return, especially as we'd always taken so much care and time to look after them in the past!.

Not on your life!, in fact I think we received two letters basically saying how sad they were to lose us, especially as it was such a good service, Oh!, one chap Rod Caird did have the decency to suggest that we had a drink the next time he was in Manchester but that was it and so our relationship with Granada came to a very sad, very unhappy, rapid end!.

For the next twelve months I did continue to work for other Television companies with Thames, London Weekend and Central being just a few, I even worked for a Scandinavian outfit on sport all of whom I must say had a totally different outlook to that of Granadas', however in the May of 92, even that work came to a very abrupt end, with the emergence of Sky Television which for us was bad news!. You see I'd worked for London Weekend Television for well over a couple of years, a period where once again as with the others I'd always been obliging, reliable and trustworthy, I'd never let them down although I must say I did enjoy every minute of the time that I worked with them.

But it was a two way relationship for there was never any doubt with them as to who they'd use for cars, as they were always very loyal and committed to me. It was a commitment that actually guaranteed the payment of my hefty mortgage and so the sufferance of the odd late payment wasn't to hard to swallow, which meant that as soon as the announcement was made, saying Sky had obtained sole rights to cover the Premier League, our hearts automatically sank!.

It was news which immediately prompted me to contact Sky Television in an effort to secure whatever work they had available in our area, a call that was greeted by a very recognisable voice at the other end. To my surprise it was a lad who'd worked for Granada Television some twelve months earlier, a lad who I'd always got on extremely well with and so in the September of that year I started working for the company albeit for only five months!, a relationship only severed as a result of a car crash which I was involved in, a crash that occurred on the 7th January 1993.

At this point in my book I'd like to return to the January of 1990, some three years ago, for although I've written about the complexities of running such a business, the chaos it brought and of course the problems employing people, so much more has occurred during that time that I have to write about it.

Looking back, what was originally supposed to be a fresh start for us in our new home, actually turned out to be the initial stages of what was to become our longest struggle to date and by far the greatest test of our undying love!, for it was a three year period that brought us both so much pain, whilst at the same time so much togetherness, as we were seemingly used by everyone as a punch bag, where we ended up being knocked from pillar to post.

To start with, those horrible people from Springclough just wouldn't leave us in peace, as three maybe four of their cars at a time would kerb crawl passed our new home in a convoy!, an experience we had to suffer for a good few weeks.

Then our listening bank with the help of our "half soaked" solicitor suddenly decided to stop listening, by automatically killing our initial enthusiasm by way of unbalancing our books and taking ten thousand pounds off us.

Tom our unbelievably gormless "not with it" accountant also had a go, by frequently not producing urgently needed figures on time, sometimes not producing them at all!.

Then there were those other modern day Robin Hoods, the insurance companies, who actually help start my downfall, by paying each one of the guilty parties who'd smashed into me, whilst at the same time forgetting all about myself, the only innocent one involved. Then having made the balls up, they forced me to settle for a ridiculous sum.

By the time we'd reached the September of 1990 we'd just about had enough, when a new rogue, a Mr Roy Walton, came into our lives care of "Yes", you've guessed it our listening bank, in what I now see was a lovely orchestrated premeditated move, intent on forcing us to re-mortgage in order to save losing our home, whilst at the same time I suspect pocketing money for themselves!.

With all this pressure and outside interference taking place in our lives, I was now toughening up and so one by one companies were buggered off, as I wasn't prepared to take any more shit!, companies such as Chloride, MEL and Loganair.

Oh yes, even Loganair, all as a result of an incident, the first of it's kind, where I met the only rude member of their staff, a man who to me, had a drink problem, who spoke to his crew and myself in a typical drunken, alcoholic manner.

No way!, I was having none of that, so I told him what he was, what I thought of him and what he could do with his threats!, where upon he reported me as I expected he would. Having said that, I also expected Loganair to contact me to get my side, but did they?, did they hell, they asked the crew members present for their opinions, all of whom had no option but to side for the man, for fear of losing their jobs, knowing they'd have to work with him in the future. You see some weeks later I was told by one of the crew involved that he would in the end see the report, meaning he'd know full well who'd said what!.

Well thank you Loganair for your loyalty and commitment, especially after all that I did for you, just be grateful that I never once reported either you or your crews to the CAA for the drunken states that they and your airline flew in, or the many other flight regulations that I witnessed you breach!. Rather ironically the pilot concerned left a few months later and so the many friendships I'd built up were lost as a consequence.

By the time we'd reached the January of 91 our long, prolonged nightmare with the Midland Bank was over and so after nearly destroying my home, my family and near enough my life I finally got the chance to tell the manager what a deceitful, lying cheat he was, well now I can tell the world, something I always promised I'd do.

They are not alone though, for a few months later The Royal Bank of Scotland also joined my list of corrupt thieves, only their actions were as a result of blatant incompetence, stupidity which near enough forced me to innocently and accidently commit fraud!, a situation brought about by their own inept staff, who opened on account in one name, then laundered cheques that should have been paid into another. Of course like all banks they denied any responsibility, even though the manager was sacked and jailed for fraud but their again that's banks for you isn't it!.

By this time Insolvency even Bankruptcy were looking far better, more realistic options, as the County Court Orders issued against both Jeannette and myself were mounting by the week.

At the time it seemed everybody under the sun was suing us, finance companies, banks, insurance companies, newspapers, "all had a go".

We even had one company Cowies of Sunderland, take us to court because I stopped a cheque I'd issued.

It was stopped as a result of the poor workmanship they'd supposedly carried out and obviously because I wasn't happy.

That was bad enough but what made matters ten times worse was the fact that their garage manager, a Mr Steve Lindley had the cheek to ask me for monies I owed him for driving work he'd carried out, whilst at the same time he was prepared to stand up in support of his employers, Cowies!, "oh yes we've seen them all!".

In the end our "efficient" accountant, Tom Hatton was once again summoned, only this time he came with an Insolvency expert, another lovely, cheerful chap, a Mr Simmons. As ever, it cost us money, only this time cash which was unsigned for, however it was a very enlightening experience, as more proof of Tom's poor performance surfaced, needless to say he eventually had to go as things by now, were looking grim!.

By the time we'd reached the Christmas of 1991 all four of the cars we'd proudly used had been repossessed, we had no accountant, no solicitor, in fact hardly anything.

And so the next twelve months were spent dodging and weaving from one car rental firm to another, as we battled on a weekly, sometimes daily basis to survive.

It was a year where the constant worry of losing our lovely home was ever present and foremost in our minds. A year where we had to suffer the indignation of bailiffs coming to the door, then the degradation of hiding behind the curtains whenever the doorbell rang.

To just about cream us off altogether our new, Whelmar – Redrow built "dream home" turned out to be another nightmare, a four bedroomed ice box which has left us with unbelievably, enormous gas and electricity bills, a house that boasts of double glazing, yet as I lie in bed each morning I am able to enjoy the sound of traffic, even people walking as they pass.

A house where warped doors and door frames are common place, which according to Redrow management can only be put down to "living" wood. Well with that sort of attitude it's no wonder that a whole host of other problems have still to be dealt with, in a house that should have been built by "Jack", never mind Redrow.

Finally, of all the "low down", cruel tricks we've encountered, by far the worse is that of veterinary surgeons, you see even our three year old, pedigree Chow has suffered, a poor animal that has done nothing to harm anyone, yet as ever there's always someone who'll benefit from another's suffering!.

I couldn't possibly leave these morons out, for their actions and attitude are nothing short of despicable, as following countless visits to various veterinary surgeons, countless pounds spent in them for operations that have been proved were unnecessary and endless amounts of trust given, we've been totally "ripped off".

To, Nolan's of Farnworth, Collinson's of Walkden and Dr Bennett from Liverpool University, thank you, each and every one of you for gladly taking our money, yet not having the decency to reply to my letters. Letters sent requesting your support for me, in my efforts to recoup my losses from the robbing sods at Mayfield Kennels who screwed me in the first place, yet sadly you're not interested, as there's nothing in it for you, which obviously means morally you're no better.

Anyhow, having well and truly ground my axe, had my say, and got rid of my anger, I'd like to return to that fateful day of January 7th 1993, the day I experienced my first ever accident involving passengers.

Not surprisingly on the day in question I was drained, as all manner of problems, apart from the major one of us losing our home ran through my tired mind, where as usual I found myself running around like a headless chicken as I tried to do hell and all, something which had become a customary feature in our daily survival routine.

However there was nothing normal about this day because Jeannette, my inspiration was in Billinge Hospital having a hysterectomy operation and I was missing her badly. As a consequence, I caused what could and should well have been a fatal car accident, an accident where six other people and a baby all miraculously escaped death.

Gladly, no thankfully!, not one of those involved was seriously injured, well that's according to the police, never the less it was only by the grace of God!.

Ironically it brought an abrupt end to my dream, a dream that as I said earlier turned into reality, then eventually into my worst ever imaginable nightmare, which by a sheer twist of destiny or fate took me back to where I'd started some six years earlier, where I'd become very sick, very tired, unemployed and very much in debt!.

It also left me feeling very guilty for inspite of the thousands upon thousands of people I'd previously looked after, those poor folk involved in that crash were casualties of not just an accident, but also of my long painful demise.

And so with Jeannette's return from hospital came a whole new way of life, which has ended up being a daily battle and a lesson in learning to survive!. Where many tears have been shed, numerous raised voices have been heard and tempers flared but more importantly through thick and thin, Jeannette, Nick and I have stuck together!.

It was a period of time where despite us both being seriously ill, I once again had the thankless task of chasing around in a desperate search for the finances to guarantee the production of this book, which brings me to present day.

As I now finish writing this, my future is more in doubt than it ever was before, as the constant battle to save our lovely home, the same one that Jeannette has worked all her life for, continues on a daily basis.

But I know that with the love and support of both Alcoholics Anonymous and Jeannette, the continuing, priceless help and patience of the Alliance and Leicester Building Society plus the trust I have, in the guidance of my God, somehow we'll make it . . . a day at a time!. SOBER!

REFLECTIONS

In the early stages of writing this book I'd often wondered how I'd feel as I worked on these reflections.

Well I feel exactly as I thought I would, I feel relieved that it's all over and I feel free!, for at last and as a direct result of the honest, hard, painful work put in, I have finally rid myself of the old heavy baggage that for far too long I've humped around with me, a burden that so painfully weighed me down.

It was luggage that no Alcoholic can afford to have in their possession for too long, if they are to continue to stay sober and I knew it! but now it's gone, I'm once again at peace with myself and free to confidently carry on with my own life.

It has also enabled me to learn, to understand and to see things that I could never have done before, with the realisation of just how much I really love my mother and father being just one of many examples.

It also taught me that I must try to forgive those many thoughtless people who have hurt us so, for they are all probably very spiritually sick people, possibly sicker than I ever was as a drunk.

And so, those many ghosts that for so long have haunted me from the past are now finally laid to rest, taking with them my anger, bitterness, resentments and hatred, so what now for the future?, what dreams do I hold now?.

The answer to that question is simple!, I pray that above all else God will keep me sober, my family healthy and that I may continue to try and help others far less fortunate than myself, to experience the peace of mind, the freedom, the hope and the promise that I on a daily basis now cherish.

If I do have anyone to thank, It would be Alcoholics Anonymous, my dear friend Colin, my mother and father, Jean my ex-wife and above all else Jeannette.

THE END . . .

(WELL ALMOST) . . .

These are what I've chosen to call my "Alternative Thank You" pages, pages dedicated to those many deceitful, lying, cheating, conniving companies and people who at some time or other "crapped" on me and mine along the way.

Bollocks to

Ex-employees:
Nigel Robinson
Frank Barlow
Andy Smith
Tony Smith
Trevor
Jane Cahill
Alan Brown
Steve Dearden
Ken Morris
Steve Lindley
Jane (Airport Agencies)
Margaret (Airport Agencies)
Damion Thornton
Mervin Miles
Peter Barlow
Don Charles
Stuart
John
Ian Jarvis
Glen Murray
Laura Dearden
Bill Deakin
Chris Brown

Sub contractors:
Jack Harwood
John Villager
Chris Brett Travel
Barry Advanced Travel
Martin Star Travel
Eric Select Travel

All of whom wanted money for nothing and in many cases, more than we ourselves were getting.

The Banks:
The Midland Bank,
especially Peter Fairclough, Colin Billington, Richard Lowrie

The Royal Bank of Scotland,
especially Shaun Phoenix, Tony Shaw, Stan Grimshaw

National Westminster Bank,
especially Richard Stidwell, Geoff Kirwin, Neil Reynolds, J. Ince, J. Armstrong

Barclays,
especially Barabra Muir, Dave Shoreman

All people, who I'm sure, have succeeded in messing up many other people's lives.

Other advisers? . . . what a joke!
Tom Hatton (Accountant), James Singleton (Solicitor), Chris Lyons (Solicitor), (Ellison Blank and Goldsmith), Roy Walton (Insurance Broker), Geoff Fincher (Insurance Broker)

More robbers in disguise:
Garner's Insurance, Royal Insurance, Eagle Star, City of Westminster, Mercantile Credit, Lloyds Bowmaker, British Credit, First National Bank, Lombard Tricity

Shabby companies I've dealt with:
A & B Motors – Big fat Alan with his cigar, Duke Hire, Cooke Brothers, District Garage – Dave Mort, Practical Car Hire, Gordons Garage Walkden – Keith Walker and staff, Cowies of Blackburn – Steve Lindley, Citroen Manchester, Riding and Kok, Langford Thomson, Denis Fletcher, A.T.S, Manchester Airport – John Newton & A. Powell

Thanks for your loyalty . . . now that is a joke!
Marks and Spencer – especially Roy Harrison, Loganair, Chloride, M.E.L., DAF, Ferranti, Granada Television: A. Mutch, Max Graesser and especially Alan Pinson (a pathetic creature), who sadly seemed to pull all the strings in the company at the time. "No wonder the standard of your programmes has dropped so dramatically".

A few other incidentals:
(Newspapers) – Jewish Telegraph, The Advertiser, Inside Publications

On a more personal note:
Redrow/Whelmar, for my nightmare home, "It's a shed".
Wigan Council, no wonder we're all in a mess.

Veterinary Surgeons:
Collinson's – Walkden, Nolan's – Farnworth, Dr. Bennett – Liverpool University

All callous, despicable, uncaring professionals who extort money from well-meaning, animal loving people, when they, as well as their pets, are in a vulnerable state.

To anybody not listed above who I may have forgotten!

Finally, an extra special "Bollocks" to Mr. Harry Ashton, Mr. Geoff Cowling (of the Salford Licensing Authority) and the residents of Springclough Drive, to whom I owe so much, for it was you who inadvertently made me even more determined to succeed and "Boy did I!" . . .